Conflicting Visions of Reform

STUDIES IN GERMAN HISTORIES
Series Editors: Roger Chickering and Thomas A. Brady, Jr.

PUBLISHED

Communal Reformation
Peter Blickle

Protestant Politics:
Jacob Sturm (1489–1553)
and the German Reformation
Thomas A. Brady, Jr.

Karl Lamprecht
A German Academic Life (1856–1915)
Roger Chickering

Conflicting Visions of Reform:
German Lay Propaganda Pamphlets, 1519–1530
Miriam Usher Chrisman

German Encounters with Modernity
Katherine Roper

German Villages in Crisis:
Rural Life in Hesse Kassel and
the Thirty Years' War, 1580–1720
John Theibault

Communities and Conflict in
Early Modern Colmar: 1575–1730
Peter G. Wallace

Conflicting Visions of Reform

German Lay Propaganda Pamphlets, 1519–1530

Miriam Usher Chrisman

HUMANITIES PRESS
NEW JERSEY

First published in 1996 by Humanities Press International, Inc.
165 First Avenue, Atlantic Highlands, New Jersey 07716

©1996 by Miriam Usher Chrisman

Library of Congress Cataloging-in-Publication Data
Chrisman, Miriam Usher.
    Conflicting visions of reform : German lay propaganda pamphlets,
1519–1530 / Miriam Usher Chrisman.
      p.   cm. — (Studies in German histories)
    Includes bibliographical references and index.
    ISBN 0–391–03944–X
    1. Reformation—Germany—Pamphlets. 2. Germany—
History—1517–1648—Pamphlets. 3. Laity—Germany—History—16th
century. 4. Laity—Germany—Religious life. 5. Pamphleteers—
Germany—History—16th century. I. Title. II. Series.
BR355.P36C47 1995
274.3'06—dc20   95–8888
                  CIP

A catalog record for this book is available from the British Library.

Printed in the United States of America

To the Circle of Strasbourg Scholars

Contents

List of Illustrations

List of Figures

Acknowledgments

A book long in the making accumulates mentors, friends and assistants. Like all my work, this book started in the *Salle de Travail* of the Strasbourg Municipal Archives, where I discussed the initial idea and the possible sources with Dr. François-Joseph Fuchs and Dr. Jean Rott, who have always provided support and understanding. Similar encouragement came from Dr. Georges Livet, Dr. Francis Rapp, Dr. Marc Lienhardt, Dr. Jean-Pierre Kintz, and Dr. Gustav Koch. Dr. Koch made available to me the pamphlets by Eckhard zum Drübel which he himself had gathered. This kind of collegiality is rare in the scholarly world and should be honored as well as recognized.

As I launched my own search for pamphlets written by laymen, I was helped by the staffs of the Bibliothèque Nationale et Univérsitaire at Strasbourg and the Zentralbibliothek in Zurich. I began to accumulate a small pile. My project could never have been realized without the work of Hans-Joachim Köhler, who had, at Tübingen, amassed a collection of 5,000 Reformation pamphlets, publishing them on microfiche. This collection made it possible to move from a level of anecdote to a database large enough for scholarly analysis. Dr. Köhler not only made his scholarly notes available to me at Tübingen, he fed and housed me while I was there—and drove me at speeds of 110 miles an hour to catch my train. His dedication to the *Flugschriften-Projekt* is an example of responsibility to the larger scholarly world which few imitate. Mostly through his own efforts, he has opened these materials to everyone working in sixteenth, century history. It is a major breakthrough in the availability of previously widely scattered sources and provides a new context for our work.

Through Köhler I learned of the work of Paul Russell, who, happily, lived rather close by. The first person to publish a study in English on lay pamphlet writers, he has been generous in giving me materials and, more importantly, in sharing ideas and insights. Gottfried Krodel kept an eye for every review and photocopied anything he thought I should know. Lee Wandel became a personal librarian, willingly looking up journals and reference works at the Sterling Library at Yale and having them at the circulation desk for me when I arrived in New Haven.

When I finished the first draft, Jane Abray took time during a sabbatical year to read the entire manuscript, making copious notes and suggestions. She helped me structure the material more firmly. Her response to the individual writers encouraged me to continue.

Several friends and colleagues read the manuscript in a later phase: Thomas A. Brady, Jr., Susan Karant-Nunn, Lee Wandel, Jo-Ann Moran, and Abel Alves, each of whom approached it from a different point of view, making their criticisms and suggestions particularly useful. Later Tom Brady accepted the book for the new series, co-edited with Roger Chickering, on German social history, a series I am proud to be a part of.

At a meeting of the Society for Reformation Research and the Verein für Reformationsgeschichte in Washington, D.C., in 1991, I met Adolf Laube and Bernd Hamm, both of whom I had known only through their published work. It was invaluable to me at just that time to be able to talk with them. They continued to help with off-prints and correspondence. Eckhard Bernstein also became a friend at that time, giving me the opportunity to discuss Ulrich von Hutten and Hans Sachs with someone truly knowledgeable.

The greatest pleasure of the work on the book was the friendship of Maria and Walter Grossman. The Andover-Newton and Harvard Divinity School library, which Maria directed, had the full set of the Köhler microfiche, and I worked there. Maria was always solicitous about my access to the fiche and careful to guide me to the best machine-reader. After several visits, I was staying with them at their house when in Cambridge. They were involved in every stage of the book. Walter was a walking bibliography, always able to tell me in what obscure journal I might track down an equally obscure writer. Maria pushed me to answer questions I did not want to face. There was a constant sharing of books and ideas over long lunches at their house or ours.

The burden of getting the manuscript onto computer disk was carried by Janet Tucker and her family. She cheerfully said she was willing to help when I began it, and she never flinched at one more round of revision. When we began, Joshua Tucker was starting pre-school. This year he entered fifth grade. Thus is the time of a book measured. Michael Tucker, equally tireless, served as computer consultant, particularly with difficult problems of computer compatibility. I am also grateful to Terry Mares of the Humanities Press for his meticulous editing of the final version. He was knowledgable, precise and invariably cheerful.

The Primary Sources bibliography was prepared by James Palmitessa, who transcribed the full titles from the title pages of the originals. Corrections were made with the skillful help of Fred Hoffer in the University of Massachusetts Computer Room. Corrections of the secondary sources were made by Fred Hoffer and Alice Izod of the University of Massachusetts History Department. As publication neared, the full titles of the primary sources had to be reduced to short titles. Gabriel Chrisman, my grandson, took on the job of making the changes on the computer for me. I have never managed to work without family labor.

Nicholas Chrisman continued our long-term discussion of the process of change. Abbott Chrisman edited the entire manuscript, trying to rescue it from repetition and ponderous sentences, and arranged for the illustrations from the Zentralbibliothek in Zurich. My husband, Donald Chrisman, has given an amazing commitment to the book, no matter how long it took to finish. His ideal of a dual professional household has never flagged. And it is I who have been sustained by his dedication.

Miriam Usher Chrisman
Northampton, Mass.

Abbreviations in Notes

AB	*Art Bulletin*
ADB	*Allgemeine Deutsche Biographie*
AHR	*American Historical Review*
ARG	*Archiv für Reformation Geschichte*
BBK	*Beiträge zur Bayerischen Kirchengeschichte*
EH	*Ebernburg-Hefte*
MVGSN	*Mitteilungen des Vereins für Geschichte der Stadt Nürnberg*
NA	*Nassauische Annalen*
OED	*Oxford English Dictionary*
P and P	*Past and Present*
RHPR	*Revue d'histoire et de philosophie religieuses*
SCJ	*Sixteenth Century Journal*
SFB	Schottenloher *Flugschriften Bibliographie* in *Flugschriften zur Ritterschaftsbewegung*
SVR	*Schriften des Vereins für Reformationsgeschichte*

Introduction:
The Laity and Their
Pamphlets—
Different Modes of Discourse

The men and women described in this book felt so passionately about the Reformation that they wrote about it. While the new theology, the changes in the liturgy, and the demand for reforms in church polity were the work of the reformers, the lay response made the changes possible. Historical research in the past tended to focus on the reformers. Only rather recently have historians examined the beliefs and ideas of the townspeople, urban elite, nobles, and knights who listened to the words of the preachers and adapted them to their own view of the world. I have tried to determine the laity's religious beliefs and their perceptions of their society using the materials they wrote themselves: dialogues, letters, reports of religious events, commentaries on the Bible, attacks on the Roman clergy, prayer books, and theological tracts. This rich literature has revealed that the laity's response may have been deeply affected by the different points of view inherent in the social hierarchy.

The lay pamphlets bring together ideas of social groups which historians have tended to separate. The history of the Reformation has been approached through studies of cities, the territorial states, or the Peasants' War, each regarded as a distinct entity, with its own antecedents and chronology. Lay pamphlets reveal barriers among rural and urban groups, nobility, and commoners but they also demonstrate the spontaneous and simultaneous response of all these groups. The Reformation did not move neatly down or up the ladder of the social hierarchy. It struck everyone at the same time. The pamphlets reveal the unrestrained response, the compelling desire for change among all levels of society. The pamphlets also make it possible to address questions like those raised by Peter Blickle, on the one hand, and Bernd Moeller, on the other, as to whether there was a common perception of the meaning of the Reformation among both townsmen and rural people or whether the movement was more accessible to city folk.[1]

1

My own interest in lay writers began in 1961, when, working in the Strasbourg Municipal Archives, I discovered a pamphlet written by a local nobleman, Eckhard zum Drübel, on how to live and die a Christian life. I wanted to include his pamphlet in my first book but I did not know where he fit. Were his ideas representative of other laymen? Was he a Lutheran? A Zwinglian? An Anabaptist? Thirty years later I can put him in context. He was unique among his fellow noblemen and developed his own concept of the Christian life. He initiated my search for other lay writers.

Meantime, a growing number of scholars were investigating the pamphlet literature. Steven Ozment cited pamphlets in his *Reformation of the Cities* to show the range of clerical and lay response to the new preaching. Robert Scribner's *For the Sake of Simple Folk* carried this much further, examining nearly 100 propaganda pamphlets by clergy and lay persons and creating a brilliant portrait of the pictures and texts that drove the Reformation message. Paul Russell was the first to concentrate on lay writers, analyzing the work of eight pamphleteers, five artisans, and three women. He placed these men and women in the context of the reformation movement in the cities where they lived, focusing on the religious ideas of each writer. Martin Arnold's published doctoral dissertation reviewed 28 pamphlets by ten artisans. Following a rigid outline, he summarized each pamphlet, describing the writer's concept of the path to salvation, the Christian life, and definition of the guiding principles of life and faith. Pursuing only these questions, the depth of his analysis was restricted. Other scholars contributed studies of a single lay author. Hans-Christoph Rublack, drawing on some 400 reformation pamphlets written by Catholic and reformed clergy and by lay persons, presented a masterful analysis of the types of anticlericalism which developed as the propagation of the Word of God became the primary concern of reformed clergy and laymen.[2] The pamphlet literature has been firmly established as an important source for understanding the Reformation. I have used it to move beyond the theological issues studied by these others to explore the social and economic perceptions of the laity and their influence on lay understanding of reformation teachings. In the portrait of the Reformation which I have painted, the reformers do not dominate the scene, with lay persons—knights, merchants, beggars—standing around the edges. Lay men and women occupy the foreground, as they did in many of the title-page woodcuts, fully conscious of their own ability to interpret Scripture, offering their own, independent solutions to monasticism, confession, and the care of the poor.

THE PAMPHLETS

The study is based on pamphlets (*Flugschriften*) written by lay persons between 1519–1530 which I gathered from the libraries in Strasbourg and Zurich and from printed collections edited by Oskar Schade, Otto Clemen, and Karl Schottenloher in the decades 1893–1929. Recent work by Adolf Laube, assisted by Anne Rose Schneider and Sigrid Loos, together with the microfiche compiled and published by Hans-Joachim Köhler et al., more than quadrupled the number of lay writings available to scholars.[3] After examining more than 400 of these pamphlets, I selected 300 which I judged to be the work of lay authors.

According to Hans-Joachim Köhler, a pamphlet

> is an independent, non-recurring, unbound publication of more than one page whose purpose is to agitate [that is, move to action] and/or to propagandize [that is, influence an opinion] and which is addressed to the masses of the public at large.[4]

The pamphlet literature of the sixteenth century cannot be readily compared with modern popular culture. Multiple channels of dissemination, oral and printed, had not yet developed, although vernacular printed books, tracts, sermons, and broadsheets were harbingers of things to come. For this study I made a narrow selection of pamphlets, which as religious propaganda cannot be assumed to represent the broader stream of contemporary popular culture. Rather, the pamphlet writers were articulate members of the reformers' audience. Their tracts show how people interacted with what they read and heard, and, as Levine has written of modern popular audiences, this "can be used to reconstruct [their] attitudes, values and reactions."[5]

Propaganda pamphlets went up like a geyser, uncontrolled and uncontrollable, a phenomenon in their own time. In the Middle Ages, there had been polemic battles in manuscript form between popes and emperors, between popes and monastic orders, between factious university professors. Franciscan preachers had taken some of these issues to the laity in their sermons, but the Reformation had a new tool: the printing press. Martin Luther and Ulrich von Hutten were among the first to understand that printers could carry their message directly to ordinary people. Other writers followed quickly. The 5,000 *Flugschriften* in the Köhler microfiche collection, most printed between 1520 and 1530, represent the work of 800 different writers, at least 120 of whom were lay. Thus the laity provided one-eighth of the troops in the propaganda battle.

My study rigorously separates the lay writers from the clergy. In the late Middle Ages, the clergy differed from the laity because they were meant to follow a more ascetic path, divorcing themselves from worldly life. Traditionally, this made them spiritually and morally superior to the laity, their lives more worthy.[6] This had begun to break down in the late fifteenth century, as groups like the Brethren of the Common Life took no vows and worked in the world. The legal distinction between lay and clergy, however, remained unchanged. Clerics were not subject to civil law and appeared only before ecclesiastical courts. Laymen consciously asserted the incompatibility between the two groups. I excluded authors with any clerical background from the study, such as Catholic priests who left the old church, reentered the world, and wrote about their experience, or former monks and nuns, with the exception of nuns writing to lay members of their families. University faculty members were excluded because many of them held degrees in theology or had taken minor orders. Men with university degrees in law or medicine were included because they had neither the status nor privileges of clerics. I also omitted Anabaptist preachers and leaders, many of whom were lay people, because their writing has been thoroughly analyzed by George Williams, James Stayer, and others.[7] The work on the Anabaptists has somewhat overshadowed the contribution of other laymen. My aim has been to describe the ideas, beliefs, and actions of a broad range of ordinary men and women as they responded to the Reformation.

Their response mirrored the vitality of vernacular culture in the years 1480–1520. The turn of the century witnessed a flood of German vernacular publication as printers in cities like Strasbourg, Augsburg, Nuremberg, and Basel sought wider markets.[8] Tales and songs which had long been part of the oral culture were printed in illustrated versions, as were Bible stories and lives of the saints. The German Bible, first printed in 1466, went through 14 editions before 1518 and is often listed in inventories taken at the death of ordinary men and women.[9] Individual books of the Bible, the account of Christ's passion, Job, and Daniel's dream were also widely circulated.[10] The German humanists expanded the world of the vernacular readers with translations of the Roman historians, particularly Livy, and editions of Terence, Virgil, and Cicero's *Rhetoric*.[11] The humanists wrote major works in German. Sebastian Brant's *Ship of Fools* was a best-seller with its sharp satire of everyday life and people. Thomas Murner provided further provocative commentary on urban and rural life. Sermons by Geiler von Kaysersberg were directed at moral and ethical behavior, asserting the need for inner, spiritual reform and penance.[12] Thus, in the decades before the Reformation, lay men and women had been challenged intellectually and had been given new tools. Many became familiar with the Bible. They had been introduced to examples of German and Roman rhetoric, which they could adopt in their own writing.[13] The vernacular culture had developed new depth.

CRITERIA FOR PAMPHLET ANALYSIS

When I began to work on lay pamphlets, I assumed all laymen were alike. Indeed, in an essay written for Geoffrey Dickens' *Festschrift* in 1980, I lumped together several noblemen, a burgher, an artist, a patrician woman, and a gardener, believing they were related simply by their lay status.[14] When I undertook a more rigorous analysis with more pamphlets, I discovered my original assumption was simplistic.

My first task was to identify the authors of the pamphlets. But how did I know they were laymen? Many of them gave their name and station on the title page or in a preface. Popular poets and song writers, following tradition, slipped their names into the last stanza of the poem.[15] Some lay writers could be located in archival documents. The search made me realize there were vast differences among the writers. To explore these, to sort out the wide variety of literary forms, and to determine common themes and attitudes, I analyzed each pamphlet according to fixed criteria with regard to genre and content. Genre distinguishes works of literature in terms of purpose and technique. The purpose of all pamphlet writers was similar, but they offered strikingly divergent arguments and drew on a wide variety of techniques.

To analyze technique, I first examined the rhetorical strategy adopted by the author: narrative, dramatic, discursive, reflective, or imitative. Narrative included accounts of an event such as the siege of Sickingen's castle or the trial of a Lutheran convert by a bishop. Dramatic strategy covered a variety of dialogue forms as well as *Fastnachtspiel*, traditional popular plays. Discursive comprised pamphlets which interpreted the new beliefs according to logical reasoning. In a reflective pamphlet the author described his or her own thoughts and feelings with regard to the church, the clergy, or social or moral issues. Imitative pamphlets borrowed their form from classical authors, the catechism, or popular models like letters from the devil, New Year's greetings, or tavern songs.

Having established the rhetorical form, I outlined each pamphlet to determine the sequence of ideas as presented by the author. Was there a logical structure which built from one proposition to the next? If it was a dialogue, did the protagonist state his beliefs clearly while the antagonist was revealed as unreasonable or confused, or did they engage in real debate? What sources did the author use to prove his point? The Bible? Luther? Other reformers? Classical authors? The church fathers? Canon law?

Analysis of language focused on word choice and grammar. What kind of vocabulary did the writer use—colloquial? Formal? Scholarly discourse? What kind of grammar—a speech-like pattern or a more formal prose style? Was the tone intimate and familiar, addressing the reader as *du,* or formal, using *Sie*? Phrases and motifs which reappeared from one pamphlet to another were carefully noted.

Content analysis considered the religious ideas expressed. A major difference was whether the author was concerned primarily with exposing the errors of the old church or with propounding the new teaching according to his or her understanding. The specific targets of anticlericalism were noted, as were the particular abuses of the clergy to which the author referred and the author's attitude toward his or her own or other social classes. Finally, the author's response to the new teaching was recorded, including the words used to define the Reformation and the concept of the source of religious truth.

When I turned to the anonymous pamphlets, I found patterns of rhetorical form, language, and content similar to those in pamphlets by known authors. Both Laube and Köhler utilized language and thematics in identifying authors.[16] Using the same techniques, I placed the anonymous pamphlets with those they resembled. Schottenloher had earlier gathered together the unsigned pamphlets written by knights.[17]

When all the pamphlets were sorted out according to rhetorical technique, language, and content, a significant pattern emerged. The pamphlets mapped the process of ideological change and provided empirical evidence of the effect of social, economic and political differences on an individual's acceptance of ideas. Social status was critical in this process because people of the same social rank often received the same education and were predisposed to the opinions and beliefs of their peers. When writing they tended to adopt similar rhetorical formulae and modes of expression. Each rank had its own convictions about the causes of the Reformation and its plan for what changes should be made. These latter were often based on the particular needs and interests of their own group.

In other words, there was a social dimension to the reception of ideas. Furthermore, the Reformation message, as it penetrated the community, magnified the differences between social groups.

THE PAMPHLET WRITERS

Five social ranks were involved: nobility, urban elite, learned civil servants and professionals, minor civil servants and technicians, and common burghers and artisans. With the exception of two members of the high nobility,[18] the noble pamphleteers came from the lower nobility and the knights of the empire. They were joined by noble women, who were more likely to write than women of lower rank. The majority of the civil servants were *Stadtschreiber*, permanent city secretaries, educated in the law, although not all had completed their university degrees. Minor civil servants and technicians had less education—some Latin school or training in their art. They were school teachers, clerks, secretaries, rural administrators, astrologers, musicians, apothecaries, and printers. The group reflects an ambivalence toward those who had technical, scientific, or mechanical skills. Society, not yet sure where they fit in the hierarchy, ranked them together. The fifth rank, referring to themselves as common burghers or artisans, consisted mainly of craftsmen: weavers, shoemakers, a wagoner, a weighmaster, bakers, tanners, and clothmakers. Others were small retailers, soldiers, and *landsknechten*. By and large these men and women had received little formal education. Most were self-educated. Yet, in the short period from 1522 to 1530, they wrote more pamphlets than any of the other ranks.

Missing from the sample of pamphleteers are wealthy merchants, members of the city councils, and peasants. I found no tracts written by individuals from the merchant class or by city councillors.[19] Yet, their concepts of reform and their understanding of the common good were reflected in ordinances they promulgated to reform the church, the monastic orders, and the poor laws. These were often published to serve as models for other cities. The elite are represented in the pamphlet literature by laws and ordinances.

Peasants were unrepresented in the study. Although peasants are mentioned in the titles of a number of pamphlets, many of these, on close examination, proved to be written by urban authors, usually reformed clergy.[20] For example, in an anonymous dialogue between Cuntz and Fritz *die Brauchen wenig witz* (who showed little sense), the two supposed peasants discussed the faculty at the University of Tübingen, naming those who opposed the reading of Scripture. They also had detailed knowledge of Luther's opponents, including the ecclesiastical appointments they held. Cuntz had read the books of Oecalampadius; he particularly admired the latter's attack on canon law.[21] In another dialogue, between a priest and a tailor, the tailor stated that he could neither read nor write, a stock phrase in these pseudo-lay pamphlets. He knew, however, that at the end of his life Thomas Aquinas had rejected his own writings and had stated that the truth lay only in the Bible.[22] The clergy, he charged, were ignorant because they read only Plato, Aristotle, Ricardus, and Occam.[23] In these and similar pamphlets, the reformed clergy, by adopting the persona of a peasant or an artisan, hoped to reach the general reader but were unable to suppress their learning. Theologians and intellectuals also assumed the voice of the *gemeine Mann*, making him the leader in the reform of church and society. The term was ambiguous then as now. Did they mean urban people or peasants or both?[24] Whichever, a lay person became the mouthpiece for a learned writer. In my search for lay writers I found more than 30 of these pamphlets, none of which were included in the study. Genuine peasant writings, the articles of grievance or compacts drawn up by groups of peasants at the time of the Peasants' War, have been collected and published by Adolf Laube and Hans Seiffert and by Tom Scott and Bob Scribner.[25] They constitute a distinctive genre which is not comparable to the polemic propaganda of this study.

The lay pamphlets make it possible to follow some popular reactions to the new theology. Most people heard the Reformation message first in sermons. A priest began to preach the Gospel to his congregation in the cathedral, a Franciscan in his convent church. Wherever this occurred, men and women of different social ranks gathered. It has been assumed that this was a unifying experience which created a joining of minds, a strengthening of the urban corporate identity.[26] In fact, this may have been the flash point which led to separation and fragmentation. Each rank heard the message in terms of its own perceptions, its own needs and demands for political and ecclesiastical reform, some of which went back over a hundred years.[27] Urban society, in particular, was a corporate body made up of distinct, sometimes insular groups whose goals were not necessarily identical. Thus, in the first decade of the Reformation in the city of Strasbourg, the reformers pressed for changes in religious belief and practices. Some patricians advocated closing the monasteries. The magistrates and the city secretaries saw the movement as a means of achieving their historic objective of bringing the church under secular control. The artisans were moved by the call to spiritual renewal but also hoped to rid themselves of the usurious demands of the clergy and the rich. It was as though the sermons of the preacher had gone out on separate telephone systems to four different centers, where the message was decoded, analyzed, restructured, then integrated into the values and ethos of each particular group. Although all the writers espoused faith against works and the primacy of Scripture, the lay pamphlets expose the differences between the ranks, revealing the issues in dispute, the presence of mutual antagonisms and distrust, and the continuation of old patterns of suspicion and fear.

THE DIVERSITY OF THE PAMPHLETS: CONTENT AND TECHNIQUES

There were clear differences in the language of the pamphlets. The upper ranks tended to use a formal style, reflecting their education. Artisans wrote as they spoke, so their pamphlets read like oral discourse. Local dialects were much in evidence. During the Reformation familiar words took on new meaning: faith; Gospel; Scripture; the Word of God; the Word of the mouth of God. These were code words which identified a person as reformed—they were the banners of belief. The pamphlets reveal, however, that the words meant different things to different people, even among those who had adopted the new faith. In the early years of the movement, the lack of precise definition made it possible for men and women to formulate their own meanings. The ambiguity opened the way to deep misunderstandings, giving rise to bitter feelings of betrayal.

Each class used literary forms familiar to it. The nobility drew up grievances, as they and others had since the fourteenth century, proclaiming the problems of the empire and the reforms that should be made. As nobles they had political power and expected to have their voices heard. They also wrote letters, addressed to persons in power, urging them to protect the new beliefs; or to their relatives and to their subjects or tenants explaining the true Christian faith.[28] Many of the letters, even intimate family correspondence, were taken to the printer and published. A private form became public. The nobility also adopted the classic dialogue format popularized by the humanists, particularly by Erasmus' *Colloquies*. The dialogues thus followed established rhetorical style. A major speaker set forth the important parts of the argument; other participants asked a few leading questions which permitted the speaker to embellish his point. Significantly, most dialogues by nobles presented only a single point of view with little exchange between the principals. In the sixteenth century it was not assumed that dialogue would present both sides of an argument. It could be used by a writer to defend his own point of view and block that of his opponent.[29]

Letters were the favored form of the urban elite. They wrote urging their relatives in monastic orders to set aside their vows. Several married women wrote to their cloistered sisters advocating the virtues of life in the world. In one case the letters were published before they were sent to the supposed recipient. Family discussion was pushed out into the public forum, indicating the way in which familial and public life were intertwined.

Pamphlets written by the learned upper civil servants, in particular the city secretaries, reflected their legal training and their feeling of responsibility for their communities. Letters were again a common form, addressed to officials at all levels of authority, exhorting them to support Luther's teaching to maintain the peace of the empire. Deeply committed to Luther, several city secretaries wrote long theological explanations of his doctrines. Others published interpretations of biblical texts or translations from Scripture. The city secretaries, serving as a link between the reformers and the magistrates, wrote the laws to establish the new church polity, close the monasteries, and create new welfare systems that reflected both the reformers' teaching and the desire of the city council to strengthen and maintain civic order.

As the analysis proceeded, one miscellany of pamphlets defied classification. It included a plea for reform of the empire, two letters addressed to Luther by the devil, a letter from Jesus Christ addressed to all Christians, several mordant attacks on the Pope and his court, and two broad programs for social and political reform. The common element in these disparate tracts was that the authors were minor civil servants, school teachers, printers, and technicians whose skills lifted them above the ordinary artisan. They were an anomalous group, without the education or authority to rank with the learned, yet sufficiently educated to be considered above the handworkers from whom most of them had sprung. This in-between position may have made them sharper, more critical, more reckless than those above and below them.

The artisans, with far less experience as writers, used almost a dozen different literary forms: songs, poems, journalistic accounts, letters, plays, accounts of the martyrdoms of reformed laymen, biblical interpretations, satires, statements of faith, catechisms, attacks against specific practices of the church, and dialogues.[30] Their preferred form, the dialogue or conversation, constituted nearly a fourth of their pamphlets. They did not adopt the classical style of the humanist dialogue. In several of these *Gespräche* written by Hans Sachs, a shoemaker, Utz Ryschner, a weaver, and a student from a similar milieu, the style of the dialogue is more like the dramatic style of the popular theater, particularly the *Fastnachtspiel*.[31] Although one speaker might have more lines than another, he or she did not dominate the piece. Furthermore, the speakers were not inanimate figures serving merely as mouthpieces for the writer. People came and went in natural ways. A new arrival was quickly drawn into the dialogue and often asked for his opinion. Perhaps the most striking difference was that people with unpopular views, such as someone loyal to the old faith, stated his beliefs and was not ridiculed. True, by the end, he was on his way to conversion, but there had been a genuine attempt to find points of agreement and arrive at consensus. The tone of these pamphlets was different, suggesting that at least some of the artisans wished to bring people together, not separate them.

Breaking with tradition and precedent, the artisans and craftsmen wrote tracts addressing purely religious topics: the interpretation of Scripture, forms of prayer, and doctrinal matters such as confession, baptism, and communion. Here the lay men and women were on unfamiliar ground. The logical argument of these tracts is impressive; equally striking are the quotations from Scripture used as proof texts. These lay persons, although they lacked formal education and few of them had professional experience as writers, were able to organize their ideas and present them clearly, often in graphic, vibrant language. Their concerns, however, were very different from those of the nobility and certainly from the clerical leadership. They wanted a simple Christianity, free of dogma, infused by the spirit of Jesus himself.

The sources each group used were distinctly different, providing a clear view into the intellectual experience, the general knowledge, and the reading of each class. I compiled figures on direct quotations and references to the sources they used including the Bible and Luther, which varied widely from rank to rank. (The figures sometimes total above 100% because 40% of the writers in a group might refer to Luther, 50% to Scripture, 20% to other reformers.) There were very few direct quotations from Luther's texts; instead he was mentioned or his doctrine was assimilated by the lay writer. Noble pamphleteers mentioned Luther in only 6% of their pamphlets, patricians in 27%, the learned upper class in 50%, artisans in 15%—a bell-shaped curve when plotted against social rank. The pattern for Scripture was entirely different: 24% of the nobility used scriptural references, 45% of the patricians, 50% of the learned and lower civil servants, and 82% of the artisans—a distribution of almost geometric increase.

The noble writers drew heavily on imperial-papal history and canon law. Together these equalled 53% of their references, while references to contemporary conditions came to only 10%. The urban elite drew mostly on Scripture and on Luther. The sources of the upper civil servants reflected their years at the university. Scripture and Luther were of central importance, at 50% respectively. Quotations from Latin classics, imperial-papal history, canon law, imperial law, and municipal law as well as Zwingli, Melanchthon, Augustine, and the lives of the saints could run as high as 20% to 30% in their pamphlets. Their education and their exposure to humanism gave them a greater range than any other group.

The overwhelming preponderance of scriptural quotation among the artisans confirms the existence of a strongly established Bible culture at the artisan level well before the Reformation. The variety and length of the quotations could not have come merely from oral exposure to the Bible. This has received little attention because the assumption has been that artisans were swung over to the Reformation by sermons. Yet, the evidence of the artisans' pamphlets shows that they owned Bibles or postills and that it was natural for them to discuss the meaning of biblical passages among themselves. An artisan could move easily from the Old Testament to the Psalms to the New Testament in one paragraph, not easy to do if one had just begun to explore the text. The artisans' knowledge of Scripture was sufficient to give them confidence to criticize the sermons and books by Roman clergy and scholars. Armed with the Bible, the artisans were willing to confront those more learned on theological matters.

GEOGRAPHIC CLUSTERING

The geographic clustering of the pamphlet writers lends further support to the findings of Brady, Blickle, Scott, Scribner, and Russell with regard to the pivotal role of southwest German and Franconian cities and rural areas in the early decades of the Reformation.[32] It was possible to locate 60 of the authors by place. Of these, 30% came from the Rhenish Palatinate and Franconia. Another 29% came from Swabia, centered on Nuremberg, Augsburg, and Reutlingen. Fourteen percent came from the upper Rhenish cities of Strasbourg and Basel. Only 18% were resident in the two Saxonies. Lay pamphlet writers centered in southwest Germany, Franconia, Alsace, and the Rhenish Palatinate.

Geographic grouping according to social and occupational rank was striking. The majority of those nobles who could be identified came from the Rhenish Palatinate, the center of the Knights' Revolt. Seventy percent of the artisans were concentrated in a triangle formed by three cities: Nuremberg, Augsburg, and Strasbourg. The strong activity in this area may reflect the proto-industrialism and the proto-revolutionary conditions in the surrounding countryside. These cities were larger than those to the west and the north. The social, religious, and political tensions were greater.[33]

The city secretaries and the minor civil servants and technicians who wrote pamphlets were more evenly distributed. The Nuremberg-Augsburg area and the Rhenish-Palatinate were still important, but a larger proportion was in the Saxonies. Despite the regional concentration of the writers, the widespread printing of pamphlets demonstrates that the audience was not merely local. The market for the pamphlets reached well beyond the southwestern areas, reflected in reprinting in other the towns and cities.

PRINTING THE PAMPHLETS

Printers played a vital role in spreading the influence of the lay writers, putting themselves and their presses at risk to do so. Pamphlets by Rhenish knights were published in Strasbourg and in Augsburg. Artisan pamphlets were widely distributed across Germany and Switzerland. The Augsburg-Nuremberg-Strasbourg triangle was the focus of publication and distribution, but northern, eastern, Swiss, and Bavarian cities printed one-third of the pamphlet editions.

From 1521 to 1528, printing or owning polemic pamphlets was dangerous. The Edict of Worms of 1521, which ordered all Luther's books destroyed, was so sweeping it could not be enforced across the empire. Nevertheless, it meant that printers were unwilling to place their name, the date, or the place of publication on their imprints.[34] For roughly 70% of the pamphlets in the Köhler microfiche collection there is no publication information on the title page or at the end; the printers have been identified only by recent scholarship.[35] Caution was essential because the authorities might strike without warning and capriciously. For example, Johann Grüninger, a well-established, respected printer in Strasbourg, published a bitterly anti-Lutheran pamphlet in 1522. Although the city council at that point had not accepted the Reform, Grüninger's whole press run was confiscated.[36] In that same year, noblemen writing from Sickingen's castle at the Ebernburg noted that if a book contained anything against the Roman clergy the cathedral canons would prevent its sale. This had apparently happened to their first pamphlet.[37] Censorship was strongest and most effective in Hapsburg lands and in areas where the bishop or prince was staunchly Catholic. In 1527, the Nuremberg printer Hans Hergot was executed in Leipzig because he had printed *The New Transformation in a Christian Life*.[38] A printer could lose his stock, his shop, or, in Hergot's case, his life by publishing a polemic pamphlet.

The danger extended to owning books as well, particularly in episcopal and Hapsburg territories. A chaplain who had books in his possession was beaten and imprisoned in the town of Miltenberg in 1523, and the books were destroyed.[39] A student at Ingolstadt was punished for having Lutheran books in his room.[40] In 1524, Caspar Tauber, a respectable burgher of Vienna, was sentenced as a heretic and beheaded because he had preached Lutheran doctrines, owned Lutheran books, and written tracts. The tracts were condemned to the fire.[41]

To discuss the printing of lay pamphlets is to discuss risk, hazard, and the inconsistency of execution of the law. Nevertheless, in the larger cities there were printers willing to endanger themselves because of their religious convictions. A few protected themselves by printing both Catholic and Protestant works.[42] The majority of those who accepted lay pamphlets also printed the work of Luther and other reformed theologians.[43]

The basic formula for a pamphlet was short and cheap except for the title pages. In the case of the reformers and other intellectuals, these were held to the essentials: the title of the treatise, the author's name, and his academic title if he held one. Exceptions were the earliest Luther pamphlets, printed between 1520 and 1521, which included a portrait of the reformer on the title pages.[44] Rather quickly this disappeared and the title page was simplified as described. Title pages of lay pamphlets, however, were more elaborate. Many of them had woodcuts, in some cases identifying the status of the writer, such as a married woman standing in front of her house or a workman in his rough cloak with the tools of his trade. Pamphlets written by noblemen carried their coat of arms as soon as these authors laid off the cloak of anonymity.[45]

The pamphlets written by artisans, craftsmen, and technicians tended to have the most complicated designs. The illustrations were related to the content of the pamphlet, like the cover of a modern paperback novel. The first illustration in this book shows the title page of A *Dialogue between a Father and a Son*, on which the father, a successful peasant, is seated in a great wooden chair, while the son, returning from the University of Wittenberg, still wears his cloak. Through the open door a servant can be seen burning an indulgence letter, an incident described in the text.[46] The weaver Utz Ryschner wrote a dialogue between a weaver and a merchant discussing a recently published treatise on confession. Illustration 6 (p. 158) shows the tradesman reading from the treatise, while the weaver has a far larger book, clearly the Bible, in front of him.[47]

These woodcuts seem to be a conscious attempt to attract the reader, to give an idea of the content of the pamphlet, to relate the pamphlet to ordinary life and attract the eye of the buyer. The woodcuts were expensive. The printer had to commission the artist to draw the picture and then pay the form cutter, who usually received a higher fee than the original artist—a considerable investment for a pamphlet of eight to 16 pages. Clearly, some printers were willing to spend more money to publish tracts written by artisans and burghers, indicating a fairly secure market for these particular pamphlets.

Relatively numerous reprints are another indication of the impact made by the lay writers. Thirty-five percent of their pamphlets were printed more than once. In most cases there were one or two other editions, but Nicolaus Herman's *Mandat Jesu Christi* went through ten editions in a year. Sixteen pamphlets were reprinted six times or more. Although my data is by no means complete, 303 reprints are listed in the bibliography. Adding first editions and reprints would give a total of 597 lay pamphlets in circulation in the 11-year period. Another indication of the importance of the market is the pseudo-lay pamphlet, which confirms the popularity of the pamphlet written by a genuine layman. Once the laymen had made their mark, the reformed clergy donned their cloak to try to attract the same readers. This attempt to imitate confirms the effectiveness of the laity as propagandists.

THE SOCIAL DIMENSION OF IDEAS

This book has two purposes, the first to place the lay pamphlets in the social and intellectual context in which they were written, the second to demonstrate how the ideas of the Reformation were changed and adapted as they were transmitted to different ranks in the social hierarchy. Together, context and transmission reveal the social dimension of ideas which helped to create the fundamental divisions of early modern society.

The structure of the book grew out of the need to place like-minded writers together to analyze their work. Until very recently, lay writers were not studied as an important component of Reformation thought. Historians would cite a single lay pamphlet to prove the wide influence of a clerical writer. For example, *Die Wittembergisch Nachtigall* by Hans Sachs has been used again and again to demonstrate the rapid popular acceptance of Luther's teaching. When I examined the work of the lay writers separately from the clergy, their independence was striking. They rarely drew on the writings of reformers. Their perception of the Reformation was influenced by the realities of their own lives. They interpreted the new ideas in terms of their social aspirations, the political conflicts in which they were involved, and their individual search for a deeper spirituality.

The process of transmission began with the reformers who called for changes in dogma, liturgy, and church polity. As their sermons and those of their adversaries were heard, as their pamphlets were read, the social dimension came into play. The ideas of the reformers moved out into the complex hierarchy of classes. Each class had its own world-view, its own perception of the community as a whole and its position within it. This determined its relationships to other ranks, whether it respected them as contributing beneficially to the whole or as making selfish, self-seeking demands. Artisans did not necessarily perceive nobles as superior to them; superior in terms of powers, yes, but inferior on a moral scale. Each class was differentiated by the education, formal or informal, which it was expected to receive. Aspirations were also highly diverse. Each class heard the message of the reformers in distinctive ways. What one group heard as a call to action another interpreted as an appeal for caution. The preaching and teaching of the reformers was molded by each social rank to fit its own requirements, its own traditional agendas.

Thus, the nobles believed that with the support of the new religious teachings, they could finally achieve their ancient goal of reforming the empire. The peasants believed that their relationships with their overlords would be changed and they would have more autonomy in their villages. The urban magistrates believed they would be able to discipline the clergy and create greater civic order and harmony. The artisans believed that Christian love would prevail and the poor would be cared for as Christ had commanded. All agreed on the need for change. How change was defined, what it should include, laid bare the fundamental divisions in the society. Each group pressed for its own solution within the limits of its political power.

The hierarchical structure which early modern society believed was the foundation of order led instead to disruption. The Reformation laid bare the process which occurred when a new idea was introduced to this system. Fundamental class divisions were present in the society before the demand for change was made. Although the new ideas were phrased as universals, each rank heard different parts of the message and revised it to fit its own need. The ideology was forced into the structure of existing social and political realities. The early Reformation produced a profusion of conflicting aims. As time passed, alliances between the political authorities and the reformers made it possible to suppress the dissension and establish a unified theology and church polity. The opening years were a period of liberation and innovation. Later the authorities struggled to limit the unrestrained expression of beliefs. Heterodoxy and nonconformity were smothered by the new, reformed orthodoxy.

FIGURE 1   Number of pamphlet editions in the sample
published in major printing centers

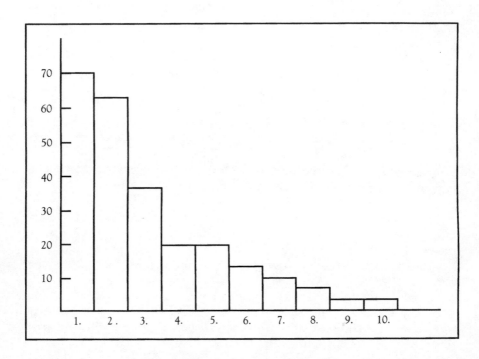

1. Strasbourg   6. Wittenberg
2. Augsburg   7. Bamberg
3. Nuremberg   8. Zurich
4. Erfurt   9. Zwickau
5. Basel   10. Speyer

Notes

(A number preceded by the symbol # refers to the full reference in the Primary Sources bibliography.)

1. Peter Blickle, *Communal Reformation*, 1992, 5. Bernd Moeller, *Imperial Cities and the Reformation*, 1972, 54–57.
2. Steven Ozment, *The Reformation in the Cities*, 1975; R. W. Scribner, *For the Sake of Simple Folk*, 1981; Paul Russell, *Lay Theology in the Reformation*, 1986; Martin Arnold, *Handwerker als theologische Schriftstellar, 1523–1525,* 1990; Rodolphe Peter, "Le maraîcher Clément Ziegler: l'homme et son oeuvre" *RHPR* 34 (1954): 255–282; Harold J. Grimm, *Lazarus Spengler: A Lay Leader of the Reformation,* 1978; Bernd Hamm, "Lazarus Spengler und Martin Luther's Theologie," in eds. Volker Press und Dieter Stievermann, *Martin Luther: Probleme seiner Zeit,* 1986, 124–136; Gustave Koch, *Eckhart zum Drübel,* 1989; Hans-Christoph Rublack, "Anticlericalism in German Reformation Pamphlets," in eds. Peter A. Dykema and Heiko Oberman, *Anticlericalism in Late Medieval and Early Modern Europe,* 1993, 461–489.
3. One of the first scholars to recognize the importance of lay writers was Oskar Schade, who included them in his collection *Satiren und Pasquille aus der Reformationszeit,* 3 vols. 1868. Otto Clemen, ed., *Flugschriften aus den Ersten Jarhen der Reformation,* 4 vols., 1907–1911, was the next one to draw attention to pamphlet literature as an important source. Half of his selections were written by clergy, a pattern followed by most editors. Another important early contribution was Karl Schottenloher, *Flugschriften zur Ritterschaftsbewegung des Jahres 1523.* Heft 53. ed. Albert Ehrhard. *Reformationsgeschichtliche Studien und Texte,* 1929. 1–29. They were followed by ed., Arnold E. Berger, *Die Sturmtruppen der Reformation,* 1931. A new, greatly expanded collection was made by Adolf Laube et al., *Flugschriften der frühen Reformationsbewegung,* 2 vols., 1983. The major collection is Hans-Joachim Köhler et al., *Flugschriften des frühen 16. Jahrhunderts,* Microfiche Serie, 1978–1987 (Zug. 1978–1987). This was the work of the *Flugschriften-projekt,* directed by Hans-Joachim Köhler, which for the first time united the important holdings of sixteenth-century pamphlet literature in then West German libraries. The directors of the project, who included Hildegard Habenstreit-Wilfert and Christoph Weisman, selected the pamphlets, filmed by teams of photographers working in the libraries. The published microfiche make available nearly 5,000 pamphlets from the Staatsbibliothek in Munich, the Herzog Augst Bibliothek in Wolffenbüttel, and the libraries in Augsburg, Donaueschingen, Dortmund, Münster, Regensburg, West Berlin, and Würzburg. Thus the wealth of these collections is opened to the scholarly world on microfiche. The present book would have been impossible without it.
4. Quoted in Steven Ozment, "Pamphlet Literature of the German Reformation," 1982, 86. See Bernd Balzer, *Bürgerliche Reformationspropaganda,* 1973, 7, for a similar definition.
5. Lawrence W. Levine, "The Folklore of Industrial Society: Popular Culture and Its Audience," *AHR,* 97, 5 (1992):1372.
6. In the early Middle Ages the term layman was more restricted, applied to the uneducated, the illiterate, or, in the idiom of the day, the idiots, which meant

the uneducated, the ignorant (*OED*). As laymen began to acquire an education, from the twelfth to the sixteenth centuries, the term was used to differentiate them from the clergy, the priests, those in orders. See Georg Steer, "Zum Begriff 'Laie' in deutscher Dichtung und prosa des Mittelalters," c. 1984, 764, 766.

7. George H. Williams, *The Radical Reformation*, 1962; James M. Stayer, *The German Peasants' War and Anabaptist Community of Goods*, 1991; Hans J. Hillerbrand, *Anabaptist Bibliography 1520–1630*, 1991. Examples of laymen who were Anabaptist leaders include Johann Bünderlin, secretary to Baron von Stahremberg (169); Melchior Hoffman, a furrier (259); Caspar Schwenkfeld, a nobleman and a knight of the Teutonic order (106); Pilgram Marpeck, an engineer (253); Peter Riedemann, a cobbler (426); Johann (Hans) Hut, a bookbinder and sexton (79); George Haug, a peasant (79); David Joris, a glass painter (346); Jacob Hutter, a hatmaker (419). All these men, drawn from lay life to become Anabaptists, wrote pamphlets and doctrinal works to define their theological ideas. The variation in their social positions and in their occupations are another manifestation of the vigor of lay intellectual life. The page references refer to George Williams, *The Radical Reformation*, 1962.

8. I used my own study of publishing in Strasbourg as the basis for this summary. See Miriam Usher Chrisman, *Lay Culture, Learned Culture*, 1982, 103. A similar pattern can be found in Basel; see Frank Hieronymus, *Oberrheinische Buchillustration*, 2, 1993, passim.

9. T. H. Darlow and H. F. Moule, *Historical Catalogue of the Printed Editions of the Holy Scripture*, 2 vols. (1911) 2, 481–485. See Chrisman, *Lay Culture, Learned Culture*, 70–74, for Bibles in inventories at death.

10. Miriam Usher Chrisman, *Bibliography of Strasbourg Imprints*, 1982, 169.

11. Ibid., 75–76.

12. Ibid., 186, 183, 15–17.

13. Ibid., 179–180.

14. Miriam Usher Chrisman, "Lay Response to the Protestant Reformation in Germany, 1520–1528," 1980, 33–52.

15. Jörn Reichel, "Hans Rosenplüt genannt Schnepperer, ein Handwerkerdichter im spätmittelalterilchen Nürnberg," *MVGSN* 67 (1980): 18.

16. In the earliest *Flugschriften* collections, such as Schade's, little attempt was made to identify the authors. Otto Clemen and the individual scholars who edited the pamphlets in his four volumes made careful identifications. Adolf Laube et al. provided model notes on authorship in *Flugschriften der frühen Reformationsbewegung*. These were invaluable in helping me to proceed with identifying the anonymous pamphlets on microfiche. Hans-Joachim Köhler noted several ways to judge whether an anonymous pamphlet was written by a peasant or by an intellectual posing as a peasant, namely, quotations from classical authors, the church fathers, or canon law. Hans-Joachim Köhler, "'Der Bauer wird witzig': Der Bauer in den Flugschriften der Reformationszeit," 1986, 11. Köhler's criteria could be applied to anonymous pamphlets possibly written by artisans. Grammatical construction was one clue, another was the type of anti-clericalism displayed. Noble authors were anti-papal, anti-hierarchy. Patricians were anti-monastic. Artisans lashed out at begging monks and priests who did not preach from Scripture.

17. Karl Schottenloher, *Flugschriften zur Ritterschaftsbewegung des Jahres 1523*, 1929, 7–9, 10, 14–15.

18. Margraf Georg von Brandenburg-Ansbach and Herzog Georg von Sachsen both

wrote propaganda pamphlets after 1526. See Hans-Joachim Köhler, *Bibliographie der Flugschriften des 16. Jahrhunderts*, Band 1, *Druckbeschreibung A–G*, 1991, entries 1291–1297, 550–553.

19. In a private communication, Adolf Laube told me that he had seen one reference to a merchant's pamphlet but was unable to find a copy.

20. Köhler, working on a sample of 365 pamphlets from the *Flugschriften* collection analyzed by subject matter, found that only 5.6% dealt with peasant life, and these with the broad aspects of peasant affairs rather than with the peasant revolt. Turning to theological pamphlets often attributed to peasant authors, he found that only one of the 12 texts was written by an authentic peasant, Hans Schwalb. But this was a question of peasant descent rather than a man living as a peasant, for Schwalb, the son of a peasant, had become the humanist Kaspar Schalbe. Köhler concludes that these pamphlets cannot be used to uncover peasant beliefs or attitudes, nor can they be used as sources on the Peasants' War. H-J. Köhler, "'Der Bauer wird witzig,'" 196–198.

21. *Ein schoner Dialogue/Cuntz und Fritz/Die brauchen wenig witz/* . . . (n.p.:n.p., n.d.), Fiche 1820/#4667, fols. Aii, Aiiii.

22. *Ein schoner Dialogus von eim/Schneider/und von einem Pfarrer/* . . . n.p.:n.p., 1524, Fiche 1820/#4668, fols. Aii^v, Bii^v-Biii.

23. Ibid., fol. Biii^v.

24. According to Grimm, the term *gemein* was used in the sixteenth century for *res publica* (Grimm, Vol. 5, 3176) and could mean everyone in the city. The individual citizen might also be referred to as *der gemein* (Vol. 5, 3186). Johann Agricola used *der gemeine Mann* to mean those urban folk who opposed the *grossen Hansen*, the magistrates and guildmasters. Ulrich Zwingli applied it to a peasant if he was a landowner and possessed several cows. Modern historians, working to identify the sources of the revolutionary movement of 1525, have debated whether the *gemeine Mann* included peasants along with urban workers and tradesmen and whether it also included the urban underclasses. Robert H. Lutz, in *Wer war der gemeine Mann?* (1979), 15, summarized the modern points of view. According to P. Blickle, R. M. and G. Radbruck, J. Buszello, G. Ritter, and R. Siegel, *gemeine Mann* included everyone who did not belong to the patriciate or the clergy. R. Endres, G. Franz, E. Hassinger, K. Kaser, W. E. Peuckert, H. Schilling, K. Blascke, and G. Schieb used it as a collective concept which includes both the agrarian and urban lower social orders. M. Haas, P. Joachimsen, A. Laube, H. W. Seiffert, A. Waas, and F. Seibt limited it to peasants and handworkers. I use it only when it appears in a pamphlet written by a contemporary.

25. These writings were often recorded or transcribed by a cleric. The Laube-Seiffert collection is a standard source. *Flugschriften der Bauernkriegszeit*, eds. Adolf Laube, Hans Werner Seiffert, 1975. *The German Peasants' War*, eds. and trans. Tom Scott and Bob Scribner, 1991, presents a broad selection of documents, peasant articles, and contemporary accounts of the Peasants' War and its leaders. Although impressively comprehensive, it contains no polemic pamphlet authored by a peasant. Köhler believes that most "Peasant" pamphlets, were written by burghers, usually clergy. See Köhler, "'Die Bauer wirt witzig'," 207.

26. Bernd Moeller, *Imperial Cities and the Reformation*, 63, 69.

27. Bernd Hamm, "Reformation 'von unten' und Reformation 'von oben': zur Problematik reformationshistorischer Klassifizierungen," 1993, 5. Robert Scribner referred to social differentiation in the response to Luther in an early article:

"Civic Unity and the Reformation in Erfurt," *P and P*, 66 (1975); 60.

28. Early introductions to the variety of noble literary forms are found in Karl Schottenloher, "Flugschriften zur Ritterschaftsbewegung des Jahres 1523, 1929, 1–29, and Wilhelm Bogler, *Hartmuth von Kronberg*, 1897. Recent studies of the rhetorical style and content of the knights' pamphlets include Eckhard Bernstein, *Ulrich von Hutten*, 1988, 84–106; Volker Honemann, "Der deutsche Lukian. Die volkssprachigen Dialogi Ulrichs von Hutten," 1989, 37– 57; Barbar Könneker, "Ulrich von Hutten: Gesprächbüchlin und Novi Dialogi," 1975.

29. R. R. McCutcheon, "The *Responsio ad Lutherum*: Thomas More's Inchoate Dialogue with Heresy," *SCJ* XXII, 1 (1991): 77–78.

30. See the bibliography in Paul Russell, *Lay Theology and the Reformation*, 1986, 266–269; Rudolf Raillard, *Pamphilus Gengenbach und die Reformation*, 1936; Klaus Wedler, *Hans Sachs*, 1976.

31. H. Brunner and E. Strassner, "Volkskultur vor der Reformation," in ed. Gerhard Pfeiffer, *Nürnberg—Geschichte einer europäischen Stadt*, 1982, 201.

32. Thomas Brady, Jr., *Turning Swiss*, 1985, 46–58; Blickle, *Communal Reformation*, xv–xviii, 12–14, 20–26; Scott and Scribner, *The German Peasants' War*, 19, 27, 28, 35; P. Russell, *Lay Theology in the Reformation*, 11. See also Manfred Hanneman, *The Diffusion of the Reformation in South-Western Germany*, passim.

33. See Thomas Brady, Jr., *Turning Swiss*, 46–58, 82–100, for unrest in southwest German cities before the Reformation. Peter Blickle, *Gemeindereformation: Die Menschen auf dem Weg zum Heil*, 1985, 21–114, describes the interplay between the peasants' movement and the burgher movement, founded on their common goals.

34. J. L. Flood, "Le monde Gérmanique," in ed., Jean-Francois Gilmont, *La Réforme et le livre*, 1990, 53.

35. Hans-Joachim Köhler, *Bibliographie der Flugschriften . . ., Druckbeschreibung*, Bd. 1, 2, 1991– 1992. Josef Benzing, *Die Buchdrucker des 16. und 17. Jahrhunderts im Deutschen Sprachgebiet*, 1963; *Lutherbibliographie*, 1965–66; See Clemen, *Flugschriften aus den ersten Jahren der Reformation*, 4 vols. and Clemen, *Kleine Schriften zur Reformationsgeschichte*, 5 vols. and Laube, *Flugschriften der fruhen Reformationsbewegung*, 2 vols.

36. Miriam U. Chrisman, *Lay Culture, Learned Culture*, 28.

37. #51, *Wer hören will wer die gantze welt arm hat gemacht*, 1522? fol. B^v.

38. Adolf Laube, *Flugschriften der Bauernkriegszeit*, 546.

39. #177, Bernhard Johim, *Warhafftig Bericht . . . wie die Christen in Miltenberg . . .*, 1523, fol. Aiii^v.

40. #152, Argula von Grumbach, *Ein Christliche Schrifft . . . daryn sie aller Christenliche Stendt und oberkeiten ermant . . .*, 1523, fol. Aii^v.

41. #269, *Warhafftig geschicht wie Caspar Tauber . . . für ein ketzer . . . und zu dem Todt verurtaylt . . . worden ist*, 1524, fol. Aiv.

42. In the case of lay pamphlets these included only Nickel Schmidt in Leipzig and Hans Schobser in Munich. J. L. Flood, "Le monde Germanique," 50.

43. Based on the pamphlets in the study, in Augsburg there were 12 such printers, in Strasbourg 8, in Nuremberg 7, in Erfurt 6. None of these men were *Winkeldrucker* with small fly-by-night presses. They were established printers. In Zwickau and Bamberg there was one printer in each city who published lay pamphlets. In most other cities—Worms, Oppenheim, Eilenburg, Wurzburg, Munich—one printer put out an occasional lay pamphlet. In these outlying cities most of the editions were reprints.

There was no discernible pattern in the repertoires of individual printers with regard to the social class of the authors they accepted, nor did propinquity play a dominant role in where an author found a publisher. There was also no established pattern of reprints. A pamphlet first issued by Ramminger in Augsburg did not promptly show up in a particular printer's office in Nuremberg, Strasbourg, or Wittenberg. Indeed, reprints of the same pamphlet might be published by three different presses in one city. There seems to have been a random element in the choice of printers or authors, except in cases like Balthasar Stanberger, a minor civil servant, whose friend, Michel Buchfürer in Erfurt, published all of his pamphlets, including one exhorting Buchfürer to publish evangelical Christian works. Johann Schott in Strasbourg published the majority of Ulrich von Hutten's German polemic pamphlets. Altogether, 58 printers can be identified who spread the ideas of the lay writers.

44. R. W. Scribner, *For the Sake of Simple Folk*, 15–20, 22.
45. *Ibid.*, 34, for a portrait of Hutten with his coat of arms.
46. #18, Anonymous, *Eynn Dialogus ader gesprech zwischen einem Vatter unnd Sohn dye lere Martin Luthers belangende* (n.p.:n.p. 1523), title page.
47. #218, Utz Ryschner, *Ain Gesprëch buchlin von ainem Weber und ainer Kramer über das Büchlin Doctoris Mathie Kretz von der haimlichen Beycht*, (n.p., 1524), title page.

1

The Social Order

SOCIAL DIFFERENCES

Social differences were visible at all levels of everyday life. A noble rode across the town square on horseback, his half armor or his velvet cloak emblazoned with his coat of arms. The grave city councilors walked to the town hall in fur-lined robes which came to their ankles. Guildsmen, by law, could not wear silk, velvet, or fur. Many of them wore leather britches as work clothes, with short tunics which made it easy to move about the work place. The fabric was heavy and coarse. Journeymen's cloaks, by law, had to cover their buttocks. Clothing announced the wearer's occupation or economic activity, gender, social status, and wealth.

Social difference was also discernible in housing. The mansions of the upper order with their spacious rooms, often with intricately carved ceilings and walls, surrounded a central courtyard to accommodate arrivals and departures on horseback and the reception of important visitors. The houses of the artisans were squeezed together on narrow streets. Their shops opened directly onto the street, separated from it only by shutters and perhaps a narrow counter. The artisan's family, their apprentices, and essential raw materials shared the interior space.

Deferential behavior was another visible expression of rank. Inferiors deferred to their superiors by standing aside to let them pass, by bowing, by removing their head covering. Submission was woven into language patterns, particularly in the formulae of formal address. Even the city council would address a superior—a bishop, a nobleman—with an expression of their humble position and their obedience. An ordinary citizen, addressing a city councilor or a civil servant, would refer to himself as "your humble and submissive servant."

Levels of education were displayed in the academic robes of university students and those who held university degrees. Boys attending a Latin grammar school frequently wore a uniform, a jacket, or a distinguishing cap. All these visible signs were merely outward symbols of a society sharply divided by birth, wealth, political authority, social status, and education. They were the perceptible marks of the distance which separated the ranks.

Differences between the groups were not only a matter of laws and regulations, of perception and custom. One of the most important factors was the experience of each group, the totality of what a person had gone through from childhood to adulthood, what had been expected of him, the limits which had been placed on his aspirations and development. The economic and social factors described in this chapter must be evaluated in terms of their influence on the experience of the individual and the group.

Traditionally, the social order was conceived as composed of the three estates: the clergy, which watched over the spiritual life of the community; the nobility, which protected it from its enemies; the third estate, which provided its material needs. By the sixteenth century, however, urban society, in particular, could no longer be visualized as one estate, a term which continued to be used although it had no legal meaning. Learned clerics, city governments, poets, and popular song writers attempted to define the divisions among the ranks more exactly so that the proper relatioships would be clear and thus order would be maintained.[1] The need to define was manifested in the constant enactment of sumptuary laws, tax ordinances, and *Polizei* ordinances which set forth the appropriate behavior for each rank and subgroup. These laws helped to form the separate social matrices. They drew the boundaries within which people lived out their lives, affecting the relationships they could have with others.

In the late fifteenth century, there were no firm criteria of who belonged to which subgroup. There was only an underlying assumption that men and women were separated by wealth, gender, power and authority, status, occupation, and education. The Nuremberg and imperial sumptuary laws enacted at the end of the fifteenth century were still amorphous, the boundary lines ill-defined, as is shown in Figures 2 and 3. The Nuremberg city councilors thought in broad terms of rich and poor, of honorable people and ordinary people. The imperial diet saw more differences among the upper ranks than the lower. The need to distinguish honorable people, essentially the governing elite, drove the city councilors and their learned lawyers to ever-increasing precision. If order were to be maintained, power and authority had to be clearly assigned. Those who wielded political control had to be identified and legitimated. Eligibility to serve in the city government (the contemporary German term was *Ratsfähig*) was precisely and legally defined. These ordinances, as well as sumptuary legislation and tax laws, are evidence that throughout the sixteenth century distinctions of rank were more sharply perceived, with the result that the ranks became more separated. The differentiation among the lay writers in this study—knights, patricians, learned civil servants, minor civil servant, and artisans—exemplifies this increasing social distance.

FIGURE 2   Ranks specified in sumptuary legislation for the German
Empire, 1497

1. The common farmer and working people in the city or on the land
2. Guildsmen and apprentices
3. Burghers who are not noble
4. Nobles who are not knights
5. Nobles who are knights
6. Princes
7. Archbishops, bishops, and other clergy

SOURCE: Johannes Phillipus Datt, *Rerum Germanicorum Novum*, *Libri* V (Ulm:
Georg G. Kühnen, 1698), 894–895. "Abschid des König liches Reichstags
donrstags nach dem sontag Esto Michi, A.D. 1497 zu Lindau gehalten."

FIGURE 3   Ranks specified in
Nuremberg sumptuary law, 1496

Honorable women and young women
Women and young women
Doctors of law and knights
Citizens or inhabitants

SOURCE: Joseph Baader, *Nürnberger Polizeiordnungen aus dem XIII bis XV Jahrhundert*,
Bibliothek des Litterarischen Vereins in Stuttgart, LXIII (Stuttgart, 1861), 96.

Sumptuary laws and *Polizei* ordinances led to the punctilious circumscrip-
tion of differences in rank, which was an urban, not a rural phenomenon.
Social boundaries in the cities were drawn on lines of wealth, political power,
social standing, occupation, and education. Entrance to the rank of the
governing elite, "the honorables," depended largely on wealth.

The ability to support one's family from rents and interest was the basis
of political power. Elite status rested on holding office in the city government.
A Nuremberg family became "honorable" if a member served or had served
in the city council.[2] In Augsburg, a small upper rank of politicians dominated
the powerful upper councils. Below them was a rank closely bound to them
but with less money and slightly lower positions, followed by a broad middle
rank of those who participated only in the larger assemblies, infrequently

summoned. The mass of small guildsmen and tradesmen were citizens but held no office or civic responsibility. At the bottom was a large underclass.[3] Social status was closely linked to the ability to exercise authority over others,[4] for the urban patriciate as for the nobility.

Occupation was a strong factor in drawing social boundaries. The elite, those eligible to serve on the city council, did not work with their hands. They were rentiers or professionals, usually lawyers. The great merchants made decisions with regard to business and gave orders but performed no manual labor. That made them honorable. Artisans and small merchants could never be admitted to the ranks of the honorables because "they worked with their hands, the craftsmen at their benches, the small merchants unpacked their own wares and sold them."[5]

Education separated the ranks but, at the same time, was a means of social mobility within the upper classes. A literary education made it possible to rise within the ranks. It was also essential to maintaining class status.[6] In Nuremberg, after 1450, members of the learned professions were admitted to the rank of honorable. Kramm found in small cities and towns in central Germany that the learned were given equal status with the merchants.[7] The question of who was learned, however, was not easily defined, and the social position of a man with a university degree, as against someone who had not completed his degree, changed from place to place. Wealth was a part of this. The learned man of good family with a private income was easily accorded his place among the honorables. The salaries of the city doctor or the pastor, often the same as the income of middle artisans, might drop them to the middle rank.[8]

The sumptuary legislation of Saxony of 1612 demonstrates how these different social values with regard to wealth, power, and education were systematized, as shown in Figure 4. Clearly, one of the problems was the status of wives and children. Were they equal to their husbands and fathers or a rank below? The classifications drawn up in the sumptuary ordinance of 1628 by the city council of Strasbourg shown in Figure 5, the culmination of a century of increased regulation, achieved scrupulous differentiation on the basis of political authority, occupation, and education.

This was how the social order was defined. But what did it mean to the community and the people? How did each group place itself in the larger order? How did it see other groups? What were the social perceptions and ethical ideals which kept a group together?

THE KNIGHTS

There were significant differences within the noble hierarchy. In Germany the high nobility controlled duchies, counties, and large holdings, over which they had complete jurisdiction. The spiritual lords; the electoral archbishops

FIGURE 4   Ranks specified in sumptuary ordinance in Saxony, 1612. Nobles
and wives and daughters

Councilors and wives and daughters
Doctors and professors and wives and daughters
Other court officials who are not university graduates or councillors, down to the secretarial level.
Wives of court officials and secretaries and their daughters.
Ministers and wives
Other persons allied to the university
Students
Court officers, bailiffs, administrators, burghermasters, and city councilors
Their sons
Their wives
Businessmen, retailers, and important (wealthy or powerful) burghers
Their sons
Their wives and children
Artisans in the suburbs
House owners who live in the suburbs
Servants
The peasant, including wife and children

SOURCE: *Policey und Kleider Ordnung des Durchlauchtiguten Hochgebornen Fürsten
and Herrn Herrn Johannes Georgen, Hertzogen zu Sachsen* (Leipzig: Johann Rosen,
1612).

of Trier, Mainz, and Cologne; the prince bishops and archbishops with large
territories; the abbots of great monasteries; and the secular lords, the Elector
of Saxony, the Duke of Saxony, the Duke of Bavaria, the Count Palatine,
were the de facto rulers of the empire. They were extending their power by
forcing the lower nobility to submit to their authority. Below them were
the counts. Below them were the lesser nobility, which included the imperial
free knights, all inferior in status. The rest of the rural community were the
peasants. Only one of these subgroups, the imperial free knights, wrote pamphlets. Two of the high nobility, as already mentioned, wrote denouncing
the political-religious controversy of the 1530s, but the great nobility kept
themselves at a distance in the propaganda battle of the first decade of

FIGURE 5   Ranks in sumptuary ordinance, Strasbourg, 1628.

Class Six:	The Magistrat Legal counselors of the city Urban nobles
Class Five (Upper):	Burgher families whose ancestors had been in the *Magistrat* for a century or more. High chancellery officials Scholars holding the licenciate or the doctorate (all professors at the university)
Class Five (Lower):	Large-scale merchants Scholars who have not taken the examination for the licenciate or the doctorate but who have gone far enough in their studies to do so
Class Four (Upper):	Chancellery clerks Customs and tax collectors Secretaries of the city commission Lawyers without a doctor's degree Teachers in the Gymnasium
Class Four (Lower):	All those elected by their guild to the Council of Three Hundred who would otherwise be in Class Three Schoolteachers Notaries Midwives Skilled Art workers Music teachers who do not play for dancing
Class Three:	Lower civil servants Common craftsmen and citizens
Class Two:	Subordinate male workers including day laborers, porters, woodcutters
Class One:	Subordinate female workers, including: Housemaids Cleaning women Barmaids Seamstresses

SOURCE: Franklin L. Ford, *Strasbourg in Transition, 1648–1789* (Cambridge: Harvard University Press, 1958), 15–16.

the Reform. They appear in the pamphlets as rulers, enforcing the law in one of their cities or towns, quelling the revolt led by the knight Franz von Sickingen. Many of them supported the reformers, as did the Elector of Saxony.

The imperial free knights were a subordinate group within the highest rank. Having served as servant knights to the emperor in the civil wars of the eleventh century, maintained by him rather than by their own revenues, they were confined in perpetuity to a lower rank. Some of them had acted as officials or administrators. The honor of knighthood released them from the bondage of service and made them freemen, eligible for all the rights, dignity, and honor pertaining thereto.[9] Yet, the shadow of their original servant status was never dispersed, in part because it continued. Their landholdings were small, sometimes only 30 to 100 *morgen* of land,[10] usually centered on the original fief granted by the emperor, increased over time by fiefs held from local nobles.

Some families, like the Sickingens, however, had accumulated considerable territory—in their case six major castles and surrounding lands. The Huttens and the Cronbergs controlled a similar number of estates.[11] These holdings were further extended by a system of joint or cooperative ownership which permitted two or more families to share the titles and revenues of properties. These created strong bonds among the families involved.[12] Although they could not compete with the wealth or military power of the counts and princes, the knights were not impoverished. They had continued to be a service nobility, holding office as military commanders or administrators under the high nobility to add to the revenues from their lands. As knights they were free, that is, able to act without hindrance or restraint. Yet, as officials or officers they had to obey orders from a noble or prince. Personal service to a more powerful lord was central to the noble ethic. The emperor and the higher nobility were the knights' patrons, to whom they owed honor and loyalty. The ambiguity of freedom within duty created unresolved conflict among the three.

THE KNIGHTS' RELATIONSHIPS WITH THE EMPEROR, THE PRINCES, THE CHURCH

In 1495, the knights' relationship with the emperor was shaken by Maximilian's attempt to reform the empire. Forced by the princes' reform party to take action, Maximilian abolished all private feuding, depriving the knights of their ancient, traditional noble right. Instead, an imperial court, the *Reichskammergericht*, was established to settle disputes. Dominated by the territorial princes, the knights believed that the court limited their political and military power.[13] By joining the emperor they could have presented strong resistance to the princes. Instead the Franconian knights demonstrated their rejection of the imperial reforms by strengthening their alliance with the upper nobility.[14]

Resentful of the princes and fearful that they would absorb their lands, knightly families nevertheless maintained longstanding, loyal relations with princely families. Hartmut von Cronberg's father was an official for the Elector Palatine and then for the Archbishop Elector of Mainz in Aschaffenburg.[15] The Sickingen family had long given service to the Elector Palatine. Sons of both families were active propagandists for the reform and leaders of the Knights' Revolt. Franz von Sickingen, one of these leaders, was in the Elector's civil service from 1508 to 1511, as *Amtmann*, the highest official in the Kreuznach district, near Mainz.[16]

The knights were often competent civil administrators, and their positions furthered their own interests. Franz von Sickingen pledged 2,000 florins in cash to the Elector Palatine to win the appointment as Amtmann. He received no salary but kept all the revenues collected in the district, including a tenth of the revenues from silver mines near the Rhine, which Sickingen used to improve his castle, the Ebernburg. Sickingen was conscientious and an effective mediator, so that the burghers brought their disputes to him. As judicial officer he granted citizenship rights to immigrants; he also took an interest in the newly established Latin school.[17] Thus he exerted considerable influence over the economic and cultural affairs of the area. Hundreds of knights served as officials to princes, dukes, and bishops in this way. They were familiar with the administration and law courts of the high nobility and developed their own judicial and financial skills. This monopoly of appointments would be lost over the course of the sixteenth century as university-trained sons of upper middle-class families offered better knowledge of the law. The knights' positions at the princely courts were no longer assured, deepening their malaise.

The church was an equally important source of patronage. Younger sons of knightly families were appointed to benefices in collegial or cathedral chapters or entered monastic orders. Many of them rose to a bishop's see or became abbot or provost of their monastery.[18] In 1500, Pope Alexander VI reserved 1,000 benefices in the diocese of Mainz for the knights. Shortly thereafter this was extended to Cologne, Trier, and Salzburg.[19] Sickingen's enemy, Richard von Greiffenlau-Vollrath, Archbishop of Trier, came from a knightly family.

THE KNIGHTS' IDEALS AND VALUES

Occupying positions of responsibility in every major institution of the empire, the knights were not an isolated group, withdrawn into a dream of the past. There were, however, fundamental conflicts in their attitudes and in their behavior. They perceived themselves as rural and viewed the urban

world with disfavor. Volker Press wrote that the average knight lived in an
agricultural world, remote from politics. He wished to preserve his lordship,
his territorial dominion, and his revenues. He resisted the princes when it
came to legal jurisdiction, taxes, and the right to maintain the public peace
on his own land.[20] This opposition did not change when a knight was engaged
in service to the emperor, a prince, or a count. Knights served the emperor
as district officials close to home or as local military protectors. In the same
way, they served local princes, counts, dukes, or bishops, giving their loyalty only to that prince, not extending it to other princes. The knight wished
to stand free on his own ground,[21] freedom and independence were his ul-
timate values.

The knights distanced themselves from the lower orders. Bitterly anti-
merchant in their attitudes, they submitted grievances to the imperial diets
requesting relief from the monopolies and high prices of the merchants.[22]
They disdained trade and commerce as unworthy and socially degrading
and showed little sympathy for urban professionals or craftsmen, believing
them all dishonest.[23] Urban people, for their part, found little good to say
for the knights. Bandit knights who robbed merchant convoys convinced
the burghers that the knights used their vaunted right to bear arms to create
disorder, bloodshed, and loss of property. As a group the knights were seen
as a menace to society.[24] Furthermore, their horizons were narrow. Except
for military service, they preferred to remain near their lands and rarely
appeared at the imperial court, where they felt inferior to the high nobility.
Nor did they attempt to create an alliance of all German knights to represent
themselves at the Reichstag or the imperial court. Alliances were always
local, with nobles from their own region, such as the Franconian *Bund*, the
Swabian League, the Rhenish Knights. The Swabian League was pro-imperial
in its policies, eventually turning against its fellow knights. The Franconian
Knights and the Rhenish Knights were formed to oppose the princes.[25] The
alliances, which worked against each other rather than together, became
military enemies, creating another set of rivalries. An obsession with individual
freedom made land more important than any other element of life, the root
of ethical values, the motivation for political activity.

URBAN SOCIETY—THE URBAN ELITE AND THE HONORABLES

The urban elite were descended from wealthy merchant families, some from
noble families who had fought for the city, some from families who had
served as high-ranking officials. By the sixteenth century, through wealth,
property, and power, they dominated the inner councils and small committees
which governed the cities.[26] Each city constitution had its own name for
these men. The term patrician was first used by the humanists, then gradually adopted by the patricians themselves because it linked them to the

Roman ruling class and fulfilled their longing to be placed on a level with the lower nobility.[27]

Most patricians were no longer active in business, although they remained as silent partners in family enterprises, particularly in trans-European wholesale trade and banking.[28] They were rentiers. Merchant families who had made their fortunes invested them in land, purchased castles and fiefs and, if possible, the title that went with them. Thus the upper urban class had established themselves in the countryside, creating close links with the knights.

The patricians' status was based on their lands outside the city walls. The majority of the governing rank were "honorables." They were wealthy, possessing a solid fortune, often set by the city at 1,000 gulden.[29] Manual labor was prohibited to them. The function of the urban elite and the honorables was to make the city laws and administer them. Their own code required a high degree of selflessness and dedication: an honorable should be above censure in financial matters, provide moral leadership, accept office in the city government, and respond to the needs of the whole community, not personal interests.[30]

PATRICIAN UNITY

Each city had exclusive social clubs through which patrician families confirmed their unity and superiority. The Strasbourg *Constoflen*, the *Herrentrinkstube* in Nuremberg, the Augsburg *Geschlechterstube* and the Lübeck Circle Association all served to delineate who counted as patricians for social and constitutional purposes.[31] The exclusiveness of the patricians, their desire to limit access to power, was epitomized in the Nuremberg Dance Statute of 1521, which restricted eligibility to serve in the *Rat* to the 42 families who were invited to dances in the *Rathaus*. The Nuremberg urban elite hoped to establish a closed urban nobility of birth. This was furthered by a pattern of endogamous marriage.[32] The most powerful group in the city held itself consciously aloof from the social interplay of urban life.

PATRICIAN RELATIONS WITH THE CHURCH

Most elite families had close ties to the church. Their ancestors, who had been great benefactors of the city churches, had built chapels, dedicated altars (endowing them with beneficed clergy), and supported monastic orders. In many cities the chapter of a major collegial church was reserved for family members of the local elite. Sons and daughters of these families were likely to predominate in the convents and cloisters. Patrician influence was evident at every level of local ecclesiastical institutions. The upper clergy deeply affected urban life, for they were not only priests, canons, or monastics but landholders, employers, lawyers, and intellectuals.

In Ulm, for example, the elite controlled the patronage to positions in

the cathedral, appointing family members to these posts. Nor was their influence forgotten in death. They had their own endowed altars in the cathedral and were buried there or in family chapels in the Dominican church,
but never in the churchyards side by side with the commoners.[33] In Strasbourg, the chapter in the church of St. Thomas, second in importance only
to the cathedral, was drawn mainly from patrician families. The women's
Dominican cloisters were reserved for the daughters of the elite.[34] In Augsburg,
benefices in the Dominican cloister of St. Katherine were divided between
Swabian noble families and Augsburg patrician families. Between 1500 and
1520, a new convent church and enclosure were built for St. Katherine's.
The men's Dominican cloister was rebuilt, all of this financed by patricians.[35] As in knightly families, the monastic orders and the chapters were
woven into the fabric of family life, through relationships carried on from
generation to generation. A patrician always had an aunt or an uncle, a
sister or brother, who was a nun or a monk.

PATRICIAN VALUES AND IDEAS

Family continuity was a principal patrician value. Every patrician was
responsible to preserve the property inherited from his parents and to add
to it.[36] He looked back with pride to his forefathers, drawing self-esteem
from the offices they had held, perhaps occupying these same offices. The
family provided permanence and stability in a world which otherwise had
few of these qualities.

Service to the city was not only a familial duty but also a religious obligation.
Patricians were called by God to lead and to govern. Christoph Scheurl, a
Nuremberg patrician, expressed this clearly: "The common folk have no
power, it does not belong to their estate, since all power comes from God
and good judgment belongs only to those who have been endowed with
special wisdom by the creator of all things. . . ."[37] The governing elite believed
they were carrying out God's will, which was to create civic unity, a city
within which each individual would subordinate his special interest for the
good of the whole. They constantly invoked the norms of peace, unity, and
concord, as well as their own obligation to serve the common good.[38] This
ideal of a *communitas perfecta*, "while it may have reached down in some
form to the lower levels of society . . . was essentially the preserve of the
dominant social groups in the state—nobles, gentry, urban patricians, the
lawyers, the clergy and the educated."[39] As magistrates the patricians attempted
to achieve this ideal by caring for the poor, by holding down the cost of
living for artisans and wage earners, and by regulating prices and preventing
speculation in grain and other food.[40]

PATRICIAN EDUCATION

Education substantiated the elite's claim to political and cultural leadership and was vital in carrying on the family interests in business and trade. The elite supported the foundation of Latin schools with a humanist curriculum. Many of their sons attended universities, spending a few years in Italy, savoring one university and then another. The Italian universities opened classical culture and humanism to these young men, who, returning to their families, continued to look to Italy as their intellectual home.[41] In city after city, small humanist circles were formed where the social and intellectual elite could share their enthusiasm for classical literature.[42] The urban humanists, conservative in their views, based their civic ethic on the Stoics. Believing their lives should be governed by reason, they endeavored to exercise self-control, prudence, and moderation in all things. These virtues were essential to the *gemeinen Nutzen* of the community because the common people were subject to passion or violence and needed to be restrained by the strong authority of their rulers. Late Roman aristocratic thought was easily adapted to the world view of the patriciate.[43] Humanism gave the traditional ethic new validity, a stronger legitimacy.

PATRICIAN ATTITUDES TOWARD OTHER RANKS

Socially ambitious, the urban elite were eager to be accepted as equals of the lower nobility. We have seen that their network extended out of the city into the rural areas through purchase of estates and titles. They were part of the urban world and the feudal world as well, both citizens and vassals. Many spent more time on their country estates than in town, because to live nobly was a criterion of nobility. Marriage created stronger links with these noble families whose acceptance they so carefully cultivated.[44]

Although they idealized the corporate unity of the community, the magistral rank sought recognition, acceptance, and respect from those above them. Their relationship with those below them, the citizens, was not important to them socially. They had some contact with guild masters who served on the city councils, but even here the patricians had served their own interests by assigning their sons and relatives to the craft guilds. Thus, the representative from a craft guild was often a member of the elite.[45] The patrician clubs, their dances, their marriage patterns show that there was little social intermingling between the guild members and the patriciate. The latter insulated themselves from the common citizen and were despised by many of them.

THE UPPER CIVIL SERVANTS AND LAWYERS: STATUS

University-trained lawyers were the administrators, advisors, and judicial officers of the city. They were councilors to the *Rat*. They maintained the city records. They drafted the laws. They served as judges, tax collectors, and accountants. The highest position was *Stadtschreiber*, secretary to the city council. These men were, in effect, the permanent governing officials. The higher ranks of the civil service required a law degree, either a doctorate or a licentiate. The high status of the upper civil servants depended on education rather than on birth or wealth.

The civil servants were part of a larger learned rank, which included theologians, priests, preachers, and university professors, some of whom occupied the same status as the upper civil servants. They shared the same education and the same training in languages, philosophy, and rhetoric. They understood each other's patterns of thought. Many of the reformed clergy were personal friends of the upper civil servants, a factor which was important in the development of the urban reformation. Much has been written with regard to the relationships between the reformers and the magistrates. The concept of the magisterial reformation is based on the existence of close ties between the two, yet there is little evidence that any reformer, except Zwingli, was a close advisor to a city council or to members of the *Rat*. There is, however, evidence of close ties between reformers and city secretaries. Jörg Vögeli, city secretary of Constance, defended the preacher Bartholomeus Metzler against the bishop.[46] Lazarus Spengler, city secretary in Nuremberg, worked closely with the reformer Andreas Osiander, although often disagreeing with him.[47] The learned pamphleteers included 12 upper civil servants—6 city secretaries, 4 upper judicial officials, and 2 medical doctors.

The learned lay upper rank, particularly those from distinguished families of lawyers and high civil servants, were in the top rank of honorables but were not patricians.[48] Clearly separated from the city councilors and burghermasters who appointed them, they were servants of the magistrates; thus, like the knights, they automatically occupied a lower status.[49] Their education, however, admitted them to the intellectual circle of the patricians and the *Ratsfähige*.[50]

FUNCTION OF THE UPPER CIVIL SERVANTS

City secretaries had broad responsibilities. In addition to acting as councilor to the *Rat*, drafting laws, and supervising the accounts, Lazarus Spengler of Nuremberg, for example, kept the minutes of city council meetings, controlled all the correspondence going out from the city council or from the small committees, kept track of all memoranda submitted by the city lawyers, and supervised the diplomatic correspondence.[51] All city secretaries were bound by oath to be loyal to the *Rat* and to the city. They were to warn the *Rat* of any impending problems (a euphemism for public unrest) and to protect the interests of the *Rat* in such crises. They were to keep careful records and maintain absolute secrecy on the council's deliberations, a secrecy not to be broken until death.[52]

Although restricted by their obligations to the city councilors, the secretaries had there were opportunities to assert their own opinions and influence the *Ratsherren*. Spengler, when writing up the decisions of the *Rat*, was closely tied to the wording of the councilors. When he wrote letters or instructions to men on diplomatic missions, however, he could emphasize his own concerns, as was true for his memoranda or supplications. A major task was to provide confidential legal advice to members of the city council, again a chance to convey his own judgment or beliefs. Spengler wrote personal letters to city secretaries and legal councilors in other cities and princely courts, often without the knowledge of the Nuremberg *Rat*. In these he expressed his own political and theological views.[53]

The upper civil servants had authority which contributed to their status. Whatever their formal subordination to the *Rat*, they were recognized as being close to the city councilors and therefore having influence and power. Both within the city and outside it, people believed they spoke for the *Rat*. Their authority was reflected in their power to draft the laws. A law was first discussed by the city councilors, but it was the city secretaries who wrote it, based on the councilors' discussion and their knowledge of the law. The mandates of the city council were a joint expression of the magistrates and the city secretaries, reflecting their concepts of justice and their desire for order. Eric Midelfort, in his study of German princely states, concluded that the evidence "demonstrated to a remarkable degree the newfound reliance of German statesmen on learned experts. The early modern territorial state was built by men ... ready to depend on bureaucrats, university trained scholars and specialized professionals in the shaping of state policy."[54] The same was true in the city states. The magistrates relied on the legal and theological knowledge of the permanent city secretaries and their staffs.

VALUES AND IDEAS OF THE UPPER CIVIL SERVANTS FAMILY

The continuity and stability of the family were of great importance to the upper civil servants, as for the knights and the patricians. They were not achieved by the accumulation of land and wealth, although property was carefully preserved and protected. Status was preserved by maintaining a high standard of education from generation to generation and by influencing appointments of family members to high offices. For example, Lazarus Spengler's father was secretary to the city council of Nuremberg from 1475 to 1496. On his early death, Lazarus returned from the university of Leipzig, was apprenticed to the secretary of the municipal court, and, in 1501, became secretary of the chancellery. In 1507, he was appointed to his father's position, secretary of the council. The same pattern held true for other city secretaries.[55]

The family ethic focused on education and service. Sons invariably went to Latin school and, in most cases, to university. Loyal service to the city increased the opportunities for children and gave them further upward mobility. The sons of city secretaries could seek their fortunes as merchants and sit in the chambers of the city councils. The learned civil servants and their families were among the most mobile people in urban society.

INTELLECTUAL VALUES OF THE UPPER CIVIL SERVANTS— HUMANISM

The learned elite helped to shape the humanism which they shared with the patricians in the *sodalitas literaria*. The civil servants were perhaps more important as agents of change than the patricians because they wrote the treatises on the reform of the church; they published the volumes of eulogies and carmens; and they translated and edited the classical authors, the church fathers, and the historical sources. The patricians tended to be rather passive members of the humanist circles, although their patronage was important. The learned upper class, lay and clerical, were the engine of the movement.

The beliefs of the patricians and the learned were the same, although the learned were perhaps more convinced than the patricians that social and religious order could be restored by a revival of learning. Their model was the early Christian church. If the moral precepts of the church were followed strictly, if ecclesiastical discipline was reinstated, the purity of the early church would be recovered. Influenced by late medieval piety, these scholarly men believed God's gift of reason meant that, despite their sinfulness, they could find a moral way of life.[56] Their search led them to Scripture and to the church fathers.

To arouse citizens to new standards of ethical behavior, Spengler wrote a guide to the moral life in 1520. He listed the virtues to be cultivated and the vices to be avoided, using examples from the classics, the Bible, and folklore. In the good life the citizen would devote himself to the welfare of the city, following his reason and humbling himself in the fear of God. He would avoid the vices of pride, revenge, gossip, and quarreling, all, it should be noted, damaging to urban unity.[57] Sebastian Brant's *Ship of Fools* was perhaps the most widely read book of the last decades before the Reformation. Brant, the city councilor of Strasbourg, lashed out at human folly, which defied reason and divine law.[58] In Nuremberg, Christoph Scheurl admonished citizens to respect the priesthood. Citing numerous historians, he wrote glowingly of the honor given to priests in Egypt, Greece, and Rome. If people followed the example of the ancients, balance and order would be restored.[59]

The upper civil servants were the intellectual leaders in their communities. Professional and dedicated, they, along with the upper clergy, studied the classical texts and the Bible, laying the groundwork for the biblical translations and commentaries of the Reformation period. Because they had been well educated, they were aware of the need for more and better instruction. They encouraged the founding of Latin schools and libraries. Their own scholarly and literary work and their demand for classical texts provided work for the printers and their presses. They were truly engaged intellectually, a factor which would deeply influence the development of the Reformation.

Upper Civil Servants' Relations with Other Classes

The upper civil servants looked upwards in the urban community. Their network was based on the honorable families, who were the people they lived and worked with. They were not admitted to the exclusive social clubs of the patricians but were taken into their intellectual circle. A study of the marriage patterns of the civil service families needs to be done. The Peutingers, for whom there is information on children's marriages, married into merchant and high official families.[60] Unlike the patricians, the upper civil servants were not drawn into rural life nor did they seem to have close relations with knightly families.

Their relationships with the burghers and the artisans constitute another major lacuna. Clearly they worked with the burghers on a daily basis, particularly those who sat on the council. They would have seen artisans as they came before the courts and when they presented petitions to the council. The artisan's reaction to them is by no means clear. Whether they included the city secretaries among the *grosse Hansen* (the big shots), whom they despised, cannot be established because the term is so general. The artisan pamphleteers castigated the "learned," meaning essentially the priests. Whether this carried over to the civil servants cannot be assumed. All classes, however, disliked lawyers. The general suspicion that the lower classes had for the upper classes probably included the upper civil servants. There was never, however, a word with regard to corruption on their part, although individual members of the *Rat* were specifically mentioned as dishonest.

Minor Civil Servants, Teachers, and Skilled Technicians: Social Position

Above the artisans and below the upper civil servants, a transitional rank reflected the porosity of the boundaries between the upper, honorable ranks and people who worked with their hands. For a small number of artisans who had received some education or had special skills, it was possible to break through the ceiling which confined the hand workers and move to another level. Although some of them attended university, they did not have degrees, thus they could not easily attain the status of honorables, particularly if they lived in a larger city. Kramm placed all the educated in one rank: "Full academics, half academics, graduates with lower and higher degrees, many non-students. [There] were officials, men from all departments of book production, city councilors and jurists, doctors and apothecaries, clergy, educated artists and musicians."[61]   Kramm described smaller cities and towns where greater equality was obtained. The upper civil servants in my study came from larger towns. I placed those with university degrees in a separate group, convinced that the kind of education they received made a difference in their status. Technical education which gave people mechanical, military skills did not provide the same level of respect. It was acquired differently. Printers and apothecaries might have had some Latin school education—some had attended university—but their technical expertise was learned by experience, like apprentices and journeymen. Furthermore, they worked with their hands. The minor civil servants' knowledge of Latin made them dependable secretaries and local administrators, but they were not regarded as sufficiently educated in law to be given responsibility for advice, counsel, or policy-making. They implemented policy, they did not create it.

The social position of many of these men was cloudy. For example, apothecaries did not have their own guild, though theirs was a specialized occupation that required considerable learning. The apothecary was often well-respected but he had to struggle against wandering quacks and charlatans, whose fake remedies undermined the credibility of his own work.[62] University-trained physicians looked down on the apothecary because he administered treatments and touched the patient with his hands, unlike the doctor of medicine, who never performed manual work or touched his patient.[63] School teachers, fairly mobile, might enter the civil service and eventually emerge as city secretaries in a smaller town. Musicians and music teachers, low in status, were burdened with a variety of functions—choir master, elementary teacher sexton. They were used to fill in where needed.[64] A military captain like Marschalk lived in his quarters, surrounded by his ill-paid mercenary troops, having little contact with the citizens of Augsburg and no social position among them.

Minor civil servants, technicians, and school teachers were also separated from upper civil servants by money. They never commanded the same pay or salaries as the rank above them, although the amount varied according to the size of the town. In a city like Leipzig, in 1550, there were three doctors, four persons in the book trade, and two artists whose 1,000–1,923 florins placed them with the upper burghers. In Wittenberg, in 1540, by contrast the city doctor and the pastor had the same income as middling artisans. In Meissen, the salaries of the schoolmaster and the city physician were below the earnings of the average artisan. In the larger cities of Saxony, schoolmasters were paid 100–120 florins a year. Music teachers were well below that at 40–50 florins. These should be compared to the reformed clergy, whose salaries ranged from 40–200 florins a year.[65]

In early seventeenth-century Strasbourg, when ranks were becoming more rigidly defined, this transitional rank appeared in the *Polizei Ordnung* as Class 4. It included school teachers, notaries, midwives, skilled art workers, "music teachers who do not play for dancing," chancellery clerks, customs and tax collectors, lawyers without a doctor's degree, teachers in the Gymnasium, and those who had been elected by their guilds to the large Assembly of the Three Hundred (Figure 5).

Socially these men were relatively isolated. They had no network of relationships with their peers, no guilds, clubs, or associations which bound them together. They occupied a layer of their own between the guildsmen and the upper burghers. The layer was thinly spread, consisting of only a few individuals in a town or city. They were often separated from others like themselves—the mercenary captain, the artillery expert, the one school teacher in town. Their special skills had lifted them above the ranks of the guildsmen from which many of them had come and placed them in a group by themselves. The irregular position of the printers and the military engineers reflects the fact that the society did not yet understand technology and technicians. There was no place for them in the hierarchy. They were a class in formation, bureaucrats and technologists who would become the basis of the modern state. Their separation may have made all the members of this group more innovative and radical in their ideas. Since they had no fixed set of values and ideas which bound them together as a rank, they could push beyond the bounds of conformity.

Of all the people in the study, the printers were the hardest to place. Their very novelty gave them a special position. Printing, furthermore, was a wonder of the age. All—literate, barely literate, illiterate—were aware that it had changed the world. If they could not read, someone at the tavern could read an account of the discovery of new islands by the Spanish king or of a battle in Italy against the French king. Printers were more than ordinary artisans because they commanded this new technology. Most of them could handle Latin, since that was the basis of any education they had received at school or at university. Because they had appeared so recently, they had not developed a guild of their own, although the art required the same passage as apprentice, journeymen, and then master. When they arrived to establish a press in a new city, they were assigned to an existing guild, often the goldsmiths or a guild which included several occupations. Their links to the intellectuals, who were both clients and customers, gave them status. I placed them in this loosely defined rank of minor civil servants and technicians because of the similarity of their education and because they were skilled technicians. At the same time, they were artisans. They shared the experience of apprenticeship and serving as journeymen with other craftsmen. They had their own confraternities or joined those of other artisans. They moved in the two groups.

ARTISANS: DEFINITION

Artisans worked with their hands. This defined their social status, placing them below the honorables, the great merchants, and the upper and minor civil servants. Like these other ranks, the craftsmen had their own internal hierarchy, based in part on the guild system. Nuremberg, home to so many of the pamphleteers, had its own organization of sworn crafts.[66] At the top of the artisans' hierarchy were the guilds, with their well-defined ranks of masters, journeymen, and apprentices. Whether in a traditional guild structure or in Nuremberg, skilled artisans lived under the regulations and the protection of their craft. Below them came those without these protections; men and women who depended on a daily wage, those engaged in occupations considered dishonorable, grave diggers, knackers, bath house workers and prostitutes.[67] At the bottom of the hierarchy, and of urban society, were the poor.

SOCIAL INSTITUTIONS LINKING THE HANDWORKERS

No institutions bound all the handworkers, as they were referred to in the documents, into a unified whole. Bonding came from their fear of poverty and their subordinate position in the political order. The guilds gave the upper artisans a sense of group consciousness, common purpose, and unity. The guilds determined the skills required of each individual artisan, taught him his craft, and supervised his work until the end of his career. Regular meetings were held, quarterly or twice a year, which all members were required to attend. An elaborate yearly banquet was the high point of guild life.[68] Religious confraternities, which might be independent of the guild organization, maintained their own altars, dedicated to a patron saint. The annual service brought all members, men and women, together for a solemn service.

The guilds or the confraternities made provision for the proper burial of deceased members, including the exact number of candles to be placed around the body.[69] The confraternities exhibited the artisans' concern for the poor and reflected their fear of descending into poverty themselves. Careful provision was made for members who fell into poverty. The fraternity might give money, supply a sister or brother with food, or arrange for them to enter a religious house.[70] Some regulations provided that a brother who needed help might go to the houses of fellow-members, where he would be treated as an honored guest and given meat, drink, and clothing.[71] Other articles provided help for non-members, the maimed, the deaf, the sick. Alms were collected yearly from the membership to distribute to the poor. Ale from the annual banquet was shared with them.[72]

ARTISANS' RELATIONSHIPS WITH THE GOVERNING ELITE

In most cities and towns, the political power of the guilds peaked during the fifteenth century. Urban revolutions in the hundred years before had given them representation on the city council and the powerful small committees of the *Rat*. After 1450, the patricians began to penetrate the guilds, and served as guild representatives on governing councils. There was no need to change the constitutions: they were subverted.[73] The political importance of guild membership had been seriously undermined by the turn of the sixteenth century, diminishing the power and the status of the artisans. An exception to this was Zurich, where the guilds, cooperating with the patricians, overthrew the merchants in 1336 and, by the end of the fifteenth century, acquired a majority voice on the town council. Artisan families rose to membership in the ruling elite in Zurich during the sixteenth century.[74]

The declining status of the artisans can be traced in city documents. In Strasbourg, the term handworker first appeared in 1308 in a chronicle. Handworkers and burghers formed one rank, differentiated from the lords, who wielded political power. By the end of the fourteenth century, the artisans had been forced out of the rank they shared with the burghers, and derogatory words began to be used to describe them: *Buben* (rogues) or *Geburen* (peasants).[75] In the city oath drawn up in 1482, the two original ranks had grown to seven, the artisans ranked sixth, the commoners seventh. Basel experienced a similar development in the perception of its craftsmen.[76]

ARTISANS' ETHICAL VALUES AND IDEALS: FAMILY

Maintaining the stability and security of the family was just as important for the artisans as it was for the upper ranks. It was, however, much more difficult to achieve. There was rarely enough money or property to provide a cushion from generation to generation. Instead, artisans passed their skills to their sons and daughters. Although the learned upper class would not have appreciated the comparison, the artisans' arrangements for training their children were not unlike the sending of sons to university.

Similarly, artisans were as exacting as the knights and patricians in maintaining the lineage of their family and their fellow guild members. Guild regulations commonly required that any person applying for membership had to be of legitimate and honorable birth.[77] Legitimacy was essential in a Christian society. Honorableness, to a guildsman, meant freedom from any hint of servile ancestry or work in a dishonorable trade. Honor, although defined differently from rank to rank, was an indispensable part of the ethic of all groups.

Guild requirements encouraged endogamy, which created a tight circle within each trade. A young journeyman working for a master craftsman was accepted as a member of the family. If he married the master's daughter he received not only continuing support from the father but also free *burgherrecht*, because his bride was a citizen. Furthermore, she had worked in the shop since childhood, was familiar with the craft, and could do her share by keeping an inventory of supplies, doing the accounts, and selling the finished product. If, on the other hand, the master died, it was usual for the journeyman to marry the widow. He acquired the shop, attaining mastership and a wife at the same time.[78] In my study of printers in Strasbourg from 1480 to 1599, approximately 65% of 27 larger printing shops were closely linked by family ties to other printers. Only five families of the 27 managed to pass their presses on down the family for several generations. Even with a direct succession from father to son, there was no guarantee that the same level of productivity would be maintained. One son went bankrupt; some sold out a few years after their father's deaths; others merely reprinted what their fathers had published earlier.[79] The stability and security of an artisan family was easily destroyed.

THE ARTISANS' WORK ETHIC

The artisans' ethic, defined by work, rested on the dignity of labor. As early as the fourteenth century, popular literature, songs, poems, and plays broke with the teaching that work was a curse arising from Adam's disobedience. Work was good. Work was honorable. To work was virtuous. This affirmative attitude was, in part, a result of the guilds and the establishment of the examinations for master craftsmen, which set standards of workmanship and guaranteed that all guild members had attained a specific level of skill. The maintenance of these skills was also required. By 1450, the weaver's guild in Strasbourg provided that five guild members should visit every house and workshop to examine completed work. Faulty lengths of cloth were taken before the whole guild and, if irreparable, burned.[80] Inspections of this sort, common in all guilds, pressured every member to meet the same standards. Since men were judged by the quality of their work, their knowledge and technique were part of their self-identity.

Illustrated books describing the work of a variety of craftsmen were popular as early as the fifteenth century. The most famous was Jost Amman's *Ständebuch*, depicting 114 different crafts, each described in verse by Hans Sachs. For each craft, Sachs spoke as the artisan, describing his special tasks. Each worker displayed his skills and was proud of the articles he made for others to use.[81]

This conviction of the value of work surfaced in the pamphlet literature. Artisan writers stressed the honesty and integrity of the laborer, comparing it unfavorably to the idleness of those who did not work with their hands.

They strongly believed that working people could better understand the new faith than the rich and the powerful, who were only interested in making money and spending it.[82] A Nuremberg artisan wrote that each person should perform his day's work, rich and poor alike, and thus fulfill the laws of God.[83] His fellow townsman, Hans Sachs, quoting from Thessalonians, stated that he who did not work should not eat.[84]

Artisans and working people developed their own values, their own code of ethics, based on practical experience. Although their rank placed them in the role of obedient servants to the governing elite, they did not honor their betters. They scorned them. The artisans perceived the upper ranks as inept, unable to meet the needs and responsibilities of everyday life.

The narrowness of the network of each rank is striking. Occupation, particularly manual labor, and wealth created barriers between groups. These were carved into semi-permanence by endogamous marriage customs which protected each rank from intrusion by another. The exception to this was the knights, whose position as functionaries gave them an active role in the courts of the high nobility and the upper clergy. Their status in the rural community meant they were sought after by the patricians who wanted to enter their rank. There was an intricate pattern of intermarriage, land ownership, and inheritance of land between these two groups. By contrast, few upper civil servants sought titles or land. They were urban people, content to keep their families in the upper rank of honorables. Intellectually, however, they had ties with the clergy, both Roman and reformed. The minor civil servants and the artisans lived in sharply restricted worlds, having only formal contacts with those above them, perhaps as lower magistrates, occasionally in a relationship of client to patron, most frequently in the market place where one was the buyer, the other the seller.

There were few occasions for the exchange of ideas between ranks. An artisan did not emerge from church, having heard a sermon, to discuss it with the city councilor. They could occupy the same public space, the cathedral or a church, together, but being members of the same audience did not mean they had the same spiritual or intellectual experience. Sullivan's study of Peter Bruegel's peasants reveals the profound chasm which separated the upper and lower classes. The former perceived themselves as dignified, restrained, noble, and hardworking in contrast to the wild, drunken, lewd, gluttonous, and morally inferior peasants.[85] The upper ranks could not believe that individuals from the lower ranks could attain the level of spiritual enlightenment which they themselves attained.

THE ORDERED UNIVERSE: THE IDEAL

How was it possible to keep society together? The answer lay in the strength of order as a value among all ranks. Most sixteenth-century people shared a common view of the nature of the universe and God's role therein. The foundation of the universe was order. No one could conceive that God had created a chaotic world.[86] If order broke down it meant that God was angry, that he had given the world over to the devil or the Antichrist. The logical outcome of this cosmology and the view of society based upon it gave disorder a supernatural dimension. The norm was order. Its loss could mean that God had let the forces of evil take command.

The biblical description of the creation lay at the base of the cosmology of sixteenth century men and women, learned, lay, scientists, and tradesmen. It was a shared constant. From emptiness and nothingness God had made order. He then placed his creation in the hands of Adam and Eve, and even when they were disobedient he did not withdraw his gift of a complete and perfect world. Every part was interdependent, each component had its particular role to play. A beneficent universe, it would seem. Yet God was still active in it, and while he might act with charity and mercy, people of the sixteenth century feared his anger—feared, above all, a return to original chaos. The wrath of God was not a figure of speech. It was imminent, a con-stant threat creating that climate of anxiety which, William Bouwsma believed, molded the thought and action of John Calvin. Bouwsma's portrayal of Calvin's feelings reveals the inner fears of many sixteenth-century people:

> He clung, at times with frantic tenacity, to the conception of a natural order that had traditionally helped human beings to feel comfortable in the world.[87]

God had also ordained the proper relationships which would establish and preserve order among human beings, based on a functional division of power and authority. Social divisions were a part of this. Certain tasks had to be done if life were to run smoothly. These were assigned to specific groups of people, traditionally exemplified by the three estates. The estates theory strengthened and legitimized the existence of different social contexts and created two centers of authority, the clergy and the nobility. They were to govern, to maintain justice and keep the peace in their respective jurisdictions. The members of the third estate were their subjects, whose duty was to obey. If each estate fulfilled its function scrupulously, order would be maintained, the common good would flourish, and unity among all groups would be preserved.[88]

The ideal of a united society did not change during the sixteenth century, which made the divisions that arose from the Reformation more contentious because each side could charge the other with undermining God's order by individual or corporate disobedience. One group, often that to which the writer belonged, was responsible and conscientious. The others were motivated by ambition, pride, and greed. God's plan could be restored only when these selfish interests were abandoned and each group accepted its proper place in the hierarchal order. While sixteenth-century people accepted unity and order as the norm,[89] belief in the norm deepened the suspicion and animosity between groups, strengthening the walls around each social class.

Notes

1. For example, Sebastian Brant, *The Ship of Fools*, trans. Edwin H. Zeydel, 1944, passim; Johannes Agricola, *Die Sprichwörter Sammlung*, ed. Sander L. Gilman, 1971, Vol. 1, 201–203; Gerald Strauss, *Manifestations of Discontent on the Eve of the German Reformation*, 1971, 89–103.
2. Berndt Hamm, "Humanistische Ethik und Reichsstädtische Ehrbarkeit in Nürnberg," *MVGSN* 76 (1989): 76–77.
3. Rolf Kiessling, *Bürgerliche Gesellschaft und Kirche in Aubsburg im Spätmittelalter*, 1971, p. 44.
4. Lee Palmer Wandel, *Always Among Us: Images of the Poor in Zwingli's Zurich*, 1990, 7.
5. Hamm, "Humanistische Ethik," 77.
6. Ibid., 78; also see John W. O'Malley, *The First Jesuits*, 1993, 209.
7. Heinrich Kramm, *Studien über die Oberschichten der Mitteldeutschen Städte im 16. Jahrhundert: Saxony; Thuringia; Anhalt*, 2 vols. (1981), 1, 313.
8. Ibid.
9. Helmut Bode, *Hartmut XII. von Cronberg, Reichsritter der Reformationszeit*, 1987, 17.
10. Helmuth Gensicke, "Der Adel in Mittelrheingebiet," 1965, 138. A *morgen* comprised 0.6 to 0.9 of an English acre.
11. Johannes Polke, "'Wiewohl es ein rühmlich und wohlgebaut Haus gewesen,' Das Ende der Ebernburg im Spiegel Hessische Dokumente," *EH* 15 (1981): 134. Klaus Peter Decker, "Die Besitzungen der Familie von Hutten . . . um 1500," 1989, 115–116.
12. Volker Press,"Franz von Sickingen, Wortführer des Adels . . .," 1989, 293; Helmut Bode, *Hartmut XII von Cronberg*, 31.
13. Hellmuth Rössler, "Adelsethik und Humanismus," 1965, 236.
14. Volker Press, *Kaiser Karl V . . . und der Entstehung des Reichsritterschaft*, 1976, 15.
15. Bode, *Hartmut von Cronberg*, 16.
16. Martin Schoebel, "Franz von Sickingen als Kurpfalzische Amtmann in Kreuznach und Böckelheim," *EH* 15 (1981): 144. The date for the beginning of Sickingen's appointment is not assured. Documents in his name appear as early as 1506. Thus his period in office may have lasted five years.
17. Ibid., 145, 146.
18. Gensicke, "Der Adel in Mittelrheingebiet," 141; Hans H. Hofmann, "Der Adel in Franken," 1965, 119.
19. Rössler, "Adelsethik und Humanismus," 244.
20. Press, *Kaiser Karl V . . . und . . . des Reichsritterschaft*, 12.
21. Rössler, "Adelsethik und Humanismus," 245.

22. Thomas A. Brady, Jr., "Patricians, Nobles, Merchants," 1978, 41. Gerald Strauss, *Manifestations of Discontent*, 1971, 190–191.
23. #101, Eckhart zum Drübel, *Vetterliche gedruge . . . lere*, 1528, fols. Bii^v–Biii.
24. #58, Hans Bechler, *Gesprech eyness Fuchs und Wolffs*, 1524, passim.
25. Press, *Kaiser Karl V . . . und . . . des Reichsritterschaft*, 19.
26. Brady, "Patricians, Nobles and Merchants," 40.
27. Ibid., and Kramm, *Studien über die Oberschichten . . .*, Vol. 1, 5, 7–8.
28. Albrecht Rieber, "Das Patriziat von Ulm, Augsburg, Ravensburg, Memmingen, Biberach," 1968, 305.
29. Hamm, "Humanistische Ethik," 78.
30. Ibid.
31. Kramm, *Studien über die Oberschichten*, Vol. 1, 11–12.
32. Patrician marriages were limited to other patrician families in the same city, patrician families in other cities, or knightly families. Hermann Mitgau, "Geschlossene Heiratskreise, sozialer Inzucht," 1968, 9–11, 15–16. Brady found that in Strasbourg marriage to patrician families in other cities was rare. Thomas A. Brady, Jr., *Ruling Class, Regime and Reformation at Strasbourg, 1520–1555*, 1978, 61–62.
33. Rieber, "Das Patriziat von Ulm . . .," 302.
34. Chrisman, *Strasbourg and the Reform*, 32–33.
35. Wilhelm Liebhart, "Stifte, Klöster und Konvente in Augsburg," 1985, 199.
36. Brady, *Ruling Class, Regime*, 41.
37. Quoted by Hans-Christoph Rublack, "Political and Social Norms in Urban Communities in the Holy Roman Empire," 1984, 44.
38. Ibid., 27, 48.
39. J. H. Elliott, "Revolution and Continuity in Early Modern Europe," quoted in Brady, *Ruling Class, Regime*, 17.
40. Lorna Jane Abray, *The People's Reformation: Magistrates, Clergy and Commons in Strasbourg, 1500–1598*, 1985, 58.
41. Hamm, "Humanistische Ethik," 70.
42. Ibid.; Chrisman, *Strasbourg and the Reform*, 51; Josef Bellot, "Humanismus-Bildungswesen Buchdruck-und Verlagsgeschichte," 1985, 343; Rieber, "Das Patriziat von Ulm, Augsburg . . .," 307.
43. Hamm, "Humanistische Ethik," 124–127.
44. Brady, *Ruling Class, Regime*, 84, 86, 127–134; Rieber, "Das Patriziat von Ulm, Augsburg . . .," 306; Brady, "Patricians, Nobles and Merchants," 40.
45. Brady, *Ruling Class, Regime*, 173–178.
46. Jörg Vögeli, *Schriften zur Reformation in Konstanz, 1519–1538*, ed., Alfred Vögeli, 3 vols., 1972, 1, Halbband, 48.
47. Harold J. Grimm, *Lazarus Spengler*, 1978, 80, 93, 114, 117; Bernd Hamm, "Stadt und Kirche unter dem Wort Gottes," 1981, 718–720.
48. Hamm, "Humanistische Ethik," 82.
49. Kramm, *Studien über der Oberschichten*, 1, 421.
50. Hamm, "Stadt und Kirche unter dem Wort Gottes," 712.
51. Grimm, *Lazarus Spengler*, 6.
52. "Pflichten und Rechte des Stadtschreibers (15.–16. Jahrhundert)," in eds., Dieter Demandt und Hans-Christoph Rublack, *Stadt und Kirche in Kitzingen*, 1978, 123–124. See also the very similar oath taken by the *Stadtschreiber* of Constance in Vögeli, *Schriften*, 1, 45.
53. Hamm, "Stadt und Kirche unter dem Wort Gottes," 711.

54. H. C. Midelfort, *Mad Princes of Renaissance Germany*, 1994, 124.
55. For Spengler see Grimm, *Lazarus Spengler*, 4–6. Jörg Vögeli, city secretary of Constance, came from a civil service family, his father having served as notary to the bishop of Constance. Christoph Scheurl, legal advisor to the Nuremberg city council, had connections to *Ratsherren* through marriage. Conrad Peutinger, city secretary of Augsburg, came from a family of lawyers and merchants. The accountant and imperial notary in Nuremberg, Georg Alt, was from an honorable family. Upper civil servants also came from middle-class stock. The father of Sebastian Brant, *Stadtschreiber* of Strasbourg, ran a large inn. His grandfather had served on the city council eight times, representing the wine merchant's guild. Jörg Vögeli, *Schriften*, 1, Halbband 39; Phillip N. Bebb, "The Lawyers, Dr. Christoph Scheurl and the Reformation," 1972, 55; *Augsburger Stadtlexikon*, 1985, 281–282; *Nouveau dictionnaire de biographie alsacienne*, 14 vols. (1984), 5, 334.
56. Hamm, "Humanistische Ethik," 128.
57. Grimm, *Lazarus Spengler*, 28.
58. Chrisman, *Strasbourg and the Reform*, 57–58.
59. Maria Grossman, *Humanism in Wittenberg, 1485–1517*, 1975, 71.
60. *Augsburger Stadtlexikon*, p. 281.
61. Kramm, *Studien über die Oberschichten*, 1, 313.
62. Ibid., 394–395.
63. Chrisman, *Lay Culture, Learned Culture*, 124.
64. Kramm, *Studien über die Oberschichten*, 1, 316, 468.
65. Ibid., 314; 316, 469.
66. Nuremberg prohibited the development of guilds in the fourteenth century. Regulation of the crafts was entirely in the hands of the city council, including the establishment of standards of work, the rules governing each craft, and the qualifications for membership. The artisans were organized into sworn crafts, each headed by a sworn master who was elected by his fellow workers but appointed by the council. The regulation of the economic activity of the individual artisan was entirely in the hands of the council. Gerald Strauss, *Nuremberg in the Sixteenth Century*, 1966, 97.
67. Rudolf Endres, "Sozialstruktur Nürnbergs," 1982, 197.
68. *English Guilds*, ed. Toulmin Smith, 1870, 178, 181, 183–184, 164, 167, 168.
69. Ibid., 161.
70. Ibid., 160, 181, 182, 166.
71. Ibid., 169.
72. Ibid., 161, 168, 183, 184.
73. Francis Rapp, "Über Bürger, Stadt and städtische Literatur in Spätmittelalter," 1980, 152.
74. Wandel, *Always Among Us*, 22.
75. Rapp, "Über Bürger, Stadt und städtische Literatur," 150–151. I am grateful to Eckhard Bernstein of Holy Cross College who translated the term *Geburen* for me.
76. Rapp, "Über Bürger, Stadt und Städtische Literatur, 154, 158–159.
77. Ellis Lee Knox, "The Guilds of Augsburg," 1981, 171.
78. Lucien Sittler, *L'artisanat en Alsace*, 25. See also Chrisman, *Lay Culture, Learned Culture*, 22.
79. Chrisman, *Lay Culture, Learned Culture*, 15, 21.
80. Gustav Schmoller, *Die Strassburger Tucher- und Weberzunft: Urkunden und Darstellung*, 1876, 18.

81. Hans Sachs and Jost Amman, *Das Ständebuch*, Facsimile Aufgabe (Leipzig: Insel Verlag, n.d.), passim.
82. #50, *Welcher das Evangelium hat für gut . . .*, fol. Aiii.
83. #90, Conrad Distelmair, *Ain gesprechbüchlein von ain Xodtschneyder . . .*, 1523, fol. Ai.
84. #223, Hans Sachs, *Eyn Gesprech von den Scheinwerken der gaystlichen*, 1524, fol. Aiiiᵛ.
85. Margaret A. Sullivan, *Bruegel's Peasants*, 1994, 10ff.
86. An exception to this is Carlo Ginzburg's miller, Domenico Scandalla, called Menocchio, who developed his own cosmology. He believed that all had been chaos. Earth, fire, air, and water had been mixed together and out of that chaos a mass had formed, in the same way cheese was formed out of milk, and worms appeared and they were the angels, among whom was God. Menocchio was called before the Inquisition for his heretical beliefs, which also questioned the virginity of Mary. The process before the Inquisition, however, dragged on for over fifteen years and it seems to me that the evidence of his fellow villagers on his cosmology indicated that they listened to him but no one was swayed from his own belief. The village chaplain himself reported that "when he was heard talking about the moon and the stars he was told to be silent." The inquisition was directed far more at his religious ideas than at his cosmology, which essentially was not believed and was not a threat to traditional ideas. See Carlo Ginzburg, *The Cheese and the Worms*, 1982, 5–6, 53, 100.
87. William J. Bouwsma, *John Calvin: A Sixteenth Century Portrait*, 1988, 33.
88. The concept of the three estates is fully developed in Ruth Mohl, *The Three Estates in Medieval and Renaissance Literature*, 1933, passim. Bernd Moeller's description of the organic community of the imperial city has become a classic. See Bernd Moeller, *Imperial Cities and the Reformation*, 1972, 43–45, 76–78. A more recent study based on the acceptance of the theory by three major sixteenth century figures is Abel Alves, "The Christian Social Organism and Social Welfare: The Case of Vives, Calvin and Loyola," *SCJ* XX, I (1988): 5–21.
89. Hans-Christoph Rublack, "Political and Social Norms in Urban Communities in the Holy Roman Empire," 1984, 26–28.

1 "A Dialogue between a father and his son with regard to Martin
Luther's teaching."

The son, returning from Wittenberg, tells his still Romanist father of the opposition to Luther. The father, quickly converted, burns an indulgence letter in the
name of Eck, Emser, and Murner. The woodcut shows the sequence: the arrival of
the son of the burning of the letter.

SOURCE: Title page of an anonymous pamphlet, *Eynn Dialogus oder gesprech zwischen
einem Vatter unnd Sun dye Lere Martin Luthers und sunst andere sachen des Christlichen
glaubens belangende.* Erfurt: M. Buchfürer, 1523. Courtesy of the Zentralbibliothek,
Zurich, Switzerland.

2

Fear of Injustice: The Warning Pamphlets and Accounts of Judicial Actions

The first lay pamphlets were written to warn Luther and other reformers that they were in peril. Taking the risk of printing their opinions, a knight, a city secretary, a nobleman's wife, an artisan, and a student were driven by their fear that these clergy might be accused of heresy, tried by an ecclesiastical court, and sentenced to be burned. This was the only group of pamphlets which cut clearly across the lines of social rank. Their unanimity demonstrated a fear of injustice which marked lay attitudes toward the legal system.

The burning of Johann Huss at Constance in 1415 remained fresh in the popular memory. Granted a free conduct by the emperor to travel to Constance and return, he had been imprisoned by the church authorities almost immediately, condemned by ecclesiastical judges as a heretic, and turned over to the civil magistrates to be burned. One hundred years later, lay people still were stunned by the violence of his death. The church had derided, mocked, and killed a pious man. Eyewitness accounts of his martyrdom were reprinted in the 1520s.[1] As recently as 1509, the church in Bern had comdemned four Dominican friars as heretics, then released them to the lay magistrates to be burned. The four had perpetrated a hoax to cheat the laity, but despite their guilt and their trickery, people reacted strongly to the burning. However wrong, they had not deserved death. Occurring only ten years before the Reformation, the story had spread in newsheets and pamphlets.[2] The event was constantly referred to in the Reformation pamphlets. Laymen saw the Dominicans as martyrs, one more example of injustice and violence by church courts.

The Legal System and Fear of Injustice

Was the lay fear based on reality? The existence of two sets of courts, church and secular, created a fundamental division which stuck like a bone in the throats of nobility, city people, and peasants alike. Originally the jurisdiction of the ecclesiastical courts had been limited to clerical persons and their servants. In the High Middle Ages, before secular courts were firmly established, businessmen brought suit in ecclesiastical courts because the judges were willing to place debtors under the ban and interdict. Furthermore, the secular courts were slower and inadequately staffed.[3] By the fifteenth century, German ecclesiastical courts had extended their jurisdiction to include wills and all religious matters, which included usury, marital cases, and non-payment of tithes.[4]

The punishments enforced by the church courts affected the religious and social life of all lay people. The major penalties were excommunication, usually referred to as the ban, and the interdict. The ban meant exclusion from the church community. The interdict forbade the reception of the means of salvation: the individual could not take part in any church service or receive communion or any other sacrament. He was not, however, excluded from the church community.[5] The church either cut the individual off from his fellow-Christians or denied him the sacraments on which his salvation depended. Designed to maintain discipline among the faithful, applying excommunication and interdict to secular offenses led to abuses. Failure to meet payments on a loan resulted in denial of the sacraments to the debtor. Indeed, contracts for loans might include a clause providing for excommunication or the interdict, and these sentences might be cumulative in case of persistent non-payment.[6]

Laymen were convinced that the scales of justice always tipped in favor of the clergy in an ecclesiastical court and that a clerical offender, except in the case of heresy, would be let off with little punishment. As early as 1314, the Strasbourg Magistrat, for example, had mandated that a priest who wounded a burgher was to be judged in a civil court, subject to the same punishment as a lay person for that offense.[7] Yet in practice the cleric could almost always escape.

For lay people, both ban and interdict were carried to extremes. When, in 1507, the clergy of Worms laid their city under interdict, they ordered the Frankfurt clergy to do the same on the grounds that excommunicated persons, namely, merchants from Worms, would attend the Frankfurt fair. Although Frankfurt had a privilege which guaranteed holding religious services during the fair, the Frankfurt clergy ignored this, and in September all services in the churches ceased. Until the end of the year, when the interdicts were lifted, no one in either city could be baptized, married, or buried with the sacraments of the church.[8] Whatever the reformers' other proposals for change, the laity wanted to be free of ecclesiastical courts, free from being banned for non-payment of tithes and other secular offenses.

The dual system also divided the process of justice. In cases involving capital punishment, the ecclesiastical court tried the case according to canon law. The secular authorities had to carry out the execution because the church could not shed blood. The lay authorities, however, could not question the decision of the church court.

It is ironic that the first lay pamphlets warned the reformed clergy of the dangers of ecclesiastical justice. They attempted to protect the reformed clergy from the exaggerated charges and excessive punishments which the laity had routinely experienced. It was not, however, the clergy who needed protection.

LAY PEOPLE RAISE THE ALARM: THE WARNING PAMPHLETS

The first warning pamphlet was written by Lazarus Spengler, secretary to the city council of Nuremberg, to support Luther's teaching and defend himself as a follower.[9] It was triggered by an overt example of papal injustice. In September 1518, Luther stopped in Nuremberg on his way to meet Cardinal Cajetan in Augsburg on October 12–14. Luther fully expected to be charged with heresy, ultimately to be burned. The interview with Cajetan turned out differently than anyone expected. The cardinal merely admonished Luther and sent him home. Returning to Nuremberg, however, Luther received a copy of a papal letter to Cajetan, dated 18 August 1518, directing the cardinal to arrest Luther and excommunicate all of his followers. Since the order for arrest had been issued three months before the interview, the Pope had condemned Luther without a hearing. The duplicity of the Pope confirmed the worst fears of Luther's supporters in Nuremberg. Spengler, writing in the first person throughout the pamphlet, defended Luther's teaching.[10] He took a major risk. It was an extraordinary act by a highly placed civil servant who was expected to preserve a neutral position. By openly announcing himself to be a defender of Luther, he exposed himself to the papal order of excommunication.

Luther's teaching, Spengler stated, was Christian, sound, in accord with reason, and based on Scripture, the only source of religious truth. Yet the Pope had proclaimed Luther a heretic because he had attacked indulgences. This could only occur, Spengler continued, because church law had totally darkened the commandments of Christ. How many blameless men, who owed perhaps three *heller*, had been banned as members of God and his church, denounced from the pulpit, and, as unbelievers, buried out in the field? Luther had freed men from this and should be praised rather declared an enemy.[11] Nevertheless, Luther's opponents continued to attack him: "So many of these dream preachers, who believe themselves to be great theologians ... fight against Luther's teaching with violence rather then with well-reasoned, honest argument based [in Scripture]."[12] By refusing to permit Luther to justify his teachings and denying him the right to demonstrate their scriptural foundation, the church under its own law could condemn him as a heretic. The theologians were hardened against him. They wrote out of envy or their own self-interest.[13]

Spengler wrote because he feared immediate action by the church. The imperial election prevented it. By the summer of 1520, however, the Pope was ready to move. The bull *Exsurge Domine*, giving Luther 60 days to recant or to be declared a heretic, was published in Rome. Johann Eck and Hieronymus Aleander were responsible for promulgating the bull in the north. Eck was given instructions, secret even from Aleander, to add names to the bull on his own judgment. He singled out Spengler, Willibald Pirckheimer, perhaps Ulrich von Hutten, and three men from Wittenberg.[14] Laymen were immediately accused as well as reformers. Eck was ordered to burn heretical writings and political manifestos such as Hutten's *Roman Trinity*, which was specifically named by the Pope.[15]

Ulrich von Hutten responded to the papal bull in a pamphlet strongly warning against the unchristian power of the pope.[16] He wrote of the danger to himself rather than to the reformers. "They take away the freedom of anyone who writes against them and since I have done so ... I am in peril of my life. ... They have sent a monk with a mandate against me and he can hunt me down with force."[17] The priests had persecuted those who preached the truth, like Huss. He hoped he would not face the same punishment and asked all men to help him struggle against the Pope's might.[18] The German people, the *landsknechten*, and his fellow knights should rise up and use their horses, halberds, and swords against the opponents of God.[19] Hutten feared he would be abandoned to his enemies.

Popular response to Eck's activity was reflected in an anonymous pamphlet written as a dialogue between a peasant father and his son, a student just returned from Wittenberg. "The pope and Thomas Murner's monks," said the son, "are Luther's enemies, as was Eck, but Luther had stood up against Eck at Leipzig." Yet, continued the son, "Eck would sell Martin for gulden as Judas sold Christ. ... He would sell Luther and all of Wittenberg to their deaths. God protect Luther."[20] Although people said that Wittenberg would be burned like Sodom and Gomorrah, the father and son believed that God would protect it, for there the Word of God was preached and taught. They prayed that God would send his grace so that his Word would go forth.[21]

Eck and Aleander maintained persistent pressure on the secular authorities. Charles V permitted enforcement of the bull in his hereditary domains so that Aleander was able to burn Luther's books at Louvain.[22] In the Rhineland, however, he encountered resistance. Although the Archbishop of Cologne had consented, the public executioner refused to light the fire without a specific imperial mandate. The archbishop overruled the executioner and the books were burned. A few weeks later in Mainz, his torch already lit, the executioner asked whether the books had been legally condemned. When the crowd shouted "no," the executioner stepped down from the platform and extinguished his torch. Aleander went directly to Archbishop Albrecht of Mainz, and the following day a few books were burned by a gravedigger with only a handful of market women to observe him.[23] Thus, at the very lowest level of the civil hierarchy, the partnership between the secular and ecclesiastical authorities was crumbling.

Eck's book burning led another student, a young nobleman named Lux Gemmiger von Heinfelt,[24] to write a poem in praise of Luther, warning against "the villainy of the Romans . . . Luther . . . consecrated as a light to Christianity . . . is hated by the pope, the priests and monks . . .[who] wish to have him secretly killed, along with the noble Ulrich von Hutten who wishes to stand faithfully by the Godly truth."[25] Gemmiger's solution, like Hutten's, was violence: "Arise Christians, we must reform [the clergy] and wipe them out with cold steel. [We should] take their property away from them and beat them on the head. . . . The Roman church has excommunicated everyone that did not freely submit to it. The pope has become so depraved that his misdeeds can no longer be tolerated."[26]

In the same year as the Diet of Worms, Matthias Zell, the people's priest in the Strasbourg cathedral, had mounted the pulpit and announced that he would preach the Gospel of Jesus Christ, beginning with the Epistles to the Romans. The bishop immediately tried to remove him from the pulpit but was stopped by rivalry among the cathedral clergy. Early in 1523, Stefan von Büllheym, probably an artisan,[27] voiced his growing concern that Zell would be arrested in a dialogue between a son and his father, entitled *A Brotherly Warning to Master Matthias*.[28] The pamphlet revealed the popular opinion in the city, the lingering fear that the bishop and magistrates would join forces against Zell. "Everything on earth is wild," asserted the son, "and the clergy cannot keep unity among themselves. . . . They quarrel and squabble among each other. . . . But there is one good man, the parish priest in the cathedral called Master Matthias."[29] The father agreed but wanted to know what the other cathedral preacher, Doctor Peter Wickram, nephew and successor to Geiler von Kayserberg, thought about Zell.[30] "He doesn't help," replied the son, "Doctor Peter just shrieks from the chancel—'murderer'"[31]

Wickram's opposition persuaded the father of the danger to Zell. Wickram was from an important family and his views would be shared by many of the magistrates. "Son," said the father, "you had better warn Zell right away

that he should not preach tomorrow. . . . You see how it goes. If the Rat at
Bern had not openly disgraced the four Dominicans, the spiritual authorities
would not [have condemned them to the burnt]. If Master Matthias falls
into the hands of the ecclesiastical courts, he will be punished. . . . They
lie when they say they will overlook him . . . he is much too learned for
them. . . . The biggest flies," concluded the father, "are rarely caught, it's
the little ones which get left in the spider's web."[32]

PROTECTION FOR THE CLERGY

After the Diet of Worms, the Elector Frederic's protection provided Luther
with an invulnerable cloak against the ecclesiastical authorities, strengthening
the position of the evangelical clergy in principalities and cities where the
Reform had taken hold. In these areas, the bishop and the ecclesiastical
courts gradually lost their force. The secular courts began to emerge as the
single judicial authority. This was made possible, in part, by the threat of
popular unrest. Artisanal riots occurred in the cities from 1522 through
1523, well before the Peasants' War, over the appointment or dismissal of
evangelical preachers. In the critical years when the Reformation was taking
hold, civil authorities in Nuremberg, Strasbourg, Augsburg, Memmingen,
Rostock, and other cities did not move to dismiss the new preachers nor
did they cooperate with ecclesiastical or imperial measures to control them.[33]
Relatively secure in their pulpits, the reformed clergy could begin to lay
the foundations of the new church, which would be formalized in church
ordinances in the late '20s and '30s.

Even in Catholic-controlled territories, the clergy could escape severe
punishment. At the University of Ingolstadt, Arsacius Seehofer, a young
cleric, was discovered to have Lutheran books in his possession. Some sort
of public trial was held, he was forced to recant, and went to a monastery.[34]
From there he managed to get himself to Wittenberg, was protected by
Luther, and later became a respected reformed teacher and preacher.[35] Argula
von Grumbach, a Bavarian noble woman, rose to defend him at the time of
his arrest. She launched four pamphlets against the university and the Dukes
of Bavaria, casting Seehofer in the role of Christian martyr.[36] It was, however,
Grumbach's husband who bore the punishment. He was forced to leave his
position at the Bavarian court and return to his family lands.[37] The layman
suffered for the action of his wife because he was responsible for her obedience. And the layman, not the University, was punished.

The clergy were shielded. The list of Lutheran clergy martyred as heretics
is short.[38] The German pamphlet literature records only a few instances of
clerics who suffered the death penalty, an event which would certainly have
been exploited for polemic purposes.[39]

RISK FOR LAY PEOPLE

Laymen did not receive the same protection but were subjected to the full force of the church's attempt to wipe out heresy. The trial and execution, in 1524, of Conrad Tauber, a burgher of Vienna, was described in detail in a pamphlet as a warning against the injustice of canon law and the contempt and bias of the ecclesiastical court.[40] Brought before the bishop's court in the heart of Hapsburg territory, Tauber was declared a threat to his neighbors and the community of God, which meant he had to be punished as an example. The articles against him "which the learned and the clergy invented and wrote for him" charged that he had denied the Real Presence, the intercession of the Virgin, and the scriptural base of purgatory, and had preached the priesthood of all believers. He had Lutheran books in his possession and had also written tracts.[41]

He was called on to confess his errors and submit to public penance, failing which, he would be proved a heretic and turned over to recant. He spoke to the congregation, absolving King Ferdinand from all blame but naming the bishop, the provost, the deacon, and the *fiscal* as the leaders of the attack against him.[42] Appealing to imperial justice, he was surrounded by the clergy and taken back to prison with excessive force. The clergy led a mob attack against him, later alleging that he attempted suicide in prison, "because that is how Lutherans behave if they are defeated." Exonerated from this by his friends, he was beheaded a few days later by the public executioner. "Tauber was killed because of the lies of the learned and the High Priests of Vienna," concluded the narrator.[43]

In cities where the Reform took hold, the magistrates used the confusion of the times to strengthen their authority. Lenient and protective toward the reformed clergy they might be, but when order was threatened, they did not hesitate to use their power against citizens whose religious activities they felt endangered the public peace. Long before the Peasants' War or Anabaptist preaching made urban uprisings more dangerous and menacing, cities were taking firm action against their own people.

In Augsburg in 1520, enthusiastic artisans attempted to prevent the consecration of holy water and salt. One was imprisoned, another exiled, while the *Rat* created "a great defense for the clergy," who were, in this case, of the old church.[44] Later that year, when hundreds of artisans gathered outside the Rathaus to protest the banishment of a Franciscan who preached the Gospel, servants of the Augsburg *Rat*, mingling with the crowd, identified 86 artisans in the crowd as dangerous. Some were imprisoned, two were beheaded. In reformed Nuremberg, in 1524, when the preaching of Thomas Müntzer and Andreas Carlstadt spread radical ideas leading outlying villages to refuse to pay tithes, the city council felt compelled to act, and forcefully.

An apprentice weaver and an innkeeper were beheaded "for conspiring to incite rebellion." Others were imprisoned and one was banished from the city.[45]

ECCLESIASTICAL JUSTICE ENFORCED

While the civil authorities pursued order harshly, the ecclesiastical courts did not stand idle. In 1523, the full fury of ecclesiastical justice was experienced by the citizens of Miltenberg, a small town near Aschaffenburg, whose overlord was the Archbishop of Mainz. Using all his powers, the archbishop extinguished reformed teaching and forced the citizens to return to the old faith. Several writers described the events and the suffering of the citizens of Miltenberg. Two of them were laymen, visitors from other cities, who happened to be in Miltenberg at the time. Miltenberg had only one church, closely controlled by its chapter canons, drawn from the sons of Miltenberg burghers. Bernhard Johim's account warned against these canons. The town had been attacked by its own clergy, sons of Miltenberg burghers, who had turned against their own people. Other cities should take heed and, following the teachings of the apostles, train their children in a craft rather than permitting them to become priests.[46]

God had sent Doctor Johannes Carlstadt, an evangelical preacher, Johim wrote, to proclaim the Word of God to the people of Miltenberg. After a year of his preaching, however, the priests in Miltenberg turned against him. The archbishop placed him under the ban. The people were enraged when this was read out in church. If Carlstadt himself had not appeared from the sacristy, dragged the priests from the altar, and locked them up in the sacristy, "God knows what would have happened to the priests."[47] A few days later, the archbishop's governor ordered the people to send their pastor away on penalty of losing life and property. Thus, "the poor humble subjects" requested Carlstadt to withdraw for a time. He left a young chaplain behind to preach God's Word. Since the canons had meanwhile fled to Aschaffenburg, the chaplain was the only resident cleric in town. The burghers, fearing that the clergy, now gathered in Aschaffenburg, would mount an attack, sent a representative to state their case but no one would listen to him.[48] Instead, the governor ordered the town to prepare stabling for 100 horses. The burghers were forbidden to wear any military equipment on pain of death. The chapter members returned, accompanying the governor when he rode into the city with his horsemen. Simple peasants from the outlying villages came in secretly by night and were hidden in the castle.[49]

Friday morning, the bell was rung and the people went as always to hear early Mass and the chaplain's sermon. The bell rang again as a signal to the governor's men still outside the town. The burghers thought it meant that they should gather at the Rathaus and proceeded there. At this moment, both cavalry and peasants came out from the castle in force, led by Count von Auerbach, the mayor, whose duty it was to protect the town. He betrayed his people, wrote Johim, "as Judas betrayed Christ." The armed men fell with naked force on the unarmed burghers, shouting "death to those who shame God's martyrs," "they must die."[50] Terrified, some of the "Christians" fled to their houses. The chapter members commanded the soldiers to invest and attack the houses and to beat the women and apprentices. The chaplain was taken to the castle as a prisoner.[51] That night the mayor locked the main gate. When the people assembled at his command the next morning, all the gates were closed and locked. The citizens had to agree to six articles on pain of loss of life or property: never again to appoint their own pastor, the pastor must be a tonsured priest, not just some untonsured chaplain they knew nothing about, to abide by the traditional services of the church, never again to read the Bible, never to write their complaints to the archbishop, and to swear loyalty to the authorities of the diocese of Mainz.[52] The citizens could neither speak nor defend their actions. They were surrounded by soldiers, who remained in the town for a long time.

Naked, armed force was brought to bear against this community, which had chosen to listen to an evangelical preacher. The old church was maintained because the archbishop had used his full powers. The authors of the accounts were moved by the injustice, the fact that the citizens were never allowed to present their case and had no means of redress. They had drawn up 27 grievances against the clergy but no one would accept them. For this reason, they had been written down by a "stranger" and given to be printed.[53] "May God give all towns who wish to adopt God's word the courage and steadfastness of the people of Miltenberg," exhorted Bernhard Johim.[54]

The laity's fear of injustice was well-founded, but the force of ecclesiastical and secular justice fell on them rather than on the reformed clergy. The latter were protected by the secular authorities as major pieces in their chess match against the Roman church. Laymen had little protection and were subject to punishment for their religious ideas both by the Roman church and by the newly powerful secular authorities. As Stephan Bullheym's father had said, "the biggest flies are rarely caught, it's the little ones which get left in the spider's web."[55]

The warning pamphlets reveal the measures taken to insure order by the Roman church and the magistrates in cities which had accepted the Reformation. Of the two powers, the Roman church was more violent in its trial and judgment of heretics like Conrad Tauber and in forcing a city like Miltenburg to return to orthodox beliefs and practices. Yet, the magistrates of cities like Nuremberg and Augsburg were also quick to move against riot or incipient rebellion and did not shrink from brutality. God had given them their authority to maintain order. The Reformation did not change their attitudes toward law and justice. It abolished the ecclesiastical courts, but the power passed into the hands of the secular authorities, who assumed responsibility for protecting the Gospel against the forces of the Antichrist. The double standard of justice inherited from the past was maintained. Force was ever-present in these years. People's fear of injustice existed as an undercurrent in many lay pamphlets. The difference between those who had power to enforce their will and those who did not remained unchanged.

Notes

1. For accounts of the burning of Huss in the pamphlet literature see: #42, *Ain schöner newer Passion* (1521–1522), fol. aiv.; #28, *Ein klarlich anzeygung und aussweysung eins Christlichen und unchristlichen lebens.* . . . (c. 1523), fol. C; #52, *Wie Hieronimus von Prag ain//anhanger Johannis Huss . . . für ain Ketzer verurtailt und//verprant ist*, and also #18, *Dialogus . . . zwischen einem Vater unnd Sohn die Lehre Martini Lutheri belangende* (1523), fol. Bii^v–Biii.
2. The many German editions of Thomas Murner's pamphlet that attacked the Dominicans are listed in Frank Hieronymus, *Oberrheinische Buchillustration 2; Basler Buchillustration 1500–1545*, 1983, 37–38. There were also popular songs about the incident: [Nikolaus Manuel], *Die war History von den Vier ketzer prediger ordens, zu Bern in der Eydgnosschafft verbant* (1509).
3. Justus Hashagen, "Zur Charakteristik der geistlichen Gerichtsbarkeit vornemlich im späteren Mittelalter," 1916, 213.
4. Helmut Cellarius, "Die Reichstadt Frankfurt und die Gravamina der deutschen Nation," 1938, 82, fn. 1; Hashagen, "Charakteristik . . . geistliche Gerichtsbarkeit," 249.
5. Cellarius, "Die Reichstadt Frankfurt," 84.
6. Hashagen, "Charakteristik . . . geistliche Gerichtsbarkeit," 246.
7. Miriam Usher Chrisman, *Strasbourg and the Reform*, 1967, 36.
8. Cellarius, "Die Reichstadt Frankfurt," 87–89.
9. Nolf Laube, et al., *Fluzschriften der frühen Reformationsbewegung*, 2 vols. (1983), 2, 512.
10. Harold Grimm, *Lazarus Spengler, a Lay Leader of the Reformation*, 1978, 35–36.
11. #246, Lazarus Spengler, *Schutzrede und Christenlichen Antwort.* . . . *eins erbarn Libhabers gotlicher Warheit . . .* (Augsburg: Silvan Ottmar, 1519; Basel: Adam Petri, 1520), Wittenberg: Melchior Lotther, 1520). The first edition of this pamphlet was published, anonymously, against Spengler's wishes. The two editions the following year bore his name (Grimm, *Lazarus Spengler*, 36). References here below are to the Wittenberg edition. Here, fol. Ai; Bii.
12. Ibid., fol. Bii. Here Spengler referred to Johann Eck, who had vaunted himself as the winner of the Leipzig debate (1519) and attempted to prejudice the Electors of Brandenburg and Saxony against Luther. Laube et al., *Flugschriften*, 1, 515, fn. 31.
13. Ibid., fols. Bii^v–Biii; Bv^v.
14. Roland Bainton, *Here I Stand: A Life of Martin Luther*, 1950, 157.

15. Hajo Holborn, *Ulrich von Hutten and the German Reformation*, 1937, reprint 1966, 148.
16. #163, Ulrich von Hutten, *Clag und vormanung gegen dem übermässigen unchristlichen gewalt des Bapstes zu Rom und der ungeistlichen geistlichen. . . .* , (1520).
17. Ibid., fol. d; fol. e^v.
18. Ibid., fol. div; fol. eii.
19. Ibid., fol. g^v.
20. #18, *Eynn Dialogus ader gesprech zwischen einem Vatter unnd Sun dye lere Martini Luthers und sonst andere sachen des Cristlichen glaubens belangende* (Erfurt: Michel Buchfürer, 1523). The text states that this dialogue took place between a student returning from Wittenberg and his father, a peasant in Thuringia. Otto Clemen accepted these self-identifications and assumed that the father had sent his son to university so that he might achieve a higher status in life. Otto Clemen, ed., *Flugschriften aus den Ersten Jahren der Reformation*, 4 vols. (1907–1911), 1, 21. I included the author among the artisans because the dialogue describes popular religious practices. The student is an example of upward mobility although his new status as a professional has not yet been achieved. Here on fol. Biii.
21. #18, *Eynn Dialogus*, fol. Bi^v.
22. Bainton, *Here I Stand*, 158.
23. Ibid., 159.
24. Laube et al., *Flugschriften*, I, 555. Laube states the pamphlet bears witness to literary connections with the Hutten circle. The name Gemmiger, he continues, suggests that of the Swabian noble family of Gemmingen, which belonged to the imperial knights and had ties with humanism. There was a Dietrich Gemmiger in Sickingen's circle. I classified Lux Gemigger as a knight in part because he drew heavily on Hutten.
25. #119, Lux Gemmiger von Heinfelt, *Zu Lob dem Luther und eeren der gantzen Christenhait* (1521–1522), fol. ai^v.
26. Ibid., fol. aiiii.
27. Büllheym has not been definitively identified. Timotheus Wilhelm Rörich, *Geschichte der Reformation im Elsass*, 1830, identified him as a member of Zell's congregation. Marc Lienhard, in his "Mentalité populaire," 1980 (see below), points to the popular origins of the poem in its references to the tavern life of the city, particularly the inn where waggoners met. I classified him as an artisan.
28. #71, Steffan von Büllheym, *Ein brüderliche warnung an meister Mathis Pfarrherren . . .*, 1523. Text printed and translated into French by Marc Lienhardt, "Mentalité populaire, gens d'église et mouvement évangelique à Strasbourg en 1522–23," 1980, 37–62. Page references are to this edition.
29. Büllheym, *Ejn brüderliche warnung*, 47, lines 175–177, 186.
30. Ibid., 57, n. 34.
31. Ibid., 47, line 207; 48, lines 220–221.
32. Ibid., 48, lines 236–239, 243–245, 250–251, 257– 259, 254–255.
33. Paul Russell, *Lay Theology in the Reformation*, 1986, 150, 152–153, 83–85; Philip Broadhead, "Popular Pressure for Reform in Augsburg, 1524–1534," 1979, 80–81; Axel Vorberg, "Die Einführung der Reformation in Rostock," 1897, 49, 30.
34. Russell, *Lay Theology*, 192.
35. *ADB*, 33, 573–574.
36. #155, Argula von Grumbach, *Wie Ain Christliche fraw des Adels . . . durch iren . . . Sendtbrieffe die hohenschul zu Ingoldstat . . . haben strafet*, 1523; #148, *An ain*

Ersamen Weysen Radt der stat Ingolstat ain sandtbrief . . ., 1523; #154, *Dem* . . .
Hochgeboren Fursten Herrn Johansen Pfaltzgrauen bey Reyn, 1523; #149, *Eyn Antwort
in gedichtss weis auz der hohen Schul zu Ingolstat* . . ., 1524.

37. Roland H. Bainton, *Women of the Reformation in Germany and Italy*, 1971, 104–
105.

38. A. W. Heckel, *Die Martyrer der evangelischen Kirchen in den ersten Zeiten nach
der Reformation*, 1828. Heckel includes Heinrich Voes and Johann Esch,
Augustinians who were burned at Brussels in 1522; Heinrich von Zutphen,
also an Augustinian from Antwerp, who had preached at Meldorf in Dithmarchen;
Wolfgang Schuh from Pölding; Matthias Weybel, who was found hanged; and
Leonhard Kässer (7–10, 20, 26, 38ff). Note: Most were in Hapsburg territory.

39. This is substantiated by Ulman Weiss's listing of the pamphlets on Reformation
martyrs in the volume *Flugschriften Vom Bauernkrieg zum Täuferreich (1526–
1535)*, ed. Adolf Laube, Annerose Schneider, Ulman Weiss (in press). Weiss
found pamphlets describing the trial and execution of five reformed clergy as
heretics and three laypersons. I am grateful to Adolf Laube for sending me this
information.

40. #269, *Eyn Warhafftig geschicht wie Casper Tawber . . . fur ain ketzer . . . verurtaylt
worden ist*, 1524.

41. Ibid., fols. Aii, Aii^v, Aiii^v, Ai^v.

42. Ibid., fol. Biii^v.

43. Ibid., fols. Biv^v, Ci^v–Cii, Ciii.

44. Georg Preu, "Die Chronik," in *Die Chroniken der Schwäbischen Städte: Augsburg*,
Vol. 6, 24, 25.

45. Russell, *Lay Theology*, 121, 156.

46. #177, Bernhart Johim, *Warhafftig bericht Bernhart Johims wie die Christen zu
Miltenberg . . . gesturmbt seyn. Anclage der Stat Miltenberg widder die Pfaffen daselbst.
Ein ander unterricht von Michel Fincken* . . ., 1523. Johim identified himself in
the text when he was questioned by the troops storming Miltenberg and said
that he was an outsider from Burgstat (fol. Bi^v). Fincken identified himself as a
"guest" in the city in his preface (fol. Cii^v). See also [Johannes Carlstadt],
Epistel an die Gemeyne zu Miltenberg den abschyd des Pfarers daselbt betreffendt . . . .
*Supplication des veriagten Pfarrers vonn wegen der Burger unnd gefanngnen zu
Miltenberg*, 1524. Not a lay pamphlet, it corroborated the lay account and is
indicative of Carlstadt's loyalty to his parish. There were at least four editions
of this account.

47. #177, fol. Aii.

48. Ibid., fol. Aii^v.

49. Ibid., fol. Aiii.

50. Ibid.

51. Ibid., fol. Aiii^v–Aiv.

52. Ibid., fol. Aiv–Bi.

53. Ibid., fol. Cii.

54. Ibid., fol. Bi^v.

55. #71, Büllheym, *Ein brüderliche warnung*, 48, lines 254–255.

Eyn hüpsch Cristenliche
vnd Götliche erinnerung vnd warnung/
so Kayserlicher Maiestat võ eynem
jren Kayserlichen Maiestat ar
men Reüterlyn/ vnd vn
dertßenigem diener
beschicht.

2   "A fine Christian and godly admonition and warning
to his Imperial Majesty."

The knight Harthmuth von Cronberg kneels in full armor before the emperor to urge him not to support the Pope. The woodcut reflects the power relationship between emperor and knight.

SOURCE: Title page of a pamphlet by Hartmuth von Cronberg, *Ein hüpsch Christenliche und Götliche erinnerung und warnung/so kayserlicher Maiestat von eynem iren kayserlichen Maiestat armen Reuterlyn und underthenigem diener beschicht.* Strassburg: J. Prüss der junger, 1520/21. Courtesy of the Zentralbibliothek, Zurich, Switzerland.

3

The Knights as Propagandists

THE LEADERS: SICKINGEN, HUTTEN, AND CRONBERG

The knights' role in the Reformation is usually equated with the Knights' Revolt of 1522–1523. Franz von Sickingen and Ulrich von Hutten having died, all the knights disappear from the stage, their performance regarded as insignificant to the Reformation movement. "Defeat," as Eugen Weber has said, "can condemn to silence, to the blacking out of people and events."[1] In this chapter, I will attempt to restore this small group of knights to their position as leaders in the very early years of the movement and give them their due as the earliest lay propagandists. As Heinz Schilling wrote, "the imperial knights were the first secular followers to stand decisively and effectively behind Luther."[2]

At least 64 pamphlets were written between 1520 and 1524 by individual knights or groups of knights. Many were reprinted two, four, six, or seven times in a three-year period. Printed in Speyer, Würzburg, Mainz, Bamberg, Augsburg, Nuremberg, Strasbourg, Wittenberg, Landshut, and Erfurt, they covered the empire from east to west and north to south. This propaganda battle helped to establish the themes of later writers. Ulrich von Hutten's pamphlets sharply attacked the priests, monks, and Roman clergy. Other knights denounced the injustice of the ecclesiastical courts. They attacked the immense land holdings of the church. Their outcry prepared the way for the shift of power to the secular courts and the later secularization of monastic and chapter lands.

The leaders of this campaign were Franz von Sickingen, his cousin Hartmut von Cronberg, and Ulrich von Hutten. 32, or nearly half, of the knights' pamphlets were written at the Ebernburg, the castle Sickingen had made his primary residence. He had used the monies received as magistrate in the Palatinate to modernize its fortifications against the destructive power of the new artillery. By 1520 he began to bring together at the Ebernburg a circle dedicated to living according to the Gospel. It was only the third evangelical community to be formed in Germany, Wittenberg being the first, the group around Staupitz in Nuremberg the second. Both the latter were led by reformed clergy. Laymen were the leaders at the Ebernburg. Ulrich von Hutten was one of the first to arrive. By 1521 Hutten, Sickingen, and Cronberg were publishing propaganda pamphlets. Others wrote jointly, publishing their work anonymously.[3] These pamphlets provide a rare example of the shared ideas of a group of writers. They reveal the opinions of the knights from 1520 to 1522, spanning the time when they believed the power of the Gospel would change the church, to the moment, probably after the defeat at Trier, when they saw themselves surrounded by enemies drawing ever closer.

It is impossible to determine what brought the group of knights together because the Sickingen archives were destroyed when the Ebernburg was demolished at the end of the knights' rebellion.[4] The varied motives that brought the leaders there by 1520–1521 can be traced. Up to that point their lives had followed the usual pattern of knightly life, Hutten's the least so. Ulrich von Hutten spent the years 1512–1514 and 1515–1517 in Italy as a university student in law. The curriculum bored him and he devoted most of his time to writing and poetry, achieving acceptance within Italian humanist circles. He did not, however, distance himself from German politics or intellectual life. When the Duke of Württemburg murdered his cousin Hans von Hutten in 1517, Ulrich plunged into his family's effort to force the emperor to punish the duke. Always the polemicist, Hutten wrote a Latin dialogue against the tyranny of princes.[5] He was also deeply engaged in the struggle of the German humanists against the conservative Dominicans. In 1517, he received the crown of poet laureate from the hands of the Emperor Maximilian, indicating not only the personal recognition of the emperor but also his protection. In 1515, he received an appointment as counsellor at the court of the Archbishop of Mainz.[6] He continued his activity as a leading humanist and polemicist. In knightly tradition, he served in a princely court. His military experience was, however, limited. He had served with his cousin Sickingen in the campaign against the Duke of Württemburg and had had a brief exposure on the battlefield in the Italian Wars.[7]

Franz von Sickingen, from a well-established family in the Palatinate, inherited numerous ancestral castles and properties on the death of his father in 1505. He married into another important Palatine family with ties to the court and to the chapter at Worms. He had little literary education. He followed family tradition in serving the Elector-Palatine, first in the war over the succession to Landshut, then becoming magistrate in the Kreuznach, one of the eight districts of the Palatinate, from 1506–1511.[8] By 1515 he had struck out on his own as a military captain for hire. Successful actions against the city of Worms and the Duke of Lorraine began to build his reputation as a fighting man. The latter action brought him into contact with the king of France.[9] In a short time he established himself as an outstanding military leader, able to mobilize as many as 10,000 men.[10] These exploits made the Elector Palatine wary, particularly when the Emperor Maximilian tried to use Sickingen to bind the imperial knights to the imperial cause. This led eventually to a rupture of Sickingen's ties with the family patron, the elector.[11] Sickingen's military prowess was known throughout the empire. The position of these independent leaders of mercenary troops was complex. They were indispensable to the princes who hired them for their own territorial wars. Feuding had been abolished by imperial mandate in 1495, but the illegal feuds of the knights were tolerated as showcases for their military talents, carefully watched by the princes for potential leaders.[12] Sickingen provided an important force for the imperial troops mustered against the Duke of Württemburg, further strengthening his ties with the emperor.[13] After 1511, Sickingen's career was heavily military; furthermore, he was deeply entangled in the complex web which impaired the relationships between the princes and the emperor. His ambition was to acquire enough lands to become a territorial prince or count himself.

Hartmut von Cronberg was born in 1488, the same year as Hutten. The Cronberg lands, like those of their Sickingen cousins, were in the Palatinate. Hartmut's father served the elector as magistrate of Oppenheim, later he was an administrator for the Archbishop of Mainz. Hartmut received his education and training as a knight at the court of the Count Palatine.[14] He inherited the family lands in 1506, at the age of 18, and received a supernumerary appointment at the court in Mainz.[15] Married to an heiress, he could build up the property and power of his family. Closely associated with Sickingen, he played an active role in most of the latter's feuds and military campaigns. After a feud against the Landgrave of Hesse in 1518, lands taken in an earlier war were returned to Cronberg, something Phillip of Hesse never forgot. Hartmut von Cronberg was his enemy for life.[16]

All three men came from conservative backgrounds, from families of wealth and standing. All followed conventional careers of knightly service. Their religious conversions were rooted in deep convictions and in their personal concepts of justice and duty. They never knew Luther personally, but their lives were inextricably intertwined with the career of the reformer.

THE YEARS 1519–1520

In 1519, the knights could feel genuine satisfaction with their position. True, the old emperor had died in early January, but nothing led them to believe the Hapsburg policy would change. Maximilian's efforts to bring the knights to his side had succeeded. They felt their place in imperial politics was secure. The princes had been restrained. In that year, the army of the Swabian League, composed of knights and hired mercenaries from the cities, had defeated the Duke of Württemburg. The knights believed they had brought a notorious law-breaker to justice. Equity seemed to have been restored between themselves and the princes, with the help of the emperor.

The election of the new emperor further confirmed their self-confidence. Fearing that the election might be subverted by the Pope or the king of France, Margaret of Austria asked the knights to provide protection for the electors when they met at Frankfurt.[17] The knights looked on this as a recognition of their ancient, traditional function, as the vassals the imperial family could trust. Their encampment before Frankfurt was a bulwark against violence, fraud, and external enemies. For Sickingen it justified his support of the emperor. He, Hutten, and Cronberg were all there at Frankfurt; indeed, there Hutten and Sickingen drew closely together for the first time.[18] All three believed that the young Charles V, to use a metaphor of the time, would place a strong hand on the rudder of the ship of state and bring it into safe waters.

Ominous clouds, however, had begun to gather. When the Pope had summoned Luther to Rome the year before, in August 1518, many nobles, including Elector Frederick of Saxony, saw this as an overt attempt to undermine the jurisdiction of a German court. Six months before the papal bull of June 1520 formally condemned Luther, Sickingen and Hutten had pledged that they would defend Luther's life. Cronberg joined them somewhat later. Sylvester von Schaumburg, together with 100 fellow Franconian knights, made the same pledge.[19] Perturbed by imperial support of the papal ban against Luther, Hutten journeyed to Brussels seeking an audience with Charles V, which was refused. On returning to Mainz, he found a letter addressed to several princes, including the archbishop of Mainz, directing them to send Hutten directly to Rome. In September 1520, to protect his family, Hutten withdrew to the Ebernburg, given shelter by Sickingen.

THE ASYLUM OF JUSTICE

Providing shelter for those who had been wronged was part of the knightly ethic. There was ample precedent for knights to take individuals under their protection. Sickingen had championed others and had written pamphlets as part of his advocacy. In 1515, he had written to justify his protection of Balthasar Slör, notary to the bishop of Worms, accused of fomenting an uprising in that city.[20] As recently as 1519, he had defended his old tutor, Johann Reuchlin, who had been subjected to "unheard of" legal processes by the Dominican order. Sickingen threatened to take over the administration of the papal judgment in Reuchlin's favor and demanded that the order pay Reuchlin's costs, stating that it was his duty as a knight to protect the weak and the innocent.[21]

In January 1521, the Diet of Worms opened. As knights, Sickingen, Hutten and Cronberg maintained their traditional loyalty to the emperor. After the election Sickingen had loaned the new emperor 20,000 gulden, without security or interest.[22] The knights believed the emperor was receiving bad advice but that when he knew the truth of Luther's books he would accept his responsibility to lead the reform of the German church. They were perhaps encouraged when Jean Glapion, the emperor's confessor, asked Sickingen to propose to Luther that he meet with the emperor's advisors at the Ebernburg rather than appearing at Worms.[23] Luther, however, rejected the proposal and proceeded to the diet.

In 1521, Sickingen continued to serve Charles V as he had served his grandfather. Even after the diet and the imperial ban against Luther, Sickingen joined the imperial forces against France, believing it was his duty. After the defeat of the imperial army left him unable to pay his men, his link to the emperor was weakened.[24] He resigned his imperial commission and in September withdrew to the Ebernburg with a group of knights dedicated to Luther and to the establishment of a Christian life founded on the Gospel. Hutten called it the Asylum of Justice, linking their mission to the restoration of justice in the land. There was a genuine feeling of excitement, of the possibility of change.

Franz von Sickingen had already started the process of change. After his conversion he had taken immediate steps to establish a new, evangelical church order in his own lands, led by outstanding reformed theologians. In 1521, he appointed Martin Bucer pastor in Landstuhl; Kaspar Aquila became the tutor of Sickingen's son, and Johann Oecolampadius was the chaplain at the Ebernburg.[25] As the knights arrived in the fall of 1521, they assumed the task of spreading the truth of the Gospel to the German people, dedicating themselves to a life of Christian action. Their optimism was reflected in a letter written in 1522 by the reformer Johannes Schwöbel of Pforzheim. He wished his friend "could hear the evangelical Christian discourse . . . at the Ebernburg. No man in orders, however spiritual . . . nor any theologian, however learned, could speak so discerningly . . . in praise of God and with regard to salvation as this group of noblemen. The game," he continued, "has been turned completely upside down. Formerly one learned the laws of God from the priests. Now it is necessary to go to school to the laity and learn to read the Bible from them. The nobility now seek the honor and love of God instead of power and wealth."[26] Cronberg described the life of the community in a letter written to Luther, also in 1522. "The spirit of God and justice have been present at Franz's house at the Ebernburg for a long time. . . . Every day a section from the Epistles and Gospels is read in German and, after Mass, one of the prophets. The same in the evening. Thus, the Word of God increases with us. . . ."[27] The knights, as their pamphlets reveal, began to assert themselves as spiritual as well as religious leaders.

It was essential to their purpose to make their own ideas known, to proclaim the truth of the new faith, and to expose the injustice of the Roman church. There were, however, differences in their objectives, even among the leaders. Ulrich von Hutten envisioned a political reform which would overthrow the usurpation of Rome. He had little interest in spiritual issues. Sickingen was genuinely committed to Lutheran doctrine and Christian practice based on scripture. He also believed that the time had come to overthrow the ecclesiastical courts and administration. He heard in the Gospel a cry for justice, for a restoration of the liberty of the knights in their own territories. Hartmut von Cronberg was a devout convert, for whom the Christian faith was the measure of all things.

ULRICH VON HUTTEN AS PROPAGANDIST

In September of 1521, Hutten had already been in residence at the Ebernburg for a year, translating his Latin pamphlets into German.[28] As a German nationalist his primary interest, indeed obsession, was to restore the empire to greatness. His aim was to defame and destroy the Pope and his Roman courtiers, using the humanist tools of scathing satire and ironic dialogue. In his pamphlets he had decried the power of the Roman clergy, not their theology. His German translations made no attempt to change this message. Unlike Sickingen and Cronberg, Hutten did not move out of his past. He used what he had written before, believing he could thus strike a blow for German freedom. Although he prepared the translations himself, the elegance of the Latin was lost. He maintained his original hypotactic syntax, one clause piled on another. This and his nominalist style resulted in a complex and diffuse German.[29] The translations were not broadly popular. *The Collected Dialogues* saw only one edition, although *Fever the First*, an amusing satire on syphilis, went through five reprints.[30]

The most important of these Latin pamphlets, *The Roman Trinity*, was a traveler's report on the iniquity of life in Rome. It summarized Hutten's major themes. He charged the Pope with grasping political control of Germany by usurping the right to crown the emperor. Thus, a free and warlike nation, inhabited by strong-willed people, had been debased, its wealth taken to support the scandalous life of the Roman clergy. The force of the pamphlet came from constant repetition of the metaphor of the Trinity: "Everything evil and sinful in Rome can be counted in threes. . . . Three things keep Rome in power, the authority of the pope, the holy place, the wealth from indulgences. . . . three things are killed in Rome, good learning, devotion to God, one's oath. . . . the visitor to Rome comes back with three things, biased knowledge, a bad stomach and an empty sack."[31] German freedom could be restored only by military force—a war against the Pope and his Romanists. Hutten boldly asserted that "the Germans were born to rule the world and were given that world."[32] A rough imitation of the pamphlet listed page after page of the "three things" people did at Rome, or three things the Romans hated, an indication of how themes were picked up and reworked.[33]

Hutten's translation of Lorenzo Valla's exposure of the fraudulent Donation of Constantine appeared in February 1520. At the same time, Hutten wrote pledging armed support to Luther from Sickingen and himself. Luther received further encouragement from his humanist friend Crotus Rubianus and the knight Sylvester von Schaumburg. Karlheinz Blaschke believed that this support was crucial in Luther's decision to come forward openly in the three reformation treatises of late 1520. His trust in the knights' pledge of protection made him fearless. Furthermore, Hutten's patriotism had a profound effect on Luther, leading him to identify the Pope as the anti-Christ.[34]

Hutten's nationalism influenced the writing of the reformer, but Luther's theology had little effect on Hutten. The *Roman Trinity*, however, served as a lightning rod for the wrath of the Pope. He linked Hutten's pamphlets to Luther's writings and placed the humanist under the same ban. When Jerome Aleander left Rome to enforce the papal bull against Luther, he carried specific instructions to burn all copies of the *Roman Trinity*.[35] Papal punishment of a cleric was extended to include a free German nobleman, something Hutten used to prove the extremes of Roman despotism. He never failed to refer to himself as a victim of papal persecution.

In the new pamphlets which he wrote in German at the Ebernburg, Hutten believed he spoke for all the knights, but his views prevented cities and other knights from joining Sickingen. He attacked the wealth and luxury of the great merchants, contrasting it to the ascetic life of the German noble, which hardly encouraged the cities to accept the leadership of the knights.[36] His radical rejection of the Roman church went too far for many of the knights. His anti-clericalism, his attacks on the worldliness of the popes were acceptable, but when he proposed that the nobility should renounce their church benefices he struck at a major base of the knights' economic and social system.[37]

Hutten addressed the pamphlets, respectively, to the whole German nation, the estates of the empire, Duke Frederick of Saxony, the imperial free cities, and the emperor. He repeated the same themes from the past. The Roman curia was a mercenary army, lying in wait to fleece the innocent.[38] Germans must rise up against these oppressors and free themselves. To each person or group Hutten pledged to lead the struggle: "Hutten will come with all he can to serve you day and night. He will not accept any pay but will die in poverty."[39]

In all these German pamphlets, Hutten invoked the papal bull and the secret instruction to place him under the ban to assert the danger of persecution of a German citizen. "I was warned I should be killed . . . at first I took it lightly. Then letters arrived from the pope instructing the German nobles to imprison me and send me to Rome. . . . Honorable lords and good friends of the German nation, would you let the innocent be forcefully punished? Where is the courage of the Germans?"[40] Writing to the Elector Frederick of Saxony, he asked "Why has Leo X ordered . . . that I should be seized and imprisoned outside German land. . . . is that the work of a bishop or shepherd of Christ?"[41] To the emperor he was even more explicit: "The pope ordered certain nobles to take me prisoner to Rome and I, your servant, plead that you will not permit this. I will be named a heretic . . . and killed because I tried to honor you and write the truth. How could you let someone be imprisoned who fought for the common freedom?"[42]

Hutten's pamphlets succeeded as propaganda. Five other writers, an artisan, an apothecary and three knights (two at the Ebernburg), praised him for his support of Luther.[43] Hutten created an image of himself as hero. As a young humanist he had sought fame as a writer in Italy and at the imperial court, but now the papal ban gave him the opportunity to soar higher, to make his own fame. The jurisdictional conflict between the Roman church and the empire was no longer an abstraction, it was personified in Hutten as the persecuted, the hunted, the man who might lose his life as Huss had lost his. The papal ban became the symbol of the power of the Pope over all Germans. Hutten linked German freedom to ending the tyranny of the church. The one, he insisted, could not be achieved without the other.[44] It was a powerful emotional appeal.

SICKINGEN'S RETURN: THE EBERNBURG PAMPHLETS

When Sickingen returned from the war against France to the Ebernburg in September 1521, his situation had changed dramatically from the days of hope and optimism in 1519. The unsuccessful campaign against the French had blemished his military reputation. By now he had loaned a total of 96,000 gulden to Charles V, and clearly it would never be repaid. The imperial court in the Netherlands was afraid that Sickingen might attempt to take imperial lands to force payment of the debt. Instead, he decided to attack the Archbishop of Trier.[45] It was not an irrational decision. Bishops and archbishops had been seen as a major impediment to imperial reform as early as the *Reformation Sigismundi*, which had called for removal of their secular authority and an end to their holding of vast properties.[46] At the turn of the century, there had been an outpouring of anti-episcopal sentiment when Berthold, Archbishop of Mainz, led the opposition to the new constitution of the empire.[47] Sickingen saw the Archbishop-Elector of Trier,

Richard von Greiffenklau, as an imperial adversary. It was believed that he had secretly backed the king of France for the imperial title, a suspicion which turned out to be true. Following that, Trier had been a strong opponent of Luther at Worms.[48] To Sickingen the archbishop appeared to be pro-French, anti-empire, anti-Luther, and thus unworthy as an elector and ruler. If he, a spiritual prince, was forced to secularize his lands, these could be returned to their rightful owners, the knights, and the church brought under the control of lay rulers. Fortified by his Lutheran convictions, certain of the imperative need to control the power of the Roman church, Sickingen was the first lay individual to act decisively against the church. If he was to succeed, he had to bring other people to his side. The propaganda campaign begun by Hutten was a first step in this larger plan.

Several other knights at the castle devoted part of their time to propaganda for their cause. A military attack on the church had to be justified. They needed to convince more knights and the cities of their need for support. The result was four pamphlets identified by Schottenloher as the work of Sickingen's supporters.[49] Modern scholars assign 1521 as the date of publication for three of these pamphlets and 1522 for pamphlet #41 which Schottenloher describes as the first.[50] He identifies #51 as the second in the series, #15 and #14 as the third and fourth.[51] The texts of the pamphlets confirm Schottenloher's order. The first pamphlet is a general statement of the new faith to teach "everything that is necessary for your soul's salvation." The clerical members of the dialogue, who have only reluctantly admitted their Lutheranism, ask to whom they should attribute the book. The noble count answers "to me." The others say no, no one will sign it, which may place its composition very close to the Edict of Worms.[52] In #51 the priestly interlocutors openly support Luther and state that they will write another book to show how the monks took the property of the nobility.[53] Pamphlet #15, which states that it is the third book which has gone out from the nobles, condemns the monks as robbers of the nobles' property. The authors conclude that they will write more to teach what the right faith is.[54] The fourth pamphlet refers to the third, stating that it will carry the argument further.[55] The pamphlets may not have been printed in the sequence in which they were written, the first being delayed, but the order in which they were written is important because it reveals the changing perceptions of the writers within a very short compass of time. The descriptions of forthcoming pamphlets indicate that the noble writers had a definite program in mind. These were not random volleys but an organized attempt to exhort people to the new faith, to justify the knights' actions, and to defend their use of violence. I refer to the four as the Ebernburg pamphlets, accepting Schoftenlubeis order.

The first pamphlet was set in the familiar world of the knights, at the castle of a count. There the count had called in his spiritual advisors, a canon and three priests, probably from parishes on the count's lands. The same group appears in all the Ebernburg pamphlets. The count was uneasy about his people, the men, women, and children who lived on his farms and in his villages and towns. Having heard of the new religious teaching, the count appealed to his spiritual councilors for instruction. What, he asked them, was the true Christian faith? The clergy refused to answer. That was not their affair, they said, it was the task of the count. Thus, the traditional roles were reversed, the definition of the faith was made the responsibility of the laity.

The count, a sympathetic and sensitive protagonist, could not immediately accept the change. He repeated his question several times. One of the priests, less patient, asked "Don't you go to church and hear what the faith is?" "Yes," said the count, "I go to church. I don't hear, however, that anyone teaches me the true faith. They simply teach I must believe what the Christian church believes, but I never hear what the church believes, so how can I know what I should believe?" He should hear the Gospel and the Word of God, said the priest, but the Mass was the true faith. The count appealed to the canon, who responded that he did not know what to say or believe because anyone who spoke the truth was persecuted. Furthermore, it was not his function, "for I am not a shepherd who should teach people. . . . There is one tree which grows and bears good fruit which is called Martin Luther. But the same tree can now never bear fruit."[56]

Having referred to Luther tangentially, the canon pressed the count to broaden his role, to extend his responsibility. He should teach his people correctly for "you are the father and the spiritual and worldly protector of the young and the old . . . and you should stake your soul for them as a true shepherd for his sheep." The count was stirred. He had taken better care of his dogs than his people. He had sinned in not providing for their salvation, now he wanted to change and become a good shepherd to them.[57]

The canon still refused to give advice, because he would be placed in great danger; he could be killed for it. "But," remonstrated the count, "as I am a pious count . . . I will call all my knights to help and I will protect and shelter you. You do not have to fear."[58] He continued to press the canon and the priests to guide him, until one of the latter relented: "We hear that you wish to [discuss] the Luther affair. We cannot, however, speak about it. The *fiscal* has forbidden it. . . . Therefore it is better to be silent than that we should talk about such things." The count rejoined, "I will have it unsilent. All four of you know that I wish to know the truth for I see the end of the world is at hand [and] I see a terrible death before me. Therefore I will hasten and I will not stop until I have uprooted the evil lack of faith." The canon finally admitted that there was a man who could tell the count everything about the true faith, but it would have to be done secretly. "Oh honorable Lord, be silent and do not name anyone with a name, otherwise he will not come to you."[59]

Nevertheless, secrecy was finally cast aside. One of the priests acknowledged that Luther had defined the truth at Worms. He had remained steadfast to the Word of Christ, knowing that the whole Christian faith stood on the Word of God. This was what all good Lutherans should believe, appealing to Christ to open their eyes and forgive their sins. The definition of faith was simple. It was all contained in the Our Father. Christ said in the Gospel, what you ask the father in my name, he will give you. Thus, each good Christian should acknowledge the father and pray to come to his heavenly kingdom. True Christian faith was to know and recognize God as father.[60]

The pamphlet described the changes the knights hoped for. The count resolved to become the true father of his people and establish justice and righteousness. The canon and priests finally abandoned their timidity and openly announced their Lutheranism. In the conclusion, one of the priests declared, "He who wished to be a good Lutheran, he may well come and join us . . . [but] we say that we Lutheran men will soon be killed by the canons and priests."[61] The threat of the Edict of Worms and the papal bull was palpable. The anxiety of the reformed clergy shifted to defiance, but that did not dispel the reality of possible arrest and trial. Fear and apprehension were the companions of the new faith in the year 1521–1522.

The simplicity of the definition of faith reflected the conservatism of the knights. They accepted the responsibility to maintain the purity of the faith of their people, as part of their patriarchal function, but they did not need a complex theology or dogma. The Word of God, which included everything Christ had said, contained a whole theology, but it could all be easily summarized in the words of the Our Father. Notably, nothing was said about justification by faith, about the sacraments or their use, about penance. Those were matters for the theologians. For these laymen, Christian truth required only a belief in God as father. It was a feudal perception: God was the lord and the individual was his vassal, who gave loyalty, obedience, and faith.

The second pamphlet, a broad attack on the ecclesiastical princes and the priests, carried further the theme that the nobility would have to assume the responsibility to restore justice and remove the oppression of the clergy. Another nobleman and a Lutheran joined the dialogue. The count and the nobleman were the protagonists, the latter portrayed as having just joined Sickingen. He asked to sit in with the others as a fool, "to help bring the truth to the light of day."[62] The role of fool was, of course, protective. The fool could say things that responsible men could not, a role not developed in this pamphlet. Instead, the fool spoke as a nobleman.

The second pamphlet addressed the problem of order. God had created a just and ordered world, which now raged with turmoil because of the usurpation of the clergy. The knights' duty was to restore God's law and command. In a world turned upside down, the knights believed it devolved upon them to turn it right side up. The priests had taught that the church was made of wood and stone. A pious, righteous man, however, believed nothing but what God had taught him. When Christ taught him the Our Father, he could have no further need, for "perfection is there in overflowing measure for his soul's sake."[63] Yet, the nobility were denied the right to share their knowledge and to teach. Noblemen, knights, and counts had become servants to the ecclesiastical princes. Some of these princes appointed good teachers, but others permitted their priests to teach and practice injustice, namely, to demand money and fees from the poor. These priests should be punished and taught to teach as Christ taught.[64]

The weakness of the nobility, wrote the knights, lay in the donation of property by noble families to chapters, monastic houses, and churches. Through these ancestral gifts, the nobles had lost their lands, their people, their taxes, rents, and money. They had been driven to go out on the highway to rob the merchants or to demand tolls, the only form of revenue left to them.[65] The nobleman stated that the ecclesiastical princes should not permit the priests to demand even more money from the people, but he doubted that would end until the Gospel was fulfilled. Christ had told his disciples that he who had two cloaks should sell one and buy a sword. Only then could another system of government be established.[66] The immediate solution was that the nobility must unite with one another and with the empire, which maintained justice. Together they must protect the poor, the widow, and orphans from the grasping demands of the clergy. "God made me a count so that I could protect the poor and I will keep my promise to them."[67] Implicit here was the use of violence. The book ended with a dedication to Luther and his knightly champion, Ulrich von Hutten.[68]

The second pamphlet repeated the ideas of the first. There was the same definition that the whole of the faith was contained in the Our Father. There was the same criticism that the clergy had not fulfilled their role of teachers. The new element was the answer to the title's question, "Who has made the whole world poor?" The clergy had impoverished Germany because they had occupied the lands of nobility, forcing the knights to become highway robbers. The authors promised another book to explain that the monks were the real robbers.

The third Ebernburg pamphlet differed sharply from the preceding tracts. The tone was scolding, shrill, violent. The spokesman was the fool, who began by reaching back to the *Jetzerhandel*, the duping of the innocent novice by the Dominicans of Bern. "The tailor of Bern," charged the fool, " was the first living martyr to be martyred . . . and it was the Dominicans who martyred him."[69] The affair was used as an example of the duplicity of the monks, their desire to build up their wealth by trickery and deceit. The monks had lied and cheated. They had told the parents of the nobility that they could not be saved without giving property to the church. How could the monks and priests be saved when they had taken land and goods unrighteously? The monks had become merchants, selling the treasures of heaven. They were also highway robbers because they held the land and the people through usury.[70] The solution was that "we all should take our land. God will give what remains to the monks and priests . . . and we will give them 30 gulden a year. If that is not enough, they should work the land."[71]

In contrast to the first pamphlet, the fool boldly acknowledged his Lutheranism. "This book was written by the lay fool who is a good Lutheran. Who then is the enemy of Luther is also my enemy and that of all pious Christian. . . ." The writer challenged the nobility to act. "If [the monks] destroyed us in the past, so we will destroy them in the future. I ask all those born from the nobility to be good Lutherans and follow the truth of Christ. So we will become rich."[72]

The pamphlet was without logic, rambling, aggressive, filled with fear. All the anxieties of the warning pamphlets appeared. The fool feared he might be burned; he feared the cities would enforce the censorship edict and no one would be able to publish anymore; he feared the imperial ban. Reasoned discussion had disappeared in ranting; the appeal to violence was more overt.

The final Ebernburg pamphlet adopted the powerful metaphor of the hunt. The priests, the monks, and the Pope were the hunters, the German people the hunted. The nobles must rise to free the land from the dogs and nets of the hunters.[73] "It would be much better if people hunted the priests and hunters out of the land . . . and hung them from trees, for they rob the land and take what is on it. If a man has no money. . . . they take flax. If no flax, they take eggs. . . . It would be better if people chased these greedy priests out of the land and [instead] served God and his holy ones who are in heaven and who do not eat."[74] The fool went farther, to propose a system for the redistribution of the land. The nobility would take back their ancestral properties, chasing the monks from their cloisters install their and children in them, "for they have high walls within which the children can be content. [Furthermore] those villages, towns and peasants originally belonged to the nobility." The redistribution of land could extend even further: "The poor people. . . . as I understand it, have very little. Therefore I think it would be good if the nobility did not delay but take their property again and in return make the land a little free. . . . Then, when the land which the monks and priests unjustly occupied is equally distributed, everyone will have enough and the evil hunters will no longer be in the land."[75] The obsession with land had not weakened. It was the main concern of the pamphlet writer, who said nothing about the protection of the new faith. The needs of the people came only in the recognition that even the poor might receive some of the clerical lands since they "had very little."

The four pamphlets reveal the gap in the Knights' understanding of the clergy, the merchants, even the people on their own lands. The knights were unable to recognize that their repeated demand for the return of church lands would sound self-serving to peasants, artisans, and merchants, that branding the monks as highway robbers would appear as self-justification.

SICKINGEN AND CRONBERG AS TEACHERS OF THE FAITH

Yet, there was more propaganda activity at the Ebernberg. In the same years, 1521–1522, that the four pamphlets appeared, Franz von Sickingen and Hartmut von Cronberg between them published ten pamphlets explaining the right doctrine and the foundations of the new faith to their own families and people. The actions and writing of Sickingen and Cronberg indicate that they were profoundly touched by Luther's teaching and that their beliefs and their religious lives changed. In contrast to Hutten, Franz von Sickingen addressed himself clearly and specifically to questions raised by the new teaching, supporting his arguments with frequent quotations from Scripture. His son's father-in-law, Dieter von Handschuchsheim, questioned the new faith on several counts. He was not sure that the Mass should be offered in both kinds nor that it should be said in a different way. He questioned whether monks and nuns should leave the cloister and marry. Finally, he did not understand why one should not pray to the saints nor why holy pictures should be destroyed.[76]

Sickingen addressed these doubts in a straightforward letter, beginning with a statement of faith. The foundation of the faith was "the mouth of the truth of Christ"; second came the rock on which he built his church; third came the Scripture; fourth, the teaching and the works of the disciples; and fifth, the preaching and teaching inspired by the Holy Spirit. The faith, then, included the Word, the Gospels, and the church. Everything else was human fables.[77] Responding first to the question of communion in both kinds, he wrote that it was hard for him to believe that his kinsman still placed more importance on human customs than on "the mouth of truth. . . . Do not blaspheme the highest Godly power as a fool, as though God in his testament of his departure . . . made an error or forgot something for our soul's salvation."[78] No, Christ had spoken the words of institution "with his godly mouth," thus forgiving our sins and offering us everlasting life. Sickingen cited the account of the last supper from each of the Gospels and from Paul's letters to justify the offering of the bread and the cup. Indeed, he concluded, "I can never understand why those priests were moved to forbid both elements to the laity and keep them only to themselves, except that perhaps they wished to feel superior to Christ or wanted to put aside the forgiveness of sins promised by Christ."[79]

He was less dogmatic with regard to how Mass should be said. Admittedly, for a long time it had been said differently from the way Christ established it, and "few men know what the right mass is." Nevertheless, Sickingen could not understand why Handschuchsheim objected to the use of German, since Christ was never secretive and had told his disciples to spread his words to all creatures, which was why he had sent the Holy Spirit.[80] The knight's position on the closing of the monasteries was forthright. Christ, he said, did not establish any other order for mankind than marriage. If he had wished to elevate the status of monks or nuns, he would have been born of a nun or a young cloistered woman.[81] Indeed, Sickingen regarded the orders as blasphemous because they set themselves up as separate sects and marked their separation from others through dress and other appearances of holiness. It was the standard argument, based on Luther's sermons and pamphlets against monastic vows.

Prayers to the saints, Sickingen wrote, broke the second commandment as well as various statements by Christ with regard to prayer, all carefully cited. With his usual literalism, he pointed out that Christ never called on any holy persons, not even on his mother. Nor had Sickingen himself read in any histories of the saints that they had instructed anyone to pray to them. "In the true Scriptures of God we are never taught . . . to call on his saints . . . but in many places we are told the opposite . . . and there is no need to dispute further about it."[82] It is worth noticing that Sickingen does not say anything about the Our Father as the true statement of the faith as his followers had. The independence of the thought of each individual knight is thus demonstrated. On the final question of images in the church, Sickingen was indifferent. If they helped people to contemplate and reflect on their lives, they were fruitful. The problem was that they tended to divert people and served an artistic rather than religious purpose. The greater problem was that men had not heard the message of Christ and his disciples even though they had access to it. Instead, they had submitted to human and papal commandments: "Those who have held themselves rightly in the struggle will not know it until they come to the house of death, then the fires of hell will creep out the window."[83]

The image of Sickingen as a rash leader who plunged into a fruitless feud against the Archbishop of Trier is not supported by this pamphlet. Its frankness, the candor of the language—all suggesting Sickingen's own hand in the writing—tell much about the quality of his mind. Sickingen was careful to differentiate between religious matters which were important and those which were not; he had arrived at his own definition of essentials. Certainly his military and political career played the major role in his life, but that does not prohibit a spiritual search. Nor does the strength of Sickingen's political ambition, his desire to establish himself as a prince, diminish the strength of his evangelical faith. From 1520, he placed himself at risk to support the Word of God. He never turned back from that and, in the end, lost his life.

His friend Hartmut von Cronberg was the perfect knight, courageous, loyal, faithful to his pledged word. He placed these qualities in the service of the Reformation, sacrificing his family lands and his material wealth for his religion. Cronberg believed the new faith required him to honor and follow the Word of God, and he set about to fulfill this in his daily life by writing to share the joy of his religious commitment, to bring others to the fountain of the pure water of the Gospel which had inspired him. The result was some 11 pamphlets, printed between 1521 and 1524.

The majority of Cronberg's pamphlets were letters which he addressed to Pope Leo X, Pope Adrian VI, the emperor, the Swiss confederates, the Estates of the Empire, the Franciscans and Dominicans, the citizens of Frankfurt and of Strasbourg, and the inhabitants of his own domain. His style was hortatory and diffuse, the words spilling out one after another, yet the reader feels the conviction behind them. He believed that if the popes and the emperor heard the Word of God, if they would truly listen, then they would accept Luther's teaching and again become leaders to their people. After he had renounced his service to the emperor, Cronberg addressed a letter to the "unconquerable, most illustrious, all-powerful Christian emperor Charles," exhorting him to live up to that title, to be not only a knight of God but also a child of God and thus surrender to God as his lord and heavenly father. "O Emperor, as you accept the fear of God, so the mercy of God will descend upon you in heaps . . . you will lose all fear of men and the devil and truly deserve the highest titles and will be undefeatable, illustrious and most mighty."[84] He pleaded with the emperor to give room to the Word of God preached by Doctor Luther. Armed with the truth of the Word of God, the emperor would be able to tear the pope away from the devil and lead him to the way of Christ, thus manifesting the greatest brotherly love.[85]

In his letter to Pope Leo X, he again appealed directly to the true Christian hidden beneath the power of the papal office. "O righteous Leo . . . I understand from many that before you were a pope you were regarded as a virtuous man. . . . You must surely rejoice with us from your heart that the true heavenly light now shines in this our fearful darkness. You must have no doubt that you will receive this superior mercy from the spirit of God . . . so that you can turn away from your father the devil . . . Our Lord Jesus

Christ is so merciful that he will accept you, if you have the grace to turn to him."[86]

Many of the themes and metaphors of Cronberg's other pamphlets are present in these passages: his belief in the Word of God as truly active force in the lives of men; the power of God's mercy; Jesus Christ as the fountain of truth; the gift of baptism which led to a universal brotherly love. Expressed in simple language, written directly from the heart, his pamphlets circulated not only among the knights but were read out to the guilds in Frankfurt and passed from hand to hand in Strasbourg.[87]

His pamphlet addressed to the inhabitants of Cronenberg was a manual of the Christian life written by a layman for lay men and women. In a letter to Jacob Köbel, the secretary of the town of Oppenheim where he had lived as a boy, Cronberg explained that he had written his pamphlet for his people because as their lord he was responsible to exhort them to obedient faith and trust in Christ.[88] The obligation acknowledged by the count in the first Ebernburg pamphlets was acted upon by Cronberg.

Cronberg addressed "each and every inhabitant of Cronenberg, old and young" and used the metaphor of darkness and light to describe the changes that were at hand. "God has visited us in our darkness in this our time through his heavenly light which is the clear Word of God which is Christ himself."[89] He hoped to show his people how to come to the light of Christ after having been "stuck" in the dark. The first step was to recognize "our sins and selfishness and call on Christ to grant us grace" to be led into his strong light. Men should renew the heavenly brotherhood created at their baptism, turning away from the world to become heirs of the everlasting kingdom. The path had been clearly laid out by God but men had trusted too much to custom, to praying to saints, to pilgrimages and other such things. Cronberg believed that people should follow nothing but the Word of God, but he was sensitive to people's loyalty to tradition, adding "we may tolerate and leave ceremonies and church customs if they are seemly until we are better informed, but we must not build on them."[90]

For Cronberg, evangelical belief rested on the two commandments of Christ, to love God and one's neighbor.[91] This knowledge could not be achieved by men's own efforts but through the grace of God and the proclamation of his Word. Thus, each individual must trust in God and call to him in faith; then the Father would grant him his grace.

Cronberg was able to describe the way to salvation simply and clearly, if with much repetition. As was true for many laymen, the heart of his faith was the Word of God. The Word contained the commandments to govern the life of each individual Christian, and was an active force which opened men to a relationship of trust in God and in God's mercy. More completely than Sickingen or Hutten, Cronberg had experienced this relationship of faith and it had changed his life. In his writing he attempted to share his experience with others, to call them to move to this new freedom.

There were no pamphlets of spiritual instruction written by Hutten, although at the very end of his life, in an appeal to the cities to help the knights, he stated that "their enemies had begun to forbid Doctor Luther's teaching as though it were wrong. They cannot bear the truth."[92] As Volker Press pointed out, there were two different streams in the earliest years of the Reform, the old current of imperial and church reform, represented by Hutten, and the new current, represented by Luther. Sickingen and Cronberg had immersed themselves deeply in the new movement. Hutten regarded Luther as a secular leader who would free Germany from the usurpation of Rome.[93] The letters of spiritual guidance show that both Sickingen and Cronberg had begun the process of Reformation on their own lands and in their own households as early as 1521. By that date, as lords they were able to achieve changes in terms of the introduction of the reading of Scripture in German, the offering of communion in both kinds, and other liturgical changes. At that time in some cities, reformed preaching was tolerated, although sometimes the preacher was abruptly dismissed. Liturgical changes such as those made by Sickingen and Cronberg were far more difficult because of the presence of bishops and the political anxiety of the city councilors. The Reformation may have proceeded more rapidly in some rural areas than in the cities in these early years.

THE KNIGHTS BROUGHT TO JUSTICE

In the summer of 1522, a large army gathered at the Ebernburg. In August, 600 Upper Rhenish knights came together at Landau and swore a brotherly oath to ally themselves for six years against the princely states. They also swore to live together in Christian brotherhood with one another and to settle disputes among them not by the newly established legal procedures but through the arbitration of their peers. Sickingen was named commander. Schilling saw this alliance as the first expression of Christian association and confederation, which would develop into the federal theology of Calvinists. The revolt spread across Germany. The Franconian knights rose against the bishop of Bamberg and Wurzburg; levies were underway in Luneberg, Julich-Cleves, and the Electorate of Cologne to strengthen the knights of northern Germany.[94]

In September, Sickingen's knights invaded the territory of the Archbishop of Trier and laid siege to that city. They were quickly repulsed, and Sickingen, defeated, was forced to fall back to the Ebernburg. The atmosphere there quickly changed. In October, Sickingen was declared an outlaw by the Imperial Council of Regency. The enemies of the knights gathered: Ludwig, the Elector Palatine, Sickingen's old patron; Phillip of Hesse, who hated Cronberg; and the Archbishop of Trier, who could now wreak vengeance on Sickingen. Both the Elector and Hesse were Lutheran supporters. Meeting shortly after the disaster at Trier, they decided to move first against Cronberg. In October they attacked his lands and his castle and confiscated all his lands and worldly possessions, which forced him into exile with his mother, wife and three minor children.[95] Hutten had left the Ebernburg in September, too ill to participate in the defense.[96] The leadership was shattered.

The expected attack against Sickingen came the following spring. The allied princes joined their forces on 22 April 1523, at Kreuznach, ironically where Sickingen had been magistrate. They had learned that Sickingen was at Nanstuhl, one of his minor castles, and were determined to catch him there so that he would not be able to reach the Ebernburg.[97] Nanstuhl had not been refortified and would be unable to withstand an artillery siege. As reported by the imperial herald Caspar Sturm, the artillery barrage was without precedent in the land.[98] In eight days the castle was in ruins. Sickingen, out on the ramparts to direct the defense, was crushed when a part of the wall gave way. Trapped within the ruins, mortally wounded, Sickingen received the three princes on his death bed when they asked to speak to him. Told that the elector had entered, he removed his cap with his undamaged left hand and tried to get up. The elector told him not to move, but Sickingen's removal of his cap was interpreted as having made obeisance to his lord. Sickingen died that day.[99]

The war against Sickingen did not stop with his death. The princes, to make an example of him, emptied his castles for booty to pay the costs of the war,[100] then destroyed them. Caspar Sturm's account of the princes' war was a propaganda pamphlet against the knights that stressed the disobedience of Sickingen. While the princes had been attacking Cronenberg, Sickingen, without sending a formal notice of feud to the elector, had taken the latter's castle at Lützelstein. Because of this breach of the peace, the princes had launched their crusade.[101] The destruction of each Sickingen castle was described by the imperial herald in detail: the surrender of the captain of the castle, the removal of all weapons and gunpowder, the plundering of movable goods, the burning of the castle, and the destruction of the fortifications. No doubt was left in the mind of the reader that a knight could not stand against the armed force of a prince and that Franz von Sickingen had deserved his fate.

The example of the princes bore fruit. Although the Franconian knights had remained aloof from Sickingen, in that same year, 1523, the Swabian League planned a military expedition against the Franconian "Robber's Nest." In January 1523, in a last desperate attempt, 400 Franconian knights meeting at Landau had vowed to come to one another's aid in case of invasion from the outside. They also attempted to plead their case at the Diet of Nuremberg but without success. After the destruction of Sickingen's castles, the Swabian League felt newly empowered and turned their vengeance on the Franconians. In less than a month they razed 23 castles to the ground, again carrying off all movable goods and property. A pamphlet with three woodcuts depicted the burning of the castles, another listed the names of the nobles who had belonged to the Franconian band,[102] which brought deep disgrace to these knights. The open publication of their names and the account of their demolished castles meant a loss of dignity and honor.[103]

Some popular songs rejoiced in the fall of Sickingen.[104] The most bitter attack was launched in a pamphlet, *Schnapphahn* (The Highwayman), written by one Matthias Slegel of Trier, who may have been a cleric. He denounced the Sickingen circle, stating that they held themselves up as good, pious Christians because they were evangelicals, but in fact they lived on robbery and violence. He derided the religious "pretensions" of the Ebernburg circle as empty "gestures" of piety. Sickingen, he alleged, was in league with the devil, not with Jesus Christ.[105]

There was deep ambivalence toward Sickingen. One writer hailed him as a champion of justice. In a cleverly composed dialogue, Sickingen, while being examined at the gate of heaven by St. George, defended himself by saying that through a poor man he had received a scriptural commandment to administer justice. Whatever love he showed to the least of his neighbors would be rewarded by God himself. He had taken this to heart and helped the poor man to obtain justice.[106] Popular songs in praise of the knights or their adversaries reflected some sympathy and support among the common folk. A song writer calling himself Nicholas Under the Red Hat appealed to all the estates of the empire to continue the struggle against the clergy, which "Franz Sickingen and his company have [undertaken] out of justice and love . . . so that the godly work of the holy Gospel will not be suppressed."[107] Jörg Graff, a wounded *landsknecht*, recalled how the nobles had established many benefices and founded many convents. These should be given to their children and kinfolk rather than to Roman clerics.[108] Songs of this sort, which were sung around tavern tables, are an indication that the courage of the knights was applauded in some urban communities.

The general attitude toward the knights may have been best recorded by one Hans Bechler von Scholbrunnen, in a dialogue between a fox and a wolf which went through seven editions.[109] The author carefully explained his metaphor. The fox was a knight who had fought for Sickingen and was now at large. The wolf was a knight who had tormented the empire until driven into exile. Where could they spend the winter months? They agreed that since they had made many enemies among the burghers and peasants in Swabia and Bavaria, there was little hope of welcome in those areas.

The Swiss liked neither the fox nor the wolf, unless they were given a lot of money. The wolf suggested Bohemia. No, said the fox, the princes and the [Swabian] league agreed with the king of Bohemia that refugee knights would be tormented. The purpose of the tract was to warn "all honest men." It would be a cold winter, and the fox and the wolf had insatiable appetites. They would be hungrier than ever.[110]

Sickingen and his knights had taken a dangerous risk. Their attempt to secularize clerical lands led them into a web of conflict. Any attack on property rights stirred up the larger question of everyone's property rights, and property was the foundation of the social order. There was also the aura which surrounded the archbishop because he represented a part of the sacral order. Sickingen was on the brink of *lèse-majésté*. He was a knight, not a prince. A prince or a group of princes might have attacked an archbishop, using the knights to do the fighting. But Sickingen was perceived as having overreached his position in the hierarchy of order. The religious commitment of the knights, furthermore, was never mentioned by the princes, perhaps because of their own Lutheran leanings. They ignored it and punished Sickingen as a disobedient vassal.

Furthermore, the knights had disobeyed the imperial edict forbidding religious matters to be discussed in print. This was a further rupture of their traditional obedience to the emperor, an act which could have been comfortable for none of them. The tie to the emperor was ancestral, a pillar of the knightly ethic, and they had lost it. Unlike the reformed clergy or the artisans who wrote, the knights had far more to lose. Their lands, their property could be confiscated. Punishment would reach their innocent families.

Yet, they took up the cause as a sacred obligation and served it with knightly fidelity. The risks knowingly taken must be accepted as a measure of the depth of their convictions and their faith in the Gospel.

Notes

1. Eugen Weber, *My France, Culture, Politics, Myths*, 1991, 8.
2. Heinz Schilling, *Aufbruch und Krise, Deutschland 1517–1648*, 1988, quoted in H. C. Erik Midelfort, "The Reformation and the German Nobility," in Hans R. Guggisberg and Gottfried Krofel, eds., *Die Reformation in Deutschland und Europa*, 1993, 347. New interest in the knight's role in the Reformation is seen in a paper presented by Victor Thiessen, Queen's University, Toronto, "Stormy Days, Peaceful Knights: Noble Writers and the Reformation," at the Sixteenth Century Studies Conference, Toronto, Oct. 29, 1994.
3. On the Ebernburg see H. Schilling, *Aufbruch und Krise*, 133. On the propaganda activities of the knights see Karl Schottenloher, *Flugschriften zur Ritterschaftsbewegung des Jahres 1523*, 1929, 2, 7.

4. Johannes Polke, "'Wiewohl es ein rühmlich und wohlgebaut Haus gewesen' . . .," *EH* 15 (1981): 134–135.
5. Eckhard Bernstein, *Ulrich von Hutten*, 1988, 65, 50–52.
6. Volker Press, "Ulrich von Hutten, Reichsritter und Humanist . . .," *NA* 85 (1974): 78.
7. Bernstein, *Hutten*, 37.
8. Volker Press, "Franz von Sickingen, Wortführer des Adels . . .," in ed., Peter Laub, *Ulrich von Hutten, Katalog zur Ausstellung des 500. Geburtstag*, 1989, 293. See also Martin Schoebel, "Franz von Sickingen als Kurpfalzische Amtmann . . .," *EH* 15 Folge (1981): 144.
9. Press, "Franz von Sickingen," 294.
10. Ibid., 296.
11. Ibid.
12. Volker Press, *Kaiser Karl V, König Ferdinand und die Entstehung der Reichsritterschaft*, 1976, 21.
13. Press, "Franz von Sickingen," 298.
14. Helmut Bode, *Hartmut XII. von Cronberg, Reichsritter der Reformationszeit*, 1987, 16, 21.
15. Ibid., 25, 32.
16. Wilhelm Bogler, *Hartmuth von Kronberg: eine Charakterstudie aus der Reformationszeit*, SVR 57 (1897): 7–8.
17. Press, "Franz von Sickingen," 296.
18. Ibid., 298.
19. Roland Bainton, *Here I Stand: A Life of Martin Luther*, 1950, 18, 148; Hans Holborn, *A History of Modern Germany*, 3 vols. (1959), 1, *The Reformation*, 141.
20. #242, Franciscus von Sickingen, *Warhafftiger bericht Francisci von Sickingen uff das ungegründt verschryben von Worms wyder inen bescheen* (n.p.:n.p., 1515), fols. Aii^v, Aiv.
21. #241, Franciscus von Sickingen, *Ervorderung und verkundung . . . an und wider provincial, prioren und Conventen prediger ordens* (n.p.:n.p., 1519), fol. Aii^v, Aiii, Aiii^v.
22. Holborn, *Hutten*, 153.
23. Bainton, *Here I Stand*, 181. See also Press, *Sickingen*, 300.
24. Karl Brandi, *Emperor Charles V*, 1965, 160.
25. Press, "Franz von Sickingen," 300.
26. #239, Franciscus von Sickingen, *Ain sendbrieff . . . dem Junckherr Diethern von Henschüchssheim* (n.p.:n.p., 1522), fols. aii–aii^v. Schwöbel wrote a prefatory letter.
27. Quoted in Bogler, *Hartmuth von Kronberg*, 63.
28. Volker Honemann, "Der deutsche Lukian, Die volkssprachigen Dialogi Ulrichs von Hutten," in ed., Stephan Füssel, *Ulrich von Hutten 1488–1988, Pirckheimer-Jahrbuch*. Band 4, 1989, 51–52.
29. Ibid., 52.
30. Ibid.
31. #170, Ulrich von Hutten, *Die Römische Dreyfaltigkeit* (n.p.:n.p., 1520), in ed., Eduard Böcking, *Opera Ulrichi Huttens Germani*, 5 vols. (1963), 4, 168, 169, 171.
32. Ibid., 156.
33. #53, *Wiltu etwas newes habenn, Lass diss büchlein nicht vor über draben/ . . .* (n.p.: n.p., n.d.) Fiche 1257/#3213, unpaginated.

34. Karlheinz Blaschke, "An den Christliche Adel," in ed., Hans-Ulrich Delius, *Martin Luther, Studienausgabe*, 3 vols. (1979–1983), 2, 90.
35. Holborn, *Ulrich von Hutten*, 148.
36. Reinhard Seyboth, "Ulrich von Hutten und sein Verhältnis zur Ritterschaftlichen Bewegung," in ed., Stephan Füssel, *Ulrich von Hutten 1488–1988*, 1988, 133–135.
37. Press, "Ulrich von Hutten," 85; R. Seyboth, "Ulrich von Hutten," 139.
38. #163, Ulrich von Hutten, *Clag und vermanung gegen dem übermässigen unchristlichen gewalt des Bapstes* . . . (n.p.:n.p., 1520), fol. aii, aii^v, aiv^v.
39. Ibid., fol. diii^v.
40. #162, Ulrich von Hutten, *Clagschrift an alle stend Deütscher Nation* (n.p.:n.p., 1520), fol. Aiii^v, Bi.
41. #175, Ulrich von Hutten, *Die verteuscht clag* . . . *an Herzog Fridrichen zu Sachsen*, fol. Aii^v.
42. #172 Ulrich von Hutten, *Uber und gegen der vorgewaltigung des Bapsts* . . . *an Keyserliche maiestat* (n.p.:n.p.), fol. aiii, B.
43. #36, Anonymous, *Ain n new gedicht*, fol. aii; #59, Ulrich Bossler, *Dialogus* . . ., fol. Biii^v; #15, Anonymous, *Das biechlin zaiget an wie der lebendig martrer sey* . . ., fol. b; #14, Anonymous, *Das biechlin hat gemacht der nar det gut lutherisch ist* . . ., 742, #119, Lux Gemmiger, *Ob einer wissen wolt* . . ., fol. ai^v.
44. Here was reason for the distance between Luther and Hutten. Luther thought in terms of Christian freedom, independent of the secular world. Hutten thought in terms of German freedom. Hutten was sympathetic to Luther for tactical reasons and because it contributed to the goal of German independence. Heinrich Grimm, *Ulrich von Hutten, Wille und Schicksal*, 1971, 107.
45. Holborn, *Ulrich von Hutten*, 180.
46. *Manifestations of Discontent in Germany on the Eve of the Reform, A Collection of Documents*, ed. and trans. Gerald Strauss, 1971, 11.
47. Hermann Wiesflecker, *Kaiser Maximiliam I. Das Reich, Österreich und Europa an der Wende zur Neuzeit*, 5 vols., (1986), 5, 3, 136–139.
48. Holborn, *Ulrich von Hutten*, 181.
49. Schottenloher, *Flugschriften zur Ritterschaftsbewegung*, 6.
50. #41, *Ain schenes und nutzlichen büchlin von dem Christen glauben*, 1522? The 1522 date may come from a notation in parenthesis on the title page of the University of Tübingen copy of the pamphlet. The date appears in the Köhler Microfiche listing, Fiche 69/ # 180 and in the Folger catalogue # 66, but these do not discuss the context of the pamphlet.
51. Schottenloher, *Flugschriften zur Ritterschaftsbewegung*, 6.
52. #41, *Ain schenes* . . . *büchlin*, fol. B^v.
53. #51, *Wer hören will* . . ., fols. bvi–bvi^v.
54. #15, *Das biechlin zeigt* . . . *der lebendig martrer*, fols. b; aiv; b.
55. #14, *Das biechlin hat gemacht der nar* . . ., 742.
56. #41, *Ain schenes und nutzliches büchlin von dem Christlichen Glauben* n.p.:n.p. 1522, Fiche 691/#180, fol. Aii, B.
57. Ibid., fols. aii, aii^v, aiii.
58. Ibid., fols. aiii^v.
59. Ibid., fols. aiv, aiv^v. The *fiscal* was the bishop's judicial officer.
60. Ibid., fols. aiv^v, B.
61. Ibid., fol. B^v.
62. #51, *Wer hören will wer die ganze Welt arm hat gemacht* (n.p.:n.p., n.d.), Fiche

221/#619, title page. Laube, p. 731, attributes this to Ulrich von Hutten. Schottenloher in *Flugschriften der Ritterschaftsbewegung* (p. 7) makes no identification. I believe this pamphlet was written by the same knights who wrote *Ain schenes . . . büchlein*. The style is not characteristic of Hutten; the references to Scripture are too frequent. The apology for the former behavior of the nobility, with its attempt to reach the merchants, does not accord with Hutten's pride and consciousness of his nobility. Here at fol. aii^v.

63. Ibid., fols. aiii^v–aiiii.
64. Ibid., fols. aiiii^v–av^v.
65. Ibid., fols. avii–avii^v.
66. Ibid., fol. aviii^v.
67. Ibid., fols. biii^v–bv.
68. Ibid., fol. bvi.
69. #15, *Das Biechlin zaiget an wer der lebendig martrer sey auff erdtrich* (n.p.:n.p., n.d.), Fiche 984/#2493, fol. aiii.
70. Ibid., fol. aiii^v, aiv.
71. Ibid., fol. aiv.
72. Ibid., fol. b.
73. #14, *Das biechlin hat gemacht der nar der gut lutherisch ist . . .* (n.p.:n.p., n.d.). In eds., Adolf Laube et al., *Flugschriften der frühen Reformationsbewegung*, 2 vols. (1983), 2, 742.
74. Ibid., 743.
75. Ibid.
76. #239, Franciscus von Sickingen, *Ain Sendbrieff . . . dem Junckherr Diethern von Henschüchssheim . . .* (n.p.:n.p., 1522), Fiche 79/#212, fol. aiii^v. See also Eduard Kück, "Zu Sickingens Sendbrief an Handschuchsheim," *Anzeiger für deutsches Altertum und deutsche Literatur* 30 (1906): 148. In this brief entry Kück notes that in Odenwald and in the vicinity of Frankfurt the term Schwäher was applied to the fathers-in-law of a couple. Thus, the Junckherr Dieter was probably the father-in-law of Sickingen's son, Schwicker. Here fols. aiii-aiiii^v.
77. #239, fol. aiii.
78. Ibid., fol. aiii^v.
79. Ibid., fol. aiiii.
80. Ibid., fol. aiiii^v.
81. Ibid., fol. b.
82. Ibid., fol. bii, biii.
83. Ibid., fols. biii^v, biv.
84. #81, Hartmuth von Cronberg, *Tzwen Brieff, Eyner an römische kaiserliche Majestät*, in Laube et al., *Flugschriften*, 2, 748.
85. Ibid., 751.
86. #89, Hartmuth von Cronberg, *Vier schrifft . . . Die erst an Bapst Leo des namens den zehenden* (n.p.:n.p., 1522), fols. aii^v, aiii^v.
87. Bogler, *Hartmuth von Kronberg*, 17.
88. #89, Hartmuth von Cronberg, *Vier schrifft . . . Die vierd an Jacoben Köbel* (n.p.:n.p., n.d.), fol. Dii.
89. #89, Hartmuth von Cronberg, *Vier schrifft . . . Die ander an die inwoner zu Cronenberg* (n.p.:n.p., n.d.), fol. Bii.
90. Ibid., fol. Biii^v.
91. Ibid., fol. C, C^v.
92. Böcking, *Ulrich von Hutten Schriften*, 3, 531.

93. Press, *Hutten*, 82.
94. H. Schilling, *Aufbruch und Krise*, 134, 136.
95. Bogler, *Hartmuth von Kronberg*, 3. Bode, *Hartmuth von Cronberg XII.*, 211.
96. Bernstein, *Ulrich von Hutten*, 140.
97. #265, Caspar Sturm, *Warlicher bericht wie von den dreyen Churfürsten and Fursten, nämlich Tryer, Pflaz und Hessen weylandt Franz von Sickingen überzogen* (n.p.:n.p., 1523), Fiche 583/#1516, fol. Aiiii.
98. Ibid., fol. Aiv^v.
99. Ibid., fols. Bii, Bii^v.
100. Polke, "'Wiewohl es ein rühmlich und wohlgebaut Haus gewesen.' . .," 134, 135.
101. #265, Sturm, *Warlicher bericht*, fol. Aii^v.
102. *Die Schlösser, die verbrannt werden sind von dem Schwäbischen Bund in Jahr 1523* (n.p.: n.d., c. 1523), SFB, #12b. *Namen und Summa derer vom Adel so auf dem fränkischen Zug besoldet sindworden* (Augsburg: H. Steiner, 1523), SFB, #12a.
103. Schottenloher, *Flugschriften zur Ritterschaftsbewegung*, 4.
104. See SFB, #6, #7.
105. [Michael Slegel], *Schnapphahn*, c. 1523, SFB, #8.
106. #19, *Dialogus der Rede . . . Fransiscus von Sickingen*, fol. aiii^v.
107. Quoted in Schottenloher, *Flugschriften zur Ritterschaftsbewegung*, 9. The pamphlet's title: *Ich bin der Strigel in teutschen land* (Fiche 279/#795).
108. #134, Jörg Graff, *In disen tractetlin sind drey hübsche lieder new gemacht* (n.p.:n.p., n.d.). Fiche 1130/#2890, unpaginated.
109. Schottenloher, *Flugschriften zur Ritterschaftsbewegung*, 16.
110. #58, Hans Bechler von Scholbrunnen, *Eyn Gesprech eyness Fuchs und Wolffs* (n.p.:n.p., c. 1524), Fiche 1378/#3633, fol. aiii, B^v, ai. Hans Joachim Köhler accepts the identity of the author as by a layman, probably urban, because of the strong anti-noble element, (personal communication with Köhler).

Ableynung des vermein

lichen vnglimpffs so dem Andechtigen Hoch
gelerten vnd Criftenlichen vatter Doctor
Martin Luther Augustiner ordens. rc.
von vielen zügelegt/jn dem das er vn
sern vatter den Babst ein Vicary
des Teüfels vnd Antecrists
rc. genant hat.

3 "Rejection of the alleged wrongs attributed to
the learned and Christian Doctor Martin Luther
by many because he called the Pope
the vicar of the devil."

Hartmuth von Cronberg stands in full armor to defend Luther before a member
of the Roman clergy. The woodcut shows the two as equal in status.

SOURCE: Title page of a pamphlet by Hartmuth von Cronberg. *Ableynung
des vermeinlichen unglimpffs so dem Andechtigen Hochgelerten und Christenlichen
vatter Doctor Martin Luther Angustiner ordens von vielen zugelegt in dem das er
unsern vatter den Bapst ein Vicari des Teüffels und Antecrists genant hat.* Strassburg:
J. Schwan, c.1524.
Courtesy of the Zentralbibliothek, Zurich, Switzerland.

4

The Nobility Define Christian
Life and Practice

FORMS OF WORSHIP

As convinced, evangelical Christians, some of the nobility faced a conflict between faith and practice. Their lives had been transformed, yet their parish church might have remained untouched. Beliefs changed more rapidly than rituals. The same priest, perhaps, occupied the chancel, saying mass on Sundays and holy days. The choir continued to sing the traditional liturgy. If a reformed cleric was on the church staff, his duty was often limited exclusively to preaching.

The same difficult choices confronted other evangelical lay women and men. Should they attend Mass or not? In its traditional form it emphasized the sacrifice of Christ, a sacrifice repeated every time a priest said the words of institution. Luther, however, taught that Christ's sacrifice was made once, upon the cross. To attempt to repeat it was blasphemy. What was the laity to do? Attend and believe in their own interpretation, or avoid Mass altogether? And what about confession? Luther had criticized the selling of indulgences, and the resulting controversy had undermined the validity of penance and auricular confession as the basis of the penitential system. But people were still expected to confess and do penance before receiving communion at Easter. Prayer presented another problem. Luther had written, and his followers had reiterated, that Christ had taught his disciples only one prayer, the Our Father, which was sufficient for all needs. But ordinary church services invoked the saints at various points in the liturgy and always included prayers to the Virgin. What, again, was the evangelical Christian supposed to do? What should he teach his children?

A handful of noblemen addressed these issues. Because one part of the body social, the church, had failed in its obligations, some of the nobility believed that they were now responsible for the preservation of public order and for proper worship in their own churches. One of Sickingen's supporters stated this bluntly. "No one," he wrote, "will undertake to root out bad teaching. It should be the duty of the ecclesiastical princes and the secular sword."[1] But the nobility themselves were not sure how to proceed. Hartmut von Cronberg reflected the mood of caution and wariness. God had instructed all Christians, he wrote, that they should do nothing against the Word of God. Christ himself "told us and established what we should do. Thus we should tolerate and leave church ceremonies, so far as they are seemly, until we are better informed."[2] The Edict of Worms prohibited any criticism of the institutions of the church, which created further apprehension among the reform's supporters. "Some say they follow evangelical teaching and call themselves Lutherans," wrote Franz von Sickingen, "but they are waiting to see what will be maintained as right."[3] Hieronymus von Endorf, a convinced evangelical, regretted the divisions which the Reformation had created. "The old and new teaching have not been brought together for a long time. . . . Unity has been broken for so long that the longer it lasts, the more things are turned upside down. . . . Even Father Martin has had one follower grow into a carbuncle [Karlstadt] and soon another will grow . . . and more evil will break out."[4]

These statements reflect the confusion and malaise that pervaded ordinary life. There was a vacuum, roughly from 1519 through 1528, when the reformers were absorbed with doctrine but the old forms of worship remained relatively untouched. Ordinances which established new orders of service began to appear in 1524 when Luther gave biblical reading and preaching the primary position in Wittenberg's parish church.[5] Much of the medieval liturgy, however, was kept. Luther believed that matters like vestments, candles, and music were externals which congregations could work out for themselves. Significantly, individual confession before receiving communion was maintained, despite Luther's strong attack against its use in the Roman church. New ordinances and the reorganization of churches in other territories and cities moved slowly. The Elector John began the task in Electoral Saxony in 1527; a synod for the purpose was called in Hesse in 1526. The Mass was not abolished in Strasbourg until 1529, the new church order was not drawn up until 1533. In cities like Brunswick, Hamburg, and Lübeck, the changes occurred in 1528 and 1531.[6]

Individual noblemen were disturbed by this divergence between evangelical doctrine and the maintenance of traditional Roman ritual. In pamphlets and in letters to their families, which they had published, they addressed the questions of appropriate rituals and forms of worship. Adam von Schaumburg described his reasons for writing on these matters in some detail. There has been "an unusual dispute among the learned and theologians . . . as to whether they should depend on Christ . . . his holy apostles and evangelists, and the four holy teachers Gregory, Augustine, Jerome,

Ambrose. . . . Against these . . . are those who preach another sect of the highest bishop of Rome, who wishes to set himself up as another God. . . . They also teach the old bunglers Aristotle, Plato, Cato and other heathen masters who are against the holy Gospel and all Christian teaching." Schaumburg had decided to write about his own beliefs, "which he had held since he was a child," not in order to dispute or to attack, but as a simple layman, "to educate poor people so that they can know what to believe." He had written his book, as he called it, in German and had it printed so it would spread afar.[7]

CONFESSION AND ABSOLUTION

Confession and penance were critical matters for these writers. Luther's attack on indulgences not only struck a death blow to the belief in penance as a sacrament, it also weakened the practice of auricular confession. Lay women and men had hated this requirement for years, and now the power of the clergy to grant absolution or to enforce penitence had been questioned. Many people no longer wanted to kneel in the confessional. The reformers wrote about the broad theological issues of confession, but provided few alternatives to the traditional practice; indeed, they tended to suggest that the laity continue to confess to a priest. Luther discussed this very early on in a *Sermon on the Sacrament of Penance*, first printed in 1519, with 14 editions in the next two years.[8] Luther differentiated between penance as punishment and penance as the forgiveness of guilt. The latter was by far the more important, "one might call it a godly or heavenly indulgence, one that only God himself can grant from heaven." Forgiveness of guilt was necessary to the Christian because it reconciled him with God, and "a person's sins no longer bite him or make him uneasy."[9] Three things were involved: absolution, the forgiveness of sins, and the faith of the individual that the absolution and words of the priest were true. Faith made the sacrament valid. Furthermore, Luther insisted, no human being had the power to forgive guilt; that depended entirely on the words of Christ and the individual's faith in them. A Pope, a bishop had no more power than the lowliest priest over absolution. "Indeed," he continued, "where there is no priest, each individual Christian does as much. For a Christian can say to you 'God forgives your sins, in the name of etc.' and if you accept that word with a confident faith, you are surely absolved."[10]

Luther envisioned the latter procedure to be used only at a moment of crisis, unexpected death, a life-threatening illness, since he continued in the same paragraph, "Even so one should observe and not despise the established orders of authority. . . . If you believe the word of the priest when he absolves you . . . your sins are assuredly absolved also before God."[11] Absolution was still the function of the priest, even if the faith of the believer was the active force. In a later work on confession, Luther merely criticized the endless cataloguing of sins, but still assumed that the individual would confess to a cleric.[12] Thus, although Luther had denied the power of the priest to absolve, since God alone possessed this power, the laity were still directed to the confessional booth.

Other reformers attempted to go farther. The title of Johann Oecolampadius' Latin treatise of 1521 summarized his message, *A Paradox, Christian Confession Is not Onerous*. Describing auricular confession as tyranny, he pointed out that three other forms of confession could be found in the Bible: secret confession to God, public confession in church, and private confession to a fellow Christian.[13] Since the book was written in Latin, its circulation among laymen was limited. Urbanus Rhegius, however, published a German manual on daily confession to God in 1522,[14] and Jacob Strauss published his *Beychtbeüchlin* in 1523. The latter, breaking with tradition more completely than either Luther or Oecalampadius, denied that penance was a sacrament and advised that the individual should "merely inform the priest of the state of their souls and receive from them, not a judicial examination, but a sure confirmation of their independent judgment" that they were free of sin. Furthermore, he stated, Christians who felt the need to confess should do so to another Christian and receive forgiveness from them.[15]

Except for Strauss, none of the reformed clergy visualized confession without a priest: only the priest could speak the words of absolution. Neither the liturgy nor the ritual of confession were changed in these early years. The reformers did not regard it as a problem requiring immediate attention.

The laity saw it in a very different light. They did not want to go to a priest to confess, knowing they could exert no control once they entered the confessional. Puzzled by the differences between the reformers and the priests, several members of the nobility, heartened by Luther's sermon on penance and Strauss's *Beychtbeüchlin*, began to build forms of corporate or private confession, their own rituals suited to the new faith. These appeared in prayer books, books of spiritual counsel, and manuals for confession. Left without direction, they attempted to fill the vacuum for themselves, their families, and their people.

The problem had begun with the indulgence controversy. If the Pope or other clergy did not have the power to release souls from purgatory, what power did they have and by whom were they given it? Ulrich von Hutten confronted the matter bluntly in 1520, stating that the Pope should not tell people how to confess, nor what they should eat.[16] He did not, however, offer any alternative to confession to a priest. The following year, he criticized both the clergy and the pope because they granted absolution only for money. The pope was the shepherd who scraped and fleeced his own lambs, giving indulgences out, taking pennies in.[17] One of the anonymous noble writers at the Ebernburg echoed the same complaint. The priests told him he must make offerings and gifts and that it was a deadly sin if he did not confess, yet he could find no commandment in Scripture that he must give a penny or confess.[18]

Lay people thus openly questioned the power of the clergy over confession. Adam von Schaumburg wrote a long pamphlet in 1522 which placed the power to forgive and to absolve exclusively in the hands of Christ and God, names which he used interchangeably. The pamphlet was supported, sentence by sentence, paragraph by paragraph, from biblical sources, the Old Testament perhaps more frequently than the New. Though long, rambling and jumbled, it had a clear concern: God alone had full authority and could forgive sins. God governed the universe jointly with Christ, and they had given the responsibility for earthly government to kings, not the clergy, but had reserved to themselves the power to forgive men's sins. The power over penance and absolution claimed by the clergy was invalid.[19] Schaumburg's interpretation of the traditional text was somewhat cloudy but he was firm in his conviction. "It is true that Christ said I will command the keys of the kingdom and what you bind here on earth will be bound in heaven, [but] it can no longer be applied to forgiveness or refraining from sin, for Christ . . . never allowed any sin but forgave. . . . Christ did not give power to forgive sins to Peter or the disciples. He appeared before them and said 'Take and receive the holy spirit and when you forgive sins, to [those] it will be forgiven.'"[20] It was the Holy Spirit, Christ in another form, not the disciples nor priests who had the power of forgiveness.

Schaumburg's explication of this text was rather typical of his use of proof texts. There was no question in his mind that he had the right to interpret the Bible for himself, and he was not restrained by caution. He jumped from Genesis to the Gospels in the same sentence, selecting exactly that part of a text which supported his argument. The context in which it appeared bothered him not at all, and he was capable of drawing his own conclusions, as in this instance, whatever the text.

He was, however, one of the first of the noblemen to provide an alternative to confession, namely, communion. "The crucifixion brought full forgiveness of all sins, thus I cannot and should not believe that the outward works of men, whether it is fasting, praying, pilgrimages or giving alms bring absolution. For Christ did enough, so wrote the holy Paul. Thus we must love God for he created us and with his death released us from original sin and made sufficient atonement for all our sins and gave us all mercy."[21] Absolution came only through Christ in communion, through the gift of his body and blood for all men and women. If one confessed to the most insignificant priest or, in great need, even to a layman, only God had the grace and mercy to grant absolution.[22] The words echo Luther's sermon, but Schaumburg's emphasis was different. As on many other points, Schaumburg was not clear whether an individual was still meant to go to confession or whether it was sufficient simply to take communion. Hartmut von Cronberg was equally vague in his letter to the people of Cronenberg: "Our needs require we must recognize our sins and selfishness and call on Christ so that he will grant us his grace and . . . [he] will unburden us from the terrible darkness so that we can be truly children of God."[23] How this was to be done was not spelled out. It was simply clear that Christ would grant absolution to all who turned to him.

A noblewoman went farther in providing a form for confession. In 1524, an honorable woman wrote to her sister Hilgart von Freyburg, expressing her sorrow that she had not been able to visit but that she had had "to take care of my little sheep." Since she could not come herself, she was sending a short confession of sin to God, "which you do not have to accept but which is my faithful advice to you."[24] Letters from women, especially noblewomen, to their sisters were fairly frequent among the lay pamphlets, although many of these involved lay women writing to their sisters who were nuns. But all these letters indicate that women were used to sharing their spiritual concerns with their sisters. There is almost always some mention of the children, some discussion of family matters, which confirm that they were indeed written by women. The intensity of their belief in the new faith is always apparent.

In this case, Hilgart's anonymous sister had created her own penitential order based on the Psalms, on self-examination, and on confession directly to God. Casting aside the traditional classification and categorization of her sins,[25] she examined not her outward acts but her inner, spiritual development, which she felt was weak and unworthy. "I am a woman," she began, "who has trespassed against all your commandments. I have never held to them in spirit, I have not considered your holy word. I have remained weak in my faith. I have not loved, praised or honored you. I take too much interest in myself. . . . I do not suppress my evil, stubborn will so that I may be obedient to your will."[26] She then turned to her outer life. She had not been true to her neighbors, nor had she shared with them the gifts God had given to her. God, she prayed, would help her to love her neighbors "without irritation or sorrow." God, she believed, would let his Holy Spirit enter her sinful heart and help her change her evil nature.[27]

Hilgart's sister was not concerned about absolution; indeed, she did not mention it. It seemed sufficient to unburden herself of her spiritual failings, her weakness, her selfishness. She did not have to be told she had been forgiven. At the end of the letter, however, she included the general confession which had been introduced in Augsburg by the reading master of the Franciscan order in that city. This was Johann Schilling, whom the Magistrat had tried to ban from the city in that same year. The confession was set off on a separate page with a heading in large type font: "A useful Confession. The open confession of a reading master of the Franciscan Order at Augsburg pronounced by the people at all sermons." The noble lady made no comment on the form or content of the confession, perhaps in deference to the rioting and unrest which had occurred in Augsburg. But it is significant that she published it and that she wanted her sister to know about this new method of open, general confession. The wording of the latter was extremely general. The first two sentences recognized the eternal power of God. The congregation then appealed—"Do not reject your heirs whom you redeemed with your red blood. But we ask you that, according to your great mercy, you will hear our prayer, for we have sinned grievously and committed evil before you."[28] The congregation were then to strike themselves on the chest and ask God for forgiveness.

The noblewoman had included two new forms of confession, private confession directly to God and general, open, public confession, but had said nothing in either case about absolution. It was a Strasbourg nobleman, Eckhart zum Drübel, who provided a form to be used by a layman to confess to another layman, as well as a form for the latter to use in granting absolution.

Drübel came from an ancient Strasbourg noble family which had held civic posts for several centuries.[29] Converted early to the Reform, he wrote nine pamphlets. In 1524, according to one pamphlet, Drübel had abandoned auricular confession. The foolish confessor, he wrote, stated that he could not grant absolution unless Drübel gave him a sum of money, then he would say a certain number of masses. When that happened, wrote Drübel, it was time to complain about the stupid priest. Christians should flee from such men and seek Christ, who would act with trust and faith and mercy.[30] Four years later, Drübel was ready to present his own version of private confession and absolution, because purgatory and auricular confession had led to great harm in all Christendom. Through confession the priests "have destroyed us and injured us in many ways in soul, body, honor and property. . . . But he who with great and pure faith confesses to him who alone can forgive sins, that is God himself and no other, that is good. It can be done at all times and hours, in all places, the more, the oftener, the better."[31] Like Schaumburg, Drübel placed the power of forgiveness solely in the hands of God but did not feel it was necessary to develop the point. He was more concerned with the form to be used.

Anyone wishing to make their confession should go to an understanding Christian brother and say to him, "I ask and wish that, for the will of God, you will hear my confession. He replies, in the same name it shall be done." The sinner then should continue, "I know myself as a poor sinner . . . I have angered God . . . left him and dishonored his holy name, have been ungrateful for his good gifts and mercy, and have also trespassed against God and my neighbor . . . breaking God's commandments many times. . . . I know I am guilty, I repent, I am truly sorry and wish for God's mercy and instruction to better my life according to the teachings of Christ . . . and to receive redemption and forgiveness of my sins and the sins of all of us."[32]

A full heading was then printed across the page, occupying three lines: "The absolution which every priest or confessor, whoever he may be, should pronounce as follows." The text continued:

> The Lord Jesus Christ through his holy suffering, death and sufficient merit, be gracious and merciful to you, record and forgive your sins, give you a Christian faith, ignite in you a Christian love and holy hope through which all desire to sin will be overcome and you will be led to all goodness. I, according to his godly command and injunction [as when he said what you bind on earth or loosen, will also be bound or loosened by me in heaven], absolve you. He, God himself, records and forgives all your sins, in the name of God the father, the son and the holy spirit. Amen.[33]

The confessor—priest or layman—should then ask the penitent if he believed if God had forgiven all his sins. If so, he was to go forth and sin nor more, using all his will to refrain from falling into wickedness. That was sufficient penance, as Christ himself had said, and not "money, money, money and do this or that and some sort of devilish works and foolish game," which had been demanded up until now. He was aware that his enemies would attack him for this and call him Eckhart zum Teuffel instead of zum Drübel, because that had happened to him before. But God would be his protector and would forgive them all. "This," he concluded, "is enough said about penance."[34]

The nobility moved more quickly than the reformers on confession. The reformers wrote on the question, the laity acted. True, Adam von Schaumburg merely developed Luther's point that God alone had the power to forgive, and did not say to whom one confessed. By 1524, however, a noblewoman had developed her own form for private confession and sent to her sister a form in public use. In 1528, Eckhard zum Drübel created a formal system which a layman could use instead of auricular confession, making it clear that confession could be made to a lay person as well as to a priest. Thus, he moved the power over confession from the hands of the clergy into the hands of the laity. Faced by their own practical needs, this handful of noble writers suggested changes in essential church ceremonies. They had assumed their right to lead.

PRAYER

Prayer was a part of the daily religious life of every sixteenth-century Christian, even if it involved only hastily murmured words in the morning, before meals, and at night. The question of prayers to the saints, particularly the use of the Ave Maria, was thus a vital concern since many daily prayers invoked the saints. Most of the noble pamphlet writers accepted the new order with regard to prayer. Franz von Sickingen, as we have already seen, was almost curt with his brother-in-law's father on the issue. As far as Sickingen was concerned, prayers to the saints were against God's commandments. If men acted against the will of God and prayed to others it would do more harm than good—"for we must remain united with him in whom all unity, holiness and salvation is found."[35] Sickingen, however, did not suggest any specific prayers. Hartmut von Cronberg also mentioned prayers to the saints as one of the customs which had misled men and diverted them from the path that God intended. People should pray directly to God, for anyone who firmly trusted in God and prayed to him "with childlike fear" would receive his grace. He included a short prayer asking God "to give us grace . . . that we should be fundamentally instructed, for then there would be no doubt about the one brotherhood which is given us in baptism and that we should be increased and maintained in brotherly love."[36] For him, like Sickingen, prayer was a means of attaining unity, both with God and with the Christian community.

Prayer to God alone was also cited by Adam von Schaumburg, who quoted the words from Exodus, "you shall pray to God alone."[37] With his customary flexibility he was able to extend this to include prayers to the saints. Men prayed to the saints, he wrote, to ask their help in earning salvation. In effect, this was not necessary because the saints were so unified with God that they never went against God's will. This, Schaumburg concluded, meant that one could pray to the saints, especially to Mary, for grace and mercy. But one could not petition them for salvation. He added a small caution. Men must have patience toward God and the saints if their help did not seem to be forthcoming; people should not then murmur against them or be angry.[38]

Hilgart's anonymous sister dealt more extensively with prayer than any other noble writer. Again, this may have been, partially, the result of a long-standing tradition of spiritual correspondence between women, the exchange of devotional poems and meditations, the sharing of common spiritual concerns.[39] The pamphlet could, indeed, be considered a prayer book, based almost entirely on the Psalms. There were, wrote Hilgart's sister, many excellent psalms "to pray for help and mercy in times of trouble." In moments of real distress she should repeat Psalms 12, 24, 53, 66, 85, 140, 141, and

122. "You do not need to pray all these in one day, but one after another. You will not have to work at it very long for the spirit of God will enlighten you. . . ." She did not, it should be noted, write out the psalms she referred to, for her sister had a psalter. She listed the penitential psalms to use when asking for forgiveness of sin, "when your reason wishes to deny its sin."[40] These were followed by psalms of joy, hope, and consolation and psalms for deliverance from her enemies.[41] The greatest of the deliverance psalms, she believed, was 143, "a powerful fire, a hammer and sword which destroys death, the devil and fleshly desire and all our enemies. . . ." With it David "had slaughtered more enemies than with his powerful sword."[42]

The noblewoman perceived prayer as a weapon against sin. Constant prayer would keep one aware of sin and wrongdoing. One of the most dangerous enemies, she believed, was one's reason. As she put it, "you may wish to lament the anguish of your reason." Since reason came between the Christian and God, it made it possible to trick yourself, to excuse yourself for sins you had committed. She counseled her sister never to go to sleep at night without "recognizing before God . . . how you have wasted the day" and asking him to forgive hidden sins.[43] The noblewoman, more introspective than any of the male writers, demanded a self-examination and a consciousness of wrongdoing which the men did not insist on. Together, however, the prayers and confessions written by these noblemen and the noblewoman indicate the independence of their religious life. Within four years of Luther's emergence as a public figure, individuals created their own forms for daily and weekly worship.

THE CHRISTIAN LIFE

Several noble pamphleteers described their concept of the Christian life and what it demanded of the believer. Adam von Schaumburg's Leyen Spiegel, published in 1522, contained Twelve Articles of the holy Christian faith, which included the Apostles' Creed, the primacy of the authority of God, the supremacy of kings over priests, and several articles on the community of saints. The last, he believed, had fellowship with God in heaven, but, at the same time, pious, thoughtful men were within the communion of saints in their life here on earth.[44] His emphasis on this was not explained. The pamphlet focused on the absolute authority of God and obedience to this authority, supported from the Old Testament. His prime example was the story of Moses striking the rock for water, which he recorded in meticulous detail. When the children of Israel murmured against Moses and Aaron because they had no water, God instructed Moses and his brother to take their rod and assemble the people, when Moses should speak to the rock so it would give forth water. Moses called the people together and said, "because of your lack of faith we will bring water from the rock" and struck twice thereon although God had not ordered him to do so, but there came forth overflowing water. . . . Then, said the Lord to Moses and Aaron, since you did not believe me that the word was as powerful as striking with the rod, and because you did not honor me before the people . . . but took the honor for yourself, as though you had anything to do with it, you will not lead my people to the promised land.[45]

The story was a late medieval favorite. The *Biblia Pauperum*, a popular volume of Bible stories with woodcuts, paired the scene of Moses striking the rock with a woodcut depicting Christ on the cross, with the blood and water of salvation flowing from the wound on his side.[46] Schaumburg, however, made no connection between the water and the salvation. It was a matter of Moses' disobedience. Schaumburg gave the text of God's reply as "you did not believe me that the spirit of the Word was as powerful as striking with the rod."[47] Schaumburg took major elements of Reformation theology, the Word of God, the importance of faith, as measuring rods for the patriarchs and prophets and as an explanation of their failure.

The clearest and most extensive manual on the Christian life was written by the Strasbourg nobleman Eckhart zum Drübel.[48] The book is important because it provides autobiographical details which are missing in the writing of other noblemen. It mirrors his likes and dislikes, his social prejudices, and his disappointment in his fellow man. Read carefully, it reveals the moral as well as the religious problems of an urban noble.

The urban nobility were a special breed. They owned houses within the city walls, and, in most city constitutions, they were represented in their own special council and were appointed to certain administrative posts. At the same time, they had their lands outside the city. Drübel's town house was in the center of the city, the wealthiest section, near the great Franciscan square. This was within the cathedral parish.[49] The family also held five villages in fief, two to the west of the city, three to the south, toward Colmar. It was in one of the latter, Hindesheim, that their castle was located.[50]

Eckhardt was born around 1478 and therefore was in full maturity during the period of the early Reformation, when he turned himself with some passion to writing in support of the new faith.[51] His youth and early manhood had been spent as a military man, which had taken him to Eastern Europe, Turkey, Wallachia, Russia, and Poland.[52] On his return, he had married the daughter of another noble family, the Fraulein von Büttenheim. They settled in Hindesheim. Seven children survived into adulthood, five boys and two girls.[53] He devoted himself to his duties as lord in his villages, but his relationship with the city was not always smooth. In 1500, he resigned his burgher rights. In 1517, he repurchased these rights and took the oath as an *ausburger*, meaning that he was permitted to maintain a residence out-side the city walls. He was assigned to one of the guilds for voting pur-poses.[54] The pattern of renunciation of citizenship followed by repurchase was not unusual among patrician families.[55] More significant was Drübel's lack of interest in holding political office or involving himself deeply in civic affairs. By contrast, his son Gabriel would hold the office of *stettmeister* seven times between 1582 and 1591.[56]

Drübel was absorbed by the religious questions of his time. The opening sentence of this first pamphlet, written between 1521 and 1523, went to the heart of the matter: "I, Eckhardt zum Drübel, am certainly not a Lutheran nor an agitator, but I am a Christian and a layman and my conscience has been uneasy for many years . . . with regard to the . . . disorder in our Christian faith."[57] Or, in another pamphlet, "I as a layman cannot grope my way to or comprehend faith at all, but I, Eckhardt. . . . announce, remind, and give a true Christian warning to all Christian leaders and government officials . . . wake up, see, and hear, not just in terms of your own interest, selfishness and kinfolk. . . . Stop the gross disloyalty, fraud and abuses which are against God."[58] The question might be raised, he wrote in a later pamphlet, whether only the anointed and ordained could preach, whether they alone could enter the chancel and instruct the people. "No, it is not so," he answered, "I can and may, I and every Christian, write, sing, say, advise, speak, teach, instruct in a Christian way." For Christ said, "wherever two or three are gathered in my name, I am there in the midst of then. But he does not specify whether these are priests or laymen. And he says 'wherever' and by this he means that all places are his . . . and thus every man should, can and may preach, announce, set forth and make known the Word of God in all places."[59]

Fortified by his convictions, confident of his mission, in 1528 Drübel wrote to his children on how to live and die a Christian life. As we have already seen, the first section of the book dealt with confession. In the second part, he turned to the question of how his children should handle their earthly goods and material needs. Drübel was deeply concerned by the economic injustice which he saw all around him both in the city and in the countryside. He was convinced that one cause of this poverty was that the church demanded money for everything. Over and over again he wrote that the most important reform was "to get the money out of the church."[60] This would lead to a better economic balance. The money which now went into the pockets of the priests (he always referred to these as the priests' "sacks"), would be available to help the poor. In yet another pamphlet he praised the new poor relief law of the city of Strasbourg. "It is with deep thankfulness that I have lived to see the Christian city of Strassburg accomplish such a praiseworthy Christian work . . . for . . . you have provided that the poor Christians and wandering, naked, sick, unfortunate people are to be taken off the highways and byways, and maintained with orderly supervision and provided with the necessities of life."[61] Other problems remained unsolved. Speculation, the sale of crops before they were harvested, led to preemption and false scarcities. It particularly affected the "day laborers, like woodcutters and harvesters, who are faithful and serious . . . and find themselves in great trouble."[62]

His concern about inequalities in wealth carried over to his children. They must shape their behavior to prevent the gap from becoming any wider. "First," he instructed them, "refrain from all unnecessary spending, such as an elaborate household, pomp, luxury, guests and expensive banquets. . . . Receive and take that which belongs to you from God and by right, and use it for Christian purposes. . . . If you have any surplus and want to use it for luxury, give it to the poor." He was wary of doctors, lawyers, and craftsmen, all of whom, he believed, took advantage of the nobility. "Hold back from all legal disputes, for every lawyer is a wolf. . . . Do not go in for building a new house, because it will be too expensive. . . . For I find my food tastes just as good, my drink is as good and I sleep just as well in my old house as I would in a new one. And night and day come just the same way as they would if I were in a great palace."[63]

Nor should they fix up their old house, because they would call in the mason and the carpenter and the latter would say that "the job could be done for fifty gulden, but actually it will cost a hundred, for what they can do in two days, they will never finish in one . . . [for] they all work together like the judges and the advocates, or the doctors and the apothecaries. . . . Guard yourself against borrowing, especially from the burghers, for they bring discord, scorn and ruin."[64] Without the context of his comments on poverty, Eckhardt's advice could be seen as the stereotype of fatherly counsel from Plutarch through to Polonius. Eckhardt's genuine conviction of the plight of the poor places it on another level. Poverty was at the root of much of the social and political unrest of his time. He believed every Christian had to take responsibility for reducing the level of privation.

Despite this concern, he was disillusioned with the peasants, who had clearly suffered from the rural uprisings during the Peasants' War.

> Leave the peasants their church festivals for truly the *gemyn Man* nearly always is false, unthankful and untrue. He is indeed to be protected [but] small thanks will be obtained from him. Observe . . . how much trust, honor and good I have demonstrated toward the common people and shown this with loans, gifts, advice and help . . . and I have undertaken dangerous things for them. What has come to me as repayment or thanks? Nothing but great unreasonableness, disloyalty and ruinous damage to your and my great disadvantage, and against my married estate, kin and

household. This has been done to me by those whom I filled day and night, giving them to eat and drink in my house. I did good to them and trusted them. . . . They and their great disloyalty were the reason I did not remarry. So be warned, do everything which you are responsible to do, but refrain from doing more. For those who behave honorably toward you, leave your door open, otherwise, keep your door shut.[65]

Drübel's faith in God did not carry over to faith in people. Indeed, his own experience in the world, as with his peasants, had made him wary and skeptical. Yet, he counselled his children "to hold everyone as a friend." Surprisingly, he advised his five sons to avoid any military service. "Do not enter of your free will in any enlistment or war. Do not spill any blood or offer your ancient honor. I, Eckhardt, your earthly father . . . travelled in many lands, kingdoms, and nations serving other emperors, kings, princes and lords and have been in terrible, horrible battles and experienced much danger. But God, my lord, alone protected and guarded me. What prince or superior gave me anything for it? No one for a minute. And if I helped a lord win ten territories, he never gave me a village for it. What is the need for us to hang our bodies and our life on a nail and to anger God thus?"[66] He was a knight turned pacifist but not out of Erasmian sympathies. Drübel's ethics were rooted not in theory but in his own life, his experience as a warrior, his encounters with his peasants, his dealings with the Strasbourg burghers.

There was one final admonition in this section. Court life was to be avoided, as he had found out for himself. "Guard against setting yourself up and from all courtly life, especially with regard to clothes. For I have seen many fools in silk clothes and golden shoes and gloves . . . for there is nothing in feathers, except for the birds. High court life is the height of folly for, dear children, to live simply is to live well."[67]

Drübel rarely quoted from Scripture—it was not necessary. He had observed life around him and he wished to share his insights with his children. He did, however, counsel them to read often and with pleasure from the Bible, including both testaments, the prophets, the Gospels, and Epistles for these were the basis of the Christian life. In sum, "in all things place God's honor first and be friendly and good with all men, but do not become close to any man, for being close creates lack of peace and anxiety. . . . The world is the world, and if anyone trusts it, it fails him. But the real strong base is God and no other."[68]

The last article of Drübel's book was devoted to his final illness and his death. He was 50 years old when he wrote the treatise; his death came 10 years later in 1538/39.[69] Preparation for death was part of his life as a Christian. His very first desire was that his children should live in peace and unity and not be torn apart by disputes over money or anything else. A similar injunction is repeated over and over again in the testament of a seigneur in

New France in 1696.[70] It may have been a conventional phrase but it revealed the deepest fears of a father.

Drübel then gave precise instructions for his last illness. No monks, priests, beguines, or lay brothers were to be permitted to come to him. Instead, one of his children should read to him,

> and especially in my dying minutes, the psalter, the Gospels and the Passion of our Lord and read faithfully. Lay me out without torments and unencumbered by all man-made ceremonies, such as holy water and wax, which are not necessary for the salvation of the soul. You should give me no idol to hold, whether made of stone or wood, also do not place any light in my hand for in heaven there is enough light, and no earthly light can shine in hell. God provides me, however, with a spiritual, inner light, true Christian faith. And do not make great lamentation over me, but be of good courage. Provide me with the Holy Sacrament and testament of Christ according to the usages of the parish of St. Lawrence of Strassburg. With this provision let me rest. You should not, or may not smear me up either with oil or grease for if the worms will not eat my unanointed flesh, let them fast.[71]

Once he was buried, nothing more was to be done, no masses, no prayers, no money to the priests. Instead, money should be given to the poor. "Food and drink, bread and meat should be prepared and distributed to all who need it, widows, orphans, women in childbed and prisoners. Or give it to a nunnery to help a common, open sinner to have money to get married. Or money might be given to a very young girl, the daughter of a poor man, so that she can marry decently. To give in this way, to receive the poor as guests in your house, that is Christian giving."[72]

Drübel was not a theologian, nor did he use the Bible to support every element of his treatise like Adam von Schaumburg. As he himself stated in the first sentence of his first pamphlet, he was a Christian and thus he felt that it was his responsibility to address himself to how one should live one's life as a Christian. He had had a broad experience of life, not all of it pleasant, but he had no idea of withdrawing from the world. The world was full of dangers and difficulties, but one was responsible to God to deal with these, and the unpleasant people who often accompanied them, in a practical way. Drübel said little about the special responsibilities of a nobleman, unlike the Ebernburg writers. His emphasis was on the care of the poor. The order of the world, God's order, required that those with more money take care of those with less. Of all the noble writers, Eckhardt zum Drübel was the most aware of others. He was direct, almost blunt in his appraisal of a problem and its solution. He was unselfconscious, willing to discuss what were clearly misfortunes and failures, open about his prejudices. Above all, he wrote from his heart.

These lay manuals showed marked differences from the pre- Reformation vernacular spiritual manuals usually written by clerics. Their emphasis had been on obedience. The *Beychtspiegel* of 1517 required obedience to one's superiors, even if they lived sinful lives. Curiously, it stated that men and women were to show honor only to the secular magistrates.[73] *The Footpath to Everlasting Salvation*, written for a knight, also stressed obedience. The knight's horse represented the world of the flesh, carnal lust, desire. The knight must control the horse, force him to obey his commands. With his saddle, bridle, and spurs the knight should drive the horse on its right path, as God forced men into patience, obedience, and faithfulness.[74] *The Footpath* spelled out in detail the ravages of death, the finality of damnation to those who were disobedient. The pre-Reformation pamphlets dealt with the need to restore order. The Reformation introduced new elements.

In the manuals that lay men and women wrote in the early years of the reform, the emphasis and the tone were different. Every pamphlet written by the nobility placed the praise and honor of God as the first, the paramount duty of a Christian. Traditional manuals were concerned with the salvation of the individual; they turned inward, considering the sinfulness of the person. The noble writers turned outward. Their lives should provide a paean of praise to God. Prayers should mount constantly to heaven. You must, said Drübel, place God's honor first. It was a different relationship, in which God demanded not only obedience but joy and acclamation, a relationship based not on self-abnegation but on a sense of man's dignity before God.

This was picked up in another theme, the theme of brotherhood and unity. Cronberg wrote of one brotherhood in baptism which united all Christians. Sickingen stated that men must remain united in him in whom all unity, holiness, and salvation would be found. Schaumburg wrote of the unity in the communion of saints. Faced by the divisions in the earthly church, they appealed to the unity which could be found in God. They translated the search to a higher level.

In looking at these pamphlets, it is necessary to search for what is missing as well as what is there. In this particular set of writings, God did not appear as threatening eternal punishment; indeed, the apocalyptical elements in the political pamphlets of the nobility were also missing. The Christian life did not mean that men and women must try to mollify God at every turn, to please him, to turn aside his wrath. These writers had accepted Luther's teaching and believed that if they had faith in God, he would respond to them. This self-confident faith is clear in their writing on confession. God was merciful, forgiving, not punitive or threatening. They feared God but they were no longer afraid of him.

Notes

1. #51, *Wer hören will wer die gantze Welt arm hat gemacht*, c. 1522, fol. Aiiii.
2. #89, Hartmuth von Cronberg, *An die inwoner zu Cronenberg*, c. 1522, fol. Biii^v.
3. #239, Franciscus von Sickingen, *Ain sendbrieff . . . sein schwäher dem . . . Junckherr Diethern von Henschüchssheim . . .*, 1522, fol. biii^v.
4. #105, Hieronymus von Endorf, *Axiomata oder sitig begerungen*, 1525, fol. Aii.
5. Harold Grimm, *The Reformation Era*, 1978, 126. Reform of the liturgy began at about the same time in other areas, for example, Strasbourg, where the reformers began to discuss the matter in 1524. See René Bornert, *La Réforme Protestante du Culte à Strasbourg . . .*, 1981, 85–121.
6. Miriam Usher Chrisman, *Strasbourg and the Reform*, 1967, 172, 216–219; Grimm, *The Reformation Era*, 128–129. A few anonymous books on "The Evangelical Mass" and on the order of the church service appeared in 1524. In 1525, the order of service used in Strasbourg was printed. See Chrisman, *Bibliography of Strasbourg Imprints*, 1982, P5.1.7, P5.1.9, P5.1.10.
7. #230, Adam von Schaumburg, *Dyses Buchlein wirdt genent der Leyen Spiegell*, 1522, fol. aii.
8. Steven Ozment, *The Reformation in the Cities*, 1975, 50. See also p. 18, for the falling off of yearly confession in the late medieval church.
9. Martin Luther, "The Sacrament of Penance," ed. and trans. E. Theodore Bachman. In *Luther's Works*, ed. Jaroslav Pelikan, Helmut T. Lehmann, 55 vols., Vol. 35, "Word and Sacrament I," 9.
10. Ibid., 12.
11. Ibid.
12. Ozment, *Reformation in the Cities*, 50–51.
13. Ibid.
14. Chrisman, *Bibliography . . .*, P5.1.3.
15. Ozment, *Reformation in the Cities*, 54.
16. #163, Ulrich von Hutten, *Clag und Vermanung gegen . . . des Bapstes zu Rom*, 1520, fol. C.
17. #173, Ulrich von Hutten, *Ain Klag über den Luterischen Brandt zu Mentz*, 1521, fol. aii^v–aiii.
18. #51, *Wer hören will wer die gantze welt arm hat gemacht*, 1522, fol. Bii.
19. #230, Adam von Schaumburg, *Leyen Spiegell*, fol. aiv^v, Biiii–Biiii^v.
20. Ibid., fol. Biii^v–Biiii.
21. Ibid., fol. Dii.
22. Ibid., Diii.
23. #89, Hartmuth von Cronberg, *Ain die inwoner zu Cronberg*, fol. Bii^v.
24. #23, *Der Gotzferchtige Eerentreiche fraw Hilgart von Freyburg seiner cristenliche aller liebsten schwester*, 1524, fol. Aii. The sister's husband is identified by the anonymous author as a *juncker*. On this basis I have assumed they were both from a noble family.
25. See Ozment, *Reformation in the Cities*, 19–31, for the lay catechism by Dietrich Coelde, reprinted 29 times between 1480 and 1520.
26. #23, *Der Gotzferchtige . . . frau Hilgart*, fols. Aiiii^v, A^v.
27. Ibid., fol. Avi.
28. Ibid., fol. Avii^v.
29. Timotheus Wilhelm Röhrich, *Mittheilungen aus der Geschichte der evangelischen Kirche des Elsasses*, 3 vols. (1855), 3, 19.

30. #96, Eckhart zum Drübel, *Ein Christlich lob und vermanung an die hochberümpte Christliche statt Strassburg* . . . (1524). Also in Laube et al., *Flugschriften der fruhen Reformations bewegung*, 2 vols. (1983), 1, 958ff.

31. #101, Eckhart zum Drübel, *Ein vetterliche gedruge gute zucht lere und bericht Christlich zuleben und sterben an meine kynder und alle frumme Christen*, 1528, fol. Aiii.

32. Ibid, fol. Aiii[v].

33. Ibid.

34. Ibid., fol. Aiv.

35. #239, Franciscus von Sickingen, *Ain sendbrieff* . . . *sein schwäher*, 1522, fol. biii.

36. #89, Hartmuth von Cronberg, *An die inwoner*, fol. C[v], Biii.

37. #230, Adam von Schaumburg, *Leyen Spiegell*, fol. Civ[v].

38. Ibid., fols. D–Dv.

39. Anne J. Schutte, "The *Lettere Volgari* and the Crisis of Evangelism in Italy," *Renaissance Quarterly* 28 (1975): 639–688, passim.

40. #23, *Der gotzferchtige* . . . *fraw Hilgart von Freyburg*, 1524, fol. Aii[v].

41. Ibid., fol. Aiii.

42. Ibid., fol. Aiii[v], Aiii.

43. Ibid., fol. Aiii[v].

44. #230, Adam von Schaumburg, *Leyen Spiegell*, 1522, fols. Bii–D[v].

45. Ibid, fol. Aii[v].

46. Lawrence A. Silver, "'The Sin of Moses': Comments on the Early Reformation in a Late Painting by Lucas van Leyden," *AB* 55 (Sept. 1973): 404. Lucas van Leyden gave this scene the same interpretation as Schaumburg.

47. #230, Adam von Schaumburg, *Leyen Spiegell*, fol. Aiii.

48. Gustave Koch, *Eckhart zum Drübel, témoin de la Réforme en Alsace*, 1989. Koch's book presents a critical edition of each of Drübel's pamphlets, including one anonymous treatise not previously attributed to him. I am more than grateful to Dr. Koch, who provided me with xerox copies of those treatises I had not been able to see. His generosity is typical of the cooperation which marks the relationships among scholars working in Strasbourg.

49. Gustav Lasch, *Ein Wanderung durch die Reformationstatt Strassburg*, 1928, 19.

50. Röhrich, *Mittheilungen*, Vol. 3, 19.

51. Thomas A. Brady, Jr., established for me the approximate date of Drübel's birth. Reading a lawsuit of 1524, he found that Drübel had deposed that he was about 46 years old. AMS, IX/1, No. 4. Philips Hagen vs. Constoffel zum Hohensteg.

52. #98, Eckhart zum Drübel, *Ein demütige ermanung an Ein gantze gemeine Christenheit*, 1521–1523, fol. aii.

53. Röhrich, *Mittheilungen*, Vol. 3, 21.

54. Charles Wittmer, *Le livre de bourgeoisie de la ville de Strasbourg, 1440–1530*, 3 vols. (1948–1961) 3, #5080, #6701. *Augsbürger* were rural nobles who had associate citizenship and were exempted from the requirement to live within the city; see Thomas A. Brady, Jr., *Ruling Class*, 1978, 72.

55. Brady, *Ruling Class*, 79.

56. J. Kindler von Knobloch, *Das Goldene Buch von Strassburg*, 1886, 375.

57. #98, Eckhart zum Drübel, *Ein demütige ermanung*, fol. aii.

58. #96, Eckhart zum Drübel, *Christliche lob und vermanung*, Laube edit., 956.

59. #101, Eckhart zum Drübel, *Ein vetterliche gedruge gute zucht, lere und bericht*, fols. Dii[v]–Diii[v].

60. #98, Eckhart zum Drübel, *Ein demütige Ermanung* . . . *Gemeine Christen heit*,

1521–1523, passim. The pamphlet is an attack on buying and selling the ceremonies and services of the church. This theme reappears in most of his works.

61. #96, Eckhart zum Drübel, *Christeliche lob und Vermanung*, 1524, Laube edit., 952.
62. Ibid., 957.
63. #101, Eckhart zum Drübel, *Ein vetterliche gute zucht*, 1528, fol. Bii, Biii.
64. Ibid., fol. Biii.
65. Ibid., fol. Cv.
66. Ibid., fol. Biii–Biii^v.
67. Ibid., fol. C.
68. Ibid., fol. Biv^v, Cii^v.
69. Koch, *Eckhart zum Drübel*, 15.
70. Pierre Boucher, "Mes Dernier Volontez," c. 1696, printed in Louis Lalande, *Une vieille seigneurie: Boucherville*, 1890, 58ff.
71. #101, Eckhart zum Drübel, *Ein vetterliche gute zucht*, fol. Ciii. The St. Lawrence Chapel is part of the Cathedral of Strasbourg.
72. Ibid., fol. Civ.
73. *Der beycht spiegel. Ein gar schön tractetlin spiegel der Bibel . . . von der erkanntnüss der sünden und etlicher tugent* (Strassburg: J. Knobloch, 1517). Chrisman *Bibliography* c5.1.25. passim.
74. #1, *Das biechlin ist genant Der fusspfadt zu der ewigen seligkait . . .* (n.p.:n.p., 1521), Fiche 1233/#3109, passim. Although published in 1521 this was a traditional manual for a knight.

Dialogus oder gefprech des Appoſto
licums Angelica vnd anderer Specerey der Appotecken An=
treffen Doctor M. Lutterers ler vnd fein anhanck ꝛc.

4 "Dialogue between the herbs and compounds with regard to
Martin Luther's teaching,"

Woodcuts of authors of lower rank often showed their work place. The author of
this pamphlet, an apothecary, has gone to his shop in the middle of the night for
medication for a sick patient. Listening at the window he finds the herbs and
compounds in the shop in a heated discussion of the merits of Luther's teachings.
The large figure in the foreground is the nightwatchman with his clapper and horn,
the signs of his occupation.

SOURCE: Title page of Ulrich Bossler's pamphlet, *Dialogus oder gesprech des
Appostolicums Angelica und anderer Specerey der Appoteken antreffen Doctor M. Lutterers
ler und sein anhanck.* Speyer: J. Eckhart, 1521.Courtesy of the Zentralbibliothek,
Zurich, Switzerland.

110

5

Angry Men, the Devil, and Social Reform

The commitment of the knights to religious reform and their appointment of preachers to their churches on their lands meant that the Reformation began to spread to rural areas as early as 1521 and 1522. This is confirmed by pamphlets from the group that included minor officials, often stationed in semi-rural areas, teachers from very small towns, and technicians like military specialists and printers. There were 15 of these writers, who on first glance seem to be particularly ill-assorted and mismatched: an apothecary, two teachers, four lower level officials, two professional military men, an imperial herald, and three printers. Most of them lived in urban communities, but sometimes these were very small towns. Their duties gave them extensive contacts with rural people. Lenski identifies the officials and professional military who worked for the governing elite as "the retainer class," emphasizing their crucial role as mediators between their employers and the common folk.[1] They had to collect taxes, act as minor judicial officials, and command them when they were serving as mercenary soldiers. Of the 15 writers, eight addressed themselves to rural problems. Their pamphlets sharply criticized the church and the lay authorities. They were the only writers who proposed broad plans for social and economic reform. Several presented elaborate schemes for Christian agrarian communities. Very few peasants, if any, wrote pamphlets. This group of writers, however, tried to describe the problems of rural society, to act as spokesmen for the peasants. They add another dimension to the knights' discussion of "the people on their lands." These writers looked in both directions, up and down the social hierarchy. Upper civil servants served as intermediaries between the Reformers and the city magistrates. Minor civil servants and technicians tried to act as intermediaries between the peasants, the lower urban classes, and the power elite. What differentiates them as a group is that they did not define change in terms of their own needs; instead, their

111

concern was for the whole community. Reeditions of their pamphlets indicate that several of them were widely reprinted and may have reached down to the artisans, a phenomenon which did not occur as frequently with pamphlets written by the nobility or upper civil servants. The minor officials and professionals played a pivotal role in popularizing the ideas of reform.

Despite the disparity in their training and occupations, they wrote pamphlets which incorporated similar points of view and developed strong common themes: firm support for Luther, dismay over factional-ism within the church, and concern for the deterioration of social conditions. They offered specific programs of social reform. No other group was so imaginative in their support of Luther. They described themselves as true Lutherans. The artisans avoided the term, referring to themselves as evangelical.

The minor officials and military men did not expound Luther's doctrines. Their aim was to show that his teaching was right and must be upheld against the errors of the pope and his Roman mob. They used dramatic rhetorical forms, letters from the devil, a letter from Christ, and descriptions of battles between Christ and the papal forces and between Christ and the devil. These pamphlets will be described first.

Ulrich Bossler was probably the first of this group to write and publish. An apothecary in Hassfurt, he was a friend of Johann Virdung, the court apothecary at Heidelberg.[2] In his introduction, Bossler wrote that for a good period of time he had served "a well-known man" who lodged great lords and princes and engaged a full-time apothecary.[3] He had received the education required of his profession, had some important connections, and was familiar with the Latin New Testament.

On March 26, 1521, almost a month before Luther would arrive to defend himself at Worms, the diet published an edict sequestering his books. It was a firm warning that the emperor and the princes supported the papal ban against Luther's work. Two days later, on March 28, Bossler responded to this censorship with an imaginative dialogue, a conversation that he overheard among the medicinal roots, plants, and herbs in his well-stocked shop. Returning to the shop at midnight to help a sick person, he heard a war of words among the herbs. He asked Virdung whether the event had been governed by the stars or whether it was the work of the devil.[4]

The title-page woodcut depicted an apothecary shop with the unguents, herbs, and roots in their decorated jars. Bossler, in a cap with long earflaps, appeared in a lower window. The fantasy was carefully crafted. Various herbs, simples, and compounds spoke in terms of their strengths and their effects. The major part of the dialogue was carried by Apostolicum, who ardently supported the Pope, and by Angelica, the spokesperson for the rest of the herbs, who favored Luther. Bossler probably chose these two for their medicinal properties. Angelica was one of the most agreeable of the herbs, used as a sweetener and an aromatic.[5] Apostolicum, so-named because it was a compound originally made of 12 ingredients, was a solution of rather harsh, astringent herbs used to cleanse or cauterize a wound.[6] "Apostolicum" was also used in medieval Latin for the Pope, particularly apt in this case because the compound spoke as the Pope, using the pronoun "I."

In the dialogue, the herbs, compounds, and simples confronted Apostolicum with the consequences of his opposition to Luther. They had just heard that the emperor, the electors, the princes, and estates of the empire had forbidden Luther's writings to be sold or read. Because Apostolicum had resisted Luther, the other roots and compounds rebuked and teased him. Using medical terms they charged that he had lost his strength and no one bought him anymore. In contrast, Luther was "well rooted" and "well grounded" in Scripture and could explain and expound Christ's Word.[7]

The pro-Lutheran side was led by Angelica. She accused Apostolicum of believing only what suited him, not the Gospel which Luther preached. Apostolicum lashed out. Angelica thought she was an angel, "the best among the herbs. I will write to our father in Rome and report to him the criminal *lèse-majesté* of the roots and simples so they may be banned."[8] The church had already hurried its ban against Luther, Angelica replied. They had done it to frighten him and now all his followers would get a good dose for their stomachs. She listed a radical set of purgatives. Apostolicum, not to be diverted, feared that Christoph Scheurl of Nuremberg would have too much influence at the Diet and wished to send a messenger to the cardinal to warn him.[9]

The exchange between the two became bitter, and the other herbs said that if they were going to discuss the matter of Luther and Christianity they would be glad to hear it, but only if it was done properly, without insults. Each side should appeal to Scripture or to reason. Apostolicum accepted this grudgingly. Maybe the plants could tell him what Luther had taught, written, or printed which was good. Nothing but the Word of Christ our savior, was the reply. Apostolicum took refuge from this in the supremacy of the Pope, quoting "Tu es Petrum." This meant that the Pope was the highest, no one could teach him or punish him.[10] The Pope was the shepherd, and all Christians were his sheep, insisted Apostolicum, citing John 10. That meant that he could put them out to pasture and shear them, cast them out or sell them. Angelica objected. That would mean the Pope had the right to sell offices in German lands. Christ had told his disciples to go out in the world and preach, but when someone like Luther obeyed his command, the Pope burned his books. The hangman at Mainz who had refused to light the fire had been right.[11]

Apostolicum continued to twist the meaning of Scripture and ignore the context in which Christ had spoken. In a final appeal, Angelica asked him to read the Gospel correctly and to interpret it according to Peter, Paul, Augustine, Cyprian, Erasmus, and Martin Luther. Apostolicum's resistance crumbled. Their well-grounded argument and teaching had gone to his heart. He asked them all to pray for him. Angelica replied that it could be solved by good medicine and by reading the Gospel, the strongest testament.

Bossler's pamphlet is evidence of the impact of the edict against Luther's books among the educated. Two days after the action taken at Worms, the apothecary had completed his pamphlet. His haste was indicative of the tension all over Germany, the convergence of attention on events at Worms. The distance by land from Hassfurt to Worms was at least 80 miles, substantially more by the river route. Yet the news must have been passed along within 12 or, at the most, 24 hours. A month before Luther took his stand before the emperor, Bossler, an obscure layman, had offered his public and loyal support, thereby risking his position and his career, like Sickingen and Cronberg.

Two years later, the polemic battle had changed very little. Luther's defenders continued to fight off his attackers. Haug Marschalck, the captain of imperial troops stationed in Augsburg, met the derision of Luther's enemies with an impassioned encomium, *On the Widely Resounding Name of Luther, What It Means and How It Is Misused*. This was not a pamphlet which set out the logic and reason of Luther's doctrines. It was directed at the opposition polemicists who disdained and mocked the reformer. No one, wrote Marschalck, honored the Christian Doctor Luther except with vindictiveness, scolding, blasphemy, and abuse. Like Christ, Luther was slandered and persecuted by his opponents.[12] They twisted his name to misrepresent him and his teaching; they said he was not the *Lauterer*, the enlightener, but the *Trüber*, the darkener, tearing the band of Christians apart and making things dark. He was, they said, the *Lotter*, the rascal, and those who believed in him and the Scripture were rascally and roguish, fallen from the faith. Finally, they said he was a *Laur*, a spy who spoke against the priests and was disobedient, refusing to submit to the ban.[13]

Marschalck turned these accusations against the accusers. It was the Roman clergy, not Luther, who had kept the Gospel in the dark. "They cannot be attentive to reason for they wish to remain in darkness. Thus they do not appear in daylight. They go to no disputations. They do not sign their names to their books. . . . They administer everything with bans, bulls, force and quarrels."[14]

Marschalck enjoyed twisting the words of the word-twisters back against themselves, but the image painted by Luther's opponents was an indication of the increasing schism within the society. The Roman Catholic population, taught by their priests, believed that Luther had obscured Christian doctrine and divided a united Christendom. Marschalck asserted—"I will give a meaning to the name Luther, but it will mean nothing to the unbelievers who are not moved by word or sign":[15]

> The name Luther is written in German with six letters
> L.U.T.H.E.R.
> L Lautere Evangelische leer
> U Uberflussige gnad des heyligen geists
> T Treulicher diener Christi
> Dz bedeut
> H Heliam welche den Endchrist verraten
> E Enoch
> R Rabbi/das er ist meister wordenn aller schrifft schender.[16]

Despite Marschalck's zeal, he had little hope that things would change. The Roman clergy remained untouched, secretive, and underhanded. Other writers in this group reflected this same mistrust and resentment.

Five lower officials and professionals wrote defenses of Luther in the form of a clash between the forces of good (Christ and Luther) and the forces of evil (the devil and the Pope). No other group of writers made this division. No other group protested so openly that the devil was the opponent to be destroyed. Heiko Oberman showed that Luther had a similar view,

> According to Luther's prediction, the Devil would not "tolerate" the re-discovery of the Gospel. He would rebel with all his might and master all his forces against it. God's reformation would be preceded by a counterreformation and the Devil's progress would mark the last days.[17]

Lurking in the background of the lower officials' and professionals' pamphlets was an assumption of intrigue. The devil and the Pope were plotting and scheming to lead people astray. The devil wanted to rule the world, as well as to destroy the church. The lower officials were persuaded that it could only end in armed conflict. In one pamphlet the devil warned Luther of the harm he had done, then challenged him, formally, to a feud. In another Christ wrote from heaven that he would defend his people against all assaults of their enemies with halberds, shields, and weapons. In a third, the Pope and his Roman mob stormed heaven to take back the keys from St. Peter. Yet another described the army of Christ, fortified in a castle, shooting at the castle of the devil. Christ's artillery was 10 shots from the Old Testament, 10 from the New. Only two of these belligerent pamphlets were written by military men. The other authors were a small-town school teacher and a music teacher. The omnipresence of the devil and his activity in the everyday world, as Oberman has shown, were part of the system of belief.[18]

Erasmus Alber was a school teacher in Oberursel am Taunus in Hesse.[19] In 1523 and 1524, he wrote two *Teufelsbriefe*, or letters from the devil. This form of satirical propaganda, found in manuscripts of the fourteenth century, was revived during the Reformation to condemn the papacy.[20] In the first of the letters, the devil interrupted Luther working on his translation of the Old Testament in Wittenberg. Luther greeted his visitor, dressed as a Dominican, in a friendly way, believing he was a papal messenger. The devil revealed his identity, warning Luther that he and the Roman clergy were angry because of the trouble Luther had made for the Pope, the devil, and the monks and nuns. If he would stop preaching against the canon law, indulgences, pilgrimages, and auricular confession, he could become a great lord. The Pope would give him a cardinal's hat and he could have his own courtesans and servants.[21]

A woodcut on the title page of Alber's second pamphlet showed the devil coming through the door, letter in hand, a hat with Mercury's wings on his head, his claw-like feet scraping the threshold. Luther looked up, rather startled.[22] The devil announced that he had been sent by Cardinal Campeggio and Cardinal Lang, then meeting at Regensburg, to deliver a formal *fehdschrift*, or declaration of war, against Luther. Following the proscribed form of such a document, the Pope's grievances were listed. There were the familiar charges. Luther's preaching had diminished the yearly income of the clergy. He had brought the Bible and the Gospel back into use which, under papal orders, had not been used for several hundred years and had been forbidden at Constance.[23] He had taken auricular confession away from the clergy, monks, and nuns, consequently they could no longer conveniently pursue their adultery, whoring, and ravishing of young women. The devil closed by announcing his public enmity and that of his followers, the Pope, cardinals, and bishops toward Luther and his followers—"We will pursue you and your followers with fire, beheading, drowning, robbery, you and your children, life, property and goods."[24]

The pamphlet was written shortly after the publication of the final decree of the Diet of Nuremberg on April 24, 1524.[25] During the sessions, Cardinal Campeggio had pressed Charles V to enforce the Edict of Worms rigorously. The diet, however, had refused to consider the religious question. Alber's two pamphlets reflect the tension of the reformed party. The first pamphlet went through five reprints, the second four, most of them in 1524. Alber had provided what many people wanted, a picture of the pious, dedicated Luther working at his desk, threatened by the devil, in contrast to the cardinals at Regensburg exerting their power to force Luther into obedience to their will. Luther against "them" was clearly impressed upon the reader.

Pamphilus Gengenbach reported an imaginary conversation among an abbott, a courtesan, and the devil criticizing both the Roman curia and Luther. Gengenbach, a Basel printer, had no ties of loyalty to Luther. The hero of his piece was Pope Adrian, whose attempts to reform the papal court aroused complaints from the abbott and the courtier. Gengenbach scourged the papal court but he also criticized Luther for his lack of Christian humility and love of neighbor. Indeed, because of the misunderstanding which the common people had of his writing, Luther had become the servant of the devil. He had stirred up jealousy and envy and had set the secular authorities against the church. As a result, much blood would flow.[26] The devil, in this case, would win. Gengenbach still believed that the papacy could reform itself.

Nikolaus Herman, an obscure music teacher and choir director in the village of Joachimsthal, turned from hell to heaven, writing a letter from Jesus Christ.[27] As in Alber's pamphlets, the letter form was carefully followed. The conclusion read: "Given at the right hand of my heavenly father in the 1524th year after my birth, Jesus Christ, the living son of God and savior of the whole world."[28] This immensely popular pamphlet went through eight editions in the year it appeared.[29] In it Jesus Christ exhorted his people, reminding them that he had saved mankind not with gold or with armies but by seizing the devil and robbing him. This had cost him his life. Now he had been forgotten and his command-ments were badly taught, but he had left faith behind as a bastion to shield his people from the devil. He had sent his officials, also his spirit, and guns, halberds, and other military equipment, but nobody had noticed the dangers for hundreds of years.[30] The devil had taken over the castle of the Christian kingdom. By this letter Christ wished to recall his people to their allegiance. He would fight his enemy again and take back what he had lost. He would help them if they called on him with true and unquestioned faith.[31] The time was at hand, the enemy was declared. The people could not prevail against the devil with man-made arms but only with spiritual weapons. "The truth [my holy Word] will be as a girdle to your soul . . . [and] the breastplate of righteousness. On your feet [will be] the armor of the Gospel. . . . But above all, the shield of faith. . . . My Word shall be a sword to protect you against your enemy. If anyone comes to you with another sword [that is, human teaching] by which you can come to heaven, do not let him in your house, do not greet him. . . . Thus I will protect you against your enemies."[32]

The appeal of Herman's pamphlet lay in its directness. Alber wrote of a cunning, designing, and devious devil, but he existed in the third person, as "he." In the *Mandat* Christ spoke directly to the reader. The pronouns used were "I" and "you." Jesus proclaimed the strength of faith and gave his promise to lead the forces of truth against the devil. It was a powerful message.

In the same year, 1524, Jörg Motschidler, a master gunner in Wittenberg, wrote a violently anti-papal pamphlet to expose the danger of the papal threat to Luther and the moral corruption of the papacy.[33] The form of

Motschidler's pamphlet was complex, bordering on the bizarre. It opened with a description of the Pope meeting with his cardinals to decide what to do with the "cursed beast" Luther. Various suggestions were made by his advisors. They agreed on a plan to storm heaven and capture power from Christ. Letters sent out to the pope's allies, with the replies, formed the pamphlet's next section. An army having been mustered, a dialogue ensued at the gates of heaven between the Pope and his forces and an angel. The pamphlet closed with a poem summarizing the meaning of it all.[34] However complicated and confusing the structure, the clear intent was to show the willingness of the Pope to use all means of violence to silence Luther.

The meeting of the Pope with the cardinals was designed to show the treachery of the Romanists, their acceptance of murder and assassination to further their cause. The Pope began by saying that Christians, especially the Germans, had undertaken to overthrow the glory and the honor of the papacy. He had answered the criticisms of the cursed beast (Luther), but had been unable to overturn his writings. They must now move to a solution. One cardinal proposed that since Duke Frederick of Saxony had protected the brute they should send people to poison the Duke, then the Germans would stop supporting the execrated monk because they would fear the power of papal mandates. The Pope could then call on the other princes to hand over Luther, who would be forced to recant by torture. If he refused, the pope could kill him secretly and say that he had gone mad. This plan was rejected by the assembly of cardinals on the grounds that Frederick was too well loved by his people. His assassination would create only greater opposition to the papacy.[35]

The next suggestion was more ingenious. They should bring the learned in all lands over to their side. The preachers in those cities whose inhabitants still supported the papal side should be paid a subsidy. If they insisted on grounding their sermons in Scripture, the papacy should set up secret printers to publish Bibles and the Gospel according to "our" interpretation. These should be sent out to all lands, and it would be announced from the pulpits that these were the right and true texts of the Old and New Testaments and the Gospel, that the old texts had been falsified by Huss and Wyclif. It would be necessary to say that the new texts had just been discovered, but this would not be difficult because the coarse and drunken Germans would never notice.[36]

A cardinal rejected this scheme because people did not believe the Pope and the cardinals anymore. The solution, he said, lay in Scripture. "You, the pope, have been given full power from heaven. So, would it not be well to visit it, since things are going so badly on earth? For if you took the heavenly power, you could kill all those who stand in opposition to your holiness by fire and force. After which things might go well for us again."[37]

There was instant agreement. Letters were sent out to the papal allies. There was some hesitation on the part of the Swiss because they did not want to fight against Christ, but they relented when reminded that "the proverb in Switzerland says, we will fight anywhere for money, even to help the devil."[38] They did not, however, want to send Christ a formal declaration of war.

Once organized and in action, the papal forces were met at the gate of heaven by an angel. The dialogue which ensued pointed to the papal misunderstanding of the nature of Christ's power. Christ had rejected earthly power and had given an example of humility to his disciples by washing their feet, said the angel. "What Christ did for his disciples, washing their feet," replied the cardinals, "that we will not do. You do not know that Christ was poor and had nothing. But we are powerful and rich with silver, gold, land and people. And what is more, and true, all emperors must kiss the feet of the pope."[39] The cardinals insisted that they be given the key to heaven which Christ had given to Peter. In addition, they wished Christ to retract some of his words. The angel replied that since they had just said Christ was poor, they must realize that he had never had the wherewithal to make a key. The key had been lost by their own selfishness, so they should now go home and think about what the key really meant. The angel, never harsh, promised that the troops should have no fear of punishment. God would lift them up out of their need, he would have mercy on them.[40] In his conclusion, Motschidler stated that the pamphlet was to show what the clergy had done and why change was necessary:

Martin has written so much that is all truth
And will remain so forever without end.
. . . .
So it is my advice, which one can see herein,
That a reformation must occur,
And [we must] examine our mortal lives
So Christ will hover over us.[41]

Motschidler's vocabulary was inflammatory. Luther was referred to as the poisonous monk, the cursed monk, or the damned monk, more powerful in the German alliterative words *vergiften, vermaledeiten, verdampten*. The Pope and the cardinals spoke of their honor, their glory, their power, all of which must be maintained. There was a cumulative energy to the pamphlet which gave the reader little chance to question the villainy of the papacy. There was only good and evil, with no ground for compromise.

The anticlericalism of the lower officials and professionals exceeded that of any other class. The nobility detested the clergy because they had taken their lands. The patricians wanted their sons and daughters to leave the convents. The artisans scorned the clergy because they had not fulfilled their responsibility as teachers and spiritual leaders. The lower officials and professionals perceived the clergy as an abomination, full of tricks and sharp practices, who would stop at nothing to achieve their goals. Through all their pamphlets, except Gengenbach's, there ran a current of conspiracy. The Pope conspired with the devil, the devil with the Pope, the Pope with the cardinals. "We have our spies in all lands," said one of Motschidler's cardinals.[42] The compound Apostolicum had said he must inform the cardinals at Nuremberg of Christoph Scheurl's opposition and of the lèse-majesté of the herbs.[43] These authors were convinced of a papal conspiracy directed against Germany and the German people.

Balthasar Stanberger, writing from "the princely castle in Weimar," undermined the Pope by impugning the source of his power, denying that St. Peter had ever been the bishop of Rome.[44] His pamphlet, published in 1523, described a meeting between Peter and a peasant. The latter, wandering over the fields to thresh, thought of all the violence in the world and thanked God that he had let his Word be proclaimed so that the peasant with his threshing stick could achieve as much as a Carthusian with his rule. A handsome man greeted him, "God thanked him and would enlighten him with his strong faith." Who was he? the peasant asked. He was Peter, a fisher of men, the stranger replied. The peasant fell at Peter's feet, asking him to intercede with Christ for him so that he could achieve everlasting life. Peter told him to stand up and stop such talk, "I am a man like you. I cannot be your helper or intercessor because Christ alone is the helper, intercessor and mediator. I cannot promise you eternal life, God must give it to you."[45]

The peasant protested. Peter was a high holy one, near to God. The Pope had said that he had been in Rome, was a prince of Heaven and the gatekeeper to Christ, so he, as a poor peasant, should show him the greatest honor. Peter expostulated. He was never more than a poor fisherman. He did not want honor and titles. The only honor he had ever desired was to write about his savior. "Therefore, by God's order, Martin Luther has arisen, my brother co-apostle of Jesus Christ, who says the truth to the pope and his followers, namely that I was never in Rome and did not rule there. They do me an injustice for they have made me into a murderer, a bloodsucker of the poor."[46]

The peasant agreed that the rule of the church was heavy. He believed that priests and monks should have to work, that nuns and beguines should take pitchforks in their hands and support themselves and their children.[47] The peasant asked about Luther. Some said Luther was right, others that he was in error. How could the people know? Luther, replied Peter, was an angel, because "he who teaches and preaches God's Word is an angel . . . or prophet of God." Luther had been sent to bring God's Word to his mistreated sheep and had made clear that everyone's hope rested in faith.[48]

The peasant wanted to know what teachings were against the Gospel. The peasants, he continued, would like to have a Peasant's Council, bringing all clergy and secular people together. There Luther's opponents could dispute with Martin himself. The people would soon see who was right and, if the flail ruled, it would not be healthy for the clergy. "The peasants must make things right again . . . become again the lords of the house and give the clergy the flail so [the] children can be nourished." Peter responded that the peasant should do only what God ordered him to do. God's will made all human thought and intelligence foolishness. Let people follow the Pope if they wanted to, but the peasant should remain with Christ and not be pulled by the devil.[49]

As early as 1523, Stanberger, a minor official, was openly writing about the possibility of peasant action against the clergy. He was careful to have St. Peter caution the peasant and admonish him to follow the orders of God, but this was after he had proposed a Peasant's Council and permitted the peasant to threaten using the flail against the clergy. The early part of the dialogue was a clear denial of the papal claim to supremacy. From his desk in the castle at Weimar, Stanberger gave his overt support not only to the angel Luther but to the peasants as well.

The tense conditions in the countryside were widely recognized among the lower officials and technicians, nor was their anticlericalism limited to the Romanists. In 1524, Heinrich Vogtherr der Älter, an engraver, deplored the conditions in rural parishes where the nobility, although reformed, had appointed ignorant men to preach the Gospel. They were, he said, just as bad as the Roman priests they were meant to replace. Vogtherr's father was a barber-surgeon and oculist. The son had similar training, but without a university degree. He became a highly skilled engraver, which led him, eventually, to be a printer. From 1522 to 1525, he lived at Wimpfen am Neckar, apparently active as an engraver. His brother Georg was one of the major reformation preachers in Fruchtwungen. In 1525, Heinrich moved on to Strasbourg, where he worked as an engraver for other printers.[50]

Clemen believed that his pamphlet *A Christian Admonition against the Lutherans Who Shout from the Pulpit* (1524) was directed against Johann Schilling, the radical Franciscan preacher in Augsburg. Laube agreed that Vogtherr's propaganda was based on events in Augsburg but believed that he sided with the more moderate Lutherans.[51] The emphasis in Vogtherr's pamphlet, however, is on village and country churches, rather than on city churches. While the relationship between the uprisings in Augsburg and the villages in the city's territories is well known, Vogtherr described rural churches controlled by the nobility. Wimpfen was not very close to Augsburg, thus Vogtherr may have been addressing the problems in the countryside around him. The significance of the pamphlet lies not so much in whether it was written in Augsburg or Wimpfen, but in the fact that an educated man, a skilled engraver, was moved by the plight of the rural communities. Even more important, he was willing to criticize Lutheran clergy.[52]

Vogtherr first praised Luther, who had been driven by God, had worked on the holy Scriptures and brought them to the light of day. He had done great good to both the upper and lower estates, opening the Gospel to all. Yet, almost immediately, certain men had raised up their heads like malicious vipers and puffed-up frogs, praising themselves as Christian evangelical priests, but then boasted, slandered, and scolded all the world. They had been accepted as good men at first, but then it was seen that the trees they planted bore no fruit. Instead, their preaching led to pride and envy rather than to the enlightenment of the poor masses of Christians.[53]

Vogtherr believed that many preachers, prophets of Baal, had adopted Lutheran teaching as a cloak to hide their villainy and avarice. They were no different from the priests they had replaced. Frauds, hucksters, money-seekers, they had nestled down among the mighty princes, lords, and nobles. Their goal was to to increase their sacks without experiencing want or suffering.[54] Christ had had no shoes, no pocket book nor a staff, but these new pompous asses had no evangelical foundation. They claimed they had read Luther's books and called themselves the protectors of Christ's Gospel, although they might never have seen the cover of a book or looked at its contents, nor understood the tiniest point. Because of them the Gospel and Luther's books were despised and obstructed. In his final admonition, Vogtherr spoke directly to these Lutheran clerics, "Don't act so high and mighty, as though you carried heaven around on its axle, and as if you alone had God's spirit in all its fullness. . . . A group of pharisees, hucksters and devils [should] not be born from the evangelical clergy."[55]

Vogtherr was indignant at the damage these selfish and arrogant preachers inflicted on their parishioners. The needy poor were pressed to the ground while the pastors maintained themselves in pomp, living on generous benefices. God had done more than just create the world, he had grasped the hoe and dung fork to show that no one should pay others to work for them. No Christians should be idle. The true evangelical preacher should willingly give all he had to the poor—his house, hearth, property, and life. Instead, these clergy spent the money for the poor on themselves.[56]

It was a bleak picture. Although the Gospel had been opened, it had been corrupted by ambitious "evangelical" preachers more interested in their benefices than in their people. Country folk continued to suffer as they had before. Vogtherr's pamphlet may have revealed the state of many villages on the eve of the Peasants' War. The Reformation had not changed the social and economic realities of rural life. The following year the Peasants' War swept across southern Germany from Styria to Carinthia in the east, to Thuringia in the north, and to Hesse, the Palatinate, and Alsace in the south. Uprisings occurred in cities as well: Basel, Constance, Augsburg, Nuremberg, Frankfurt.

Haug Marschalck took the other side. In 1525, after he had helped to defeat the peasants in the territories surrounding Augsburg, as the captain of the imperial troops in the city, he wrote a dramatic account of the uprising. To him the Peasants' War was part of a continuing struggle between Christ and the devil, in which he had been directly involved. Marschalck had led his troops against the Duke of Württenburg in 1519, against the peasants in 1525. Later he would fight against the French in Italy.[57] He was not a learned man. In a dedicatory letter to one of his numerous pamphlets he explained that he had been taught the Word of God by the learned preachers of Augsburg. He had listened to their sermons, then asked questions. They had willingly shown the relevant Scripture to him. Back in his quarters, he had looked up the biblical passages himself.[58] His system had been successful. He had a sure grasp of his texts and his scriptural references were never extraneous or irrelevant. Biblical cadences gave his writing an energy of its own. It should be noted that he wrote *The Sharp Cannon* between the campaign against the peasants and the campaign in Italy. A lonely man in a tent, he appealed to his fellow-men to follow God instead of the devil.

Citing scripture, Marschalck described the battle between the truth of God and the wiles of the devil. As he put it, "I have undertaken a short writing drawn from Holy Scripture against the false Christians who . . . under the appearance of God's Word, wish to protect their uprisings. . . . Therefore, I have called the book after the casing of the cannon of the city of Nuremberg, for the cannon is such . . . that no one can stand before it. Just so it will be shown in this pamphlet that no attack by the devil or his mob can stand against the violent, strong bombardment of Holy Scripture."[59]

The struggle was presented entirely in military terms. There were two castles, God's and the devil's, the former fortified and based on the love of God, thus on the rejection of oneself; the other fortified with self-love, even to the rejection of God. Each castle had its own battle cry: the one, unity and peace; the other, riot and violence. Each city had its own cannon, its own leaders and captains. The captain of the castle of God, none other than Jesus Christ, charged that the devil protected himself behind an imaginary Christian freedom, basing his laws on this spurious freedom to impress the *gemeinen Mann*. His troops then sallied forth and shot their evil arrows against the magistrates, thinking they would attain freedom. The devil's horde could be destroyed by three things: the strong shot of the Old Testament, the forceful shot of the New Testament, or a barrage from both testaments showing how God had punished division and rebellion.[60]

Marschalck described the battle, shot for shot, first from the Old Testament, then from the New. Moses, he wrote, fired the first shot in Genesis 13: 6–9. When Abraham and Lot no longer wanted to live near one another, Abraham had said to Lot, I pray you, let us have no division between us, for we are brothers. "So you see," interjected Marschalck, "Abraham, the pious patriarch, did not want to have divisions between his shepherds and his brother's shepherds. What then should we Christians not do to avoid such quarreling and rebellion? I say we should give up everything we have before we give cause for such a rebellion."[61] The New Testament shots stressed peace with one another, for, as in one body all its parts are in harmony with one another, so it should be in the spiritual body, that no one part makes another suffer.[62]

The 20 shots, Marschalck wrote, were a manifestation of the power and force of Jesus Christ the King, who mediated to prevent violence. Thus, the rebels should join in unity, in the bond of peace, for misfortune had always fallen on the heads of those who led the rebellions, for example Lucifer, Korah, Dathan and Abiram, Ephraim and Jeptha.[63] The futility and unrighteousness of revolt was strongly asserted, supported entirely from the Word of God.

Marschalck shared the fear of conspiracy which had been present in Alber's and Motschidler's pamphlets, but he believed it was the people who were guilty of plotting. He gave his own description of how the revolt occurred, how men were drawn into the peasant armies. The common man fell because of his own selfishness, ignoring the common good.[64] God, however, promised the best fruit to a peaceful heart, "so when someone comes to you and whispers in your ear to plan a revolt, treat him as though he wanted to burn your house down."[65] The world was full of dangerous plotters, faithless, recreant men, with crooked mouths, a wink in their eye. They congregated with their feet, they spoke with their fingers, they made evil strikes with their hearts. These were the kind of "evangelical" men who led revolts.[66] Then there was the secret tale-bearer who created unrest and anger. He was like a torch set to wood which lit the fire. He too must be driven from the house.[67]

The picture of men meeting in dark corners, whispering in the streets and taverns, "congregating with their feet," was yet another indication of the mood which had taken hold in the land by 1525. The euphoria of the earliest years of the reform had dissipated, to be replaced by anxiety, mistrust, a fear of one group toward another. A handful of men, including a former episcopal administrator and an unknown Nuremberg burgher, began to think in broader terms. Aroused by the conditions around them, depressed by the failure of the Peasants' War, they proposed fundamental social and political reforms, outlining programs for a more just and equitable society. An eloquent plea of this sort had been made in 1520 or 1521 by the anonymous author of *Love God and Serve Him Alone*: "We are all created equal on earth, no one better than another, none nobler than another, none more handsome than another. Jew, heathen, gypsy, Turk, Christian, all come from the same clod of earth. This same creation no one must despise, scorn, make fun of . . . nor [fail to] take care of its needs."[68]

In 1523, *The Needs of the German Nation*, known as the Reforms of the Emperor Frederick III, spelled out specific steps to achieve this more just and equal society.[69] The pamphlet contained 13 articles, each presented separately with an explanation or exposition of what changes would be required. This formal organization is an indication that it was written by someone familiar with legal forms. At the end, the writer noted that "we are all gathered at the Diet"—the Diet of Nuremberg in 1523?[70]

The writer did not call for sweeping changes. He looked for the restoration of proper relationships, idealized from the past, not a revolution. His first article concerned the clergy. They should all be in order, in their correct rank, without respect to birth, inheritance, ability, or intelligence. Their duty was to praise God and to reveal the Word of God correctly to the common man; thus all parishes should be supplied with an honorable priest so that poor Christians would not be without a shepherd. The priests should receive their food and drink, and their needs should be taken care of. The buildings of the church should also be kept in order.[71]

Similarly, the nobility should conduct themselves according to their station as ordered in the empire. They should obey the law, so that the poor man on his land would be left untroubled and maintained "in his human freedom."[72] In the cities, all the communes and *Gemeinde* should be governed without regard to their old freedoms, customs, traditions or oaths, but instead according to Christian freedom and natural reason, so that all men would be equal and middling (*leidlich*). Thus the *gemeynen nutz* would increase among the poor as well as the rich. The authorities in all cities would be responsible to provide for the artisans and other workers. All should be paid wages to cover their costs and their labor. A moratorium on debt would be proclaimed so that all goods pledged to the rich would be returned to their rightful owners. Thus, "with brotherly love and the common need, no one would have to worry that anyone would lose his wages and his property. With such provisions all the estates in the empire will come out honorable and be able to progress, [because] the selfish needs of each commune are broken."[73]

The remaining articles proposed to limit the power of the great merchants, and, by dimishing the influence of doctors of law in the courts and in all affairs of justice, to limit the centralization of the courts. Similarly, clerical control would be restricted in princely and city councils. There was the usual call for centralization of customs, a common currency, and common weights and measures.[74] The *Norturfft* was a typical fourteenth-century program of social reform, looking back to an irrecoverable past.

In 1523, Pamphilus Gengenbach, the Basel printer, made a proposal for reform.[75] Although his earlier pamphlet had supported Pope Adrian, the success of the First Zurich Disputation changed him. The Zurich city council had confirmed Ulrich Zwingli's right to proclaim the Gospel. Gengenbach hoped this would lead to a reform among the clergy and the laity throughout Christendom. The pamphlet, *The Three Christians*, purported to be a conversation after the disputation between a Roman Christian, a Bohemian Christian, and a Turkish Christian who had met at an inn.[76] It bears the signs of being hastily cobbled together, perhaps drawing on pamphlets available in Gengenbach's shop. The account of the nobleman echoes the pamphlets put out by Sickingen's circle. Gengenbach's nobleman complained that the souls, bodies, and property of the Germans were all in the hands of the Roman clergy.[77] The Bohemian Christian was given very little space. Gengenbach may have copied from the numerous biographies of Huss which appeared in the pamphlet literature after 1520. The articles of faith of the Hussite church were summarized, but there was no discussion of social changes or reforms.[78]

Gengenbach's emphasis was on the Turkish Christian and the Serbian city where he lived. By 1523, the establishment of a common chest to take care of the poor had become a significant part of the program of the urban reformation. The Turkish Christian's common chest, however, went well beyond anything that had been proposed or inaugurated in Germany. His city had achieved a communal utopia. The Christian order they enjoyed was a new accomplishment, said the Turk.[79] In the past, things had been very bad in Turkish lands. "If a hen went out on the street, it belonged to the clergy . . . they tithed every pig sty." But the Christians had fought a long war against the Turks. No Christian powers had come to their aid. Finally, they negotiated a peace which permitted them to keep their Christian faith and govern themselves, paying only a yearly tribute to the Turks. The war led to a reorganization of the city. Because the monks had not helped during the war, their convents were closed down. A pious pastor had drawn up a new order to govern both clergy and laity. The order stated "that the salvation of every Christian lay in two things, first, in the love of God, second, in the love of one's neighbor. Everyone had to obey this or be severely punished, and they had started with the clergy."[80]

The new laws provided for the defense of the city and the care of the poor. All church property, whether in land, tithes, or usury, was put together in a common house and a common sack. These revenues were used to support the clergy and to provide for their training. A House of the

Knights of Christ was created. Fifty nobles were always in residence, each receiving 100 gulden from the common sack, whose duty was to protect the city, to practice knightly exercises, and to study. One presumes they studied Scripture, because the clergy were chosen from among them. Fifty burgher children were also chosen to live in the House of Knights: 25 sang the church services, the others studied any university they chose but were dedicated to the city, like the knights.[81]

There were no poor people in the city nor on the land. No foreigners, men or women, were allowed to beg in the city. Everyone who could work was required to do so. "He who will not work is forbidden the land." Orphans, men, and women who had fallen on poor days, whether they dwelt in the city or on the land, as well as people who had no craft, were placed in the house of the common chest and were supported. The boys were taught a craft. Money from the common sack was distributed to the poor so that the peasants did not suffer if their crop failed; other poor were helped according to their circumstances.[82] Gengenbach broadened the reformers, proposal for a common chest to create an ordered community which met the economic needs of all its citizens. Public funds were assigned to the nobility to train them for war and as priests.

The originality of Gengenbach's community lay in the House of Knights. To support the nobility and train them for military duty and as pastors ignored established class lines and functions. Was it an attempt to say that the nobility should be responsible and dependent on the city? They would no longer possess private wealth but would be supported by public funds. In a sense this echoed the requests of the knights for the return of their lands, but provided them with a salary instead of landed wealth. Gengenbach envisioned an extended community which integrated the nobility, the clergy, burgher children, and the poor, blurring traditional lines of rank. The goal was the fulfillment of the two great commandments, the love of God and of one's neighbor.

The most radical programs for reform were written after the Peasants' War. Michael Gaismair and Hans Hergot both supported the peasants, Gaismair as a leader. Afterward, despite the rout of the peasant forces, Gaismair and Hergot drew up careful, considered plans for a reform of society based on the communal holding of property. It is noteworthy that these plans come out of this intermediate social rank. Although the artisans wrote in eloquent detail of the problems of the poor and the unemployed, they offered no solution except Christian charity. The upper civil servants and one nobleman supported the establishment of a common chest, but it was the middle rank of the hierarchy which envisioned a new social order. Both writers lost their lives because of their radicalism.

Michael Gaismair's plan for a new order, never printed, does not meet the criterion for a *Flugschrift*, but his influence on Hergot makes it essential to outline his program. Gaismair had served as an administrator for the Bishop of Brixen, leaving his post to join the peasants when the revolt broke out.[83] He was elected commander of the peasants' army in the Tyrol in May 1525. Despite the failure of the movement, perhaps because of it, in 1526 he drew up a *Landesordnung* for a new Tyrol, which was preserved in manuscript and has been published frequently in recent times.[84]

Gaismair's purpose was to honor God and serve the *gemeinen nutz*, a phrase repeated over and over again. First, a godly community had to be established. Godless people who persecuted the Word of God were to be forced out, ridden out of the land. From then on, all things were to be based on the holy Word of God, and everybody would live accordingly. God's Word should be truly and honestly preached in "Gaismair's Landt," any other preachers, sophists, and canon lawyers being run off, their books burned. Images in the churches would be destroyed. A learned pastor would be established in every parish, supported by the tithe. Tithes left over would go to the poor. Cloisters and the property of knightly orders would be turned into hospitals.[85]

The core of Gaismair's order was the parish. The parish preacher was the leader of his people. If God's commandments were known, people would have need of little else. Like the author of the *Teutscher Nation Notturfft*, Gaismair was deeply concerned about equality. Like that author he recommended the abolition of privileges or "freedoms," so that no person would have an advantage over another. This would be achieved, in part, by tearing down all city walls and all castles so that there would be no segregated units but only villages. This, he believed, would abolish pride and prevent insurrection because there would be complete equality in the land.[86]

Legal procedures would be simplified and justice made available to the lower classes. Judges chosen by an appropriate local person, such as the pastor, could be supported with least cost to the community. Judges and eight jury men would be elected yearly. Court would be held every Monday, and no appeals would be permitted to a higher court because this led to more expense. A university was to be established in the community as the administrative center of the *Land*. Only the Word of God would be taught, and three professors, learned in Scripture, would always sit in the governing body.[87]

Gaismair had farsighted plans for developing the economy of the Tyrol. The chief administrator would be responsible not only for defense but also for the maintenance of roads, mountain passes, bridges, waterways, and dikes. Swamps and other wasteland would be improved and made arable, new crops would be introduced, and vineyards would be developed as in Italy. A special section on mining and the mining industry brought the ordinance to a close.[88]

It was, despite its brevity, a detailed, pragmatic plan. The economic section was unique. The ideal, to honor God and the common good, was translated into specific changes to create an egalitarian society. At no time did Gaismair, the former bishop's administrator, quote from Scripture, but it is clear that he envisioned a village economy in which property was shared as in early Christian times. His proposals to force out all those who did not agree and to abolish cities were prophetic of utopias to come.

The following year, 1527, Hans Hergot, a Nuremberg printer, published a pamphlet, *On the New Transformation of a Christian Life,* which he may have written himself.[89] Based on the same principle of "everything for the honor of God and the common good," Hergot developed a detailed plan down to the last cow. The system, based on community of property, provided for the education of children outside their own families as well as reeducation for those who refused to conform. The religious element in Hergot's community was far stronger than in Gaismair's.

Hans Hergot wrote that as a poor man he wished to proclaim that God would now humble all estates, villages, castles, chapters, and cloisters and would establish a new "transformation," in which no one would say "this is mine." The cities would be brought low, noble birth would disappear, and the monastic orders would lose their cloisters, tithes, and rents. The divisions in the reformed movement would also disappear. All would be united. All property would be used in common. This would occur, wrote Hergot, because Christ had said, in John 10, that there would be one shepherd and one sheepfold.[90]

The new system would be based on a unit of land called the *Flür,* sufficient in size to support its people and a church. The church would be the center of the community, to which everyone would belong. The head of the church would be "the provider of the house of God" and would also act as village chief or mayor.[91] The land would be free of all tithes and dues, although it would be granted to the people by the nobility, who would live under a disciplined rule like the Carthusians. Those who had sinned or were unwilling to accept these changes would live in a separate house until they repented and were willing to join the community. Although the cities would be reduced to rubble, essential artisans would live in each *Flür,* but would have to follow correct practices, seeking not their own selfish ends but the *gemeinen nutz.* So the words of the Our Father would be fulfilled, "and we will take to heart the words our Lord so often said 'our, our, our.'"[92]

Several *Flür* created a *Land,* whose lord was chosen by the pastors. Twelve *Länder* made up a quarter. A university would be established in each quarter, one to teach Greek, the second Latin, the third Hebrew. The quarters were referred to by the language taught, the Greek quarter, etc.[93] At the universities, where men would learn to honor God and the common good, all the books needed for the community would be there. The university men would arrange for church services to be held in every *Flür*, more of them and better than those in any cloister. Small children would be taken to church when young, and the church provider would bid those adults with the best conduct to bring them up as their true father to the honor of God and the common good. Female children would be given to pious women from the same house.[94]

The plans for the new community were interrupted by a bitter attack on learned men in the princely courts and the cities, who judged their knowledge to be greater than God's knowledge. God, wrote Hergot, had had nothing to do with learned men when he was on earth. Instead he had gone to poor fishermen and tax collectors.[95] The wisdom of the learned was to kill the peasants. If they had taught people correctly, the Peasants' War would not have come about. However, no one should ever believe that the War happened because of books or writing. It had come from God. "I believe," he continued, "that God will never again arouse the peasants against their lords because [by the revolt] God did good things for the nobility and the learned but they have been ungrateful."[96]

Hergot ended with a striking image: "There are three tables in the world. The first is overflowing and has too much on it. The second is moderately laid with a comfortable amount of what is essential. The third is totally wanting. So those from the overflowing table come and wish to take bread from the needy table. From this conflict arises, and God will overthrow the superabundant table and the humble table and maintain the middle table."[97]

Both Gaismair and Hergot lost their lives shortly after the publication of their pamphlets. A directive dated 13 June 1526, from the authorities at Innsbruck to the governor at Nellenberg, thanked the latter for his report on Gaismair. A physical description depicted Gaismair as a tall, haggard, thin man, 34 or 35 years old, with a seemly countenance, a shaved head, very eloquent in his speech.[98] Forced to leave the Tyrol, he was welcomed by the Venetians and received a good pension because, under the League of Cognac of 1526, Venice and Austria were enemies. It was, however, impossible to protect Gaismair adequately, and he fell to an assassin's knife.[99] Hans Hergot was pursued by Luther, who complained that the printer was publishing false copies of his New Testament. It was also believed that Hergot had published Thomas Müntzer's attack on Luther, *Hochverursachte Schutzred*, which may have been clandestinely printed by one of Hergot's journeymen on his master's press. The *Neuen Wandlung* was another matter. The book made its way to Leipzig, where it was bought by students. The university, the city, and Duke Georg became embroiled as to who should discipline the students. Hergot was arrested and executed. No materials with regard to his trial remain in the city records.[100]

The lower officials and professionals were frustrated, often angry men.

Placed in the very middle rank of urban society, they could see the social and economic needs of the urban working class and the peasants. They were, however, unable to initiate policy and were forced to deal with the delays and ineptitude of the bureaucracy above them. Haug Marschalck wrote letter after letter to the city council of Augsburg asking them to pay his men.[101] Michael Gaismair, after serving as secretary to the Bishop of Brixen and, later, as tax collector in Klausen, was moved by the conditions he saw to forsake his career and join the peasants in 1525.[102] The tone of their pamphlets was often strident and biting. All were bitterly anti-papal, anti-monastic, anticlerical. The vehemence of their attack on the papacy was matched only by Ulrich von Hutten, but his tirades were more personal. He hated the Pope because he had been placed under the papal ban. Alber, Bosler, Gengenbach, and Motschidler attacked the Pope as the embodiment of evil, the stand-in for the devil. The Pope as personally responsible for the demise of Christendom was dramatically depicted in Motschidler's description of the Pope and his cardinals meeting in council. The difference in tone from the artisans' pamphlets is notable. The minor officials and technicians thought in confrontational terms, while the craftsmen avoided discord. Almost always, at the end of an artisan pamphlet, there was an attempt to reconcile, to bring opposing sides together. Not so among these men.

The lower professionals and officials were highly critical of the judicial system, the arrogance of lawyers, the high cost of taking a case to court. These were common complaints at the time. Strauss referred to lawyers as "a profession under indictment" in these decades. They were regarded as quarrelsome, crooked, and greedy men who dragged out cases for years in order to enrich themselves.[103] They had no respect for papal courts nor for the canon law. They despised the great merchants. The *Need of the German Nation* called for the abolition of the great merchants and their trading societies. No one should be permitted to invest more than 10,000 gulden in an enterprise.[104] This attitude was expressed in other programs for social reform, where the cities were to be destroyed to be replaced by an agrarian economy. The writers scorned the learned, whom they perceived as sophists who wished to play with God's Word or to disregard Christ's commandments. The simplicity of the disciples, the fact that they came from the lower class and were coarse, unrespectable people, was a theme repeated by one writer to the other.[105]

Despite their genuine conversion to Lutheranism, few members of this group wrote about their spiritual life, nor did they try to disseminate Lutheran theology. They seldom mentioned justification by faith, grace, or the working of God's mercy. Only Haug Marschalck and Balthasar Stanberger revealed their inner religious ideas. The former wrote two pamphlets on the Word of God which were, in essence, a biography of Jesus, the embodiment of the *Verbum Dominum*. In moving and eloquent language, Marschalck described the birth at Bethlehem as a beautiful, holy *Reichstag*, which made heaven and earth rejoice. All should stay in peace until the Word of God had grown and born fruit through the tree of Christ, which is in all men.[106] In the second part he described Jesus' life as a teacher and the crucifixion. Following his example, people should not be concerned with outward things nor depend on human reason, human faithfulness, or human ceremonies. Rather, they should let God work in all things.[107] Stanberger wrote an exhortation to faith and love of one's neighbor in impassioned religious language.[108]

More than any other rank, the minor officials and technicians believed that the solutions to disorder and injustice were political and social. The power of the Pope had to be destroyed and with it the power of the clergy. As was the case with the knights, Gaismair's and Hergot's plans for change should not be regarded as those of impractical dreamers or radicals. Their proposals, sweeping and visionary though they were, grew out of constitutional experiments in Upper Swabia, the Black Forest, Alsace, and Franconia during the Peasants' War of 1525.[109] They are evidence, as well, of the powerful attraction exerted by the Swiss Confederation in southwest Germany.[110] Like the knightly pamphleteers in 1520–1522, the minor official and the printer still were convinced that change was possible. Their plans reflected the belief that there were valid and practical alternatives to the traditional landlord-peasant relationship, in particular strong communal associations based on rural or urban communes with power to elect officials, particularly pastors and judges. A territorial organization would knit these units together in an assembly representing the different estates or a federation based on the Swiss model. At all levels, the laws would be based on the principles of godly law.[111] Constitutions of this sort had been put in place by the Christian Association of the Allgäu, Lake Constance, and Beltringen, and by the Salzburg peasants in 1525.[112] They were revolutionary proposals of reorganization but providing new norms of order, namely, godly law as the fundamental principle of government and a political system which could assume the functions traditionally in the hands of feudal lords. These constitutions had furnished an effective organization for the peasant armies and received support from the territorial towns, particularly in the Tyrol, Württemberg, and Thuringia, where the majority of townsfolk joined the peasants.[113]

The Gaismair and Hergot pamphlets are important because they show the links between the rural and urban areas. Both writers were urban men, yet, as Blickle has said, Hergot's *New Transformation* "carried the political ideas developed during the Revolution of 1525 to their intellectually most compelling conclusion."[114] The suburban areas of territorial towns and some of imperial free cities had firmly backed the peasants, in part because their economic circumstances were equally precarious.[115] Both groups, peasants and the lower urban ranks, shared a common vision of an equitable society based on Christian laws assuring justice to all. This was also a common theme of the pamphlets written by the artisans.

Notes

1. Gerhard Lenski, *Power and Privilege*, 1966, 243, 246. See also, Peter Blickle, *The Revolution of 1525*, 1981, 116–118.
2. Max Steinmetz, "John Virdung von Hassfurt," in ed., Hans-Joachim Köhler, *Flugschriften als Massenmedium* . . ., 1981, 360.
3. #59, Ulrich Bossler, *Dialogus* . . . *des Appostolicums Angelica* (Speyer: Johann Eckhart, 1521), fol. Aii.
4. Ibid.
5. Sarah Garland, *The Complete Book of Herbs and Spices*, 1979, 204, 272, 249.
6. Hieronymus Brunschwig, *Das ist das buch der Cirurgia* (Weiler im Allgau: Editions Medicina Rara Ltd., n.d.), fol. cxviii.
7. #59, Bossler, *Dialogus*, fol. Aii[v].
8. Ibid., fols. Aiii–Aiii[v].
9. Ibid., fol. Aiv.
10. Ibid., fols. Aiv[v].
11. Ibid., fols. Bii[v]–C, below fol. Ciii[v].
12. #205, Haug Marschalck, *Von der weyt erschollen Namen Luthers* . . . (Strasbourg: A. Farckel, 1523), Fiche 10/#41.
13. "Zum ersten haben sye sich bedacht zurechen an seinem namen . . . er heyss nit der lauterer/sonder der trüber/er mach des Christenlichen glaub trüb, welcher lang lauter sey gewesen. . . . Zum anderen/sprechen sie/er heyss der Lotter/unnd die ihm und der schrifft glauben synd lotterisch/bübisch. . . . Zum letzten sprechen sie, er sey ain Laur . . . wol ungehorsam seinden Bann nymmer volgn/wol zu aynem lauren wedenn.[11]
14. Ibid., fols. Aii–Aii[v].
15. Ibid.
16. Ibid., fols. Aiii[v]–Aiv.
    L = Loud (clear) evangelical teaching
    U = Unrestrained (overflowing) grace of the Holy Spirit
    T = True servant of Christ
    These mean:
    H = Helias who revealed the anti-Christ
    E = Enoch
    R = Rabbi, that he has become master of all blasphemers of Scripture
17. Heiko Oberman, *Luther, Man between God and the Devil*, 1989, 12.
18. Ibid., 10.
19. #55 Erasmus Alber, *Absag/oder Vehd schrift des Lucifers an Luther zu gesandt*, in Otto Clemen, *Flugschriften aus den ersten Jahren* der Reformation, 4 vols. (1907–1911), 3, 359.
20. Ibid., 356.
21. #57, Erasmus Alber, *Schöne Dialogus von Martino Luther und der geschickten*

Botschaft aus der Hölle (n.p.:n.p., 1523). Summarized in Otto Clemen, *Flugschriften*, 3, 357–358. This was identified by Alfred Götze, the sub-editor, as Alber's first pamphlet (358).

22. #55, Erasmus Alber, *Absag oder Vehdschrifft* . . . (Speyer: Johann Fabri, 1524); Clemen, *Flugschriften aus den ersten Jahren*, 3, 363. Title page.

23. Ibid., 365.

24. Ibid., 365–366.

25. Ibid., 359.

26. #126, [Pamphilus Gengenbach], *Ein kläglichs gespräch* . . . *von einem Apt, Curtisanen und dem Teüfel, wider den frommen Pabst Hadrian* (Basel: P. Gengenbach, 1522), in Clemen, *Flugschriften aus den ersten Jahren*, 3, 5, 21.

27. *ADB*, 12, 186.

28. #158, Nicolaus Herman, *Ein Mandat Jhesu Christi an alle seyne getrewen Christen* (n.p.:n.p., 1524). Fiche 1062/#2680, fol. Biii^v.

29. Clemen, *Flugschriften aus den ersten Jahren*, Vol. 2, 253–255.

30. #158, Manuel, *Ein Mandat* . . ., fol. Aii, Aii^v–Aii.

31. Ibid., fols. Aiv^v–B.

32. Ibid., fols. Bii–Biii.

33. Otto Clemen, *Kleine Schriften zur Reformationsgeschichte*, 1897–1944, 5 vols., 4, 117.

34. #209, Jörg Motschidler, *Ein Underred des Bapsts und seiner cardinalen* . . . (n.p.:n.p., 1524), in *Satiren und Pasquille aus der Reformationszeit*, ed., Oskar Schade, 3 vols. (1863), 3, 75–100.

35. Ibid., 76–79.

36. Ibid., 80.

37. Ibid., 81.

38. Ibid., 90.

39. Ibid., 94.

40. Ibid., 95, 96.

41. Ibid., 98, 100.

42. Ibid., 80.

43. #59, Bossler, *Appostolicums*, fols. Aiii^v–Aiv.

44. The reference to Stanberger's position in Weimar comes from the title page of his pamphlet #259, *Ein Epistel oder Sendtbrieff Balthasar Stanberger* . . . *seinem geliebten bruder in Christo Michel Buchfürer aus den Furstlichen schloss gen Erffurdt zu geschriben* (Erfurt: Michel Buchfürer, 1523), Laube, Vol. 1, pp. 222–225. The letter exhorts his friend, the printer Buchfürer, to have faith in Christ, to love his brother, and to be zealous in the printing of the Word of God. Since Stanberger's pamphlets were addressed to a popular audience and lacked the structure and formal legal reasoning of the learned civil servants, I have assumed he was a secretary or clerk rather than a counselor or an official at the court.

45. #257, Balthasar Stanberger, *Dialogus zwischen Petro und aynem Bawrn* . . . (Erfurt: Michael Buchfürer, 1523), Clemen, 3, 200–201.

46. Ibid., 201–202.

47. Ibid., 202–203.

48. Ibid., 205, 207.

49. Ibid., 211–212.

50. François Ritter, *Histoire de l'imprimerie alsacienne, au XVe et XVIe siècles*, 1955, pp. 281–288; ed. Adolf Laube, et al., *Flugschriften der frühen Reformationsbewegung, 1518–1524*, 2 vols. (1989), 1, 488.

51. Laube et al., *Flugschriften*, ibid.
52. #274, Heinrich Vogtherr der Älter, *Ain Cristliche anred unnd ermanung sich vor den grossen Lutherischen Schreyern und Cantzel schendern zu verhütten* . . . (Augsburg: Heinrich Steiner, 1524). Ed. Laube et al., *Flugschriften*, 1, 487.
53. Ibid., 480.
54. Ibid., 481. Laube et al., point out, in fn. 8, p. 489, that, according to Thomas Müntzer, suffering was essential to the attainment of perfection.
55. Ibid., 485–486.
56. Ibid., 481, 485.
57. Paul Russell, *Lay Theology in the Reformation*, 1986, 127–128.
58. #202, Haug Marschalck, *Das heilig ewig wort gottis/was das in ym krafft* . . . *erwecken mag* (Zwickau: n.p., 1524), Fiche 1111/#2836, fol. Ai^v.
59. #204, Haug Marschalck, *Die Scharf Metz wider die, die sich evangelisch nennen und doch dem Evangelio entgegen sind*, 1525. Clemen, *Flugschriften aus den ersten Jahren*, 1(3), 105.
60. Ibid., 105–107.
61. Ibid., 108.
62. Ibid., 114.
63. Ibid., 121–122.
64. Ibid., 107.
65. Ibid., 109.
66. Ibid., 111.
67. Ibid., 115.
68. #25, *Hab Gott lieb unnd diene im allein* (n.p.:n.p., 1520–1521), Fiche 612/#1576, fol. Bii.
69. #47, *Teütscher Nation notturfft: Die Ordnung und Reformation aller Stendt ym Römischen Reych. Durch Kayser Fridrich den driten* . . . (n.p.:n.p., n.d.), Fiche 531/#1355. The author of this pamphlet is still unknown. Just before the conclusion, at the end of the articles, a name appears: "Georg Rixner genant Jherusalem Römischer Keiserlicher Mayestat und des reychs Ernhalt," fol. Eiii^v. H. Werner, "Die sogenannte' Reformation des Kaisers Friedrich III', ein Reichsreformplan der westdeutschen Ritterschaft" (1909), however, attributed the pamphlet to Hartmut von Cronberg. Karl Schottenloher, in *Flugschriften zu Ritterschaftsbewegung* (1929), rejected this on the grounds that the emphasis on the free development of the common good and the poor man, as well as the advocacy of the cities, removed Cronberg as a possible author. Robert Lutz, in *Wer war der Gemeine Man?* (1979), attributed it to an unknown Nuremberg burgher. O. Schiff "Forschungen . . . Bauren Krieges," (1919/20) was inclined to believe it came out of Nuremberg, written by Georg Rixner, a herald in the service of the Count Palatine Frederick, *Statthalter* for the Reichsregiment in Nuremberg, 1521–1523, a view supported by Klaus Arnold, "Reichsherold und Reichs reform," 1984. Laube et al. in *Flugschriften*, 2, 788, concluded that no final determination could be made. Tom Scott and Bob Scribner, in the *German Peasants' War* (1991), 259, attributed it to Friedrich Weigandt, an official of the elector of Mainz in Miltenberg, which is the attribution I accept.
70. #47, *Teutscher Nation notturfft*, fol. Eii^v.
71. Ibid., fol. Aii^v–Aiii.
72. Ibid., fol. Aiii^v. "Und im sein menschlich freyheit auch gehalten werde."
73. Ibid., fols. Bi–Bii.
74. Ibid., fols. Biii^v–Eiv.

75. For biographical information see K. Lendi *Die Dichter Pamphilus Gegenbach*, 1926, and R. Raillard, *Pamphilus Gegenbach und die Reformation*, 1936.
76. #130, Pamphilus Gengenbach, *Von dreien Christen*. *Dem Römischen Christen*. *Dem Böhemschen Christen*. *Dem Thürkischen Christen* (Basel: P. Gengenbach, 1523), Laube et al., *Flugschriften*, 1, 239.
77. Ibid., 228–232.
78. Ibid., 237–238.
79. Laube et al., *Flugschriften*, 1, 230, identify the area as Serbia, the city was perhaps on the Morava.
80. Ibid., 233.
81. Ibid., 234.
82. Ibid., 236–237.
83. Lutz, *Wer war der gemeine Mann?* 34.
84. "Michael Gaismair's Tiroler Landesordnung," 1526, in Adolf Laube and H.-W. Seiffert, eds., *Flugschriften der Bauernkriegszeit*, 1975, 586.
85. Ibid., 139–140.
86. Ibid., 139.
87. Ibid., 139–140.
88. Ibid., 141–143.
89. #157, Hans Hergot, *Von der newen wandlung einen Christlichen Lebens* (Leipzig: Michael Blum, 1526 or 1527), in ed., Laube and Seiffert, *Flugschriften der Bauernkriegszeit*, 547–557, 642–643. Hergot's authorship is questioned by Blickle, but he states that the pamphlet can be accepted as connected with the Peasant's War (*The Revolution of 1525*, 1981, 150). Laube and Seiffert, *Flugschriften der Bauernkriegszeit*, 642, accept the attribution to Hergot. Hergot had been linked to the radicals of the Reformation by the publication of a Thomas Murner pamphlet in 1524. He traveled in an extended territory, selling books and buying manuscripts. This gave him contacts in Saxony, Zwickau, and the area near Ulm. Between 1524 and 1526, he brought out seven illustrated editions of the New Testament. My thanks to Heidi L. Eberhardt for this information.
90. #157, Hergot, *Newen wandlung*, 547.
91. Blickle, *The Revolution of 1525*, 151.
92. #157, Hergot, *Newen wandlung*, 549.
93. Ibid., 550–551. See Blickle, *The Revolution of 1525*, 151–153 for graphs and a description of this early representative system.
94. #157, Hergot, *Newen wandlung*, 548.
95. Ibid., 552–553.
96. Ibid., 555–556.
97. Ibid., 557.
98. *Der Deutsche Bauernkrieg*, *Aktenband*, ed. Günther Franz, 1935, 338, #162.
99. ADB, 8, 314.
100. *Ibid.*, 12, 212.
101. Fr. Roth, "Wer war Haug Marschalck, genannt Zoller von Augsburg?", BBK, 6, 1900, 230.
102. ADB, 8, 313.
103. See Gaismair, *Landesordnung*, 140; #157, Hergot, *Newen wandlung*, 552–553; #47, *Teütscher Nation Notturfft*, fol. Biii–Ciiii; #209, Motschidler, 78. See also Gerald Strauss, *Law, Resistance and the State*, 1986, 8–13.
104. #47, *Teütscher Nation notturfft*, fols. Dii–Dii^v.
105. #25, *Hab Gott lieb unnd diene jm allein*, fol. Bii; Marschalck, #200, *Edles Schönes*

lieplichs Tractatlein von den . . . *ewigen wort* (*Verbum Domini*), fols. Aiv^v, Bii; #124, Gengenbach, *Der Ewangelischburher*, fol. Aiii^v; #56, Alber, *Gesprech büchlein von einem Bawern* . . ., 215– 216.

106. #200, H. Marschalck, *Edles schönes lieplichs Tractatlein*, fols. Ai^v, Aiii.
107. #202, H. Marschalck, *Das heilig ewig wort gottis* . . ., fol. Aiv^v.
108. #259, B. Stanberger, *Ein Epistel oder Sendbrieff*, passim.
109. P. Blickle, *The Revolution of 1525*, 155.
110. Thomas A. Brady, Jr., *Turning Swiss, Cities and Empire, 1450–1550*, 1985, 5–7.
111. P. Blickle, *The Revolution of 1525*, 155.
112. Ibid., 97–99; 101–103.
113. Ibid., 117.
114. Ibid., 153.
115. Ibid., 118.

5   "A letter from an honorable married woman to a cloistered woman with regard to a sermon on certain Holy Scripture which the cloistered woman burned."

A nun, sitting in a well furnished cell, burns a sermon sent to her by her married sister. The pamphlet is written in the form of a letter.

SOURCE: Title page of a pamphlet written by a patrician woman entitled: *Ain Sendbrieff von einer erbern frawen in Felichen stand an ain Kloster frauen, gethon über berümung ettlicher hayliger geschrifft in sermon begriffen. So die Kosterfraw verbrent und darauff ain lange ungesaltzne geschrifft zu ursach erzelt hat.* N.p.: n.p., 1524.
Courtesy of the Zentralbibliothek, Zurich, Switzerland.

6

The Urban Elite and the Convents

THE URBAN ELITE

The cities were separated from the countryside not only by their walls but by their way of life, their economic activities, and their political position. In the imperial free cities like Augsburg, Strasbourg, and Nuremberg, where most of the pamphlets were written, the princes and the emperor had less direct influence than they had in rural areas. Technically, the free cities were politically autonomous, making their own laws, sending their own diplomats, sending representatives as observers to the Diet of the Empire. They could enter alliances with the princes, to whom they were not subject. Smaller cities were ruled by the prince of their territory but had their own constitution, their own city council, their own elite. The city wall defined urban people politically. It drew the boundary which made the citizens free men.

The governing elite, sometimes calling themselves patricians, dominated urban social, political, and ecclesiastical life. Some were noble, owning land outside the city, engaging in military life as knights, and also participating actively in the government of the city. Others came from mercantile backgrounds but had accumulated sufficient wealth to live entirely on income from lands and investments. All patrician families were closely tied to the church. Their ancestors had been some of the great benefactors, building chapels, dedicating altars, endowing these with benefices, supporting monastic orders. In many cities the chapter of one of the major churches was reserved for family members of the local patriciate. Convents were also dominated by the sons and daughters of elite families. Roper found records for 136 women who were members of Augsburg convents from 1517 to 1550. Of them, 40% came from elite families.[1] Though only a small minority of the urban population, the urban elite were present at every level of power, secular and ecclesiastical.

Pamphleteers from the elite were a tiny cohort of seven people, who reflect the social diversity within the group. Eckhard zum Drübel and Matthias Wurm von Geudertheym were members of the urban nobility in Strasbourg. Drübel, whose pamphlets were discussed in a preceding chapter, lived as a knight on his lands. He wrote nothing about the convents. The Wurm family, only recently ennobled, held no offices in Strasbourg. Kaspar Nützel, on the other hand, was a powerful member of the Nuremberg city council. Bernard Rem, from a minor and politically uninfluential Augsburg elite family, was organist to the Fugger family. The other three writers were women, two of whom wrote anonymously. One called herself "a convert," the other, using the conventional designation of the patriciate, referred to herself as an "honorable" married woman.[2] The third woman was Bernard Rem's cloistered sister. The striking element of this group of pamphlets is their sharp focus on monastic life, five attacking it, one a defense, one establishing a new reformed rule. Why this concentration of interest? The Reformation had a particular effect on the patricians. These families had a large proportion of family members in convents, and when the cities began to take over the monastic orders, it was their sons, daughters, brothers, sisters, nieces, and nephews who were affected. Faced by these changes, a few of the patricians who had swung over to the new faith wrote to their relatives setting forth the truth of the new doctrines, urging them to give up convent life and rejoin the family in the world. Several of the letters, written in response to letters from the cloister, provide a unique opportunity to hear a genuine dialogue, each person setting forth their own convictions. The chapter will begin with the longest of these pamphlets, a letter which metastasized into a 120-page treatise. The more intimate family exchanges will follow.

The elite were well-educated, and read Luther's writings eagerly. For those who accepted the new faith, the doctrine of justification had particular meaning. Absorbing this teaching and applying it to their own lives, they saw the benefactions of their forbears and the lives of their relatives in convents in a new light. Monastic life and the gifts to the church in the past, they believed, were works performed without faith. Although they could not repair the mistakes of the past, they could change the present. They believed that their sisters, brothers, daughters, and sons living behind convent walls were doomed to everlasting damnation. They sought interviews with them, sent Lutheran books, and wrote letters, which were sometimes published as pamphlets. It is characteristic of their group cohesiveness that they directed the propaganda to their own circle. Except for Matthias Wurm von Geudertheym, they made no attempt to reach out to their subjects, the ordinary burghers, or the artisans. Their pamphlets, while intimate and familial, were addressed to a public audience. As Wiesner has pointed out, the family was a public institution in the sixteenth century. Family decisions were also political decisions, especially for the elite.[3]

All the urban elite writers had read Luther's *Judgment on Monastic Vows* and his *Sermon on Marriage* and had been influenced by them. The thesis of the former treatise was that monastic vows violated the first commandment by displacing faith with works and elevating the founders of the orders above Christ himself, and, of the second, that the vow of celibacy was against God's work in the creation of mankind. Marriage with its responsibilities and difficulties was holy and godly.[4] Although the writers did not slavishly follow the outline of Luther's presentation, they hoped to communicate his ideas to their cloistered relatives.

MATTHIAS WURM VON GEUDERTHEYM AND HIS SISTER

Two of the letters were written in 1523, two years after the appearance of Luther's *Judgment on Monastic Vows*. Matthias Wurm von Geudertheym of Strasbourg wrote to his sister, in the convent of Saint Nicolas in Undis, a Dominican Convent of the Observance, sometime after 24 February. He wrote out of concern that she and the other nuns had misunderstood the books he had sent her and believed that Luther's teaching was disruptive and dangerous.[5] In a friendly and unthreatening way, he expressed his anxiety over her continued belief in the efficacy of works and her blindness with regard to the real nature of the vows of chastity. He hoped she would gradually turn from the commandments of men to obey the commandments of God.[6] There is no indication of his sister's response, but in the same year Wurm wrote to his fellow patrician, Eckhard zum Drübel, exhorting him to remove his two daughters from the convent, since he planned to withdraw his sister. Wurm, together with his brother Peter, had placed his sister in Saint Nicolas in Undis, believing that she would not only find salvation for herself but would also serve God with prayers, fasting, and vigils. Now, however, after reading the Bible for himself, "I have decided to take my sister out of the cloistered life, if she herself truly consents after suitable examination . . . and since I know that you also gave two daughters to the cloister . . . [I hope] you will undertake to free your children from their worldly selves and ungodly imprisonment."[7]

These simple sentences covered up a convoluted web of law suits and strife between the Wurm family, the convent, and the bishop. They poignantly illustrate the entangled relationships between the elite and the church and the elite's presence in chapters and convents. One person's conversion to the Reformation affected the whole family. No one could act freely or independently.

The Wurm family had risen only recently to the patriciate. Matthias' father, an imperial secretary under Maximiliam I, had been knighted by the emperor and received in fief part of the village of Geudertheim. The family continued to maintain residence in the city of Strasbourg. Conflict with the church ensued from property owned by the convent of Saint Nicolas in Undis within the fief of Geudertheim. The convent owed the Wurms an annual payment that, for reasons unknown, the nuns refused to pay after 1511/12.[8] Wurm and his brother brought suit but received no satisfaction. In retaliation, in 1517 the brothers ceased to make the annual payment due to the convent for their sister. The prioress responded with a suit against the brothers in the episcopal court in Strasbourg, threatening them with excommunication if they did not meet their financial obligations. Despite intervention by the imperial sub-bailiff and the Strasbourg *Rat*, matters deteriorated further when it was charged that the steward of the convent had slandered the Wurm brothers. A noble friend pledged to protect them in a feud against the convent. The nuns turned for support to Franz von Sickingen, whose daughter was in the convent. Matthias Wurm, to speed up the two law suits, put himself under the protection of Charles V when he visited the city.[9] Thus, the failure of the convent to pay their feudal obligation and the failure of the family to pay their sister's annual payment embroiled the city government, the episcopal court, outside nobles, and the emperor. Payment of the feudal levy to the Wurms seems to have been finally settled by the Strasbourg *Rat* in 1522; at least no discussion of the matter appears after that date.[10]

Wurm, however, still refused to make the annual payment for his sister. Instead, he mounted an attack with his pen. His pamphlet *Balaam's Ass*, published in 1523, denounced excommunication in cases of debt. Excommunication, he wrote, had been instituted by Christ to punish evil and vice and to bring a sinner to repentance. It did not apply to the collection of money, a usage that had been created by the clergy and constituted a human rather than a divine law.[11] Wurm ended by asserting that all members of the clergy who wished to be Christian should be subject to the secular authorities.

PATRICIAN CRITICISM OF MONASTIC VOWS

These were the circumstances behind Wurm's pamphlet on monastic vows, a remarkable work that reflected a deeper knowledge of the Bible than that of any other lay writer. Not only was he totally familiar with the Gospels and the Epistles (he had clearly read Paul thoroughly and analytically), but he moved from one book to another in the Old Testament with the ease of a trained theologian. He was one of the few lay persons who used the historical books, Kings, Chronicles, and so on, as sources.[12] He cited major prophets like Isaiah and Jeremiah, as did many others, but he also quoted minor prophets like Hosea, Amos, Malachi, and Zacharias.[13] He was a learned man who had seriously studied the biblical texts. Self-serving though he may have been in his struggle with the convent of Saint Nicolas in Undis, he had experienced a genuine conversion to the new faith and believed in the righteousness of his cause.

The book was professionally presented. He listed the principal arguments at the beginning, on the verso of the title page, as an outline of the treatise, which he carefully followed. Although influenced by Luther, Wurm placed greater emphasis on the idolatrous element in monasticism than Luther had. Of the 13 articles, the most important follow:

> That chastity is a gift of God, therefore no one may swear to God to be chaste.
>
> That poverty and obedience . . . are not in accordance with the Word of God.
>
> That saints should not be worshipped, nor should likenesses be made of them.
>
> That men should follow the holy faith and not works. That Christ is our interceder and representative before God.
>
> That God wishes only one offering from us, and that is praise and men should avoid foolish oaths.
>
> That cloister people imbibe idolatry, live in the tomb and sleep in idolatrous temples.[14]

The text expanded each of these articles by providing voluminous scriptural support for his theses. Although supposedly he directed his remarks to his sister and zum Drübel, once he began the text these individuals were forgotten. The treatise was a general, thorough exposition of his principal points, sometimes enlivened by the vigor and bluntness of his language. Describing the begging orders, he wrote that they consumed the support of the truly poor "with their vermin, wasps, flies, gnats. With their sects, gangs, and brotherhoods . . . they consumed the rapacious worms and swarms around them until they gnawed at the noble grain of God's Word and destroyed it with their lies and dreams."[15] The most important element of his thought was an implicit spirituality, a denial of a bodily aspect of God. This became apparent first in his rejection of images: "We should have no visible images and we should not represent any spiritual pictures . . . for we cannot see a likeness of God. He speaks to us within through his holy speech, he must be understood only spiritually." His citation, as one would expect, was John 1. He applied the same principle to reject prayers to the saints, which were outward and blasphemous; ceremonies, because they were an abomination to God; and monastic rules, which sought to please God with things, "cells, cloisters, cassocks, coifs, wooden shoes."[16]

In his conclusion he returned to this concept of the spiritual essence of God. The monks and nuns had built on sand, so their works and church practices would be rejected by God because they were against his Word. "For the chief article is faith, which will not suffer any of these things. For

what men see which is visible, they cannot understand. Christians, however, are converted to faith in God in spirit alone and not by appearance."[17]
At the very end of the treatise, Wurm returned to zum Drübel, exhorting
him again to take his daughters from the cloister. He, Wurm, had published his treatise so that his sister, Drübel's daughters, and many others
could be freed from the prison of the cloister.[18]

The other patrician writers drew freely on Luther's *Judgment on Monastic
Vows*. They criticized the conventuals, as Luther had, for claiming that
they followed a better way of life than ordinary people.[19] They criticized
the ceremonies and prayer life of the nuns, echoing Luther's comment that
"they stand in rows to worship God like dumb pipes."[20] Bernard Rem wrote
that when a nun prayed or sang the Psalms in Latin, she was like a parrot.[21]
The converted sister compared the convent's singing or chanting to a miller's donkey, adding that the prayer her sister had sent for the new-born
baby was as full of devotion as a piper, lacking understanding or piety.[22]
They all believed, and stated, that the conventual system emphasized works
instead of faith, and thus their sisters would be damned in eternal life.[23]

Like Luther, family members deplored the divisions among the orders,
their rivalry with one another, the disunity they had created. Each writer
scolded the nuns because they called themselves by different names and
cherished their separate identities. Luther had dealt with this rather simply. It was contrary to the laws of God, he wrote, "when people have cast
aside the name of God, established their own, and were no longer called
Christians but Benedictines, Franciscans and so forth. They boast of their
names and of their father founders more than they do of Christ."[24] The
honorable woman linked the orders to Paul's admonition against sects. He
had said that people should not call themselves after Peter or Zephas or
Apollo, but "then you cloister people come, one belongs to Saint Francis,
Saint Dominic, Saint Augustine, Bernard, Benedict, Jerome, Clara, Katherine,
Brigitta and more without count."[25] The converted sister referred to the
same verses of Paul but elaborated and embellished the confusion of the
orders further.

> How much holier is one of these sects than another? Franciscans, lesser
> brothers, greater brothers, some in wooden shoes, others in leather shoes,
> the third on stilts. . . . This order is reformed, the other is left free. This
> one is from the rule of the father, the other is from the rule of the other
> father. He wears black, another white, the third grey. He does not han-
> dle money. He does not touch the plough in the field. The third does
> not touch any of the women in the alleys.[26]

As far as the lay people were concerned, all these differences were trivial
and unimportant, leading to ridiculous rules and arrogance by monks and

nuns, who considered themselves superior. It is clear from the repetition from one writer to the next that this was a major source of resentment and ill-will. As family members, they were no longer willing to be assigned an inferior status. Christ, and Christ alone, was the true master. No Christian could follow any other master, nor pray to anyone else, nor honor anyone else. Matthias Wurm von Geudertheym put it bluntly:

> You have vowed all your vows against Scripture, for when one vows to another except God alone, whether it be Peter, Paul, James, Augustine, Francis, Benedict, Dominic, John or whatever the most holy is, it is truly idolatry, as though it were Baalim, Astaroth, Berith, Dagon, Asterthes, Moloch, Beelzebub . . . or Beel.[27]

MARRIED WOMEN WRITE TO THEIR CLOISTERED SISTERS

Because the pamphlets were based on an exchange of letters between family members and the convent, each contained its own inner dialogue between the woman in the world and her cloistered sister or between a brother and his sisters and daughter. In the pamphlet *A Convert Answers a Letter Sent by a Convent Nun to Her Married Sister*, the convert was replying to a letter from her cloistered sister asking whether she and her husband had become Lutherans. The Mother Superior and the other nuns wanted to know. In her reply the married, converted sister was defensive, self-consciously justifying her new faith, assertively advocating the married estate against the empty rules of the convent. She condemned her sister and the others in the convent as ill-informed, ignorant of scripture, clinging to a liturgy they did not understand.

The letter began conventionally. The nun had written to wish her sister, her husband, and their children a good, holy New Year. New Year's wishes were a custom observed at all social levels. The nun added that she was distressed because she had received no reply, and she and her Mother Superior were worried that perhaps her sister and her husband had become Lutherans.[28] The married woman thanked her sister for her good wishes to the newborn baby. She then continued, "I acknowledge first that Jesus Christ is our redeemer and sanctifier. . . . Therefore, dear sister, you can see what kind of people my husband and I are; if we are Lutheran, Pauline, Petrine, Apostolic, Hussite, Guelf or Ghibelline. Christ is the name we bear. We are named after him."[29] This was a clear example of the unwillingness of those who had turned to the new faith to accept the name of Lutheran. In part this stemmed from the fact that Luther himself had condemned the use of his name by his followers. They were to call themselves Christian.[30] "Lutheran" was also used derisively by the Romanists. One can hardly emphasize enough the importance of names and naming during the Reformation. A name defined one's life.

The evangelical convert went on to scold her sister. What strange fantasies did cloistered people have about the multitudes outside the cloisters? Did they think that people no longer knew God? Was the nun afraid that her sister would be led astray by false teaching? Christ had revealed himself to shepherds, not to cloistered women, nor to Herod's or Caiphas's women. Indeed, he had not revealed himself to Herod, the bishops, cardinals, or monks. He did not want them to find him.[31]

Removing her sister from the position of the direct heir of Christ, the converted sister took her place. Christ considered all who accepted him, fed him, and sheltered him as the children of God, his heirs. To those who believed in him he said, "I am the door." She pushed this further, placing those in the world on a level of equality with the spirituals. The commandments of God were naturally known to all Christians, who did not have to be monks, nuns, cardinals, popes, abbots, or abbesses. It was not a matter of wearing cowls or hats, of eating meat or fish, of living with a husband or without. There was not one word in God's law with regard to monks or nuns.[32]

There was a final thrust. The nun had written that she sent wishes to the newborn with a "poor" prayer. "Yes, to be sure," answered her sister, "it is a poor prayer. It is as devout as something coming out of a bagpipe."[33] She concluded by admonishing her cloistered sister to accept the one commandment of God, to love him with all her heart, soul, and might, and to think carefully about this letter. "All of us have groped in blind error, but especially you cloister people with your presumptuous spirit. God enlighten us and give us mercy . . . this I desire and I pray to God to forgive you and your worthy lady prioress and your whole convent."[34]

The inner dialogue of the letter indicates a rather passive stance by the nun, an aggressive posture by the reformed, married sister. Nothing indicates that the nun was trying to force her views on her sister. She had written a standard New Year's greeting, expressing her pleasure over the new baby, enclosing a prayer for her or him (the baby was never referred to by name), and indicating her concern that her sister and brother-in-law had become Lutheran. For a cloistered woman it would be natural to be anxious in this regard. Although the married sister used terms such as "dear beloved sister," "dear sister," this was often when she was being particularly critical. "Dearly beloved sister, your letter to me is based on the judgment of the human spirit which still dwells within you." "Tell me, dear sister, in whose name are we received into the world at our birth?"[35] "Dear sister" was disparaging rather than a term of endearment. The letter was mean in spirit. As the letter was full of biblical citations, and the sister exhorted the nun to read the Scripture for herself, the latter was clearly literate and capable of understanding what she read and sang in the daily services. The evangelical convert was at once dogmatic, unforgiving, and condemning. She treated her sister as inferior spiritually and intellectually. It is not clear whether she expected the nun to leave the convent, but she inferred that the latter was incapable of making her own decisions. Because she was in the convent, she was infantalized by her sister.

The "honorable woman in married estate" had more to complain about but was more sensitive and aware of her cloistered sister's feelings. The nun had written to tell her she had burned the sermon which had been sent to her. The honorable woman first apologized that she, the younger sister, living in the world, should attempt to instruct her older and wiser sister who was, besides, a nun. But the book of Daniel had stated that sons and daughters would prophecy, and so it had occurred. Holy Scripture and the knowledge of truth having now descended on the young, she must scold the nun, in a sisterly way, for burning the sermon, which was based on Christian teaching. The nun had written that it was full of evil, with good mixed in. The younger was concerned that her sister could recognize only the evil elements and had closed herself to the good.[36]

She also worried about the false teaching which the nun accepted. Christ had taught faith, hope, and love. Those should be planted in everyone whether they lived in convents or not, whether they lived in a spiritual or worldly way. To discover the falseness of her comments, the cloistered sister should read the Bible zealously, "beginning, middle and end."[37] The nun had written about cloistered life and its vows in the belief that people who went out into the world, leaving this behind, would be damned like Judas. The nun had pointed out that if what her sister had written was true, then God had treated their ancestors and elders wrongly because he had not let his holy Scripture be explained to them. Why would God have permitted them to err? The honorable woman replied, "I answer, how do we know what God wishes to work with his wonders in these last days?.... Think, that no man one, two, three or four hundred years ago knew about the world or could describe the wonderful islands or [the] marvelous men [found there].... This has happened in forty years because of the discoveries of the Queen of Portugal and Spain. And the spices known to our ancestors only in Venice, now come to Germany from the Netherlands."[38] The argument that nothing could be changed, because that was what their ancestors had done, would be attacked also by the upper civil servants. The honorable woman, with her reference to the New World, helped to undermine the sanctity of tradition.

The nun was conservative and traditional. She had, she wrote, entered the convent, made her profession, and had thus given herself to God. Her sister cautioned her. "You speak as though this was according to your will but you, like all Christians, gave yourself in baptism to God and only to

God. Now you have given yourself to human laws."[39] Instead of the freedom Christ had given to men and women, convent people insisted on human rules and regulations and special clothes and headdresses. How many people in the world, with dear, beautiful children lived better lives than those in convents?[40]

There was a brief ending. The younger sister had previously written suggesting that her sister leave the cloister. The latter had replied that she must accept what God had given and asked her sibling not to advise her to leave. If a nun was in the cloister unwillingly, the nun believed, she should be imprisoned or put in chains. The honorable woman was shocked. Where had she found that in holy Scripture? Nevertheless, she asked the nun to take her letter in the best way, to consult and learn the holy Scripture and to write her more about these things.[41]

The contrasts between the letters of the married sisters are striking. The one was dogmatic and self-righteous, alternately scolding and blaming her rather passive sister. The other nun was hardly passive, having burned the book and strongly stated the superiority of convent life. Her younger sister wanted her to leave the cloister, but there was no attempt to force her. She reached out with tenderness and a degree of understanding about deciding to leave. Yet, in neither case was family feeling put forward as a major factor. The salvation of souls was at stake. That was far more important than their earthly relationship.

A Patrician Scolds His Sisters and His Daughter

The next letters do not require a search for the inner dialogue because the exchange was frank and open. Bernard Rem, patrician and organist to the Fugger family in Augsburg, wrote to his daughter Veronica and his sisters Barbara and Katherine, who were in the local convents of St. Katherine and St. Nicholas. In St. Katherine's, the largest women's convent in the city, 50% of the nuns came from the Augsburg elite. Nearly 80% at St. Nicholas came from the upper rank.[42] Rem's letter, which he had printed, was dated 15 August 1523. Katherine replied for herself and her niece; Bernard printed that letter and his response, dated 11 September 1523.

Bernard's salutation was fulsome. They were all sisters and brothers, children of one heavenly father, so he felt great responsibility toward them. Out of Christian love he felt he must share his suffering and cares with them, and hoped they would take this with good will.[43] He began with a brief review of monasticism in Christian life. Many people, he wrote, had high regard for the cloistered life, as though the cloister was the house of Lazarus, where Mary Magdalene had sat at the feet of the Lord and received his teaching. These people also believed that cloistered people had chosen the best way, and that they would not have to suffer in the afterlife.

Bernard admitted that both Jerome and Chrysostom had written about monastic life, but it had been different in their time, not restricted by vows or demands of chastity but a way of teaching holy doctrine and obedience to Scripture. Even so, Christ had never written nor taught about such a way of life. Everyone was to take the common way to a Christian life. "Truly, since Christ said 'I am the way,' it is well to think that he who abandons the way, goes in error."[44]

The rest of Bernard's letter set forth the errors of convent life as lived by his female relatives. They were in great danger, surrounded by enemies, first among whom was the devil, who had every opportunity to stir up wicked thoughts. They had no means of attaining a good life because they did not hear Scripture, nor did they read it. They read Latin (books unspecified) but did not understand it. Indeed, a nun reading a Latin psalter was no better than a parrot. Their second enemy was their own flesh, for no cloister, no high wall, no desert could separate them from their flesh or from the world. They praised virginity but did not know if God had given them the gift of chastity or not. Thirdly, they trusted in their own works, as though they were holier than others or in better standing with God. They did not understand God's righteousness, which came from faith, not from works. They could not achieve salvation through their works but only through faith in Christ.[45] Bernard closed his letter in the hope that they would read Scripture and learn from it the right way to God and the nothingness of their own works.[46] The letter went to the printer at the same time he sent it to his daughter and sisters. By the time they received it, they knew it had been printed.

Sister Katherine answered for herself and her niece, Veronica, both in St. Katherine's cloister. No further mention is made of the sister Barbara, who must have been at the convent of St. Nicholas. Katherine's reply, calm but firm, stated her opposition in the opening sentences. She told Bernard to beware of the false prophets who Christ had warned would come in sheep's clothing but who were actually ravening wolves.[47] Her use of this citation at the very beginning of her reply is noteworthy. It was quoted by more lay writers than any other set of biblical verses, usually to condemn the Roman clergy. Did Katherine know that? Was she turning the words of the reformed writers back on her brother, from the pamphlets he had sent?

She wrote with dignity, attempting, not always successfully, to forgive his harshness. "You come with many good words," she wrote, "but you must not think we are so foolish as to place our hopes in the cloister or in our works. Our hope is in God's law. He is the true Lord and the rewarder of all things. We willingly serve him in the cloister rather than in the world." Rem was not to worry about whether they would go to heaven or hell; that was in the hands of God. Rather, he should think of himself so that he would become a good Christian. He should not swear in God's name, nor eat meat on Friday or Saturday. Although this was not part of the teaching of Christ, she acknowledged, Rem had tried to take a mote out of their eye, when he had a big beam in his own.[48]

It was apparent that the women had had difficulty with Bernard before. Katherine said she was aware that he had told her and Veronica that it would be the same or better if they were in the temple house than in the cloister. This seems to have referred to a house of prostitution.[49] He should look in his heart and think before he spoke out. Now he had taken the letter addressed to them to the printer. She was deeply disgraced by this. "The printer certainly cannot think very well of you. . . . Did you not have other offspring to print? . . . Why did you not let him print about you and others like you?" She knew, however, that he would always justify his actions and that it did not matter to him. She and Veronica would suffer gladly with the help of God, who had suffered so bitterly for them. God forgive him everything.[50] He had written, however, that he would like to come to see them. If he could not come in friendship, he should stay away. If he wanted to straighten them out, they did not need him. He was not to send any more letters. They would not accept them. Her last sentence was: "We also have many good books."[51] There was no closing or signature.

Bernard did not do what she asked. He printed her reply on 11 September with his own rejoinder, expressing surprise that she had rejected his letter written in Christian truth. Furthermore, she had insulted him by calling him a false prophet. He had tried to warn her and did not regret that the bitterness in her heart was turned against him, hoping that she would turn to God and that faith would grow in her.[52] God wanted men and women to share each other's burdens, but his sisters and daughter had cut themselves off from the needs and grief of others.[53]

Bernard answered his sister's objections point by point. She had rejected his poor prayer that she turn to the Gospel, which was insulting. Whether she wanted him to do so or not, he would always pray for the salvation of her body and soul.[54] Worse, she had let her anger push her to a wicked attitude. She had made too much of his remark about the temple house, when what he had meant was that she should not condemn completely even an open sinner, since God's judgment was hidden. He would rather be an open sinner, like the tax collector in Luke 18 who was so despised by the Pharisee, yet God had forgiven him. Similarly, it was written in Matthew 21 that tax collectors and whores who believed the Word of God would enter heaven before the chief priests and the elders. Bernard's major fear continued to be that his sister and daughter would believe that they were pious and devout and would not, could not, recognize their own sinfulness. "Once you have seen yourself as a sinner and carnal in Christian truth, then you will be able to direct your life according to the Word of God which alone is our light and rule to godly life."[55] He knew they had many books, but they should forsake all of them for the Bible, for only there would they find true knowledge of Jesus Christ. He closed by urging them to read Paul so that they would recognize the uselessness of their works.[56]

The tone of Bernard's second letter was less condemning, and he made some attempt to establish a peaceful relationship with his sister, yet he rejected every one of her arguments, still with the implication that she wrote out of ignorance. Furthermore, he published her reply to him, along with his second letter, despite her strong objections to his printing the first letter. He had not really changed his attitude or his opinions. The letter was a self-justification in which he twisted her meanings to suit himself.

PRIVATE RELATIONSHIPS AND THE REFORM

Can these letters be seen as examples of the patriarchal relationship which is considered to be the pattern of Early Modern family life?[57] The sample of five letters is far too small to provide an answer. The variations in tone which have already been noted may reflect the personality of the writer or the particular nature of the relationships within one family. The cloistered women had all been removed from their families, perhaps years before, and had been taught to accept the convent and the mother superior as the focus of their emotional and spiritual lives. They were adults, living in an independent community. It is clear that none of them wanted to change. What would it have been like to return to the house of Bernard Rem? The surprising element, perhaps, is that their brothers and sisters felt they had the right to condemn their relatives, to focus their zeal for reformation on one individual whose entrance into the convent had almost certainly been a familial as well as an individual decision. That decision had been made in the past. Now the nuns were to accept the family's advice to leave. It is this expectation of obedience which reveals the patriarchal nature of the elite family. Significantly, it could be expressed by a woman, a sister, as well as by a brother or father. The emphasis for all these writers, however, was not familial love or affection but the salvation of their sister's soul. The doctrine of justification by faith meant that people had to change their way of life. The elite applied this in their own families, hoping to rescue members who had been placed in convents, to open their hearts to the Gospel and thus guarantee them everlasting life.

Certain questions remain unanswered. Were the letters genuine, written by family members to one another, or merely a propaganda form? The general answer is that they were authentic family correspondence. Matthias Wurm was certainly writing to his sister and his friend, Eckhard zum Drübel.

The Rems were unquestionably writing letters back and forth. The honorable woman's letter may be validated by the sister's burning the book, which provides evidence of an actual incident. The recurring concern about the newborn baby in the married woman's letter is the strongest evidence that it was a familial letter written by a woman; a male writer would not continually refer to the baby.

The second question is why these family letters were published. As discussed in the introduction, letters were one of the most usual forms of propaganda among the upper classes and the learned. It was a form they habitually used. They published the pamphlets to persuade other members of the elite who had relatives in convents. Significantly, the published letters were written only to nuns. I did not find any letters to monks exhorting them to leave the monastery, with the exception of one letter written by a former nun to her brother still in orders.[58] The family did not feel responsible for their sons and brothers in the same way. They presumed that they were capable of making their own decisions. Women were not. No matter what their age, they required guidance to reach a decision. Gender difference could hardly be more explicit than in these pamphlets.

Roper believed that in Augsburg the Reformation incorporated "the guild ideals of household and family," strengthening the existing patriarchal position of the guild master with a code of discipline based on civic control of marriage and morals passed in 1537. The reasoning of all the lay writers bears out Roper's thesis of a desire for closer family control of cloistered women.[59]

The resistance of individual nuns and their convents indicates how mistaken their families were and how ineffective their propaganda efforts. Despite the books that were sent, despite the letters, some of the cloistered women held to their way of life. Among the nuns mentioned in these letters, we can be sure only that zum Drübel's daughters were living at home by 1528.[60] Wurm went to his sister's convent in March 1523, with 30 men, to try to force her to leave. She refused. In a later manuscript letter, she pleaded with her brothers to leave her alone and to pay the annual pension.[61] St. Katherine's maintained its independence through the Reformation; presumably Veronica Rem remained. By contrast, Felicitas Peutinger left St. Katherine's in defiance of her family's loyalty to Catholicism.[62] Some nuns did not easily accept the new familial ethic.

OFFICIAL ACTION AND THE CONVENTS

The debate between family members and their cloistered sisters became a struggle between the cloisters and the city magistrates. In many cities, the city council moved to close the cloisters in 1523 or 1524, taking over administration of the convent property. For example, in Strasbourg the

Franciscans voluntarily laid aside their cowls and were joined by four of the women's convents, the wealthier and more fashionable houses. The nuns were given pensions by the *Rat* and were free to live as they pleased.[63] Three women's convents remained, and these nuns provided a determined resistance to all attempts of the magistrates to close them down. As late as 1525, the city secretary visited each convent and informed the nuns that their habits, their prayers, and their vows would not make them holy. It was the same argument the pamphleteers had used. The women gave the same reply as the nuns in the letters. They wished to remain in the cloister. The *Rat* called on the relatives of the nuns to plead with them but with no effect. Finally, in May 1525, the council closed down the convents by edict, offering life pensions to all who would leave. On 24 June, the relatives arrived with horses and wagons to take their sisters, daughters, and aunts home.[64] Life in the world did not appeal to the women. In less than three weeks, by 11 July, after delegations from the families had appealed to them, the cloister administrators proposed to the *Rat* that those women who did not wish to remain in the world should return to their convents. By 9 September most had returned.

Their decision reflected social and economic realities as well as their religious convictions. As former nuns they could not easily find a place for themselves in "the world." Monks could become preachers, school teachers, or enter the printing trade, among other possibilities, but none of these alternatives was open to women religious. Furthermore, marriage was rarely an option for the older nuns. Men, particularly among the elite, married young brides.[65]

The city council was determined, however, to provide the returned women with learned preachers, and there was constant friction over their daily celebration of the Mass. Again the nuns prevailed. The *Rat* sent in reformed preachers to expound the Gospel. The nuns received them in stony silence. The traditional services continued to be observed.[66]

In 1524, the Nuremberg city council moved to take control of the monastic orders. An inventory was made of the properties, those who wished to leave were permitted to do so, a pension was provided for those who remained. Kaspar Nützel, one of the most influential members of the city council, was appointed guardian of the convent of St. Clara. Besides serving as city treasurer, the highest elected office, he was a learned, educated, conscientious magistrate.[67] He crystalized the ideas of the patrician pamphleteers in 29 articles outlining a plan to reform the convent according to Lutheran principles. The lives of the nuns were to be carefully regulated by their guardians, and the "human laws" of the orders would be overridden by city ordinances. It was an overt assertion of secular power over institutions of the church. It is too simplistic to conclude that what the governing elite could not achieve by persuasion, they achieved by legislation. Never-theless, the arguments in the pamphlets reappeared in the laws enacted to control the convents, as Nützel's articles demonstrate.

Nützel was fully aware that his plan would seem harsh to the nuns. He justified his action in the first paragraph: "I have undertaken with God's help to perform a Christian duty and although my duties . . . will not be desirable to you, yet out of Christian and brotherly love I can in no way neglect [that] the eternal, merciful God wishes to tear some of you out of the jaws of Satan."[68] His first concern was that the younger sisters in the cloister should receive instruction in God's Word and that all the affairs of the convent should be ordered according to Christ, not according to hu-man laws and rules. Thus, the abbess and the prioress and the nuns should pray for a strong, upright, true faith and for the grace of Christ. Nützel was directing these admonitions to Charitas Pirckheimer, the gifted humanist and strong defender of the old church.[69] A Christian preacher should be appointed to preach God's word daily, in the morning and in the after-noon, a half an hour on work days, a full hour on holy days. Because no one could be saved except by the Word of God, books by Luther, Melanchthon, and Pomeranus should be made available to the nuns both in Latin and in German. Regular services were to be left in place but read-ings from Scripture were to be substituted for some of the prayers at mat-ins. A list for readings during meals included not only Luther and Melanchthon but also Matthias Wurm von Geudertheim's *Trost Clostergefangener*.[70] Thus, a laymen's book received recognition. Nützel's aim was to encourage young nuns to leave the convent, one of his reasons for including *Trost Clostergefangener*. His articles provided that no young woman was to be held against her will. If she wished to leave she should be permitted to do so, with the knowledge of her parents and friends, meaning her relatives. She was to be allowed to take the main part of the money she had brought with her when she departed.[71] Returning the dowry of a young nun was a substantial blow to a convent. The patrician pamphlets had addressed them-selves to the spiritual fate of their cloistered sisters and daughters but had said little about the diversion of family money to the convents. Nützel, obviously, with the support of the Nuremberg city council, was restoring money to the wealthiest families in the city. He gave short shrift to the older women who did not want to leave. The convents should become schools. The nuns who remained should assume the responsibility of teaching Christian honor and learning to young children.[72]

The closing of the monasteries and convents was one of the first major changes in the cities which became reformed. In most cases it proceeded smoothly because there was little support from the laity for the monastic orders. The patricians whose children and relatives were affected had publicly criticized the convents. The artisans and lower classes were equally willing to shut down the monastic houses. They despised the begging orders because of their greed and usurious practices, and they looked on the women's convents as bastions of privilege which flaunted the power of the elite.[73]

Kaspar Nützel's articles revealed the sacrifice involved for the conventual women. Until the Religious Peace of Augsburg, the sisters lost their right to determine their membership in many cities. No new novitiates could be accepted. In those decades, the nuns were restricted in following the religious observances of their order. The secular authority had successfully inserted itself within the walls of most urban religious communities. The Reformation goal of discipling the monks and nuns had been achieved.

Before discussing the larger program of the city authorities for establishing discipline and order, it is essential to look at the artisans' concept of how justice and order should be attained. We move, then, directly to the artisans' pamphlets.

Notes

1. Lyndal Roper, *Holy Household: Women and Morals in Reformation Augsburg*, 1991, 208.
2. I have identified "the convert" as a member of the urban elite on the basis of her learning. She writes of the Mother Superior as an equal. The Mother Superior would have been in most cases from the urban elite or from a noble family. In the text I refer to the anonymous writer as "the convert" or "the converted woman"; the other I call "the honorable woman."
3. Merry Wiesner, "Beyond Women and the Family: Toward a Gender Analysis of the Reformation," *SCJ* XVIII, 3(1987): 316.
4. Martin Luther, "Judgement on Monastic Vows," in Jaroslav Pelikan et al., eds., *Luther's Works*, 56 vols. (1955–1976) 44, *The Christian and Society*, I, 249. Martin Luther, "Vom ehelichen leben," 1522, in *D. Martin Luthers Werke. Kritische Gesamtausgabe*. 10 band: 275, 297.
5. #281, Matthias Wurm von Geudertheim, *Christlich Schreiben so ain Evangelischer bruder seiner schwester . . . zugeschicht*, 1523, states that Matthias had received the letter from his sister, to which he is responding, on St. Matthew the Apostle's day (February 24), 1523; fol. Aii.
6. Ibid., fols. Aii^v; Aiii^v; Aiv^v; Ciii^v.
7. #283, Matthias Wurm von Geudertheim, *Trost Clostergefangner*, 1523, fol. Aii^v.
8. Jean Rott, "De quelques pamphlétaires nobles-Hutten, Cronberg et Mathias Wurm von Geudertheym," in *Grands Figures de l'humanisme Alsacien*, 1978, 140. Reprinted in Jean Rott, *Investigationes Historicae*, 2 vols. (1986), 2, 575–586. My references are to the 1978 edition.
9. Ibid.
10. Ibid., 141.

11. Ibid.
12. #283, Wurm von Geudertheim, *Trost Clostergefangner*, fols. Biv, D, Hiv.
13. Ibid., fols. Iii, Kiv[v].
14. Ibid., fol. A[v].
15. Ibid., fol. Biii[v].
16. Ibid., fol. Cii[v], Eiv[v]–Fi, Giii[v]–Giv, F.
17. Ibid., fol. Liv[v].
18. Ibid., fol. M[v].
19. #213, Bernhard Rem, *Ain Sendtbrieff an ettlich Closterfrawen zu sant Katherina und zu sant Niclas in Augsburg*, 1523, fol. Aii. #43, *Ain Sendbrieff von Ainer erbern frawen im Eelichen stat an ein Klosterfrawen*, 1524, fol. C. #13, *Ayn bezwungene antwort uber eynen Sendtbrieff eyner Closternunnen an ir schwester im Eelichen standt zugeschickt*, 1524, fols. Aiii; C.
20. Luther, "Monastic Vows," 325.
21. #213, B. Rem, *Sendtbrieff*, fol. Aiii[v].
22. #13, *Bezwungene Antwort*, fol. C[v].
23. #213, B. Rem, *Sendtbrieff*, fol. Aii[v]; #13, *Bezwungene Antwort*, Bi[v]–Bii[v]; #43, *Erbern Frawen*, fol. Aii[v].
24. Luther, "Monastic vows," 378.
25. #43, *Erbern frawen*, fol. D.
26. #13, *Bezwungene Antwort*, fol. Bii.
27. #283, Wurm von Geydertheym, *Trost Clostergefangner*, fol. Liv[v]. The false gods listed were mostly from the Old Testament. Baalim was the general name for the deities of Canaan. Astaroth (Ashtaroth) was the Hebrew form of Astartes, the Semitic goddess of fertility and love. Berith was the abbreviation of Baal-Berith, local god of Sechem. Dagon, god of fertility, is mentioned in the Old Testament as one of the chief gods of the Philistines. For Asterthes, see Astaroth. Moloch was the Canaanite god of fire. Beelzebub=Satan. Beel=Baal.
28. #13, *Bezwungene Antwort*, fol. Ai.
29. Ibid., fol. Aii–Aiii. Note that this is almost a random list, ending with the traditional political divisions between the papal and imperial parties, making the point that names were irrelevant.
30. Luther, D. Martin. "Eine treue vermahnung zu allen Christen, sich zu vorhuten for auffruhr unnd emporung," 1522, in *D. Martin Luthers Werke, Kritsche Gesamtausgabe*. Band 8: 685.
31. #13, *Bezwungene Antwort*, fols. Aiii–Aiv.
32. Ibid., fol. Aiv[v], Bi[v].
33. Ibid., fol. C[v].
34. Ibid., fol. Civ.
35. Ibid., fol. Aii, Aiii.
36. #43, *Sendbrieff von Ainer erbern frawen*, fols. Ai[v]–Aii.
37. Ibid., fol. Aii[v].
38. Ibid., fols. Bii[v]–Biii.
39. Ibid., fol. Dii.
40. Ibid., fols. Biv, Civ[v].
41. Ibid., fol. Diii[v].
42. Roper, *Holy Household*, 208.
43. #213, B. Rem, *Sendtbrieff an ettlich Closterfrauen*, fol. Aii.
44. Ibid., fols. Aii[v]–Aiii.
45. Ibid., fols. Aiii–B[v].

46. Ibid., fol. Bii.
47. #214, [Katherina Rem], *Antwort zwayer Closterfrawen*, fol.Ai^v.
48. Ibid., fol. Aii.
49. This is implicit in Bernhard Rem's *Gegenantwort*, where he states that they misunderstood him. He only meant that they should not criticize an open sinner. *Gegenantwort*, fol. Bii^v.
50. #214, [Katherina Rem], *Antwort zwayer Closterfrawen*, fol. Aii.
51. Ibid., fol. Aii^v.
52. #214, Bernhard Rem, *Gegenantwort*, fol. Aiii–Aiii^v.
53. Ibid., fol. B.
54. Ibid.
55. Ibid., fol. Bii^v.
56. Ibid., fol. Biv.
57. Lawrence Stone, *The Family, Sex and Marriage in England, 1500–1800*, 1977, 216–217; Miriam Slater, *Family Life in the Seventeenth Century: The Verneys of Claydon House*, 1984, 30–31; Steven Ozment, *When Fathers Ruled: Family Life in Reformation Europe*, 1983, 50–54. Roper, *Holy Household*, 27–28.
    Thomas A. Brady, Jr., "'You hate us priests': Anticlericalism, Communalism and the Control of Women at Strasbourg in the Age of the Reformation." in eds. Peter A. Dykema and Heiko Oberman, *Anticlericalism in Late Medieval and Early Modern Europe*, 1993, 167–172.
58. *Eyn kurtze antwort einer Ordens schwester/irem natürlichen bruder karteuser ordens zugeschickt/uber seyne Christliche und Ewangelische leer und ermanung* (n.p.:n.p., 1523).
59. Roper, *Holy Household*, 54–56.
60. #101, Eckhard zum Drübel's *Ein vetterliche/gedruge . . . zucht/lere und bericht an meine kynder...*, published in 1528, includes advice to his daughters.
61. Jean Rott, "De quelques pamphlétaires nobles . . . ," 142–143.
62. Roper, *Holy Household*, 210.
63. Miriam Usher Chrisman, "Women and the Reformation in Strasbourg, 1490–1530," ARG 63 (1972): 165.
64. Ibid.
65. cf. Merry E. Wiesner, "Ideology Meets the Empire: Reformed Convents and the Reformation," in eds. Andrew C. Fix and Susan C. Karant-Nunn, *Germania Illustrata*, 1992, 192.
66. Chrisman, "Women and the Reformation," 166.
67. Jonathan W. Zophy, *Patriarchal Politics and Christoph Kress 1484–1535 of Nuremberg*, 1992, 107. The pamphlet was written under the pseudonym Philadelphus Noricus. Otto Clemen made the identification of Nützel as the author in *Kleine Schriften zur Reformations geschichten*, 5 vols. (1982–1984), 2, 295–296.
68. #212 [Kaspar Nützel], *Wie alle Closter und sonderlich Junckfrawen Closter in ain Christlichs wesen möchten durch gottes gnaden gebracht werden*, 1528, fol. Aii.
69. Ibid., fols. Aii–Aii^v. See also Zophy, *Patriarchal Politics*, 108.
70. #212 [Nützel], *Wie alle Closter*, fols. Aii^v–Aiv.
71. Ibid., fol. Bii.
72. Ibid., fol. Biv.
73. Roper, *Holy Household*, 211.

Ain gespꝛech büchlin/von ainem Weber
vnd ainem Kramer über das Büchlin Doctoris
Mathie Kretz von der haimlichen Beycht/
so er zū Augspurg in vnnſer frawen
Thům gepꝛediget hat:
im M̃: D̃: X̃Xiiij:

Vtz Rychßner Weber:

6   "A discussion between a weaver and a shopkeeper with regard to the book by
Dr. Matthew Kretz on secret confession."

Here a weaver and a shopkeeper discuss the sermon published by a local priest.
The shopkeeper purchased the sermon and reads it to his friend. The weaver answers the priest's arguments from his Bible, shown open in front of him, The domestic setting is simple and believable.

SOURCE: Title page of a pamphlet by Utz Rychssner, Weber. *Ain gesprech büchlin
von ainem Weber und ainem Kramer über das Büchlin Doctoris Mathie Kretz von der
haimlichen Beycht so er zu Augsburg in unnser frawen Thum geprediget hat im 1524.*
N.p.,n.p., 1524.
Courtesy Staats-und Stadtbibliothek, Augsburg, Germany.

7

The Artisans, Scripture, and Christian Practice

THE ARTISANS DEFEND THEIR RIGHT TO INTERPRET SCRIPTURE

To the artisan pamphleteers, the Reformation meant the Gospel. The preaching of the Gospel by the reformers had opened a new world to them. Previous movements for change at the lower levels of society had looked backward, toward a restitution of old customs, old laws. When the reformers appealed to divine law, there was a change in perception and "a new horizon of expectations . . . the joint and equal responsibility of all citizens and residents to the will of God" was reaffirmed in the decades before the Reformation."[1] It prepared the way for the new preaching of the Gospel, which revived the belief in the covenant community that lay at the base of city constitutions. The preachers restored the Gospel as the source of law. Jesus and his disciples were revealed as humble people, concerned about the poor and the lowly, scornful of the learned. This convinced the artisans that the Roman priests had hidden the Gospel from them, making it impossible to know the truth. The priests had trampled the Gospel underfoot and laid it in the dust, wrote one popular poet. Given to the people by the mercy of God, Luther had now restored it and the cities had been reformed by pious pastors. Another writer, who described himself as a menial, charged that "human teachers" had led people around, showing them the wrong way. Pious, simple, plain folk had greater understanding of the faith than all the doctors in the land. It was the duty of evangelical Christians to make the Gospel known.[2] Jörg Graff, a blind *Landsknecht*, wrote that the truth lay imprisoned and the Christian faith restrained. "We have been blinded by the learned who turned God's word upside down."[3] No one wrote more eloquently of the imprisonment of the Gospel than Haug Marschalck, the mercenary captain. It was a common theme among all ranks:

[The] cardinal, bishops, professors, begging monks . . . sat before the door.

The Gospel imprisoned, the Scripture kept in the dark. . . . There came
to the tomb, God be praised, three Marys—Martin Luther, Andreas Carlstadt
and Phillip Melancthon. They saw an angel, the Christian prince, Duke
Frederick of Saxony who said "whom do you seek here?" . . . The holy
Scripture, God's Word said the youngest among them.[4]

That artisans openly published their opinions in pamphlets bearing their
names was a revolution in itself. Lay men and women, particularly artisans,
were not meant to have opinions. They were meant to work, to live sober
lives, and to accept the rule of their superiors. They had despised the clergy
for years but had expressed this only in popular songs and plays, sung or
acted in taverns. Now their pamphlets were printed and sold by the printers, booksellers, and in the market place. If the clergy would not or could
not teach the Scriptures, the artisans would take on the task themselves.
The learned might dismiss them, saying they had no right to interpret Scripture, but the artisans stated their right to teach and interpret, citing biblical passages which justified their action. They had to defend this claim
against the clergy and the magistrates.

The craftsmen asserted that their own superior knowledge of Scripture
obliged them to correct the errors of the priests. Bastian Goltschmit, self-
identified as a burgher of Worms, described his encounter with one of the
city's clergy. Brother Mathias, a Dominican prior, had preached on certain
articles which were not based on Scripture, at least Goltschmit had not
been able to find the proper references. Goltschmit had written a New
Year's book for Mathias to bring him the correct, godly Word, asking for
instruction with regard to the articles. The prior had refused, even when
asked twice. Goltschmit then had requested the honorable *Rat* to answer
his questions, but they dismissed him with "great pride and arrogance." Rebuffed
but persistent, he had left the book for Brother Mathias to read, but the
latter refused. Goltschmit next publicly censured the Dominican, stating
before witnesses that the brother had led the *gemein Volk* astray. At that
point, Mathias complained to the *Rat*, asking that Goltschmit be restrained.
Reproved by the *Rat*, Goltschmit published his book. "Whatever they say
about [Mathias] being a Magister or Doctor," Goltschmit insisted, "it is still
to be presumed that he cannot prove his articles from Scripture."[5]

Hans Füssli, a Swiss bellfounder, wrote a long criticism of a pamphlet by
Hieronymus Gebwiler, director of the cathedral chapter school in Strasbourg. "I was moved to answer Gebwiler's little book, despite my lack of
education, and the learned may laugh at me for I do not know rhetoric and
have not written much, except what was needed for my craft. But even if I
were learned, [Gebwiler's] book is in error, and all mixed up and entangled
in itself." Some sections, he continued, were too long, with too many words,
and these he had summarized. "Thus I have answered it so that people can

see how the schoolmaster and the Christian church . . . erred so badly. . . .
I have shown the heavy burdens the learned have laid on the poor sheep,
ruling with tyrannical force, bidding and forbidding, laying burdens on us
as though we were Hungarian oxen, burdens they would not have touched
with the tips of their fingers."[6]

Hans Sachs, a shoemaker, was an established popular poet and dramatist.
The best educated of all the artisan pamphleteers, he had attended Latin
school for eight years. Early drawn to Luther, he used his literary gifts to
champion the new faith and to criticize social relationships. The characters
in his dialogues exposed the stereotypes of the time. An encounter between
a canon and a shoemaker revealed the conflicting perceptions of the clergy
and the artisans:[7]

> *Shoemaker*: I have just written a book about your church services and
> teaching to explain them to the *gemain man*.
> *Canon*: What does a shoemaker know about such things? He works
> with leather, not with Scripture. . . . I must tell you it is not proper for
> the laity to occupy themselves with Scripture.
> *Shoemaker*: Didn't Christ say in Matthew 7, guard yourselves from false
> prophets . . . and Paul in Philippians 3 warned us to look out for the
> dogs. If it isn't appropriate for us to know the Scriptures, how will we
> recognize such things?
> *Canon*: That belongs to the bishops, as Paul says in Titus 1. . . .
> *Shoemaker*: Yes, but they don't do that. They do just the opposite.
> *Canon*: What can you laymen learn? Many of you can't even read.
> *Shoemaker*: Christ said, "You are all learned in God."
> *Canon*: Yes, but there is an art to it. Why otherwise have universities?
> *Shoemaker*: What university did John graduate from? He was just a fish-
> erman, like Mark.
> *Canon*: They had the holy spirit.[8]

Part of the irony of this exchange was that Sachs had proved that the
canon could not read very well himself; he had to call on his handyman to
read the Bible to him. Yet the canon's prejudice remained, his conviction
that the laity were illiterate.

Like Sachs, Sebastian Lotzer, a journeyman furrier, appealed to Scripture
to support his right to read and interpret the Bible. He advised his father
not to worry because his [Sebastian's] book had been slandered by some
Gross Hansen, (big shots).[9] Like certain benighted Pharisees they had stated
that the laity should stay away from holy Scripture because they could not
understand it. They had acted just as angrily and harshly with the mild
Jesus.[10] Christ, Lotzer asserted, had given men enough understanding to
comprehend him. In Proverbs the writer had asked, "Who are the wise?

Who are the learned in Scripture? Who are the scholars of the world? Had not God revealed the emptiness of the wisdom of the world?"[11] Lotzer declared the teaching of the learned was hollow. The roles were now reversed. The laity were responsible for discovering and teaching the truth.

Hans Staygmayer, a baker, chose different texts. In his pamphlet, laid in a tavern discussion, a monk asked Stagmayer why he was so clever when he had never gone to a university. The baker replied the clergy still treated the laity as the Jews had treated Christ, quoting John 7, "Who has the authority if he is not learned? Do you not know that [Christ] promised we would all be learned?" He then quoted Christ's words from Matthew 12, "I scorn the wisdom of the wise and the learning of the world I will overthrow."[12] Each of these artisans had justified his right to read and interpret the Bible from his own knowledge. Each had had to learn by himself.

Scripture was the only source used by the artisan writers. They did not quote from sermons by reformed preachers nor from pamphlets written by Luther or other reformers. The artisans' singleminded focus on the authority of Scripture makes clear the diffusion of biblical knowledge. Even a cursory reading of these pamphlets impresses the modern reader with the breadth of the artisans' command of Scripture. No common texts were used over and over by the different writers. Each had read the Scriptures himself and chose the texts he believed were the most appropriate. The lay reformation could not have occurred without a foundation of vernacular Bible preaching and reading, which reached back to the Hussites, to the printed vernacular Bibles of the last decades of the fifteenth century, to the sermons of Catholic reformers like Geiler von Kaisersburg. The humanist Jacob Wimpheling observed in 1505 that the ordinary people of Strasbourg read both the Old and New Testaments in German. Artisans read the Bible in their guild halls and discussed particular passages.[13] Scripture, whether received orally or through the printed word, was all pervasive in the lives of the artisan population.

THE ARTISANS' USE OF BIBLICAL TEXTS

Having asserted their right to read and interpret the Bible, the craftsmen incorporated Scripture into their pamphlets in diverse ways. Some merely compiled a set of texts or verses which they believed were important and had them printed up; others commented on a selected text; others quoted at length from Scripture to defend a particular position on baptism, prayer, or monasticism.

Two men self-identified as artisans printed biblical texts: Hans Gerhard, a weighmaster at Kitzingen included the texts of the Ten Commandments and the Our Father in his booklet on the Christian faith; Clement Ziegler, a Strasbourg gardener, wrote a commentary on the Our Father which also contained the text.[14] The first section of Gerhard's pamphlet was in the form of a catechism, "Why are you a Christian?". The catechumen answered, "Because Christ dwells in me, rules my life and influences me." "Confirm that," responded the catechist. "The holy apostle Paul said in Galatians 2, I do not live now, but Christ lives in me, for what I live in the flesh, I also live in the faith that the Son of God loved and gave himself for me."[15] The catechumen then went on to cite other texts from the Epistles. This style was followed for the first six pages of the pamphlet, in which every article of the Reformed faith was supported from Scripture. Gerhard, the weighmaster, knew the passages that would explain what the faith was, how one should practice that faith, and its fruit, namely, the love of one's neighbor. The pamphlet is remarkable for its simplicity and clarity. Not all artisans could handle scriptural texts as well and as lucidly. Ziegler gave the text of the Lord's prayer, but his own commentary overshadowed the text.

Hans Greiffenberger, a Nuremberg painter, wrote a commentary on the Christian's need to turn away from the world. He was almost overwhelmed by his references. One was never enough.

> Christ says in John 16, among other words to his disciples, such I have spoken to you, that you may have peace in me. In the world, however, you will have tribulations, but be consoled for I have overthrown the world. These words, dear brothers, the holy apostles took truly to heart for in these words are the armor which Paul speaks about in Ephesians 6. . . . David speaks of the hope in Psalm 23, when I walk through the shadow of death, yet I will not be afraid for thou, God, are with me. And Psalm 27, the Lord is my light and my salvation. And Psalm 30, Lord I have put my hope in you. These same anchors all the chosen and all friends of Christ and God's children have had, as Paul showed consolingly and clearly. . . .[16]

Further on, Greiffenberger struggled with the text from Romans 7, where Paul wrote that while the law is spiritual, men are carnal, sold under sin, "for I do not do what I want, but I do the very thing I hate" (RSV). Greiffenberger attempted to make the text clear by parenthetical glosses which led to almost total confusion.

> So I do that which I do not wish, so I conclude the law is good [although I do not and cannot hold to it]. So now I do not do the same [which is against the law] but the sin that dwells in me, for I know it is in me, in my flesh, does nothing good [that means satisfactory in German]. I have the desire but I cannot bring it about.[17]

Greiffenberger's exposition approached incomprehensibility, yet he was sure that the struggle between the spirit and the flesh would end in victory for those who chose the spirit. The worldly who submitted to the flesh and lived according to their reason and their own will were totally outside God's words or commandments.[18] Here Greiffenberger confirmed the artisan's distrust of reason. He made a division between spirit, which was godly, and reason which was human and subject to error.

Clement Ziegler's pamphlet on images set forth its scriptural foundation and Ziegler's method on the title page: "A short register and excerpt from the Bible, in which one learns what idolatry is. . . . Collected by Clement Ziegler, gardener in Strasbourg."[19] Ziegler collected from the Old Testament as well as the New, overwhelming his readers with texts. "Some there are," he began, "that say people only call images 'idols' out of pride. Then God must have been mistaken out of pride, for he said we should not make any images nor pray before them, Levit. 25. . . . Did you not hear what James said? Idolatry is unclean. Acts 15. . . . Do you not know that God forbade his people to make images so they would not scorn? Deut. 4. . . . and Paul's soul was angered when he saw all the images in Athens."[20]

The ruin of all peoples and their lands, all the torments and punishments which mankind had suffered were, according to Ziegler, the result of idolatry. Those who worshipped idols in former times had been visited by plagues, as Paul had warned in I Corinthians 10. Ziegler reviewed current practices, the presentation of offerings to images, the worshipping of images of saints, the idolatry practiced in the convents and monasteries. In each case Ziegler had the relevant text, his citations reflecting a thorough knowledge of the Bible with quotation after quotation from different chapters of Deuteronomy, Romans, Daniel, Isaiah, Jeremiah, Baruch, Malachi, Exodus, Micah, and Ezekiel.

Ziegler directed part of his at offerings made to images in the churches, specifically forbidden by Paul (I Corinthians 8). Instead of doing this, people should take care of the true saints by gathering up their food and giving it to the poor, as those from Macedonia and Achaea had done (Romans 15).[21] Ziegler defined idolatry as anything that turned people away from God his commandments. God could not be worshipped with material objects but only through prayer and service (Matthew 4).[22] The pamphlet, more than the short texts from the Bible that he had promised on the title page, was an exhortation against false practices of worship.

Hans Nagel, a tanner in Klingnau, wrote a pamphlet on faith in God, who alone could save, and on baptism. He presented biblical texts to support these tenets without commentary or any other interpretation. The words of Scripture were enough. The section on faith included texts from the Old Testament, primarily Genesis and Exodus, and from the Epistles, particularly Romans.[23] In the section on baptism, too, Nagel did not present the texts in chronological order but jumped, from Jesus baptizing in Judea, back to Jesus receiving baptism, and to other texts emphasizing the significance of baptism. Each text was headed by a citation (not always correct) giving the book and the chapter number. He attributed a text from Luke 3 to Luke 11, and one from Acts 2 to Acts 3, but the texts were correct, and reading them together was a powerful statement on baptism as a keystone of the teaching of Jesus and his disciples.[24]

The most professional and ambitious biblical commentary came from a Memmingen furrier, Sebastian Lotzer. In 1524, the city council had begun to permit certain changes in religious observance, including communion in both kinds. Some citizens, as well as peasants from nearby villages, refused to pay taxes in late 1524 and early 1525. Lotzer was asked by the Memmingen city council to serve as secretary to the villagers in their negotiations with the councilors. With Christopher Schappeler, the reformed preacher in the city, Lotzer summarized the peasants' grievances in *The Twelve Articles*, which clearly expressed the goals and aspirations of the peasants and were widely adopted by many villages during the Peasants' War. In June 1525, the Swabian League attacked the villagers and the city. Lotzer and Schappeler were forced to leave for Switzerland, where Lotzer disappeared.[25]

Lotzer's pamphlet, *An Exposition of the Text for the Twentieth Sunday after Trinity* (the parable of the wedding feast) was dedicated to Schappeler. The date 1524, suggests the tract was written during the crisis period. Its purpose was to show "the way in which men have trust in themselves, take charge of their spirituality, depend on their works, just as did the Pharisees (Luke 18)."[26] Lotzer believed that men should trust only in the Word of God.

Unlike other artisan writers, Lotzer interpreted the text allegorically, giving a metaphorical meaning for each person and event in the text. The text, Matthew 22, described the king who arranged the wedding feast for his son and then sent his servants to invite the wedding guests. As Lotzer said, it was a frightening story to all those who did not accept the word of God. Almighty God the King had prepared the wedding between his son Jesus Christ and his spouse, the true Christian faith.[27] The messengers sent by the king were the prophets, who proclaimed the invitation to the Jews, but they did not wish to come. God sent other messengers saying everything was ready, the oxen had been killed and the fatted calf. These messengers were the holy apostles, who carried the Gospel to the entire world, but people ignored them and went to their fields and workshops. For, contin-ued Lotzer, the Jews were always so deaf and stubborn they would not ac-cept the holy Word of God, although everything had been done to proclaim it. So Christ chose another people.[28]

Then, God was angry and he killed the murderers who had refused his invitation and burned their city, informing his servants that the wedding was now really ready. They went out into the streets and by-ways and brought in everyone, good and bad. When the tables were full, the king found one man who had no wedding clothes and asked him why he had come. The man was speechless but the king's servants bound him hand and foot and threw him into outer darkness. For when the kingdom of God is fulfilled, the sinners will come and be separated from one another. Those who do not wear the proper wedding garments of the true Christian faith will be thrown by Christ into outer darkness, for many are called, but few are chosen. The time was at hand, Lotzer concluded, the axe was laid on the root of the tree. Men must leave off the darkness of works and draw toward the Lord Jesus Christ who, would bring true understanding of his words.[29]

In Lotzer's view, the world was divided, between Jew and Gentile but also between the Gentiles who accepted the Word of God and those who ignored it, who continued to seek worldly power, wealth, and honor and did nothing about their neighbor but thought only of themselves.[30] The coming of the kingdom would bring not peace but division. Sinners would be destroyed, and only those chosen by God would remain. Although theologically undeveloped, the doctrine of divine election was apparent throughout Lotzer's exegesis. The second coming of Christ and the end of days were clear to Lotzer. Thus men should act promptly.[31]

These interpretive pamphlets reflect the self-confidence of the artisans. They made the *pro forma* statement that they were not learned men but they judged their own interpretations of Scripture superior to the learned because they were based on the Word of God.

SCRIPTURE AND CHRISTIAN PRACTICE

In another set of pamphlets the artisans applied their biblical knowledge to the practices of the Roman church, like the ban, penance, confession, and absolution. Many of these were written as conversations or dialogues between two or more artisans. Had these conversations actually taken place? Probably not. The writers used the device to authenticate their pamphlets. A religious discussion with like-minded friends was a normal activity of everyday life. Robert Scribner found evidence of them taking place at spinning bees, in taverns, at the workplace, within circles of kinsfolk and friends.[32]

The setting for one dialogue was the open highway. Two day laborers were walking from their village to work in the town. The author, Conrad Distelmaier, a Nuremberg mechanic, described the scene: "As I came upon them on the road, they started to talk about what they had heard . . . in the priest's Passion Sunday sermon. . . . As I listened I realized that people are trying to scare us . . . by saying that common day workers and craftsmen should not have the Bible read to them. . . ."[33] Two pamphlets were set in taverns: a song and a dialogue between a monk and a baker.[34] Four pamphlets had domestic settings: a father and son talking at home,[35] Hans Sachs' dialogue between a shoemaker and a canon at the door of the latter's house, another Sachs dialogue at a shoemaker's house,[36] and a discussion between a weaver and a shopkeeper in the shopkeeper's house.[37] The settings were a means of making the discussion believable to the reader.

Unlike the nobility or the urban elite, the artisans did not suggest alternatives to the Roman sacraments of penance, confession, and communion. They inquired whether there was scriptural authority for them. The primacy of Scripture over the church and by implication over the pope, bishops, and councils lay at the heart of the artisans' faith.

THE BAN

Despite the new preaching, the ban remained. It continued to arouse hatred and fear among workers and craftsmen, who could be banned for a mere non-payment of tithes. In one pamphlet, a peasant complained that he had been banned and publicly cursed by the priest because he had owed one pint of wheat. He had paid it, but when the same priest "was not able to fill up his chests," he demanded more and banned the peasant again.[38]

There was extensive commentary on the ban in the conversation reported by Conrad Distalmaier between a sawyer and a woodcutter walking to the sawmills from their village. The woodcutter was worried because his friend the sawyer had said he would no longer obey the ban. Hadn't he heard the village priest, in his Passion Sunday sermon, say that St. Peter, a prelate of the church, had cut off Malchus' ear? That meant that any priest should cut off a rebellious person who did not obey the laws of the church, and no one should communicate with the banned.[39] The sawyer responded by explaining the context of the biblical account. Before it happened, he said, the disciples asked Christ, "Lord, shall we smite [the soldiers] with the sword?" but before Christ could answer them, Peter cut off the ear. "He had received no order from Christ, he did it in his own rashness. . . . Peter sinned because he had no authorization from Christ and that is why Christ told him to sheath his sword."[40] It seemed to him, continued the sawyer, that the priest very conveniently left out that part so that no one could point out the error and he could retain the ban. Furthermore, he added, Christ put the ear back on and cured Malchus. The woodcutter replied that certainly the priest had not told the whole story and that the sawyer's explanation was better.[41] The sawyer had not merely criticized the ban, he had invalidated it.

In the same sermon, the priest had preached on the need for confession. This annoyed the woodcutter because the priest, himself, did not hear confessions and his assistants did not have complete powers of absolution. Could the sawyer help him? The latter, quoting David, Isaiah, and Ezekiel, replied that the Lord forgave all who turned to him. Did this mean, asked the woodcutter, that he needed no dispensation, that God would forgive his sins for his own sake if only he showed true faith in his mercy? Truly that was right, said the sawyer, for when we are in need we should turn to Christ, for he said "come unto me all you who are heavy laden and I will give you rest."[42]

CONFESSION

Confession was a major concern for the artisans, as it was for the nobility. Each rank repudiated the legitimacy of auricular confession, but they supported their refutation from different scriptural texts. In Hans Sachs' dialogue between a canon and a shoemaker, the canon demanded to know why the Lutherans never confessed. The craftsman replied that it was not commanded by God in the Old or the New Testament. The canon denied that. Christ had said, in Luke 17, "Go hence and show yourself to the priest." The shoemaker retorted that if that meant confession it was unusual German. The canon would have to have better scriptural proof. That was impossible, said the cleric, because what God commanded and what was contained in Scripture was a miserable, rambling thing.[43] Confession was ordered by the holy fathers in council and thus established by the church. The shoemaker pointed out that the only valid council had been held by the apostles at Jerusalem (Acts 15). The councils called later had created much trouble in Christendom by promulgating too many rules and establishing the ban. Here Sachs drew a firm line between Scripture and the laws of the church. The gap between the layman and the cleric was rammed home when the canon admitted that he had never heard of the apostolic council in Jerusalem.[44] The canon claimed Luke 17 (Christ's command to the lepers) as a proof text, but the shoemaker rejected it as too vague. Sachs gave no other texts with regard to confession.

Utz Rysschner, an Augsburg weaver, provided detailed Scriptural proof to deny the obligation of confession to a priest. He wrote in response to a published sermon by Matthias Kretz, the Romanist preacher in the cathedral. The priest had defined the various kinds of sin and then spoken of the need for confession, with scriptural references. His friend, a shopkeeper, had purchased the sermon and invited the weaver to his house so he could read it to him.[45] The weaver looked up the biblical references as the two of them studied the sermon together.[46] The weaver rebutted Kretz's use of Scripture, proving again and again that the passages could be construed differently. Open confession, read the shopkeeper, occurred in two ways. First, that the sins were open; also confession and absolution were open. This form was described in Matthew 18, "If your brother sins against you, then reprove him. . . ." This the Lutherans called evangelical confession. The weaver disagreed. According to the pure Word of the gospel, this rebuke was not public but a secret, godly, brotherly warning. If someone refused to accept such an admonition, one could only commend him to God and leave him to his judgment, but without such a warning no good order could be established.[47] The Bible passage cited, according to the weaver, had nothing to do with banning or confession. The shopkeeper admitted his ignorance. He had not read enough to know how the councils ordered penance for sin or how this had been established. The weaver asked, rather angrily, what the apostles had commanded for penitence. As for himself, God gave him the grace to recognize his sin and thus also gave him repentance.[48]

The shopkeeper persevered with reading the sermon, which had more biblical references. The weaver's explications of the texts appear below. Texts cited are given in the footnotes from the revised standard version of the Bible.

> *Shopkeeper*: Listen to Numbers 5. The text proclaims confession clearly. Men or women [says the text] who [render] themselves sinful shall confess their sins, and the whole chapter speaks of priests.[49]
>
> *Weaver*: Dear tradesman, we will look up the chapter and read whether this is so. Yes, I find it so written. If a man or woman sins against a person and thus goes against the Lord, they have sinned and should admit the sin they have done and atone for it with a sum of money. I understand that this way, if I have sinned against God and man, I should admit it, but we should never give an offering for it like money or cows or calves but [rather] a pure heart. It says nothing in here about confessing all sins, words, deeds and thoughts to the priest. Christ said to his disciples [John 20], those whose sins you forgive, they will be forgiven, and those whose you retain will be retained. [Kretz] makes a big deal of this, how men must confess to the priest, as though in these words God gave them the power of forgiveness of sins and established them as judges. . . . However, as Christ says in Luke 6, you must be merciful as your father in heaven. You shall damn no one, so that you will not be damned, forgive so that your father will forgive you. . . . Thus, if they wish to judge us and ban us . . . they themselves are full of sin . . . and take all power in their hands against the Word of God.[50]

This is a typical use of a priest's sermon as the center of a discussion between laymen. Both the shopkeeper and the weaver wrestled with the meaning of the texts the priest had used. The weaver found other citations to repudiate the priest's teaching.

Hans Füssli, the Swiss bellmaker, also discussed the Numbers 5 text. In his commentary on Jerome Gebwiler's defense of the Roman church, he wrote that the church had put too much stress on penance. Even when one confessed, whether the sin was great or small, one was considered to be given over to the devil. The granting of penance had become a huckster's market, in which absolution was available only to the very worst and was proffered only for money. "Thus," he continued, "they have no real scriptural proof thereon and do not want to demonstrate it for that reason, however, they may point out that it can be found in the book of Numbers, chapter 5. 'You should acknowledge your sin and he who has been sinned against should be given a fifth part more of the principal.'"[51] This, remarked Füssli, resembled the penitential system as practiced, except that now it was all secret and the extra fifth went to the priest. "If [Gebwiler] wanted to establish confession on this text, then he was cleverer than Christ himself, who had never thought of it with a single word and thus did not ordain it was necessary for salvation."[52]

Rysschner's weaver had been willing to accept that the Numbers text required some kind of confession, but not the full confession demanded by the Roman church, and certainly no money should be involved. Füssli was unwilling to admit the validity of the Numbers text, except as it showed the corruption of current practice, that the priests absolved only those with money. As for New Testament texts on confession, Füssli said they did not exist.

The two pamphlets provide insight into the process of cultural diffusion at the popular level. Both men commented on printed books, in their possession, written by learned defenders of the old faith. Thus, the preaching and writing of the Roman priests was important as a catalyst, important enough for an artisan to buy a book which he then refuted. In the Rysschner pamphlet, the protagonists read a sermon that had been preached. The oral message had been printed, and they discussed it orally, but the weaver checked the preacher's textual references against the Bible. The printed text of the Bible was used as verification. The weaver had his own way with Scripture. Once he verified its if he did not agree with the text, he sidestepped, offering another, better text from the New Testament. He did say, however, that if he could really read Kretz's sermon carefully, he would provide an answer to all the superfluous decrees of the church councils and the fathers.[53] Füssli did not bother with verification. Disagreeing with Numbers 5, he said that Christ had never said a word about confession. That, for him, ended the argument. Both of these artisans, in their own way, were differenting between the old law and the new. Rysschner's weaver was willing to accept the need for confession, though he would not confess to another man nor to a priest, but only to Christ, who was God-man and priest. He stated explicitly that the Old Testament requirements did not apply to Christians, because the Jews had not been praiseworthy teachers but had misled people and turned Christians in the wrong path.[54]

The weaver stated that Christ had suggested confession four times. First, concurring with Isaiah 43, he had said that God alone could forgive sins. Second, Christ had recounted the parable of the open sinner, who said

"Lord have mercy on me, a miserable sinner" (Luke). Third, in the parable of the prodigal son, the subject had said, "Father I have sinned against God and against you. I am not worthy to be called your son, make me the least of your servants." Fourth, in Matthew 6, Christ taught us to say, "Father, forgive our sins, as we forgive those who sin against us." "That," said the weaver, "I think is the right and true way to confess."[55] Rysschner did not spell out the difference between the old law and the new, but clearly for him the words of Christ annulled the Old Testament.

Hans Staygmayer, a baker of Reutlingen, wrote a lively dialogue between a monk and a baker, the former having come to collect the Easter tithe of eggs.[56] The conversation went from fasting to confession. For quite some time, said the baker, there had been a division over the teaching of Occam, Bernard, and Bonaventura with regard to whether confession had been established by men, meaning the church. Now the clergy wanted to have an agreement that God had established it, and if people asked for proof they said that Christ had talked about it with his disciples, but they had never written it down.[57] The monk replied that Christ had established confession to a priest because he had said to the lepers, "Go, show yourself to a priest," thus establishing auricular confession.[58] This was the same verse from Luke 17 that Hans Sachs had rejected. The baker also refused to accept it as sufficient scriptural proof. It was a few words said to a small group, he declared.

Nevertheless, replied the monk, if he wished to be saved, he must confess, as Ambrose and Duns Scotus had required. Further, James 5 instructed men to confess to one another. The baker was willing to accept this form, pointing out that both Jerome and Augustine had also recommended the practice of one sinner confessing to another sinner. If the baker did so, retorted the monk, he would be banned. The baker replied that if he were right in his own heart, the ban would be meaningless. He would find comfort in the prophets.[59] Staygmayer accepted one of the scriptural texts offered and added to it from the church fathers. Although he thus acknowledged that confession was established by the church, as well as by the apostle, he maintained his independence. He would confess to a fellow Christian, even if it meant the ban.

The contrast between these artisan pamphlets and those of the knights on confession is striking. The knights believed they should develop alternative forms of confession. Several of them proposed confession by one layman to another, yet none of them referred to scriptural precedents. The artisans were clear about two things. They had no intention of continuing with auricular confession and they insisted on scriptural proof. Where Scripture mentioned confession, they were careful to limit it to open public admission of sin. By no means were they willing to grant the power of absolution to the priests. It is difficult to determine whether these lay writers felt burdened by the demands of the confessor, as Steven Ozment has suggested.[60] They strongly objected to the secrecy of auricular confession, which they felt resulted in unfair advantage being given to the rich. None of the pamphlets in this study made any mention of the rigorous and prodding questions contained in the confessional manuals discussed by Ozment. The artisans did not write that they had been tyrannized, except by the demands of the clergy for money. The sense of the pamphlets, as I read them, is that auricular confession had become irrelevant to their lives. The clergy had lost the respect of lay men and women. If the pamphlets were representative of the larger artisan community, many confessionals must have stood empty by 1524.

PRAYER

The artisans' attitude toward confession was similar to their attitude toward prayer. They did not want to be told what to pray or how to pray. They wanted to speak their own thoughts directly to Christ or to God. Again in contrast to the knights, they did not write prayers for others to use. Instead, they warned against this. Prayer was an intensely personal communication, the heart of a Christian's life. Heinrich Vogtherr the Elder, the printer, criticized the reformed clergy who would not let individuals pray as they wanted but insisted on congregational prayer. The cleric "will not permit that when a heart so desires, the person speaks at the beginning or end of the pastor's prayer to express his own petitions."[61] Hans Sachs made a similar point that true prayer meant to pray to God spiritually. Churchgoing and praying at certain hours was just outward show. Christ said, in Matthew 4, you should pray to God and serve him alone.[62] This echoed the words of a song by the *landsknecht* Jörg Graff: No one could serve God for him, he must do it himself. If a lord had a knight, the latter must follow him. He, Jörg Graff, had only one lord.[63]

Hans Greiffenberger, the Nuremberg printer, had much to say about prayer. It was the devil who fooled men by providing them with pretty words to say and nice little prayers and beautiful confessions. Christ had told his disciples, in Matthew 6, not to pray with many words and phrases, for God knew each individual's needs before he prayed. Nor should men pray in front of other people, since this was only pretence and had no foundation. Each should pray privately, in seclusion.[64] Prayer was not a matter of words of the inner spirit. Despite this warning, Greiffenberger gave an example. "A man might thus speak his heart: 'Oh God, I am a poor human, what great depravity is planted in me. I pray to thee, Oh God, that thou will have mercy on me. Whatever should come, let it be as it may.'"[65]

Pamphilus Gengenbach, the Basel printer, faced an inner conflict in advocating prayer to God alone. In 1520, he had become a member of the Brotherhood of the Knights of the Shield, a confraternity dedicated to honoring the saints, especially the Virgin Mary.[66] Though a lay person, he wrote his pamphlet, *Der Evangelischburger*, as a sermon, in which he described the errors not only of the church but also of ordinary Christians. Prayers to the saints were wrong because Christ had said he and the father were one; thus, we should pray only to our brother Christ, because men's hope was in God alone, not in the saints.[67] If one wished to honor the saints, it should be done by honoring God. Only the Lord's prayer should be used. The Virgin Mary, however, was different because she was created and chosen by God, had fulfilled the prophecy of Isaiah, and had been honored by the sending of the angelic messenger. Thus it was proper to honor Mary with the angelic greeting, Ave Maria.[68] One is reminded of the knight Adam von Schaumburg, who condoned prayers to the saints because they were so united with God that they would never go against his will.[69]

Gengenbach's desire to keep the Ave Maria was a human reaction. He could willingly give up some customs, but the Ave Maria was too central to his own prayer life. Compromises of this sort were probably present in the religious thought and conduct of many people. Some changes were easy to accept, but personal exceptions were made. The pamphlets reveal these exceptions and force us to realize that few individuals accepted the Reformation precisely as it was preached by Luther, Zwingli, Bucer, or Bugenhagen. They had their own personal beliefs and rituals.

The variations among the artisans about what should be done in public and what in private are important. All of the pamphleteers rejected auricular confession, in part because of the secrecy involved. Yet they were critical of public prayer and rejected prepared prayers, except for the Lord's prayer, whether said by a Roman priest or a reformed preacher. They opposed any elite discourse which might be used to exert power over them. They did not want a pastor to pray for them, because he would come between them and Christ and break the spiritual relationship.

COMMUNION

The strength of biblicism among the working class was manifested in Clement Ziegler's pamphlet on communion, published in 1524. Ziegler was a Strasbourg gardener (the title always appeared on the title pages of his pamphlets), who described his work to enlighten the ignorant: "Certain brethren coming from afar have noted that in a lot of other cities, notably in Augsburg, they don't know what a gardener is. I want it to be known that I am a peasant, working the earth to grow onions, turnips, radishes and hemp."[70] The gardeners, who would now be called market gardeners, formed a large guild in Strasbourg.[71] In 1524, Ziegler had a conversion experience, perhaps when he escaped drowning after a flood of the fields. He believed Christ had saved him and began to preach to his neighbors and to peasants in outlying villages. "Why shouldn't I give my life to the whole community," he wrote, "even if there are dangers in doing so. Because God helped me out of the deep waters in 1524 . . . [when] I had received help from no one. But it was the name of Jesus Christ that helped me."[72] He wrote more than nine pamphlets between 1524 and 1552,[73] explaining that although he was an uneducated peasant and no one would be interested in him, they should be interested in the Word of God.[74]

Even Ziegler's early works revealed a deep familiarity with the Bible, suggesting that he may have participated in Bible readings with his fellow gardeners in their guild hall. Whether he owned a Bible himself we do not know, but his quotations from the Old Testament were drawn from a pre-Lutheran translation, his New Testament citations from the Lutheran translation.[75]

In 1524, he addressed his treatise on communion to "all who preach the Word of God with zeal and Christian earnestness." He was writing to bring forward the terrible errors which all Christendom suffered with regard to the body of Jesus Christ.[76] Luther's first German treatise on communion had been published in 1521, followed by another in 1522 and two more in 1523. Martin Bucer, the Strasbourg reformer, had responded in Latin in 1524, and in a German treatise in that same year.[77] Since Bucer strongly rejected Luther's doctrine of the Real Presence, Ziegler was familiar with the controversy. His text makes it possible to follow his reasoning and to observe his use of biblical texts:

> It is clear that the Sacrament, as it is called is . . . a great abuse. It makes me wonder, indeed, who thought of the word Sacrament which is not found in the Scriptures, for Christ himself took the living bread and called it his body when he said "Take and eat it, for this is my body. Drink, that is my blood of the New Testament." Thus, one should call it the body of Christ, and his testament, and Christ's supper and not the sacrament, for that is against the Word of Christ. And it is a man-made commandment which has established this . . . for if you read the whole New Testament from the beginning to the end you will find no foundation for it. . . . The words which he spoke at the Last Supper have never really been interpreted clearly for us. Because it is clearly written, "when they were seated Jesus took the bread, and gave thanks and broke it." That was his consecration and he thought . . . he had given us an example . . . that we should also consecrate ourselves with a thanksgiving.
>
> Now, pious Christians, listen well, because the opposing party has taught us the bread or the body of Christ is not bread but flesh. Oh, God in heaven that we should understand so little. Because Jesus Christ made it very clear . . . "The body is of no use, the spirit is the living power." But

that God is a spirit and also a body, I will shortly, dear brethren, explain to you.[78]

Ziegler drawing on the Old Testament, gave examples of how God had appeared in a cloud, as a voice, but never in the flesh. He carried this on to the New Testament and in both cases gave supporting scriptural citations. So, he concluded, "we should be content with the words of Christ, for he gave us a clear Scripture by which we should stand . . . that Christ will not be found in outward things but in spirit."[79]

Ziegler's understanding was deeply spiritualist and Zwinglian. The doctrine of transubstantiation, he believed, drew men away from the effective power of Christ and thus distanced them from God. He was able to marshal his ideas in forceful prose, supporting them with apposite scriptural texts. The pamphlet revealed his ability to persuade, an ability he used in rousing the peasants before the Peasants' War.

The artisan pamphleteers wanted an unstructured church, without any sacraments but baptism and communion. The function of the church was to preach and teach the Gospel, therefore only one cleric was needed—a preacher. They did not want the clergy to do more. They could confess their sins to one another; absolution could come from God alone. Prayers should come from their own hearts, not from devotionals. The sacramental church no longer had a place in their lives.

Notes

1. Heiko Oberman, *The Dawn of the Reformation*, 1986, 158–159.
2. #30, *Ein new Christlich lied . . . das verantwurtet den Gots lesterer schmehung . . .*, after 1525, fol. Aii. #50,*Welcher das Evangelium hat für gut . . .*, fol. Aiii^v, Aii.
3. #134, Jörg Graff, *In disem tractatlein sind drey hübsche lieder . . .*, fol. A^v.
4. #205, H. Marschalk, *Von der weit erschollen Namen Luther . . .*, fol. Aii.
5. #133, Bastian Goltschmit, *Ein underweisung etzlicher artickel, so bruder Matteiss, prior der prediger closters zu Worms, ungegründt in heiliger gschrifft, offentlich gepredigt hat . . .*, 1525, fols. ai^v– aiii.
6. #115, H. Füssli, *Antwurt eins Schwytzer Purens*, fols. aiii^v, aii^v– aiii.
7. Eckhard Bernstein, *Hans Sachs*, 1993, 23, 41–47.
8. #221, Hans Sachs, *Disputation Zwyschen ainem Chorherre und Schuchmacher*, 1524, fol. aii–aii^v.
9. The term *Gross Hansen* (always capitalized in the original) is literally translated "Big Johns." It was used frequently by the artisans to describe the upper ranks—the rich and powerful. It was a slang phrase which I have put into modern slang.
10. #187, Sebastian Lotzer, *Ain christlicher sendbrief darin angezaigt wirt, dz die layen macht und recht haben von dem hailigen wort gots reden, lern und schreiben . . .*, 1523, fol. aiv^v.

11. Ibid., fol. B.
12. #261, Hans Staygmayer, *Ain Schoner Dialogus oder Gesprech von aynem Münch und Becken, wolcher die Oster ayer Samlen wollt*, 1524, fol. Biii.
13. A. G. Dickens, *The German Nation and Martin Luther*, 1974, 148, 151. Rodolphe Peter, "Le Jardinier Clément Ziegler . . .," 1954, 265.
14. #132, Hans Gerhardt, *Schöne Frag und Antwort, Was ain warhafftiger Christenn der recht Glaub, unnd seyn frucht sey.*, 1525; #288, Clement Ziegler, *Ein fast schöne auslegung der Vater Unser*, 1525.
15. H. Gerhardt, *Schöne Frag und Antwort*, fol. aii.
16. #141, Hans Greiffenberger, *Eintrostliche ermanung den angefochten im gewissen, von wegen gethoner sünd . . .*, 1524, fol. aii.
17. Ibid., fol. aii^v.
18. Ibid., fol. aiii^v.
19. #289, Clement Ziegler, *Ain Kurtz Register, und ausszug der Bibel in wolchem man findet was Abgoterey sey, unnd wa man jeder suchen soll. Colligiert durch Clement ziegler Gartner zu Strassburg*, 1524, title page.
20. Ibid., fol. ai^v.
21. Ibid., fol. Aii.
22. Ibid., fol. Aiii^v.
23. #210, Hans Nagel, *Von dem Glawbenn Gotes Der allein selig machett, und nur von hymel geben würdt: Von dem Tauff Christi*, 1525, fols. Aii–Avi.
24. Ibid., fols. B–Biv, see especially Bii and Bii^v.
25. P. Russell, *Lay Theology in the Reformation*, 1986, 86–88.
26. #186, Sebastian Lotzer, *Ayn ausslegung uber dz Evangelium . . . der . . . zwayntzigisten Sontag nach der hayligen Trivaltigkait . . .*, 1524, fol. Aiii.
27. Ibid., fol. Aiii, Aiv.
28. Ibid., fol. B.
29. Ibid., fol. Bii, Bii^v.
30. Ibid., fol. Aiii.
31. Ibid., fol. Bii^v; #189, S. Lotzer, *Ain hailsame Ermanunge*, Laube edit., 252.
32. Robert W. Scribner, "Oral Culture and the Diffusion of Reformation Ideas," in R. Scribner, *Popular Culture and Popular Movements in Reformation Germany*, 1987, 56–59.
33. #90 Conrad Distelmair, *Ain gesprechbuchlein von aim Xodtschneider und aim Holtzhawer*, 1523, fol. Aii.
34. #61, Jörg Breuning, *Drei gar nützliche lieder*, n.d.; #260, Hans Staygmayer, *Ain Schoner Dialogus . . . von eynem Münch und Becken*, 1524.
35. #18, *Dialogus . . . zwischen einem Vater und Sohn . . . Luthers Lehre belangende*, 1523.
36. #221, Sachs, *Disputation zwyschen ainem Chorherre und Schuchmacher*, 1524. #222, Hans Sachs, *Ain Gesprech aines Evangelischen Christen mit ainem Lutherischen*, 1524.
37. #218, Utz Rysschner, *Ain gesprech buchlin von ainem Weber und ainem Krämer über das Büchlin Doctoris Mathie Kretz von der haimlichen Beycht*, 1524.
38. #18, *Dialogus . . . zwischen einem Vater und Sohn . . .*, fol. Biv.
39. #90 Conrad Distelmair, *Ain gesprechbuchlein von aim Xodtschneider . . .*, fol. Aii^v.
40. Ibid.
41. Ibid., fol. Aiii.
42. Ibid., fols. Aiv, B.
43. The word is *elende*, which means miserable, pitiful, wretched. It was used in

the sixteenth century to describe the poor who wandered from town to town. I have taken poetic license here to extend it to mean rambling. The canon's meaning is that the Scripture is too vague.

44. #221, Sachs, *Disputation zwyschen ainem Chorherre und Schuchmacher*, fol. Bii^v– Biii.
45. #218, Rysschner, *Ain Gesprech buchlin*, fol. Aii^v.
46. See Robert Scribner, "Oral Culture and the Diffusion of Reformation Ideas," 54–55.
47. #218, Rysschner, *Gesprech buchlin*, fols. Aii^v–Aiii.
48. Ibid., fol. Aiii.
49. Numbers 5:6–7: "When a man or a woman commits any of the sins that men commit by breaking faith with the Lord, and he is guilty, he shall confess his sin which he has committed and he shall make restitution for his wrong, adding a fifth to it."
50. #218, Rysschner, *Gesprech buchlin*, fols. Aiii^v–Aiv^v.
51. #115, Hans Füssli, *Antwurt eins Schwytzer Purens über . . . Meyster Jeronimi Gebwiler*, 1522, fol. Aii^v.
52. Ibid.
53. #218, Utz Rysschner,*Gesprech buchlin*, fol. B.
54. Ibid., fol. Bii, Bii^v.
55. Ibid., fol. C, Cii.
56. #261, Hans Staygmayer, Beck an Reutlingen, *Ain Schoner Dialogus oder Gesprech/ von aynem Münch and Becken/wolcher die Oster ayer Samlen wollen*, 1524, fol. Aii.
57. Ibid., fol. Aiii^v.
58. Ibid., fol. Aiv.
59. Ibid.
60. Steven Ozment, *The Reformation in the Cities*, 1975, 22–32.
61. #274, Heinrich Vogtherr der älterer, *Ain Cristliche anred*, 1524, Laube edit., 1, 484.
62. #221, Sachs, *Disputation zwyschen ainem Chorherre und Schuchmacher*, fol. Bi^v.
63. #134, J. Graff, . . . *Drey Hübsche lieder neu gemacht*, n.d., fol. Ai^v.
64. #142, Hans Greiffenberger, *Ein Warnung vor dem Teüffel der sich wider ubt mit seinem dendelmarkt*, 1524, fol. Aii^v.
65. Ibid., fol. Bii^v.
66. Karl Lendi, *Der Dichter Pamphilus Gengenbach: Beiträge zu seinen Leben und seine Werken*, 1926, 15.
67. #124, Pamphilus Gengenbach, *Der Evangelischburger*, 1523, fol. B^v– Bii^v.
68. Ibid., fols. Cii–Cii^v.
69. #230, Adam von Schaumburg, *Leyenspiegell*, fols. Civ^v–D.
70. Quoted in Rodolphe Peter, "Le jardinier Clément Ziegler," 1954, 13.
71. Thomas A. Brady, Jr., notes that agricultural guilds for market gardeners and wine growers were particular to Alsace (*Turning Swiss*, 1985, 12). Since Ziegler lived in an urban community and belonged to a guild, I have placed him with the artisans.
72. Peter 17.
73. The complete bibliography of Ziegler's works appears in Rodolphe Peter, "Le maraîcher Clément Ziegler," *RHPR* 34 (1954): 256. See also Primary Sources bibliography, 287–291.
74. R. Peter, "Le maraîcher Clément Ziegler," 260.

75. Ibid., 265.
76. #291, Clement Ziegler, Gartner zu Strassburg, *Von der waren nyessung beid leibs und bluts Christi*, 1524, fol. Aiii.
77. Miriam Usher Chrisman, *Bibliography of Strasbourg Imprints*, 1982, 326 (P3. 11. 13); *Martin Bucer's Deutsche Schriften*, ed. Robert Stupperich, 7 vols. (1960–), 1, 191.
78. #291, Ziegler, *Von der waren nyessung*, fols. Aiii^v, B.
79. Ibid., fol. Biii.

Disputacion zwischen ainem Chor
herzenn vnnd Schüchmacher
darin das wort gottes vnd ein recht Crist
lich wesen verfochtten wirtt.
Hanns   Sachs.
M   D   XXiiij.

Ich sag euch / wa dise schweigē / so werdē die stein schreie. lu. 19

7 "Disputation between a canon and a shoemaker in which the shoemaker
   defends the Word of God and a true Christian life."

A shoemaker delivers a new pair of slippers to a canon at the latter's house. The
shoemaker remarks that he has just written a book to explain the Roman church
services to the common man. The canon attacks him as a Lutheran and an
evangelical.

SOURCE: Title page of a pamphlet by Hans Sachs, *Disputacion zwischen ainem
Chorherren unnd Schuchmacher daraus das wort Gottes und ein recht Christlich wesen
verfochtten wirtt*. Augsburg: M. Ramminger, 1524. Reproduced with permission of
the Folger Shakespeare Library.

8

The View From Below: Order in a Divided Society

THE ARTISANS' VIEW OF THE WORLD

Like the upper ranks, the artisans wanted an ordered world. As they looked up the hierarchical ladder, however, they saw a divided society. In their pamphlets and in petitions addressed to the city council, they consciously differentiated between rich people and the *gemeinem armen Mann*; between merchants and putting out masters who oppressed workers and piece workers; between usurers and debtors; between "My Lords and the common citizens"; between rich burghers and peasants; and between lay people and priests.[1] In their minds, society was polarized between wealth and poverty, power and the lack of it. The world was further fragmented by those holding or demanding special privileges: foreign clergy, nobility, whores (the priests' concubines) and foreign workers.[2]

The concept of the *gemeinen Nutz* was not part of their thought pattern; none of the artisan pamphlets I read used the phrase. O'Malley pointed out that the *gemeinen Nutz* was not drawn from the Bible but reflected the political concepts of Greek and Roman writers. The artisans wrote of the *Gemeinde*, the commoners, or the *gemeinem armen Mann*.[3] They believed it was the duty of the upper ranks to take care of the lower ranks, a duty only rarely performed. Other phrases were used only by the artisans. They saw the rich and the clergy accumulating great *Haufe*, hoards or piles of money and goods. The clergy were described as having "full sacks" and "full bellies," living in luxury while the poor men ate chaff.[4] These metaphors, repeated from writer to writer, reflected a physical image of wealth and possessions at the top which they, the common men and women, would never share.

The Reformation, as they saw it, caused further separation. Although the majority of the artisan pamphleteers favored the Reform, they deplored the discord which led to the breaking up the Romanists, the Lutherans, and

181

the Evangelicals into sects, a phenomenon they feared. The artisans were the only pamphlet writers in my sample who described these factions, their behavior toward one another, the tension they created in the community. Other ranks recognized the differences between those who remained loyal to the old faith and those who converted to the new, but did not take notice of the emergence of new religious groupings and the conflicts among them. This was a significant difference. The knightly pamphleteers enumerated in detail the errors and abuses of the Roman clergy but did not describe the relationships between themselves, as Lutherans, and the Romanists, except in a reference to efforts of the latter to prevent publication of their pamphlets. The knights believed the Roman clergy should be forced to accept the new faith and to give up their wealth and privileges. They assumed that the people on their own lands would be won over to the Reform by preaching. They did not conceive that the community might split.

The patricians wrote of the divisions within the family, between those who lived in the world and their relatives in convents. They believed the latter would leave their cloisters to join their families. Neither the minor civil servants nor the upper civil servants concerned themselves with the effects of religious partition of the community. Only the artisans described the impact of divisions created within families, within the work place, among friends and neighbors by the new teaching.

Individual artisan writers used a variety of terms for the different factions. There were "God's people" and, in opposition, the learned, who said that only they could understand Scripture.[5] There were Romanists and Lutherans; Romanists, Lutherans, and Evangelicals; Evangelicals and Roman courtesans; as well as partisan humanists who were enemies of God.[6] Division affected the artisans more than other ranks. The knights, the patricians, the upper civil servants all had means of controlling the world around them. The artisans had no right to take the initiative. They had to wait for decisions made from above. They felt vulnerable and unprotected. Their solution to the problem of division reflected the limits of their influence. They thought in terms of their parish, within which they should be free to elect and dismiss its own preacher. Hearing the Word of God, the members of the church would be able to recreate a unified Christian community.[7]

THE CLERGY AS A SOURCE OF DISORDER

The greatest source of disorder, according to the artisan writers, was the Roman clergy. Their criticism, again, differed from that of other ranks. They did not attack the theological base of the convents like the patricians. They did not write sharp, scathing satires like the minor civil servants, nor violent polemics like Ulrich von Hutten. Their satire was tempered, as shown in a satirical song describing the Pope's conversion to the new faith—how he now aspired to follow God's Word. He no longer asked for money but bewailed his sins with weeping eyes. The bishops ran to find the poor and gave them heaps of what they needed. All the clergy were now shepherds, so Christendom would move ahead. It was a new story, concluded the author, and people might think it was a joke, but he preferred to sing of the holiness of the priests. It was painful to repudiate them.[8] The last comment was characteristic of the artisans, who were less confrontational and more irenic than other ranks.

The artisans' major criticism of the clergy was directed against local clerics and issues which directly affected them. They scolded the rural clergy as well, because they saw them as particularly avaricious and grasping. Some of their criticisms were general. The clergy made everyone pay for church services, including baptism. The sacraments were sold for money, thus the priests had turned the churches into a horse market or flea market.[9] The priests set a bad moral example; they were drunk and lived openly with mistresses and prostitutes.[10] The behavior of the local clergy was described in particular detail. Jörg Graff, the blind *Landsknecht*, itemized the wealth of the monks. Many a cloister had an income of 18,000 gulden to spend annually, he said, and a throng of administrators: the abbot, a judge, a tax collector, a manager, a master cook, a cellarer, and a steward. The monks ate loach, a delicacy, and fine grains, grilled fish and crab, with much wine and white bread, while the poor man had to live on hash and chaff.[11] The learned clergy had taken over the best cities, markets, and castles, pushing aside the citizens and the common people.[12] Hans Ulem complained that the monks bought up all the food so that children and pregnant women could not get hens or eggs at the market. Artisans, returning home at night, could find nothing to buy because it had all been taken by the priests.[13] The greed of the clergy, as far as the artisans were concerned, translated into shortages of food.

Steffan Büllheym, the Strasbourg artisan, in his warning to Matthias Zell, listed the latter's enemies by name, parish by parish. There was the priest Lawrence with his fat wife; the canon at Old St. Peter; the Dominican Thomas Schwein; the vicar of the cathedral and the priest at St. Martin's church.[14] He included in his condemnation the priests' concubines, who, as he said, were the same as beneficed clergy because they shared the salaries of their partners. Büllheym believed these women obstructed change. He had no sympathy for them, indeed he insulted them. Frau Beatrice, the female "pastor" at St. Nicholas, he said, had big, fat legs. Another would cry if priests were forced to marry. Only one of these women did he describe as pious.[15] The artisans lived their daily lives with these priests, whose immorality, they believed, undermined their own families and corrupted the community. They could not withdraw to their mansions or to their lands outside the city like the patricians and the honorables. They knew the intimate details of their priests' lives and the way they fulfilled their calling. And they kept track. Dietrich Butzbach, a guildsman from Leipzig who was in Worms at the time of the Diet of 1521, wrote a letter to a friend instructing the latter to read it "to all the good *gesellen* [companions] so they would know how the clergy were behaving." It was like Rome, he said, with murders, robbery, and beautiful women. Although it was Lent, no one was fasting, but they whored around, eating meat, hens, doves, milk, and cheese. It was like life at the Venusberg.[16]

The level of religious life in the villages, the artisans wrote, was even worse. The village priests were the most ignorant of all the clergy, they wrote. They scorned the peasants, wanting only their money. In a satirical poem by a popular writer, the village priest announced that the village headman had died, so all should be joyful. There would be a big banquet with the priests from the neighboring villages at the head table. The peasants would honor the departed by giving money for vigils, soul masses, and anniversary masses, money which the priests could use for themselves. So, concluded the priest, "Rejoice [you] priests when a rich peasant dies."[17]

Hans Ritter listed the demands the clergy made on common folk. They had to bring meat, bacon, oil, sausage, eggs, capons, hens, cheese, pigs, and sheep. They had to pay a penny tax for every animal, cow, donkey, or horse. All this had to be brought to the church or the cloister.[18] The artisans' pamphlets described the details of daily urban and village life much as they appeared in the paintings of Hieronymus Bosch and Pieter Bruegel the Elder. Satirical and critical of the feasting peasants, they used food as a means of measuring the difference between the ranks. Bruegel's peasants' wedding feast was meant to show the vulgarity and gluttony of the lower classes.[19] In fact, they were "feasting" on bowls of porridge. Food was constantly on the minds of the lower ranks. Ordinary artisans had enough to get by on, but the day laborer and the poor did not. They perceived the clergy and the wealthy as gorging themselves with food, taking it from the mouths of the men and women who needed it.

PRAISE OF THE REFORMERS AS RESTORING ORDER

Artisan pamphleteers believed that the Reformation would change these conditions. They flocked to hear the preachers' sermons, not only because of their enthusiasm for the Gospel but because they thought the reformers would restore order to the church and, thus, to the community. Their first pamphlets praised the Reformers. As early as 1521, Hans Füssli, the Swiss bell founder, and his friend Martin Slegel wrote in praise of the highly learned men Erasmus and Martin Luther, who had become true Christian shepherds. Luther was compared to a herald because he had opened up the fountain of the Gospels.[20] A popular poet composed a New Year's poem—a common form—listing the reformed clergy who proclaimed the Word of God and taught men to trust in Christ. Martin Luther had again brought the Word of Christ to the light of day. Zwingli in Zurich preached the righteousness of God. There was a fine preacher named Dr. Paulus in Sélestat, and Matthias Zell was in Strasbourg. Leo Jud and Dr. Thomas Wittenbach were well instructed. In Bern there was a fountain of holy Scripture.[21] Together these men would lead people to the true Christian faith. The list is an indication of the knowledge of an ordinary person about the Reform. Another poet described Luther as an angel who had revealed God's Word loudly and openly. The truth was now known and could not be split by a hair.[22]

The most important of these pamphlets was Hans Sachs' *The Wittenberg Nightengale*, which went through seven editions in 1523, the year of its publication.[23] The pamphlet was a summary of Luther's Ninety-five Theses. Sachs stated his purpose clearly in the introduction: He had written a short summary for the common man so that he could know the godly truth and compare it to the human lies with which the church had misled people. Typical of Sachs, he wrote that it was also for those who did not accept the Word of God but despised it and persecuted it. He hoped they would be enlightened by the mercy of God and would accept the consolation of the Gospel.[24] He described at length the abuses of the Roman church. Everything the clergy demanded was based on human fable, but now the papal power had been overthrown by Dr. Luther's writing, and the holy Scripture had been proclaimed orally and in writing. Christ fulfilled the law, wiped clean the stain of sin, and won God's grace for men. By faith in Christ, men were now joined in the spirit of God and could give themselves entirely to God in spirit and truth.[25] Sachs believed at this point that once the new truth was known, the church would see the error of its ways, the old abuses would disappear, and a strong, new church would emerge.

DIVISIONS WITHIN THE CHURCH: NEW DISORDER

Instead, the Reformation led to the division of the church between the old and the new, becoming a new source of disorder instead of a remedy for past errors. Like the other ranks, artisans were faced with choices. Should they stay in their parish church, where there was no preaching? Should they attend another church to hear one of the new preachers? It was a personal decision each had to make, but it affected the family, the workplace, the neighborhood. The consequences of choice, the uncertainty, the tensions created were reflected in a set of pamphlets which described choices made and the artisans' discomfort with division and what they regarded as factionalism.

Sebastian Felbaum described the trials of a faithful Catholic. People, he wrote, now said that man's salvation rested in trusting God and in faith. They wanted to rob the church of all its goods and called the church services *büberei*, tricks. Poor Christians like himself were laughed at and shamed.[26] He appealed to the Pope to wake up from his sleep. The Lutheran wolf was eating the sheep, while the cardinals and the bishops did nothing. Christ's sacrifice had been destroyed by the arrogance of the clergy and their simony— no one could argue about that. Each must now reform himself. Felbaum then appealed to the emperor, Charles V, to protect Christians with all his princely goods. The Lutheran sect must be eliminated because they wounded many hearts through hatred and envy. The princes must remain loyal to the emperor against the Lutherans, who wished to overthrow peace and order.[27]

It was not easy for those who followed Luther either. An author who described himself as totally poor, working as a menial, heard people talking about Luther at work. Some said he was good. Others said he was bad. Some pretended to be good Christians because they thought by doing so they could gain an advantage. Such people helped to oppress the truth and bring it to mockery and shame. Those who really wanted to hear about God were derided and made fun of.[28] The fear of being scorned or mocked was an undercurrent of the artisan pamphlets, and had appeared in the warning pamphlets discussed earlier. The menial here felt he had been rejected by his fellow workers. A sawyer objected that anyone who spoke of God was called a "corner preacher," an epithet which in some areas could lead to punishment by the church or the civic authorities. If people openly acknowledged Christ, he said, they were called Lutheran or Evangelical. What did the devil wish to accomplish with all this? Why were people being stirred up against each other?[29]

The name to be used for the converted indicated people's sensitivity to factionalism and the desire not to be associated with such divisions. This was clear in some of the patrician pamphlets. There was the same hesitation among the lower ranks to call themselves or others Lutheran. In the dialogue between a father and his son, the father was won over to the new faith and said he would be a good Martinist. The son corrected him. He was neither a Martinist nor a Petrine; he should name himself after God. People had been misled for so long, they no longer even thought of the name Christian. But there was yet a better name. Jan Huss had brought the Evangel to the light of day, therefore, those who accepted the new faith should call themselves evangelical.[30] This, written around 1522, was an important, carefully defined use of "Evangelical," which later took on other meanings. Knights writing at that time called themselves Lutherans. Artisans shied away from Lutheran, tending to associate it with the magistrates and the honorables. No artisan in this sample called himself a Zwinglian. They tended to use Evangelical throughout their pamphlets.

The problem was best described by Hans Sachs, in a 1524 pamphlet entitled *A Discussion between an Evangelical Christian and a Lutheran, in Which the Bad Ways of Some Who Call Themselves Lutheran Are Shown and Corrected in a Brotherly Way*.[31] That it hit a responsive chord is reflected in 10 reprints of the work in its first year of publication.[32] The dialogue described the conflicts that had arisen between Peter, a Lutheran; Hans, an Evangelical Christian; and Ulrich, the Romanist father-in-law of Peter. Ulrich had come, unexpectedly, to his son-in-law's house on a Friday to find the whole family and the apprentices eating sausage. Shocked, he had scolded them all, and since then he had not spoken a word to Peter. Peter defended his right to eat meat on Friday and was unwilling to listen to any other point of view. Hans admonished him. Clearly his father-in-law was not yet ready for evangelical freedom. It was far more important to maintain a loving relation-ship with his relative than it was to reject him and cut him off from the family because he was unwilling to accept a new custom. Eating meat was no more than a custom, it was not important to living an evangelical life.[33]

Peter dug in his heels, quoting one scriptural passage after another, as well as referring to Luther's *Freedom of a Christian Man*. No one, he said, had the right to pass sentence on his individual freedom (1 Corinthians 4). He had been freed by Christ and would not permit himself to be bound again under any servile yoke (Galatians 5).[34] He was not going to let any old man or woman determine what food he ate, when Christ had made all food free. Peter was dogmatic, unbending, convinced of the rightness of his actions, which he supported from Scripture. Hans repeated again and again that Peter's freedom was not as important as showing love to his father-in-law. Peter should willingly carry Ulrich's burden, which meant accepting his weaknesses. More important, Peter should rid himself of anger and live according to Christ's commandment, "I give you a new commandment, that you should love one another as I have loved you . . . love is the real proof of a Christian."[35]

Ulrich's arrival destroyed Hans' attempts at mediation. The tension between son-in-law and father-in-law was expressed in Ulrich's greeting, "God greet you, you Lutheran people."[36] When Hans invited him to accompany them to the preaching, Ulrich replied that the preacher should be hung as a heretic, for he taught that people should not pray, nor fast, nor serve the saints, nor confess, nor hear mass. Ulrich had heard nothing good from the Lutherans. A whole tableful of them had been at his son-in-law's house, and he had not heard a good Christian word among them. His son-in-law wanted Ulrich to behave as he, himself, did with his journeymen, but they taunted people and teased them. They blamed the Catholics for everything, leaving them helpless to reply.[37] Ulrich's complaints strengthened Peter's anger. He became more aggressive. If people did not convert to the new faith they should be forced to do so; "It would be better if we hit them with our fists" to prevent the land from being taken over by the Babylonian kingdom.[38]

The disorder within the community was exposed. The Lutheran Peter and his friends were shown as obstructing the propagation of the evangelical truth. Luther had revealed Christian freedom to liberate those who were imprisoned, and at the same time he had warned his followers that they must refrain from aggressive, angry, improper behavior. Yet there were those "who wish to call themselves Lutheran and seek in Luther a cloak for their improper behavior," as Hans said, addressing Peter. "You have brought the Christian man Doctor Luther to be slandered because of your own immoderate behavior."[39] Furthermore, these excesses had caused many to flee the evangelical teaching and to remain in their old errors.

The Catholic Ulrich agreed that if the Lutherans advocated moderate change, decently and modestly, without screaming and shouting, and without mockery, those who now ran from them would praise them.[40]

Hans hoped the divisions could be solved by mediation. In his eyes, both the Lutherans and the Romanists had adopted extreme positions. The Lutherans had shown too much zeal and had not respected the feelings of their opponents. The Catholics had been obstinate and stubborn. True Christianity would be achieved by accepting the teaching of the Gospel, specifically the commandment of love. It was not a matter of externals, like what one ate or drank. Love was the proof of a Christian life.

Sachs' pamphlet reflected the importance of appropriate conduct in the artisan world. Sachs did not address the theological differences in belief—those could be assimilated within an individual's conscience. But overt changes in behavior, particularly behavior which threatened the equanimity of one's neighbor, were dangerous. A certain level of civility was essential. Several artisan pamphleteers criticized others for mocking and taunting their adversaries, indicating that ridicule was used to control the artisans, although it was intensely disliked. Sachs disapproved of humiliation or derision in any form. Now it was being used by all sides. Sachs made no appeal to the *gemeinen Nutz*, but he was aware of the fragility of urban life and believed that harmony had to be maintained.

Conflict, however, continued. In 1524, the administrator of the Bishop of Constance issued a mandate restoring the traditional usages of the church in an attempt to silence the Lutherans. All persons were required to fast. The sacrament was to be administered as before. There was to be no teaching in corners, no discussion of Lutheran matters in taverns. The community of Lucerne quickly objected to the episcopal mandate, which had been promulgated without their knowledge and should be examined to see if it agreed with the teachings of Christ. Taking each article in turn, they rejected it as against Christ's words.[41] If the bishop went ahead with the mandate and hardened his heart like pharaoh, then "things should be according to the will of God."[42] It was a veiled and ambiguous conclusion.

As late as 1528, Jörg Ziegler, tailor and brother of the Strasbourg gardener Clement Ziegler, criticized so-called converts, who ran to hear the preachers and heard good counsel but never put it into practice. The principles of evangelical teaching had to be applied to everyday life if the divisions would disappear, because each individual's life would be consecrated to the love of God and his neighbor.[43] Ziegler's solution to disorder was love of neighbor.

THE ARTISAN'S VIEW OF THE FUNCTION OF THE CHURCH

The duty of the church was to preach and teach the Word of God. That was the view of most of the artisan pamphleteers, pointed out in pamphlet after pamphlet. "The clergy do not take care of their flocks. They fleece [them] and leave the Gospel behind," wrote one popular poet. "We need good pastors who teach the Gospel unmarred by human teaching," said a son to his father.[44] The failure to preach was crucial because it was through the Word that men and women were opened to faith and, thus, could achieve salvation. Several artisans explained the relationship between Word and faith. Hans Füssli, the Swiss bellmaker, wrote that "Christian and brotherly love is only found where God's Word is proclaimed. Thus, pray that God will not take his Word from us."[45] Bastian Goltschmidt accused his Dominican opponent because his apostles were Origen, Nicholas of Lyra, Scotus, Aquinas, and Narrenstoteles (Foolstoteles). He pleaded with the prior to abandon human teaching and teach the will of God. "You say men should not talk about the Gospel over wine or in the guild halls but only in church. This means you do not know what the Christian church is. It is not in stones or a cloister. The church is gathered by God's Word. . . ."[46]

The artisan pamphleteers believed that the divisions in the church would be resolved by God, not by human effort. They rejected human competence, human reason, and free will. God would empower individual men and women by the Holy Spirit. Those who were thus transformed would be witnesses to the new faith and a light to the world. Change would come through the inner enlightenment of each individual, not from changes in the law or changes in institutions. The schism in the church, Hans Greiffenberger wrote, was between those who had been called by God, the faithful, and those who had not received faith. Those with faith could teach and preach, not with clever, human words but with the wise words of the Holy Spirit. Like Sebastian Lotzer in the preceding chapter, Greiffenberger had adopted the concept of divine election. Citing Jeremiah 31, Greiffenberger wrote that God would inscribe his words in the hearts of the faithful so that no one would need to be taught by men.[47]

Recognizing that the Roman clergy were not going to give up their positions or power, and that the church was split, the artisan pamphleteers struggled to understand why God would permit this. Why didn't all of their fellow citizens hear the Gospel as they did? A writer who signed himself "a burgher of Nuremberg" attempted to answer this. His written style shows that he was not from the upper ranks. Neither his grammar nor his organizational skills give evidence of formal schooling, but he had read his Bible and was willing to set forth his own interpretations. He titled the pamphlet *The Struggle between the Inner and Outer man*,[48] and, having explained this conflict, went on to describe the new man in Christ and the old man. These figures of speech were used to write about the division between the reformed and those who remained in the old church. It was a matter of God's omnipotent will. God determined who would hear the Gospel and who would not. Like Greiffenberger and Lotzer, he believed it was a matter of divine election.

It was essential for salvation, he began, to be born again. No one could become a child of God unless he were newly born. This occurred, however, not by the will of the flesh, nor even by the will of God, but only by God. God, as a spirit, entered into the individual but did not change into flesh with all its desires, aspirations, fears, anger, denials, despair, or dreams. The flesh continued to produce its own fruits, compelled by its tainted nature. The spirit of God, at the same time, directed its own pure works, which conflicted with those of the flesh in an external struggle, one against the other.[49] The spirit was faith given in the new birth, through the Word of God. Thus, Christ lived within those who believed in him. They became new men. The old men, by contrast, offended against God's commandments and believed God to be a tyrant. They were directed toward hell and would never attain salvation. Christ lived in the hearts of the faithful. They were his habitation as "the Virgin Mary was for the nine months."[50]

There was a mixture of theological concepts. The burgher incorporated elements of the doctrine of divine election. God decided who would be saved and who would not. Men's actions showed to which side they belonged. A faithful man would do no evil because he was protected by God. The man without faith, however, was unjust, loving and hating the things he should not. He was damned forever by God.[51] To this the burgher added a complete separation of the spirit and the flesh, emphasizing the worthlessness of the flesh. The more he wrote, the more explicit he became. The Aristotelian philosophers and debaters who depended on human laws and teaching, opposing the Gospel, would not enter the kingdom of heaven, through the narrow gate, up the narrow stairs. But those who believed in Christ should fear neither hell nor the devil. Even though a man were left totally without help, God would provide him with food, drink, and clothing, as he had ordered from eternity.[52]

The absolute necessity of hearing God's Word received further expression in the petitions and articles which the lower ranks drew up requesting preachers for their churches. As in Lotzer's *Twelve Articles*, the request for the appointment of preachers was usually the first article. To the lower ranks, the Gospel was the Reformation.[53]

THE RICH AS A SOURCE OF DISORDER

There was, however, another source of disorder besides the church—the rich. No one in the lower ranks could openly criticize the patricians, the city councillors, or decisions made by the city council. The pamphleteers, nonetheless, undertook to describe the chasm which separated the rich from ordinary people. The artisans' general perception was that the rich, the *hochen Hansen*, the big shots, fleeced the working man of his money and had too much power. The artisans were inexorably tied to these men, locked into a debtor-creditor relationship because they had to borrow to buy raw materials or equipment. Like the clergy, the rich charged usurious rates of interest. The artisan could rarely free himself from debt. His only hope was that the wealthy would lose their pile or receive punishment in the world to come. The belief that wealth was unfairly gained was a basic maxim of the artisans. The peasant father reported that his pastor had said that the rich and the priests had gathered the goods of the poor and stored them in their own houses. His son replied that the rich would suffer as a result. God exalted the lowly, and the *hochen Hansen*, with all their false piety, would not be saved.[54] The anonymous menial worker believed the same thing. Rich people collected a great pile of rents, wheat, wine, and money, which was against God and the *gemeinem armen Mann*, the poor common man. The rich cared only about their property and their bellies, but, he continued, the powerful would be set down from their thrones, "as had happened in our own times." The riches of the wealthy would erode. They would be damned for eternity.[55] In both these cases, the division between the rich and the poor would not be solved on earth. The poor would receive their reward in the world to come. The solution was faith.

Hans Sachs, the most eloquent spokesman for his fellow-artisans, was unsparing in his criticism of the rich. In his dialogues he described precisely the economic injustices which plagued ordinary workers and their families. His first attack, published anonymously in 1522, was on usury. A peasant confronted a burgher with the inequalities of wealth. Where, the peasant asked, did the burgher get all his money? It was very simple, the rich man replied, he loaned 20 gulden to a peasant on the security of land worth 100 gulden. Every year, the peasant had to pay him one gulden. He would do this for several years, then something would happen so that he couldn't pay it, and the burgher took the land.[56] The peasant replied, that was usury. Christ had told men to help one another in need and to lend to one another. No one should take a profit from money loaned out, because it was usurious. If that were so, replied the burgher, how could he make his pile? The peasant concluded, "I hear clearly that you have a different God than the poor. We have our lord Jesus Christ who forbade loaning money for property. But it has come to the point that wherever there is property it will be pledged by the people . . . [the lender takes] the interest until there is nothing left."[57]

Hans Sachs' pamphlet . . . *ein Argument der Römischen wider das Christlich heüflein den geytz betreffend* was published in 1524, shortly after the peasant uprising in the villages controlled by Nuremberg.[58] In his dialogue *The Evangelical Burgher*, Sachs had limited his criticism to the working class world. His target was the "so-called Lutherans" among the artisans who wanted to make changes too quickly and who behaved too aggressively. Now he broadened his range to attack the rich burghers who had proclaimed themselves Lutheran but had not carried their new faith into their lives. It was an attack on the Lutheran city council and the magisterial rank.

Change in Nuremberg had been initiated from the top. The city council, dominated by patrician and great merchant families, fighting hard to control appointments to the two parish churches, won the struggle in 1480.[59] As early as 1521, the council had supported the appointment of a Lutheran preacher, Andreas Osiander, to the parish church of St. Sebald; similar appointments followed. In 1524, the year this pamphlet was published, a German version of the baptismal service was in use and the Augustinian prior was saying mass in German.[60] Furthermore, the council continued to support the changes in the face of the papal officials and Catholic princes who had convened in the city for the Diet of 1522.[61] The city would seem to have been reformed, yet, in the *Römischen* dialogue Sachs attacked the rich evangelical burghers because they had not put the Gospel into practice. By putting his criticism in the mouth of a Roman cleric, Sachs made it more biting.

"Look in the mirror of your heart, Lord Rich Burgher," said the Roman priest to Juncker Reichburgher, "how you are overcome with avariciousness. Your new evangelism turns your eyes outward only, toward us monks and priests. You say we alone are avaricious, but you forget about yourselves. . . . You buy up everything you can think of in advance, wine grain and salt, all of which are hoarded to make a profit for yourself."[62] That was a proper practice if done to provide food in times of dearth, but not to profit the buyer. Similarly, rich men got together in partnerships and bought up large stocks of merchandise, like spices, and then, having created a monopoly, they raised the price of the goods.[63] There were other unfair practices; false weights, complex accounting systems which confused the small man, "reckoning up things too fast," paying five gulden in interest on a loan of 100 gulden. Worse, continued the priest, the workers were oppressed by the putting-out merchants. The craftsmen took their work home, then the master came around and found fault with it. "The poor artisan stands shaking by the door, his hands clenched, keeping quiet so he won't lose favor with the merchant."[64]

The merchant could settle for as little as he wanted, and the poor man lost money on his labor. To make it worse, employment was unsteady. In the winter, the workers were numb with cold and had to accept any work they could get, otherwise they sucked bones in the marketplace. In the summer, they were overworked and driven by the masters.[65] The priest concluded that the rich man might think he had received the evangelical Word but he did not understand the work which had to accompany it. Without love, the Word was an empty shell. The rich burgher and his fellow evangelicals had created no change. They had had the Word of God preached for a long time, but neither their lives nor the society had been changed.[66]

Sachs revealed his anger and indignation in this pamphlet. By temperament a moderate man, in his earlier dialogues he had always played the role of the mediator. According to Winfred Theiss, economic, religious, and political changes made Sachs fearful of chaos and disorder. He maintained the traditional urban belief in peace, order, and reason, and believed these norms had been renewed in the pure Word of God preached by Luther. The Christian faith could provide a standard of right action for the magistrates.[67] In the *Römischen* pamphlet, I believe, Sachs abandoned his moderate position. He drew a sharp line between the merchant-patrician upper rank and the common burghers and artisans. The interests of the latter groups had been jeopardized. Klaus Wedler believed that Sachs hoped to create an alliance of plebeian burghers, peasants, and artisans against the merchants and patricians.[68] Certainly, Sachs was not convinced that the support of the reform by the upper ranks rested on religious belief. In his mind the appointment of reformed preachers to the city pulpits was one more example of the exercise of their power and domination. The Reformation had given them the chance to consolidate their previous political gains. Sachs did not define the Christian life by what men said but by their actions. The merchants and patricians failed as Christians because they had ignored, neglected, and scorned the poor. "You have betrayed the poor and taken from them like robbers. . . . Your silver and gold will not help you on the day of the wrath of the Lord."[69]

The issue to the artisan pamphleteers was not articles of faith but behavior—civic and religious behavior. As Robert Scribner has pointed out, "the Reformation was less a matter of doctrine than of working practical belief."[70] It was not enough to proclaim one's acceptance of the new faith, that faith had to be reflected in one's life.

TOWNSPEOPLE ARTICULATE THEIR AIMS: ARTICLES OF THE COMMONERS

As the Peasants' War spread in 1524 and 1525, southwest German cities and towns were drawn into the conflict, particularly in the area centered on Strasbourg, Augsburg, and Nuremberg, where the artisan pamphleteers were most active. "Townspeople not only offered . . . 'solidarity,' but they decisively participated in and supported the consequent revolutionary movements. Hence we find in the so-called *Artikelbriefen*, or peasant manifestos, the common political platform of town and country."[71] Most cities ruled the villages around them. The peasants hoped to bring the lower urban classes into the revolt, and those ranks joined them in Memmingen, Strasbourg, and Heilbronn. The city folk who threw in their lot with the peasants were often day laborers and journeymen. The alliances between urban and rural people varied from one territory to another. Some imperial cities like Strasbourg and Nuremberg bent every effort to control their guild members and prevent them from joining the revolt. Under the banner of the Swabian League, Hapsburgs and some princes united against the peasants and the urban commoners. In other princely towns, by contrast, townsmen made up the majority of the "peasant" armies. In the Tyrol, Württemberg, and Saxony, the towns were quick to declare their support of the rebels but were slow to send reinforcements.[72] In a few cities the peasants sparked an urban rebellion which spread from the lower ranks to the guilds, who, with the support of the burghers, were able to take control of the city government. Frankfurt was one such case. There was a factor of size. In smaller, territorial towns the poorer workers joined the peasants or supported their programs in the territorial diets. The goal of the peasants and the urban folk was the same, to restore the balance between the rights and duties in the covenant community God had intended.[73]

During the rebellion, articles were drawn up and published by urban communities and their dependent villages. The changes which they requested, the priorities given were similar to those already put forward by the artisan pamhleteers. The primary demand was the same as that of Sebastian Lotzer's *Twelve Articles*. The original read:

> Article 1. We should henceforth have the power and authority for the whole community to choose and elect its own pastor, and also have the power to depose him should he conduct himself improperly. The same

elected pastor should preach the holy Gospel to us purely and clearly, without any human additions to doctrine and commandments. For constantly preaching the true faith impels us to ask God for his grace that he may instill in us the same true faith and confirm it.[74]

The request was not revolutionary. The right of the village to elect their pastor had been established as early as the fifteenth century in central Switzerland. This spread to the villages of the upper Rhine and the upper Danube in southwest Germany, although it was carried through in only a few cities.[75] With the Reformation, the peasants wished to cut the old ties of the lords' patronage and to create a church based on the whole community by electing their own pastor.[76] Although the commoners in the cities were not as successful in establishing elected pastorates, the lower ranks clearly wished to assert their right to choose their pastors and to regulate the latter's behavior, as appeared in their articles. They wanted control of their religious life.

In 1524, the village of Wendelstein, a dependency of the city of Schwabach, drew up precise standards for the behavior of the new pastor. The common people spelled out the order they wished to be established and maintained. The articles were sent both to the *Rat* at Schwabach and to the man who had been chosen to be their pastor. The villagers wrote that the pastor was to recognize that he was not the lord over his people but their servant. He was to preach the Gospel and the Word of God loud and clear, according to the truth, without any human additions.[77] He was to distribute the sacraments according to the testament of Jesus Christ, and in no other way, and to handle baptism openly and in such a way that people could understand and remember it. If he did not do these things, the parish would know that he was not only an untrue servant but a ravening wolf, and they would not tolerate it. He could accept the conditions or not, that was up to him.[78] It is significant that the commoners of Wendelstein wrote only about communion and baptism. They made no mention of confession, penance, or absolution, which they seem to have believed were no longer to be used or practiced—a belief common among many of the artisan pamphlets. The newly chosen pastor was willing to accept the request of his future parishioners and took over the pulpit at Wendelstein.

During the year before, 1523, the burghermaster, *Rat*, and commoners of the town of Chur issued a similar mandate with regard to the behavior of beneficed clergy. No clerical person could hold a benefice in absentia. This was to insure that all such positions would be in the possession of educated persons who would be responsible for proclaiming the Word and teachings of Christ to the common man.[79] No priest could pass his benefice along to anyone in his family, nor could he preside at the death bed of a citizen and take his testament. That was to be done by laymen. No persons, whether a priest against a priest, a priest against a lay person, or a lay person against a lay person, could be cited before a court or laden with the ban. Instead, they should work these matters out among themselves, "taking and giving justice."[80] The only exception was in marital cases. The articles were drawn up by the commons to protect each other and to pledge together their lives, their honor, and their property.[81] The articles were a communal effort to abolish the abuses of clerical appointments and to protect the citizens from the jurisdiction of ecclesiastical courts and from domination by the clergy when drawing up wills.

Similar articles were formulated by the town of Münnerstadt, which was under the rule of Wilhem von Heneberg and the bishop of Würzburg. Again, the first article stated that the preacher of the Word of God was to be elected by the Christian community and assembly of Münnerstadt, "which will have power to elect and dismiss preachers and pastors as often as there is need and it so pleases them."[82] The second article provided for the establishment of a public school, where the children of all citizens would be taught without charge and instructed in the Christian Gospels, "so that each child will be better prepared for a trade or some other employment, according to his ability."[83] In Bamberg, the citizens and peasants joined to issue a brief set of articles confirming the need to establish preaching the Word of God "freely, unobscuredly, purely and clearly."[84]

Viewed within the context of the artisan pamphlets already discussed, these articles demonstrate the broad understanding shared by the peasants and artisans of the goals of the Reformation. Both groups believed that the solution to their social and religious problems would come from the Gospel. Their major goal was to chose their own pastor, who would preach the Gospel. People would hear the Word of God, his grace would open them to faith, and the community would then live in Christian love and unity as the pamphleteers had explained. Equally important, the community would come to express the will of God. The right to appoint a pastor meant far more than the substitution of preaching for the mass: It meant the creation of new, self-governing communities, controlled by the commoners.[85] Michael Gaismair's plan for the Tyrol is regarded as a utopian program of reform, yet it embodied many of the thoughts and beliefs of peasants and townsmen, systematizing them for a whole region. As Oberman has stated, to dismiss these ideas as "utopian" is to prophesy from hindsight, to dismiss "the ideals of the late-medieval city-state with its religous covenant theology," because by 1530 it could no longer free itself from the power of the princes. In the same way, one should not deny the desire of the rural people to reconcile the reality of their living conditions with the freedoms available to urban dwellers. The demands made by the lower ranks, urban and rural, were not new. They seemed practical and achievable. The basic unit in the commoners' articles and in Gaismair's plan was small—a parish, a guild, a commune, which would provide a measure of corporate identity and self-government within the larger city or the territorial state. Blickle refers to the merger of the goals of the peasants and townsmen as the Communal Reformation, emphasizing that "the first phase of the reformation was a communal movement."[86]

THE CARE OF THE POOR

The new church community, bound together in Christian love, would manifest that love by taking care of the poor. The laws and pamphlets written in support of poor laws show the hope for a more equitable distribution of wealth. In 1522, the city of Wittenberg published a new poor law providing that henceforth all taxes and rents of the cloisters, priests, and artisans' guilds should be gathered together and placed in a common chest for the poor. An earlier ordinance of 1520–1521, drawing from Luther's *Letter to the Nobility*, had banned begging.[87] Later, in 1521, the town council drew up a law which established a common chest. The following year, although Luther was still at the Wartburg, the council worked closely with him and with Andreas Bodenstein von Carlstadt to fashion an ordinance based on evangelical principles. It designated the sources of funds for the common chest and provided for their use not only for poor relief but also to support the reformed clergy, schools, and churches.[88] The ordinance of 1522 decreed that no begging would be permitted in the city. Those who could, should be trained for work. Those who were too old or sick would be supported from the common chest. The chest was also to be used for loans to poor handworkers who could not earn an adequate wage, to be repaid without interest. If the worker could not make the payment, the loan was to be forgiven.[89] Widows, poor young women, and the children of the poor were to be supported by the chest, and, significantly, if the monies collected from the churches and guilds were not sufficient, everyone, whether a cleric or a citizen, would have to contribute yearly to the fund. Those citizens and inhabitants who could not pay the full amount of their ordinary taxes were to receive help from the common chest. They would have to pay only one-third or one-half of the required amount; the rest would come from the chest.[90] The Wittenberg law provided far broader support than laws which would be passed later. It conformed to the artisans' vision of the Christian community. Furthermore the account books of the common chest show that income flowed steadily into the chest from 1526 to 1548,[91] and that payments were made according to the law to pay for the poor in the hospitals, to purchase wood, to pay for in-house relief, to pay the salaries of ministers and school teachers, and to make interest-free or low-interest loans to Wittenberg's citizens.[92] These loans were not restricted to the poor. Martin

Luther himself, as well as Lucas Cranach, the richest man in town, and the burghermaster then in office (1521–1522), drew loans from the chest.[93] Thus, the common chest served as a bank, as had been customary with hospital and charitable funds in earlier centuries. Yet, the charitable purpose was not forgotten in Wittenberg. In 1538 and again in 1539, more than 20 florins was loaned to the clothmakers as a group.[94] The regular payments of poor relief continued.

Reaction to changes in the poor laws appeared in popular poems and dialogues. One of these poems was written by an artisan calling himself N. Fassnacht, "unknown under his mask." He addressed the poem to Wolff Christofel, *Amtman*, (district judge) and the magistrates of Schwabach, praising them for the new poor law of 1524. Although criticized by some, the poet believed that the law showed the authorities' devotion to the evangelical truth, "because the poor would now receive love from them and would be taken care of as Paul had written in Galatians 6, that we should all bear one another's burdens, and in Matthew 25 Christ had said that whatsoever one did for the least of his brethren was done for him." The *Rat* could further help their poor, struggling subjects by supplying them with an evangelical preacher who would proclaim the Word of God and instruct people how to honor and serve him.[95] Although they would be criticized for establishing a common chest and prohibiting begging in the church, if St. John were still alive and saw the needs of the poor he would take care of them with alms, rents, taxes, and money, so that God's commandments would be fulfilled. The *Rat* should remain firm and give a good example by placing chests and boxes in the churches.[96] The opposition wanted the money to be spent maintaining church buildings and cloisters and on masses and benefices, which were works of the devil that oppressed the poor. If the *Rat* acted in a truly brotherly way, they would receive the praise of common people, not only during their lives but also after death. Christians were the true temples of God, not buildings.[97]

The poor as the temples of God was an important metaphor. The artisans asserted again and again that food, shelter, and sustenance should be given to living temples, not to buildings nor to the dead. The iconoclasts in Zurich used the same argument. They destroyed the images in the churches, where oil lamps were kept burning, because, they said, the images "ate up" the money which should have gone to the poor.[98] A woodcut on the title page of a pamphlet by Zwingli affirmed the artisans' concept of the relationship between Christ and the poor. Christ, in the center of the picture, moved with outstretched arms toward a group of poor, lame common folk, led by a beggar who reached out to Christ. The mirror action, Wandel wrote, was a visual expression of the poor as the "images of God" whom Christ welcomed. The love of God was given actual, representational form.[99]

Articles drawn up by the common people of Frankfurt in 1525, when they briefly controlled the city council during the Peasants' War, provide an important index of the measures ordinary men and women believed were needed to create the Christian love and concern which Christ had commanded. In the introduction the authors noted that the unrest in the city was the result of the clergy, monks, and priests, who had not wished to have the holy Gospel revealed. The belief that the fundamental source of disorder was the Roman clergy still persisted. "Now," they continued, "since we are obliged to obey God rather than man, it is necessary that we put an end to these godless practices and initiate a godly and brotherly undertaking for the praise and honor of Almighty God and of his Holy Word and of Christ our Lord and for the furtherance of fraternal unity and [begin] by reforming ourselves, so that others will not seek to trouble and reform us."[100]

The object of the ordinary townspeople was to discipline the Roman clergy and protect the poor and the lower ranks. First, the council and commons would have the power to appoint the parish priest in the city church and other churches. The priest was to preach the pure Word of God and the Gospel, so that people could be strengthened in their faith.[101] To bring order among the clergy, the begging monks were to be expelled. Those clergy who remained in the city were to accept the duties and responsibilities of citizens, including the watch, guard duty, paying taxes, and the jurisdiction of the civic courts.[102]

The provisions for the poor, detailed and practical, provide an insight into conditions. The city excise tax on foodstuffs should be cut in half. All grain should be sold on the open market to prevent speculation. Similarly, the distribution of wood should be fairly made. Those with horses and carts should not cut the larger trees, leaving only the stumps for the poor. The commune should have the right to free grazing on all common lands.[103] Specific requests were made to increase the pay of day laborers so that they could earn a decent wage. Prices on items such as milk were to be controlled. No one should have to pay the small tithe anymore.[104] All legacies and alms should henceforth be paid into a common chest, already established to feed the poor.[105] The Frankfurt Articles were compassionate and reflected Hans Sachs' belief that the poor suffered not by their own will but through misfortune.[106]

Clearly, the artisans and common people believed that practical measures could improve the conditions of everyday life for the day laborers and the poor. It was not a question of providing only for the indigent. The authors of these articles believed that many people among the lower ranks were inadequately paid, could not secure the food they needed at a fair price, and did not have the firewood for cooking or heat. If the city authorities were going to secularize the wealth of the churches, money which had formerly gone to the care of altars, lamps in chapels, masses for the dead, the money should be redirected to the citizens and inhabitants who lived in discomfort and need. Church funds could be invested in education and training of apprentices and journeymen, so that they would be able to support themselves. Other funds could provide capital for craftsmen and shopkeepers, to keep them from falling into the cycle of debt and loss of property. The workers' vision of reformation was based not on abstractions but on the conditions of daily life and the needs of those around them. Neighbors were part of the social and economic network, which allowed them to survive a period of economic crisis without turning to public assistance.[107] Their network, however, was smaller than that of other ranks. Knights and patricians depended primarily on their kin. Artisans, because of their mobility, were often removed from their immediate families and could expect only minor material aid. Jütte stated that "the available evidence suggest that for the labouring poor, their neighbours, rather than kin or outsiders, were the single most important source of help in times of family hardship."[108] Love of one's neighbor was more than a pious phrase to the artisans. It meant maintaining their community. It was this they sought in the new covenant theology.

Notes

1. #50, *Welcher das Evangelium hat für gut*, n.d., fol. aii[v]. #220, H. Sachs, *Dialogus der Römischen*, 1524, unpaginated. Submission of the Guilds of Strasbourg, 1525, in Robert Scribner and Tom Scott, eds., *The German Peasants' War*, 1991, 191; #224, H. Sachs, *Hie kompt ein Beüerlein*, 1522, Lenk edit., p. 141; #270, M. Ulem, *Merckt ir leyen*, 1522, fol. aii; #118, Gemeyn von Frankfurt, *Sechs und viertzig Artickel*, 1525, Artickel 2, fol. Aii.
2. #118, Gemeyn von Frankfurt, *Sechs und Viertzig Artichkel*, Artickel 45, fol. Biii. Submission of the Guilds of Strasbourg, 1525, Scribner and Scott, *Peasant's War*, 191.
3. See John W. O'Malley, *The First Jesuits*, 1993, 167. For the artisans see #93, Dorfmeister und Gemeind zu Wendelstein, fols. Ai[v], Aii, Aiv; #216, H. Ritter, *Welcher gern wissen well*, passim; #270, H. Ulem, *Merckt ir leyen habt euch in hutt*, fol. Aiii[v]; #50, *Welcher das Evangelium hat für gut*, fol. aii[v]; #134, J. Graff, *Tractatlein . . . drey hübsche lieder*, fols. ai, ai[v], aiii; #227, H. Sachs, *Die Wittembergisch nachtigall*, fols. Aii, Aii[v].
4. #216, H. Ulem, *Merckt ir leyen habt euch in hutt*, fol. aii[v]; #224 [H. Sachs], *Hie kompt ein Beüerlein*, Lenk edit., p. 142; #31, *News lied von bekerung der Geistlichen Stand*, fol. ai; #50, *Welcher das Evangelium hat für gut*, fol. aii[v]; #134, J. Graff, *Tractatlein . . . drey hübsche lieder*, fol. Aiii.
5. #18, *Dialogus . . . Vater und Sohn*, c. 1522, fol. aiii.
6. #30, *Ein new christlich lied*, 1525, fol. aiii; #222, H. Sachs, *Evangelischen . . . Christen*, 1524, passim; #18, *Dialogus . . . Vater und Sohn*, fol. biii[v], bii.

7. #118, Gemeyn von Frankfurt, *Sechs und viertzig Artickel*, 1525, fols. Aii–Aii^v
8. #31, *News lied von bekerung des Gaistlichen Stand*, fols. a^v–aiii.
9. #36, *Ain n new gedicht des da spricht*, fol. aiii^v; #71, S. Büllheym, *Brüderliche Warnung*, fol. Aiv.
10. #36, *Ain n new gedicht*, fol. Aiii^v; #134, J. Graff, *Tractetlein . . . drey hübsche lieder*, fol. a^v; #270, H. Ulem, *Merckt ir leyen*, fol. aiii.
11. #134, J. Graff, *Tractelein . . . drey hübsche lieder*, fol. aiii.
12. *Ibid.*, fol. aiii^v.
13. #270, H. Ulem, *Merckt ir leyen*, fol. aii^v.
14. #71, S. Büllheym, *Brüderliche Warnung*, fol. Biii. For identification of the clergy mentioned see Marc Lienhard, "Mentalité populaire, gens d'Eglise et mouvement évangélique à Strasbourg en 1522–1523 . . .," in *Un temps, une ville, une Réforme*, 1990, 59–59, nn. 49–56.
15. #71 Büllheym, fol. Biii^v; fols. Biii–Biv.
16. #73, Dietrich Butzbach, *Neu tzeytung vom Reichstag tzu Wormbs*, 1521, Laube et al., *Flugschriften, der Frühen Reformations bewegung*, 2 vols. (1983), 2, 1286.
17. #29, *Das Eesonet Papistisch, Das Eesonet Lutherisch*, fol. Aii.
18. #216, Hans Ritter, *Welcher gern wissen well*, fol. Cii. This pamphlet, which consists of a dialogue between poverty and charity, was misfiled in my *Bibliography of Strasbourg Imprints* as a joke book.
19. Margaret Sullivan, *Bruegel's Peasants*, 1994, 29–33, 36.
20. #116, H. Füssli and M. Slegel, *Das hond zwen Schweytzer bauren gemacht, Für war sy hond es wol betracht* (Zurich: Christoph Froschauer, before 1521), fols. Aiii^v–Aiiii^v.
21. #17, *Dis ist ein spruch von der Evangelisch lere* (n.p.:n.p., n.d.), Fiche 1311/#3400, fols. Ai^v, Aiv.
22. #35, *Lieplicher schöner auszug in gesetzts weysz . . . von ersten anfangs von ainen Engelschlichen leerer* (n.p.: n.p., n.d.), Fiche 1311/#3400, fols. Ai^v, Aiv.
23. #227, H. Sachs, *Die Wittembergisch nachtigall* (Nürnberg: n.p., 1523). See Primary Sources bibliography for other editions.
24. *Ibid.*, fols. Aiii–Aiv.
25. *Ibid.*, fol. Biv, C.
26. #111, Sebastian Felbaum [von Breten], *Ein nutzliche rede, frag und antwort von dreyen personen sich uben in lutrischen sachen* (Strassburg: Johann Grüninger, 1524), Fiche 1027/#2588, fols. Aii^v–Aiii.
27. *Ibid.*, fols. Di^v–Dii.
28. #50, *Welcher das Evangelium hat für gut*, fols. Aii^v–Aiii.
29. #90, Conrad Distelmair, *Ain gesprechbuchlein von aim Xodtschneyder und aim Holtzhawer* (n.p.: n.p., 1523), fol. Aiii^v.
30. #18, *Dialogus . . . Vater und Sohn*, c. 1522, fol. aiiii^v.
31. #222, H. Sachs, *Ain Gesprech aines Evangelischen Christen mit ainem Lutherischen . . .* , title page.
32. Bernd Balzer, *Bürgerliche Reformationspropaganda: Die Flugschriften des Hans Sachs in den Jahren 1523–1525*, 1973, 157.
33. #222, H. Sachs, *Gespräch aines Evangelischen*, fol. Aii.
34. Ibid.
35. *Ibid.*, fol. Aii^v, Aii, Aiii.
36. *Ibid.*, fol. Aiii^v.
37. *Ibid.*, fols. Aiii^v, Aiv, B^v–Bii.
38. *Ibid.*, fol. Aiv^v.

39. Ibid., fol. B^v.
40. Ibid., fol. Biv.
41. #102, Eydgenossenschafft zu Lucern, *In disem büchlein findt man etliche mandat wider die newe emporunng des Glaubens* . . . (Nürnberg: Hans Hergot, 1524), Fiche 567/#1447, fols. Aiv^v–B.
42. Ibid., fol. Eii^v.
43. #292 [Jörg Ziegler under pseudonym Hans von Schore], *Was steben ir da mich zgaffen an* (n.p.: n.p., n.d.), in Jean Rott, "Après sept années de prédication évangélique, où en était les Strasbourgeois en 1528? Le pamphlet de Hans von Schore," *Investigationes Historicae*, 2 vols. (1986), 1, 531.
44. #36, *Ain n new gedicht*, n.d., fol. aii^v; #18, *Dialogus* . . . *Vater und Sohn*, c. 1522, fol. aii^v; See also #30, *Ein new Christlich lied*, after 1522, fols. aii–aii^v; #71, S. Büllheym, *Brüderliche Warnung*, fol. Aiv; #90, C. Distelmair, *Xodtschneider und Holtzhauer*, 1523, fol. Aiiii; #134, J. Graff, *Tractetlein* . . . *drey hübsche lieder*, n.d., fol. a^v.
45. #115, H. Füssli, *Antwort eins Schwytzer Purens*, 1524, fol. Oiii.
46. #133, B. Goltschmit, *Underweisung etlicher artickel*, 1525, fol. Cii. See also #125, P. Gengenbach, *Der gestryfft Schwitzer Baur*, 1522, fol. ai^v; #132, H. Gerhard, *Schöne Frag und Antwort*, 1525, fol. aii.
47. #139, H. Greiffenberger, *Ein Christenliche Antwordt denen/die da sprechen/das Evangelion hab sein kraft von der kirchen* . . . , fol. Aii^v.
48. #48, [Burger zu Nürnberg], *Ein tractat* . . . *wie der inwendig und usswendig mensch wider einander und bey ander sein* (n.p.:n.p., 1524).
49. Ibid., fol. ai^v.
50. Ibid., fols. aii–aii^v.
51. Ibid., fol. aii^v.
52. Ibid., fol. aiv^v, bi^v.
53. Peter Blickle, *Gemeindereformation: Die Menschen des 16. Jahrhundert auf dem Weg zum Heil*, 1985, 111.
54. #18, *Dialogus Vater und Sohn*, fol. B.
55. #50, *Welcher das Evangelium hat für gut*, fols. aii^v–aiiii.
56. #224 [H. Sachs], *Hie kompt ein Beüerlein zu einem reichen Burger von der güldt, den wucher betreffend* (c. 1522), Lenk, 141.
57. Ibid., 143.
58. Klaus Wedler, *Hans Sachs*, 1976, 79.
59. Irmgard Höss, "Religiös Leben vor der Reformation," in ed., Gerhard Pfeiffer, *Nürnberg-Geschichte einer europäischen Stadt*, 1982, 139.
60. Gerhard Pfeiffer, "Entscheidung zur Reformation," in Pfeiffer, *Nürnberg-Geschichte*, 148–149, 150.
61. Ibid.
62. #220, H. Sachs, *Ein Dialogus des inhalt ein argument der Römischen wider das Christlich heüflein den Geytz auch ander offenlich laster etc. betreffend* (Nürnberg: H. Höltzel, 1524), Fiche 1537/#4000, unpaginated.
63. Ibid.
64. Ibid. This was not an exaggeration on Sachs' part. See Michel Mollat, *The Poor in the Middle Ages*, 1986, p. 165 for a description of the ways in which the putting-out entrepreneur cheated his workers.
65. Ibid.
66. Ibid.
67. Winfried Theiss, "Der Bürger und die Politik zu der zeitkritischen Dichtung von Hans Sachs," 1976, 90.

68. Klaus Wedler, *Hans Sachs*, 1976, 84.
69. #220, H. Sachs, *Ein Dialogus . . . der Römischen wider des Christlich heüflein*. See also Eckhard Bernstein, *Hans Sachs*, 1993, 47, on Sachs' disillusionment that the new faith would bring social change.
70. Robert Scribner, "Preachers and People in the German Towns," in Scribner, *Popular Culture*, 1987, 123.
71. H. Oberman, *Dawn of the Reformation*, 1986, 155.
72. P. Blickle, *The Revolution of 1525*, 1981, 109, 112, 115; James M. Stayer, *The German Peasants' War and Anabaptist Community of Goods*, 1991, 32–33.
73. P. Blickle, *The Revolution of 1525*, 115: H. Oberman, *Dawn of the Reformation*, 157, 160.
74. Scott and Scribner, *The German Peasants' War*, Documents 125, 253–254. See also A. Laube, and H.-W. Seiffert, eds., *Flugschriften aus dem Bauernkriegszeit*, note on Lotzer, 567.
75. P. Blickle, *Gemeindereformation*, 1985, 180–182.
76. Ibid., 109–111.
77. #93, Dorfmeister und Gemeind zu Wendelstein, *Fürhalten den Amptleüten zu Schwabach und irem new angeen dem Pfarrherrn gethan*, 1524, fol. Aii^v.
78. Ibid., fols. Aiii–Aiv.
79. *Artickel so die zwen Pündt, desgleichen Bürgermeister, Rath und Gemayn der Stat Chur mit sampt den vieer Dürffen und der Herschaft . . . samtlich mitainander zuhalten angenommen* (n.p.:n.p., 1523), Fiche 1019/#2572, fol. Aii.
80. Ibid., fols. Aii^v, Aiii, Aiii^v.
81. Ibid., fol. B^v.
82. Scott and Scribner, *The German Peasants' War*, Documents 65, 177.
83. Ibid.
84. Scott and Scribner, *The German Peasants' War*, Documents 68, 181.
85. P. Blickle, *Communal Reformation*, 99.
86. H. Oberman, *The Dawn of the Reformation*, 160; P. Blickle, *Communal Reformation*, 100, 108.
87. Laube et al., *Flugschriften*, 2, 1035.
88. Robert Jütte, *Poverty and Deviance in Early Modern Europe*, 1994, 106.
89. #256, *Ordnung der Fürstlichen Stat Wittemberg*, 1522, Laube et al., *Flugschriften*, 2, 1033.
90. Ibid., 1034.
91. Stefan Oehmig, "Der Wittenberger Gemeine Kasten in der ersten zweieinhalb Jahrzehnten seines Bestehens (1522/23 bis 1547)," Part 1, "Seine Einnahmen und seine finanzielle Leistungs-fähigkeit. . . ." *Jahrbuch für Geschichte des Feudalismus* 12 (1988): 263–268.
92. Ibid., Part 2, "Seine Ausgaben und seine sozialen Nutzniessen." *Jahrbuch . . . des Feudalismus* 13 (1989): 174–179.
93. Ibid., 160–161.
94. Ibid.
95. #110, N. Fassnacht [pseudonym], *Dem Edlen und Vesten Ersamen und weysen Wolff Christoffel von Wissenthaw genannt Amptman Bürgermaistern und Rathe zu Schwabach bekannt* (n.p.: n.p., 1524), Fiche 1316/#3427, fols. Aii–Aii^v.
96. Ibid., fol. Aiii^v.
97. Ibid., fols. Aiv^v–B.
98. Lee Palmer Wandel, "The Reform of the Images: New Visualizations of the Christian Community at Zurich," ARG, 80, 1989, 113.
99. Ibid., 121–123.

100. #118, Gemeyn der Statt Franckfort, *Sechs und viertzig Artickel*, 1525, fol. Aii.
101. Ibid., Article 1, fol. Aii^v.
102. Ibid., Articles 3–4, fol. Aii^v.
103. Ibid., Articles 7, 9, 19, 22, fols. Aiii, Aiii^v, Aiiii^v.
104. Ibid., Articles 28, 29, 40, fols. Aiiii^v, Bii^v.
105. Ibid., Article 14, fol. Aiiii.
106. #220, H. Sachs, *Dialogus . . . der Römischen*, 1524, unpaginated.
107. R. Jütte, *Poverty and Deviance*, 83.
108. Ibid., 96.

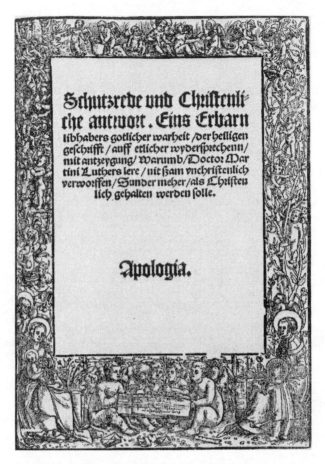

8 "Defense and Christian answer by an honorable admirer of
the godly truth of Holy Scripture."

Lazarus Spengler's defense of Luther, published in 1519. Note that the printer
has used Renaissance borders available in his shop. A scene of the Holy Familly
and St. Anne appears at the bottom. The title-page ornamentation has nothing to do with the content of the pamphlet. The use of this kind of border
was usual for pamphlets written by the reformers and their humanist supporters.

SOURCE: Title page of a pamphlet by Lazarus Spengler, *Schutzrede und
Christenliche antwort. Eins Erbarn libhabers gotlicher warheit der heiligen geschrift
auff etlicher wydersprechenn mit antzeygung Warumb Doctor Martini Luthers lere
nit szam unchristenlich verworffen Sunder mehr als Christenlich gehalen werden
soll.* Augsburg: S. Ottmar, 1519.
Reproduced with the permission of the Beinecke Rare Book and Manuscripte
Library, Yale University.

9

The City Secretaries and the Magistrates Legislate the New Order

The city secretaries were in the most delicate position of any of the pamphleteers. They were sworn by oath to be loyal to the city council, and in the early years, 1519–1522, there was no city council whose members had all converted to the new faith. A secretary who wrote in support of Luther and his teaching risked losing his lifetime appointment.

The secretaries' function as counsellors, and the magistrates' function as law makers, meant that both had to speak for the whole community. The artisans, the technicians, and the minor officials could give their own, individual opinions, but the city secretaries had to create an order acceptable to all the different ranks in the city. They had to mediate the differences we have observed, yet, as lawyers they were regarded with suspicion by many, who believed that as a group they were dishonest, tricky, cunning, and always favored the rich and the powerful against the poor. To be effective they had to rise above these prejudices.[1] I have placed their pamphlets and the laws which they helped to draft at the end of the study because they determined the final form of the urban reformation. The ideas of the other pamphlet writers were transitory. These were the formulations which had lasting influence.

There were four city secretaries and a handful of learned, university-educated professional men, doctors of medicine or lawyers, who became pamphleteers. Among the four were Benedict Gretzinger, city secretary of Reutlingen; Jakob Schorr, *Landschreiber* at Gutenberg for the Count Palatine; Lazarus Spengler, city secretary of Nuremberg; and Jörg Vögeli, city secretary of Constance.[2] It is noteworthy that three of the largest imperial cities were represented. Reutlingen was an important smaller center of the new movement.

The secretaries' pamphlets contrasted with those of the other ranks, which dealt with matters of concern to the writers: the knights' demand for church lands; the urban elite's censure of the convents; the artisans' criticism of the local clergy and their demand for care of the poor; the minor civil servants' scathing attacks on Rome. The city secretaries attempted to restore order to the fragmented communities described by the other orders. They were sober, judicious, skilled in the art of the possible. Between 1519 and 1525, four of the five city secretaries wrote pamphlets defending Luther and his doctrines. As Rome pressed its case against Luther, their defense was a courageous act. Cities like Nuremberg and Augsburg, in particular, wished to maintain peaceful relations with the emperor and did not want to be drawn into a quarrel with the church. The secretaries demonstrated independence and commitment.

THE DEFENSE OF LUTHER

Lazarus Spengler met Luther in 1518, when Luther was traveling to meet Cardinal Cajetan in Augsburg. The circumstances have already be described in Chapter 2. The Pope had called the meeting after he had issued orders for Luther's arrest. Repelled by this duplicity and by Johann Eck's attack on Luther at the Leipzig debate, Spengler wrote a defense of Luther.[3] The pamphlet reflected the change in tempo in the Lutheran matter after the Leipzig debate. Until then the "quarrel" was still within the church. Except for a disputation in Heidelberg in 1518, and his meeting with Cajetan, Luther had continued as a professor at Wittenberg, publishing only a few Latin sermons. Eck had broadened the battlefield at Leipzig, forcing Luther, who had not been meant to participate at all, into a debate on the issue of papal primacy. Finally, Eck had pounced on Luther's chance mention of the "Bohemians" to label his opponent a heretic like Huss.[4] The general opinion, magnified by Eck's own claims, had been that Luther had been vanquished in the debate. Spengler's *Defense* was an attempt to refute that defeat and prove to the learned Luther's superior knowledge of his sources and the biblical foundation of his doctrine.

He began bluntly: "I am suspected by some," he wrote, "and openly accused of being a disciple of Doctor Martin Luther . . . whose teaching and preaching [these others find] is too greatly praised and followed. . . . So I ask that [they] should listen to the teachings and circumstances which have moved me to consider Luther among the champions of the holy faith."[5] Luther's teaching and preaching, he insisted, were "Christian and sound and in accord with reason . . . all that he has . . . written and taught . . . he has based on the Holy Gospel, the sayings of the holy prophets and the holy Paul." Yet he had been attacked by preachers who based themselves only on Thomas, Bonaventura, Scotus, and other scholastics. They feared that if these teachings were denied and the Christian church considered to have been in error, it would be shameful. Spengler deplored this. There had always been differences of opinion among pious men. The church fathers had disagreed and opposed one another. Human teaching would always be subject to error, only the teaching of Christ was true, firm and not to be doubted.[6] "Many of the mistakes of our preachers and teachers are . . . due to the fact that . . . they adulterate, weaken and reduce the Scripture to nothing."[7]

If Christ returned to earth, Spengler continued, the priests would find that he would censure many human teachings. Spengler knew pious, highly learned and educated people who complained that the scribes, when writing the postills, had not given the slightest savor of the spirit of the text in their interpretations. For instance, they interpreted the text of Jesus cleaning the leper, in Matthew 8:2–4, to mean that Christ gave the power of confession to the priests.[8] Spengler called on the humanists, skilled in translation and textual analysis, to reject the traditional commentaries. This was an important step in legitimizing Luther's teachings. He had heard "many admirable, highly learned persons say they were grateful to God that they lived in this hour when they could hear Doctor Luther and his teaching". In contrast to these learned men, the "false preachers" troubled the simple, unlearned folk with their incompetent opinions, making them think they must depend on their works instead of the grace and love of God.[9] They "lay so many nets and ropes around our consciences that it is not really possible to flee from them."[10]

Men such as Johann Eck, however, prevented the truth from spreading. It was amazing that those who held themselves to be *lux mundi* and the great teachers of the church would not permit Luther's preaching to be openly disputed, but limited discussion to the learned in the universities.[11] If Luther was wrong, a debate among the learned was not the way to root out error.[12] That could only be done by an orderly council, called together by the rules of the Roman church.

Spengler's defense was strong, simple, and intensely personal. He hoped to penetrate the barriers which the Roman church had erected against the so-called heretic. Spengler appealed to the learned Roman clergy on scholarly grounds, affirming the validity of the Bible as the source of Christian truth and the reasonableness of Luther's teaching. His arguments, however, revealed the depth of the divisions which already ruptured the learned community. Bonds of mutual respect and trust had been snapped and would not be restored.

Jorg Vögeli, city secretary of Constance, revealed the breach which had opened between him and his "Christian companion," Johannes Brack, a priest. Vögeli wrote to his friend to defend Luther, declaring that when the

Bible was explained by learned priests it had remained dead to him.[13] Luther's books, however, had illuminated Scripture and given him hope that he could come to God through faith. Yet, his friend Brack changed this hope to doubt by preaching that Luther and all who read his books were heretics. Vögeli had written to Brack asking him to point out the heresies "with his finger," but the latter had refused to reply. Vögeli then wrote to another friend, "and so, more than before, I aspire to Lutheran teaching where it is the same as the Gospel and thus not Luther's but Christ's."[14] Luther had protected the faith and explained it for all men. Yet Brack, from the pulpit, had stirred up the people of the world to revolt against God and had admonished them to remain in the old faith, threatening that otherwise they would be hanged. If Brack was so convinced of Luther's errors, he should point them out so that laymen would avoid them but could still nourish themselves from holy Scripture.[15]

Vögeli's letters were more informal, more impassioned than Spengler's pamphlet. He was just as learned as his friend Brack, but he placed himself in the position of spokesman for all the laity. The reformed city secretaries gave themselves a new role—to protect the Word of God, as Luther had, and let it go forth to the common people.[16]

More than any other group, the city secretaries gave Luther their personal and public support during the critical six years in which the Reformation took shape. Year after year, they defended Lutheran doctrine in carefully reasoned pamphlets. They created a strong Lutheran presence at the top level of government in important German free cities. Their pamphlets circulated among their own colleagues and in magisterial and intellectual circles across the empire, influencing the thinking of men with political power. The city secretaries helped to legitimize Luther's teaching to the governing elite and the intellectual elite.

THE CITY SECRETARIES DEFINE SECULAR JURISDICTION

As noted in Chapter 2, on the warning pamphlets, the dual jurisdiction of secular and ecclesiastical authorities had been a thorn in the flesh for the city councilors for centuries. Efforts to curb the clergy went back to the thirteenth and fourteenth centuries. Consistently the magistrates had tried to make the resident clergy subject to the city laws. They were continually obstructed by the ecclesiastical courts with their claim to exclusive jurisdiction over the clergy. That claim had to be invalidated before the cities could make any move to reform the church. The city secretaries questioned the division of power between church and state in their pamphlets. What were the lines? On what were these divisions based? How should they be maintained?

The secretaries examined the relationship between secular and spiritual powers by the light of the Gospel. Well-read in canon as well as civil law, they acknowledged both authorities, but questioned the exercise of the spiritual prerogative and attempted to limit its jurisdiction. Some writers believed that the worldly rulers should assume all power because the clergy had abdicated their right to govern. Others criticized the worldly magistrates as well, for not following in God's path. Jacob Schorr, secretary to Ludwig, the Count Palatine, asserted that the Pope had claimed for himself the high priesthood and had placed secular rulers under the church. This was against all Scripture.[17] There could be no supreme power in the church, nor could it claim legal powers, because Jesus Christ alone reigned over the church.[18] Kings, for their part, ruled over their people, but as their servants, because they must be obedient to God and carry out his will.[19]

Hieronymus Brandeck, writing to a magistrate at Coburg named Conrad von Armstat, addressed all magistrates and rulers "in these troubled times." Spiritual authorities—the Pope, bishops, and prelates—were necessary, but they should govern spiritual not worldly affairs. In practice, they were so busy with the latter that they never even thought about their spiritual responsibilities. The secular authorities, for their part, slept or lay feeble and infirm in these critical times. They should rouse themselves and call a council to bring about a Christian Reformation.[20] Brandeck doubted it would occur. The clergy were afraid that if they preached the truth they would lose their benefices. The secular magistrates were also silenced by fear. Now they would have to lead others to the truth.[21]

Spengler defended the secular authority against the charge that civil uprising would result if they permitted the teaching of the Gospel. Instead, he confirmed their legislative and judicial powers.[22] According to the Epistles of Peter and Paul, all secular authority was ordained by God and could not be opposed. However, if rulers denied the Word of God, "the secular sword ordained by God will no longer cut."[23] This frequently happened because "no governor thinks that he must live according to the good and needs of others but only for himself."[24] Similarly, the "so-called" spiritual estate opposed the Gospel and were interested only in maintaining their own honor, status, power, and wealth.[25] The proclamation of the Gospel was the foundation of civil order and the primary function of both the spiritual and secular authorities. Spengler acted on this precept, refusing to execute the papal and imperial mandates of the Edict of Burgos against Luther, "because these things do not have anything to do with Luther or any other man's teaching but they concern the Word of God and our faith."[26] The judgment pronounced by the Nuremberg city council on that occasion stated explicitly that in any matter concerning God and his holy Word "we are responsible to God to be obedient, rather than to any human magistrates."[27] According to this, every law, in principle, depended on God's law, and the reformed jurists began to develop a law based on reformed theology, just as canon lawyers had built on the theology of the Roman church.[28]

WHO HELD POWER OVER THE CHURCH?

The foundation of the claim of the Roman church to authority lay in the Gospel text of Matthew 16:15–19 (RSV):

> And Jesus asked the disciples . . . "who do you say that I am?" Simon Peter replied, "You are the Christ, the Son of the Living God." And Jesus answered him, "Blessed are you, Simon Bar-Jona! For flesh and blood has not revealed this to you, but my Father who is in heaven. And I tell you, you are Peter, and on this rock I will build my church and the powers of death shall not prevail against it. I will give you the keys of the kingdom of heaven, and whatever you bind on earth shall be bound in heaven, and whatever you loose on earth shall be loosed in heaven.

In this one sweeping passage, according to traditional Roman theology, Peter was made the foundation of the church; he received the keys of heaven and the power to determine who would be saved and who would be damned. It was a claim to full moral and spiritual authority. The Roman church alone could forgive sins on earth, determining the individual's acceptance or rejection in heaven. The sacrament of penance and the practice of contrition, confession, absolution, the concept of purgatory, and the practice of selling indulgences were based on this text. New meanings for the words "rock" and "keys" were vital to break the hold of the old church. Several of the city secretaries applied their biblical knowledge to the task. Their interpretations reflect their own study of the Bible and their humanist training.

The issue was drawn by the bishop of Constance, probably after 1524 (the pamphlet is undated). The bishop had published 33 articles against the reformed preacher, Bartholomeus Metzler. Three of the articles accused Metzler of "speaking against the keys of the church; declaring them null and void; saying that the spiritual powers of the pope, the cardinals or any other bishops and prelates were not greater than that of any other priest and that all men were priests and could consecrate the elements."[29] Jörg Vögeli, city secretary of Constance, wrote to defend Metzler. He addressed himself to Dr. Johann Schluppf, the priest at Überlingen, since, he wrote with some irony, he felt he did not stand high enough to speak to a priest anointed by the Pope.[30]

Vögeli wrote there was only one spiritual power, one key, and one sacrament of the Christian church. Thus, the highest titled priest was no better than the lowest. The church which claimed power over morality in the name of Christ and in the name of the keys was wicked and had robbed the true church, to which the keys had been given. Metzler had wished to free the true believers from imprisonment by the human keys.[31]

The keys of the church, that is the power to bind and unbind all sins on earth, were not given to Peter, to James nor to any other apostle but mandated to the Christ-like church in common. The Christ-like church, I say, not to the one that goes under the name of Christ.[32]

Vögeli supported his argument that the keys were held in common by all true Christians from Matthew 16. Christ, he said, spoke to all his disciples together when they asked him questions. Peter, when he said "You are the Christ," spoke for all the disciples, not as their chief, for none was different from another. Similarly, Christ promised that he would give the keys to all of them, certainly not to Peter, because Peter had turned at that time to Satan. Here Vögeli referred to Peter's rebuke to Christ that he would be killed, and Christ's reply, "Get thee behind me, Satan." The common promise to the disciples, Vögeli continued, was repeated after Christ's death and his return. He had breathed on the disciples, saying "Take now the holy spirit, those whose sins you forgive on earth will be forgiven also in heaven, those whose sins you retain will be retained in heaven." The keys did not belong to any one person but were the gift of the Holy Spirit, and the power to bind and unbind came through the Holy Spirit and Scripture.[33] Vögeli's interpretation took the power of absolution out of the hands of the clergy, returning it to Christ, to the Holy Spirit, and to the whole Christian church. The keys to the kingdom of heaven were in Scripture, opened by the power of the Holy Spirit. They had never been given to men. Furthermore, the church knew no rank but humility, no legal authority but mercy and love, no pleasure but suffering and serving Christ.[34]

Jacob Schorr, secretary in Gutenberg to Ludwig, the Count Palatine, was asked by the latter to advise him on the validity of Luther's teaching. Schorr apologized that he could not cover all the points involved in the conflict but had dealt with those regarding the power and authority of the church, which seemed to him the most important.[35] "The church of God is common," he affirmed, meaning "it is united by the belief in Christ, that you are in him and he is in you [John 17; Galatians 3] . . . which unity is not bodily but spiritual [I Corinthians 12]."[36] Luther and the Pope did not agree on how the church was built. The Pope wanted to build it on St. Peter but had no scriptural support for this "except by interpreting the saying in Matthew 16, 'on this rock I will build my church' as though Peter was meant thereby."[37] Luther, on the other hand, wished to build the church on Christ, which he could prove from good, strong Scripture. "Item. Matth. 7, . . . 'who hears my speech and follows it is like the clever man who builds his house on rock.'"[38] The traditional interpretation of Matthew 16 was overturned by saying that Luther's teaching was undeniable and could not be contested without blasphemy or lying against God.[39] Christ was restored as head of the church.

Schorr went on to explain the difference between the power of the church and the high priesthood under the old law and the new. Under the old law, it was outward and temporal. Now, "there was the spiritual, eternal priesthood of Christ, in which all who enter Christ through faith shared."[40] The Pope's claim to the high priesthood was against Scripture, because "in the Christian church there is no living, supreme power or outward ruling regime, also no legal authority or any other worldly organization as in outward things."[41] Schorr proved his point with linguistic evidence. The term "rulers" could also be translated in Greek as "pastors or shepherds," and that was what was meant in the New Testament. Neither Christ nor the apostles had envisioned a worldly regime wielding power over individual Christians. No one had the right to compel another person to follow his will. The shepherd should take care of the flock of Christ, without forcing them, without shaming them, but by leading them to act voluntarily and willingly.[42] The power of the clergy lay not in bidding or forbidding but in caring. Thus, the keys and the power to bind or to loose should be understood as nothing more than to open and close the kingdom of heaven with the gifts of the Holy Spirit—the Word, faith, understanding, and love.[43] By arguing from Scripture, the lawyer- secretaries undermined the foundation of the church's claim to power. They did not quote canon law. They quoted the Gospel passages on which the authority of the Roman church rested, and demolished the accepted interpretation.

THE FUNCTIONS OF THE TRUE CHURCH

The city secretaries believed that the major function of the church was to teach and preach the Word of God. As Lazarus Spengler put it, "Outside the Godly world . . . all things are confused, inconsistent and dissolved. Each person can now understand on which rock he places his foundation and trust as a Christian."[44] Gretzinger made the Roman clergy as responsible as the reformed pastors for teaching and preaching. "All bishops, guardians and overseers of the people or priests, however they are named, [their] major duty is to proclaim the pure Word of God. If they do not wish to do this, the office will be removed."[45] Vögeli's defense of Metzler was based in large part on the latter's sound preaching of the Gospel, according to the truth, which brought people out of the captivity of Egypt into Christian freedom.[46] Thus, the upper civil servants would seem to have been at one with the artisans in their desire to elect preachers for their own parish churches. But new questions of authority arose. The city secretaries did not adopt Luther's teaching on the priesthood of all believers; indeed, they were careful to limit preaching to educated, ordained clergy. Jörg Vögeli, for example, in his defense of Metzler, denied that the latter had said that all men were priests and had the right to consecrate the elements, as one of the articles had charged. Vögeli asserted that Metzler "did not want to speak of this, especially before [people] had built a firm belief in Christ. [They had to be fed] on the milk food of the faith before [they were] given stronger food."[47] Metzler had declared that there should be no difference among Christians with regard to their status but that there was "nevertheless an undeniable official order with regard to the duties of priests."[48]

Benedict Gretzinger explained this difference clearly, maintaining, like Vögeli, standards of order and hierarchy. All children of the New Testament, he wrote, were made priests through Christ, so everything was common in the priestly office. Everyone could make offerings to God, pray for each other, and teach one another the Word of God.[49] "But although they are all equal, the same office should be given to certain men who are bidden, so that men will have the knowledge to attend to that office," thus no one would abandon their duties or neglect the people and create disorder.[50] Jacob Schorr also believed that the clergy had to be called to their office. They were pastors, shepherds caring for the flock of Christ, called by the holy spirit.[51]

The city secretaries accepted the ideal of the equality of all Christians but with definite limitations. The church was to be guided by educated Christian men whose function was to proclaim the Word of God. The role of the pastors was circumscribed. They had no power and no reason to intervene in worldly matters which had created so much turmoil in the past. The *Kirchenordnungen* of the late '20s and '30s would limit the powers of the clergy in just this way. No powerful new church would be allowed to rise from the ashes of the old. The death of the Old Law encompassed not only the law of the Old Testament, it included the law of the Roman church as well.

The concept of function, of performing ordained duties, influenced the attitude of the upper civil servants toward the Roman clergy. They deplored the arrogance of the clergy, their inordinate claims to power and status, but the important element was their failure to proclaim the Word of God. Jacob Schorr was sharp in his comments. He complained that the priests had not grounded their faith in the true Gospel and had not asked for God's help to find the right way. Instead, they left the people without a good example to guide them.[52] The clergy were thieves and murderers who had entered the sheepfold and used force and violence against the sheep. They had fulfilled the prophesy describing the Anti-Christ.[53] This attitude toward the clergy was exemplified in a verse account written in 1521 by a burgher of Erfurt, identified by Laube as being close to the Erfurt city council.[54] In mid-June of 1521, the university students in Erfurt rioted against the city clergy and destroyed many of the houses occupied by the chapter canons. The students were joined by peasants coming in to market and by the common folk of Erfurt.[55] The burgher made it clear in his account that while a riot was hardly the maintenance of peace and order which the magistrates usually advocated, the clergy had gotten what they deserved. The students had been, if anything, restrained, and their actions were laudable. Each student group had used its own password to prevent robbing or plundering. Afterwards, the canons had paid a stiff fine, 5000 gulden or more, which was counted with halberds.[56] The amount paid was, in fact, 10,000 gulden, a good deal more than the poet's estimate, and it was *Schutzgeld*, money paid to the city for military protection rendered. The canons had avoided such payments for years. Thereafter they had to pay taxes on their houses, taxes on their meals, and 4% to 6% interest on their outstanding debts.[57] One brief incident of violence made it possible to force the clergy to assume the financial responsibilities they had so long avoided. The process of bringing the clergy under the secular authority had begun, and was applauded by a person of upper rank.

THE NEW ORDER

The city secretaries' critical attitude toward the clergy and the Roman church shaped the advice they gave to the magistrates and informed their discussions concerning the need for change and the means of achieving it. Order and the public peace were uppermost in their minds. The civil servants' pessimistic view of human nature, acquired in the late phase of humanism, had been confirmed by Luther's doctrine rejecting free will. Men and women, they believed, were utterly powerless to achieve their own salvation. It devolved upon the shoulders of the city council to establish an order which would enable men to struggle against the old Adam and turn to God. As Benedict Gretzinger wrote, "Since all things occur according to godly providence, it is not possible to have freedom of our will . . . no one is good except the only God."[58] Man's powerlessness, continued Gretzinger, made it impossible for him to fulfill the commandments of God. He could only hope for God's mercy.[59] The city secretaries did not share the belief of the artisans that the commoners were capable of maintaining God's order by themselves. Intervention by the secular authorities was essential. Law was the instrument to establish the faith, to protect it, to strengthen it. The laws passed, often published in pamphlet form, reveal the political and religious aims of the city secretaries and the magistrates.

An example of the difficulties involved in moving from theory to action can be found in the opposition experienced in Constance in establishing preachers in the churches. The Mass was not replaced, but preaching was given new emphasis that made it possible to introduce the new doctrines without overtly changing the services. The city council passed an edict appointing preachers in 1524. Two years later, the burghermaster and council

were forced, because of opposition, to reaffirm that edict, and they carefully spelled out their reasons in an official defense.[60] "For the honor of
God and the furthering of Christian truth," they had established a rule for
the preachers who were to preach from the chancel nothing but the holy
Gospel, completely, clearly, and according to Christian understanding, "without
any mixture of human additions" and while abstaining from "fables and
disputatious matters."[61] Jörg Vögeli probably drafted the law, whose evangelical purpose was clear. The city council had appointed preachers and
assumed the right to legislate the content of the preachers' sermons, a matter
previously in the hands of the church.

Dissent came from Brother Anthony, vicar of the provincial Dominicans, who preached publicly against Scripture and against the order of the
city council. The council called on him to dispute the matter with his
peers, the clergy. He refused, saying he would not debate the issue locally
but only at the university of Paris, Cologne, or Ingolstadt, all loyal to the
Roman church. The matter went on from there. The council appealed to
the bishop to arrange a friendly discussion between Brother Anthony and
the Constance preachers. At the invitation of the bishop, the Constance
preachers went to Baden, but nothing was accomplished. So, continued the
edict, "we gathered all the preachers together and asked them to decide
and interrogated them according to what decision they wished to make and
therewith came to a good decision, that we would remain by the decision
we had made."[62] The procedural process was important. They had asked for
help from the bishop, but his disputation at Baden had been unsuccessful.
The city council had then been forced to make its own decision, which,
typically, was to maintain the position already taken.

Brother Anthony was informed that from then on he could preach nothing but holy Scripture. The councilors had no doubts about their authority.
"Far be it from us," they concluded, "that we should not be accountable for
our preachers but [we] should elect a judge of God's Word, according to
the Christian faith ... ordered in holy Scripture. As Christian people we
have recognized that God's Word is judge and lord of all creation. And
now ... nothing should be understood by Christians but the Word of God
and holy Scripture ... nothing according to human reason and wisdom."
Their action was based on their responsibility as Christians.[63]

The response of the intellectual elite to the appointment of preachers
was well described in a pamphlet recounting events in the Swiss towns of
Klingnau and Wallis. Heinrich Scharpf of Klingnau wrote to a friend from
university days to tell him "how things stand with the holy Word of God
among our profession and whether it is increasing among the common folk ...
You must know that everyone here and in the surrounding area wishes to
talk about nothing else ... and finds great joy therein."[64] There were several

pastors and preachers in the region skilled in speaking on the Word of God; opposition came only from the Dominicans and Franciscans, who hoped they "could wait the affair out." For this reason, Scharpf had asked another friend, Otto Karg, to write about several men from their same profession who had helped people to find out how they should conduct themselves with God, especially with regard to auricular confession.[65]

Four honorable men had been talking together in Wallis as to whether they should confess during the coming Lent. They had heard that no one in Zurich and other places confessed anymore. They then called on Lucius Steger, who read the Bible a lot, to advise them whether confession was necessary to their salvation.[66] Steger answered that according to his understanding, it was not necessary. What they should do was to help the poor and love their brothers, for love was expressed in mercifulness to one's brother.[67]

Steger continued that confession to priests had no foundation in Scripture. Instead, people should recognize their sins and confess to one another. If an individual had sinned, had cheated a merchant, an artisan, or a peasant in any way, he should go directly to that person and give him his offerings rather than giving them to a priest. He should make restitution saying, "Dear brother or sister, I have sinned against God and you . . . and I have injured you. Now I come to you and ask you . . . for the sake of the salvation of your soul and my soul, that you will forgive me and that which I took from you unjustly, I will return to you . . . also I will reconcile myself with you in a brotherly way, so pray to God for me and I will also do that for you."[68] Confession, for Steger, not merely a matter of words, was to be based on acts of reconciliation, the restoration of a damaged relationship. It involved individual Christians, and no priest was necessary.

By 1524, the Word of God was being heard in many cities and towns through the efforts of the city councils, reinforced by the writings and support of the city secretaries and other members of the intellectual elite. Petitions to the emperor and other authorities and requests for a church council had gone unanswered. The magistrates had taken the secular sword in their own hands.

FOR THE HONOR OF GOD AND IN BROTHERLY LOVE—THE POOR LAWS

Care of the poor gave the magistrates and the city secretaries one of several opportunities to carry the Word of God into practice. The closing of convents and the monasteries made new facilities available for public use. Luther had written that care of the poor should be the responsibility of city governments. New welfare laws were enacted in many cities and towns beginning in 1522, a decade before the ordinances which would establish the reformed churches. The poor laws, on the one hand, demonstrated the Christian faith of the governing elite; on the other hand, they reflected traditional ways of thought and attitudes.

Who were the poor? Did they include the poor described by the artisans—the indigent, the beggars, and those who could not find work or whose wages were below the level of subsistence? The laws written by the city secretaries and the magistrates were limited to the indigent. This was a break with the medieval tradition, which had seen the beggar as a privileged person, sanctified by the piety of a Christian like St. Martin. During the fifteenth century, begging had begun to be recognized as a public burden. The magistrates of Strasbourg had specified as early as 1411 that the poor must work if they could. Only those who could not work because of illness or some other calamity were permitted to beg. Disillusion with the medicant friars strengthened the negative attitude toward begging.[69] This continued with the Reformation.

Early in 1520, Luther denounced begging in his *Long Sermon on Usury*.[70] His *Address to the German Nobility* (1522) called for the abolition of all begging. "Every city should take care of its own poor, and admit no foreign beggars by whatever name they may be called, whether pilgrims or mendicant monks."[71] Luther thus reinforced the link between lay beggars and begging monks. Care of the secular poor, he wrote, should be the responsibility of the city councils, who should appoint an overseer of the poor to take care of their needs. They might not be as well cared for as in the old days, when they could seek shelter in a monastery, continued Luther, but that was their own fault. "He who wishes to be poor, should not be rich, and if he wishes to be rich, let him put his hand to the plow.... It is enough if the poor are decently cared for, so they do not die of hunger and cold."[72] Among the higher ranks, poverty was perceived to be the result of indolence and sloth.

Traditionally the deserving poor, those worthy to receive alms, were poor unavoidably, not by choice. Throughout the Middle Ages, according to Mollat, an individual had to be "struck down by sickness, age, or misfortune, physically or mentally incapable of earning a living" if he were to receive aid from the community.[73] Several models for the administration of poor relief were available to the magistrates. In the thirteenth century, cities in northern France and the Low Countries maintained Poor Tables, where food was distributed to the needy, paid for from city revenues and pious bequests. In 1290, the city of Mons established a Common Alms, which united church and secular bequests under a city administrator. A list was drawn up of those eligible to receive help and a token given to them in proof of their eligibility. Another group received aid on an irregular basis. Later these groups were differentiated by insignia on their clothing.[74]

The demand for poor relief escalated during the early years of the Reformation. Bad harvests and high prices were a pattern in south German cities in 1517 to 1518 and 1526 to 1530. Poverty, as we have seen, was a grim reality in Augsburg and Nuremberg. Efforts to reorganize the welfare system by consolidating scattered funds began as early as 1522 in cities like Strasbourg and Nuremberg, where the city secretaries helped to draft laws which enabled the magistrates to assume control of all forms of alms. The welfare laws abolished begging and provided for the indigent only. A welfare office was established with an administrator to distribute funds to those proved worthy.

The Nuremberg ordinance of 1522, establishing a common chest, exemplified the official attitude. Although the roots of the new welfare system lay in the thirteenth century, the city councilors believed they were creating a more Christian society, based on brotherly love. Indeed, the Nuremberg council ordered that their new law should be printed to serve as an example for similar action in all states, cities, or communities.[75] Their purpose was broadly stated: "The honorable Rat of the city of Nuremberg, to honor God and in recognition of all Christian ways, by virtue of God's commandment to hold the true faith in God and brotherly love towards our neighbor . . . from now on will undertake to support all the poor and needy people and have drawn up a Christian ordinance as follows. . . ."[76]

Their first concern was to free Nuremberg from the beggars who came in from many lands and took alms away from the needy of the city. They were to be turned back at the gates. No foreigners would be permitted to beg in the city.[77] The poor within the city were regulated by welfare officers, with four men to assist them. Their first task was to register all the poor who had the right to receive alms. The welfare assistants would check among their neighbors to determine whether they were persons of good habits, not thieves, gamblers, or pimps. Each member of a household who passed the morals test would receive a badge to be worn at all times. No person wearing such a badge could enter a tavern. If a married couple had separated they must resume life as a couple to become eligible. The number of poor children attending the city schools was reduced. The three larger schools were to admit only 40 children, the two smaller schools 30 and 10, respectively. The children would have to wear their badges at school.[78] As a sole concession to the working poor, any money left over in the common chest after the needs of the poor were met was to be loaned out to poor craftsmen of good moral behavior.[79]

The authorities were seemingly unaware of the constraints they had laid on the poor. There was no indication that they recognized any humiliation associated with wearing a badge either by adults or by school children. Wandel has written "the badge was . . . a sign marking the 'deserving' poor, deserving not only of alms but of membership in the community. It was worn by those . . . who were moral according to the standards of each Christian community.[80] The Nuremberg magistrates' belief in the Christian justice of their act was confirmed in their conclusion: "Since our own salvation rests finally on upholding God's commandments, which bind every Christian person to the same brotherly love towards his neighbor, so we . . . admonish many, through the love of our lord Jesus Christ, to take part in this praiseworthy and Christian undertaking and to give money in the churches and chest as established."[81] It was not, however, the love of neighbor advocated by the artisans.

Laws drawn up in Kitzingen in 1523, in Leisnig in 1523, and in Strasbourg between 1522 and 1524 were similar. All required registration of the poor. All required the poor to wear a badge. In all cities, the welfare administrators were expected to monitor the moral behavior of the welfare recipients.[82] The Kitzingen law affirmed that the action had been taken to honor God and fulfill his commandments, especially the commandment that out of brotherly love no Christian should let his neighbor beg.[83] What did brotherly love mean? A pamphlet written by Hans Herbst, a judge in the city of Schwabach, provides some insight into the multiplicity of meanings of the phrase. His dialogue supporting the founding of a common chest in that city was the only pamphlet written by an upper civil servant in the popular style of a *Fassnachtsspiel*.[84]

There were four protagonists in the piece: Brother Henry, a former monk who took the position of the evangelical clergy; a master weaver, who praised the city authorities; an apprentice, who echoed his master's opinions; a woman carder, who strongly opposed the new law. Brother Henry brought the news of the establishment of the common chest to the weaving work room. The master gave thanks to God that now the poor would be taken care of. The carder's first reaction, however, was that the administrators would use the money for themselves, the one for his metal-working shop, the other for his brewery. The master replied, that would be impossible, they were both good Lutherans.[85]

The carder continued her criticism. People would waste what they had needlessly, thinking that when it was gone they would be supported by the common chest. They would have no security because no one would help such wasteful people. Her argument confirmed the need to closely control those who received alms. Brother Henry, however, admonished her gently. Such people should consider the love of God and their neighbor. Christ had said that men should love one another as he had loved them. "No one," continued Brother Henry, "has greater love than he who gives his life for his friend." "Christ laid down his life for us," retorted the carder, "but our city council would do that with great difficulty."[86] The carder then pointed out that the common chest would care only for the indigent who could not work.[87] The master pointed out that the word "common" meant that all the needs of the community could be met by the common chest, including such things as repairing the churches if no other money were available. This went well beyond the provisions of the law, but the master had faith in the magistrates. They would not handle the money as the monks and nuns had, but wisely and well and they would certainly consider every need in an orderly way.[88] The apprentice responded enthusiastically that the common people would willingly help with their lives and with their property. They must all have love, concluded the master, for love was the root of all things.[89]

The pamphlet bears witness to the depth of misunderstanding among the learned civil servants, the magistrates, and the common citizens. The author, an upper civil servant, spoke through the mouths of the former monk and the master weaver, who supported the traditional definition of the poor, wrapping it in the ideal of the common good, without regard to the needs of the working poor. The carder, while voicing the standard fear that a welfare system would make everyone lazy, nevertheless reflected the abiding distrust of the lower classes of their superiors, their assumption of corruption within the city council, and the belief that poor relief should not be limited to the indigent. At the end of the dialogue, as at the conclusion of a *Fassnachtspiel*, she accepted the common chest and the new, evangelical teaching. She went off to roast a chicken and make beer soup for everyone. Her resistance, however, showed that brotherly love as defined by the upper civil servants and the magistrates could only be maintained as an abstraction. Herbst, the learned upper civil servant, spoke in terms of the common good. In practice that meant control of the beggars and the marginal working class. It would mean, as the Nuremberg ordinance stated in its final article, that the churches and streets would be sober and clean, unencumbered by poor people wandering around, and that would please everyone.[90]

The dialogue reveals the gaps that existed between the social classes, their fundamental differences in perception with regard to their society, and the changes the Reformation might bring. In the artisans' pamphlets there were no references to the common good, the *gemeinen Nutz*. They spoke of the Christian community founded in the Word of God, with multiple references to the responsibility of the authorities to take care of the poor in brotherly love. By contrast, pamphlets by the upper civil servants and the laws of the city councils spoke of the honor of God, brotherly love, the *gemeinen Nutz*, order, and discipline. These norms, "the principles legitimizing social action," as Rublack called them, had been internalized by the governing elite for centuries. It was their responsibility, profoundly felt, to maintain the peace, unity, and tranquility of the community.[91] The norms concealed the overt social and economic differences within the city. By invoking them the magistrates could suppress conflict.[92] Moeller earlier idealized the urban reformation as the result of a unified world view. Each city formed a "sacral corporation" representing the highest aspirations of its citizens. Each citizen believed he was a part of this larger whole and accepted his part in contributing to the welfare of the entire community.[93] These perceptions and attitudes continued to determine the content of the laws and decrees passed by the city councils.

The artisans' pamphlets, however, make it clear that the norms were meaningful only to the governing elite. For them, brotherly love was an abstraction, meaning a generally Christian attitude toward the commoners. The artisans did not believe their superiors were motivated by the common good, nor did they think in abstractions. They described eloquently the divisions they saw around them. Brotherly love, to them, meant the actual physical care which Christ had given to the poor and needy.

The city secretaries served as the link between the reformers and the magistrates but were not involved with the lower ranks. Particularly in the early years of the movement, the reformers were close to their parishioners and used their support in the campaigns against the mass and against the monastic orders. The city secretaries advocated these causes in their pamphlets but made no effort to take part in the popular movement. Indeed, they were careful to avoid such actions. They did, however, develop close relations with the reforming preachers. The city secretaries identified themselves very early with Luther and expounded the correctness of his doctrines to the intellectual elite. By joining the reformers in emphasizing the failures of the Roman clergy, the civil servants were able to push reluctant magistrates onto a path of action. In drafting the legislation on the appointment of preachers and the new poor laws, the city secretaries became the architects of the Reformation, removing leadership from the reformers. The maintenance of order was placed firmly in the hands of the secular authorities.

Notes

1. G. Strauss, *Law, Resistance and the State*, 1986, 10.
2. The pamphlet *Zu Kayserliche Maiestat . . . Doctor Martin Luthers lere . . . ware antzeig*, 1520, was long attributed to Jacob Köbel, city secretary of Oppenheim, because of a short conclusion written by him. In 1962, Joseph Benzing established that the pamphlet was a reprint of an anonymous work published in Augsburg in that same year. I listed the pamphlet in the Primary Sources bibiography at

#179 with Köbel's name in brackets to make it clear that it was not Köbel's work. Köbel was a printer as well as serving as city secretary. He printed this pamphlet and several Luther pamphlets. His primary interests were mathematics, astrology, and astronomy. He does not appear among the city secretaries in this chapter.

3. Adolf Laube et al., *Flugschriften der frühen Reformationsbenegung*, 2 vols. (1983), 1, 512, place the composition of the *Schutzrede* after the Leipzig debate.
4. Ernest G. Schwiebert, *Luther and his Times*, 1950, 398, 402–403, 407–409.
5. #246, L. Spengler, *Schutzrede und Christenliche Antwort*, 1519, Laube et al., *Flugschriften*, 1, 501.
6. Ibid., 502, 503.
7. Ibid., 504.
8. Ibid., 503.
9. Ibid., 505.
10. Ibid., 508.
11. Ibid., 508.
12. Ibid., 509.
13. #271 Jörg Vögeli, *Dry missiven ains layeschen Burgers zu Constanz . . . den pfarrer zu Almanssdorff*, 1524, Ed. Alfred Vögeli, *Jörge Vögeli Schiften*, 3 vols., 1972, 2, Heft 1, 471. See H.-C. Rublack, *Die Einfuhrung der Reformation in Konstanz*, 1971, 14–15, for a summary of Vögeli's influence on the Reformation in Constance.
14. Ibid., 472.
15. Ibid., 473–475.
16. Ibid., fols. Biv–Bi^v. See for similar arguments: #146, B. Gretzinger, *Beschirmbüchlein*, 1524, passim; #271, J. Vögeli, *Dry Missiven*, 1524, passim, and his *Schirmred*, n.d., passim; #244, L. Spengler, *Kurtzer Begriff*, n.d., passim, and his *Haubt Artikel*, 1522, passim.
17. J. Schorr, *Ratschlag*, fol. Aiv.
18. Ibid.
19. Ibid., fol. Aiv^v.
20. #60, H. Brandeck, *Nützliche Ermanung*, fols. B^v–Bii^v.
21. Ibid., fol. Bii.
22. #248, L. Spengler, *Verantwortung . . . etlicher Argument*, 1524, fols. Civ^v–D^v.
23. Ibid., fol. Civ^v.
24. Ibid.
25. Ibid., fol. D.
26. Quoted in Walter Zimmerman, *Die Reformation als rechtlich-politisches Problem in den Jahren 1524–1530/31*, 1976, 42.
27. Ibid.
28. Ibid.
29. #272, J. Vögeli, *Schirmred ains layeschen Burgers . . .*, c. 1524, fols. A2–D3^v.
30. Ibid., fol. A2.
31. Ibid., fol. D4.
32. Ibid., fol. E1.
33. Ibid., fol. E^v.
34. Ibid., fol. D4^v.
35. #238, J. Schorr, *Ratschlag*, fol. Ai^v.
36. Ibid., fol. Aii.
37. Ibid.
38. Ibid.

39. Ibid., fol. Aii^{v}i.
40. Ibid., fol. Aiii.
41. Ibid., fol. Aiv.
42. Ibid., fol. Aiv^v.
43. Ibid., fols. Bii^v–Biii.
44. #248, L. Spengler, *Verantwortung*, fol. aii.
45. #146, B. Gretzinger, *Beschirmbüchlein*, fol. Cii^v.
46. #272, J. Vögeli, *Schirmred*, fols. A2, A2^v, A3^v.
47. #272, J. Vögeli, *Schirmred*, fol. D4.
48. Ibid.
49. #144, B. Gretzinger, *Beschirmbüchlein*, fol. C^v.
50. Ibid.
51. #238, J. Schorr, *Ratschlag*, fol. B.
52. Ibid., fol. Ai^v.
53. Ibid., fol. B^v.
54. Laube et al., *Flugschriften*, 2, 1320.
55. Ibid.
56. #72, Burgher zu Erfurt, *Ain new Gedicht wie die gaistlichait zu Erffordt gestürmbt ist worden*, Laube et al., *Flugschriften*, 2, 1318–1320.
57. Ibid., 2, 1320.
58. #144, B. Gretzinger, *Beschirmbüchlein*, fol. Aii; Aiiii^v. See also #244, L. Spengler, *Kurtzer begriff*, 10, 12–13.
59. #144, B. Gretzinger, *Beschirmbüchlein*, fol. Av.
60. #251, Stadt Constanz, *Burgermeiysters unnd Rat der Statt Costentz verantwurtung etlicher maren, die über sy und über die predigen dess worts Gottes . . . ausgangen sind*, 1526. For another example of an edict establishing preaching, see #250, Stadt Bern, *Gemein Reformation: und verbesserung . . . Gotsdienst . . .*, 1528.
61. #251, Stadt Constanz, fol. Ai^v.
62. Ibid., fol. Aiii.
63. Ibid., fol. Bii.
64. #178, Ottmar Karg und Lucius Steger, *Ain grÿme grosse Ketten*, 1524, fol. Ai^v. The word I have translated as "profession" is *Art*, used in the late Middle Ages to describe the learning of the schools and, by extension, learning, scholarship. These were men who had received law degrees. Their status as colleagues, sharing their art, is constantly mentioned. It is also evident they were not clerics.
65. Ibid.
66. Ibid., fols. Aii^v–Aiii.
67. Ibid., fol. B^v.
68. Ibid., fols. Ai^v, Aiii.
69. M. Chrisman, *Strasbourg and the Reform*, 1967, 270.
70. Martin Luther, "Ordinance of a Common Chest, Preface, 1523," transl. Albert T. W. Steinhauser, in *Luther's Works*, 45, *The Christian in Society*, 2, 161.
71. Martin Luther, "An Open Letter to the Christian Nobility," transl. Charles M. Jacobs, in *Three Treatises*, 1943, 81.
72. Ibid., 82.
73. Michel Mollat, *The Poor in the Middle Ages*, 1986, 295.
74. Ibid., 140.
75. #254, Stadt Nürnberg, *Christliche Ordnung . . . von dem hussarmer*, 1522, title page.
76. Ibid., fol. Aii.
77. Ibid., fols. Aii; Aiv^v.

78. Ibid., fols. Aiii–Aiv.
79. Ibid., fol. B^v.
80. Lee Wandel, "Social Welfare," *Oxford Encyclopedia of the Reformation*, forthcoming.
82. #254, Stadt Nürnberg, *Christliche Ordnung*, fol. Biii.
82. #252, Stadt Kitzingen, *Ein Cristenliche Ordenung der Betler halben*, 1523; #253, S. Leisnig, *Ordnung eyns Gemeynen kastens*, 1523. This was drafted by Luther. For Strasbourg, see M. Chrisman, *Strasbourg and the Reform*, 278–280.
83. #252, Stadt Kitzingen, *Cristenliche Ordenung*, Laube et al., *Flugschriften*, 2, 1078.
84. #22 [Hans Herbst], *Ein gesprech von dem gemeynen Schwabacher Kasten*, 1524. Hans Herbst is identified as the author of this anonymous pamphlet in Dieter Demandt und Hans-Christoph Rublack, *Stadt und Kirche in Kitzingen*, 1978, 55.
85. #22 [Hans Herbst], *Ein gesprech*, fol. Ai^v.
86. Ibid.
87. Ibid., fol. Aiii.
88. Ibid., fols. Ai^v; Aii; Aii^v.
89. Ibid., fol. Aii^v.
90. #254, Stadt Nürnberg, *Christliche Ordnung*, fol. Bii^v.
91. Hans-Christoph Rublack, "Political and Social Norms in Urban Communities . . .," in ed. Kaspar von Greyerz, *Religion, Politics and Social Control*, 1984, 25, 38–41.
92. Ibid., 52–53.
93. Bernd. Moeller, *Imperial Cities and the Reformation*, 1972, 45–47.

Conclusion

The lay writers who turned to the Reformation were united in their dedication to the new faith, a faith which they believed came by the grace of God, conveyed by his Word. Scripture was the source of religious truth, knowledge of it essential to salvation. Many of them defended their right, as lay men and women, to read and interpret the Bible for themselves. The reform they envisioned was a society based on order and justice as preached in the Gospel. Differences in the social circumstances of each rank meant that movements as separated in their aims as the communal reformation, the Knights' Revolt, the Peasants' War, and the magisterial reformation could develop. All drew their inspiration from the same words.

The Gospel is a revolutionary document. In a few years of preaching, Jesus condemned the hierarchy of the high priests and their domination of the Temple in Jerusalem, creating instead a teaching priesthood.[1] Coming from a poor village in the northernmost part of Palestine, he taught that the rich and powerful would be overthrown, their places taken by the poor and the humble.[2]

The lay pamphleteers believed that Jesus' message had been imprisoned by the Roman clergy for centuries. Those who heard the Gospel from the pulpit and read it in their own Bibles in the years between 1519 and 1523, found it new and overwhelming. But each rank in society heard it differently, within their own social context. The result was a series of simultaneous revolutions, occurring at the same time, but separate. Separate because the concept of order and justice diverged widely from rank to rank, based on variant definitions of community. All the pamphleteers agreed on the necessity of reform of the Christian community. But who made up the Christian community?

The knights viewed community in terms of their own lands, their family, and the people living on their lands. Ancient loyalties bound them to other knights. Their larger sphere included the emperor, the empire, and the upper nobility. The cities lay outside this; merchants and artisans were alien elements not to be trusted. Community for the knights meant their peers and their peasants. The knightly pamphleteers, however, were some of the first to respond to Luther's teaching and preaching. Sickingen and those who followed him accepted Luther's condemnation of the Pope and the Roman church, believing that the Christian church had to be cleansed as Jesus had

227

cleansed the Temple. The scriptural basis of their revolt lay in Jesus' rejection of the hierarchical nature of Judaism. They pushed beyond this to
justify taking the lands of the church into their own hands. With this they
lost the chance of backing from other ranks. A landed knight, in the eyes
of the lower classes, had no claim to further wealth, even the unfairly gotten
wealth of the church. The first revolt of the Reformation did not receive
broad support and was quickly crushed from above.

The minor civil servants and technicians accepted and promulgated both
revolutionary messages preached by Jesus. Ardent in their hatred and scorn
of the Pope, they recommended the overthrow of Rome and all its courtesans.
Several of them took up Jesus' call for social and economic equality, and
vigorously advocated the destruction of the cities and the establishment of
agrarian communities where all would find work in manual labor, led by
dedicated preachers of the true Word of God. Man-made laws and customs
would be replaced by godly law.[3] Although several members of this group
served as leaders in the Peasants' War, their aims were too radical for their
time. Those who had assumed leadership lost their lives. The Peasants' War
was suppressed by Catholic and Protestant nobility alike.

The revolutionary voice of the Gospel was heard clearly by the artisans.
The dissolution of the Roman church would mean that they could build a
communal church based on the parish church, controlled and directed by
the parishioners themselves.[4] Like the minor officials, artisans defined community as working people, those who worked with their hands. In some
instances this included the peasants. Reading the Scriptures led the artisans to extend their vision beyond their own guild to include the unemployed and, particularly, the poor. They believed that the time was at hand
when the rich and the powerful would be overthrown and Jesus' vision
would be achieved. There would be neither rich nor poor, powerful or powerless. Instead, all would work together as brothers and sisters in a true
Christian community. Their brief alliance with the peasants to achieve this
communal revolution failed, suppressed by the city magistrates and the military
forces of the nobility.

The urban elite and the city secretaries perceived community in terms of
their city. Order meant that each rank fulfilled its obligations of work and
obedience to their superiors. Justice meant that the laws of the city were
carried out and peace was maintained. The Christian stoicism of the early
humanist movement, its later Augustinianism and traditional legal formulae, continued to define their attitudes and determine the content of their
laws and decrees. Radical change being foreign to their purpose and their
thought, they believed in a Reformation which would restore order to their
city. Following the example of Jesus, they would purify a corrupt church
and establish a disciplined clergy who would reinvigorate the spiritual and

moral life of the city.[5] They would honor God and care for the *gemeinen Nutz*, which included providing for the needs of the deserving poor. Their ideal, as Moeller wrote, was the *civitas Christiana*, a holy city founded on the laws of God.[6] It was this magisterial reformation which was the most successful.

In the years 1519 to 1530, the Reformation was not a single, unified movement. Instead, the preaching of the Gospel set off a series of revolutions. Each revolution had its own system of ideas and purpose which led men and women to act. Each followed its own pattern of events. Each failed. The changes made after 1525 by the urban magistrates and the princes in the structure and ceremonies of the Roman church were only half of the Reform envisioned by lower ranks. Their deep longing for control of their own religious life and for fundamental social change was repressed. The message of the Gospel was tamed by the powerful.

Notes

1. John Dominic Crossan, *The Historical Jesus*, 1992, 355, 356.
2. Ibid., 273–275.
3. Peter Blickle, "Biblicism and Feudalism," 1979, 142.
4. Peter Blickle, *Communal Reformation*, 1992, 25, 50.
5. Bernd Moeller, *Imperial Cities and the Reformation*, 1972, 92.
6. Ibid.

FIGURE 6 PAMPHLET AUTHORS LISTED BY SOCIAL RANK

Each entry gives the source for the most accessible identification. The abbreviations used for the Primary Sources bibliography are also used here.

NOBLES, KNIGHTS

Cronberg, Hartmuth von
  Knight. ADB, 17, 189–190.
Drübel, Eckhart zum [Eckhart zum Treubel]
  Knight, urban noble. Koch.
Endorf, Hieronymus von
  Knight. H. Holstein, Zeitschrift für Kirchengeschichte 10, 3, (1889): 453–462.
Freyburg, Hilgart von
  Noble. Self-identified.
Gemmiger, Lux
  Knight. Connections to Hutten circle. Laube, 1, 555.
Grumbach, Argula von [Argula von Stauffen]
  Noble. R. Bainton, Women of the Reformation in Germany, 97ff.
Hutten, Ulrich von
  Knight. E. Böcking, ed., Opera Ulrichi Huttens.
Landschad von Steinach, Hans
  Knight. ADB, 35, 670–675.
Niclas unter dem Rotten Hütt [pseudonym]
  Noble, defender of Sickingen. J. Halle, Antiquariatskatalog, #70.
Obendorf, Kunz von
  Noble. Schottenloher, Ritterschaftsbewegung, 5.
Schaumburg, Adam von
  Noble. Self-identified; see also Folger Library, Catalogue, #686.
Schenck von Stauffenberg, Jacob
  Noble. Ozment, Reformation in the Cities, 83.
Sickingen, Franz von
  Noble, military leader. ADB, 34, 151ff.
Anonymous author of #11, Absag brieff des Fürsten dyser wyder Martin Luther.
  Catholic nobleman. Schottenloher, Sachs/Höltzel, #5, 250.
Anonymous author of #15, Das biechlin zeiget an wer der lebendig martrer sey.
  Noble supporter of Sickingen. Schottenloher, Ritterschaftsbewegung, 7–8.
Anonymous author of #21, Dise der Graven: herren Gemainer Ritterschaft.
  Manifesto of Frankish nobility sent to the Diet of Nuremberg. Schottenloher,
  Ritterschaftsbewegung, 5.
Anonymous author of #14, Der gut frumm Pfaffennahr.
  Noble supporter of Sickingen. Schottenloher, Ritterschaftsbewegung, 8.
Anonymous author of #28, Klarich Anzeigung und Ausweysung.
  Knight. Identified by text: knights and nobles will replace the clergy as rulers of
  the land. Peroration to the German nobility.
N. von N., Anonymous author of #40, Der Ritterschaft brüderlich Vereinigung.
  Noble. Self-identified.
Anonymous author of #41, Ain schenes und nutzliches büchlin von dem Christlichen
  glauben.

Noble. Schottenloher, *Ritterschaftsbewegung*, 6.
Anonymous author of #46, *Teütscher Nation beschwerd*.
   Noble. Noble grievances presented to the Diet of Nuremberg, 1523.
Anonymous author of #51, *Wer hören will wer die gantze welt arm hat gemacht*.
   Noble. Noble supporter of Sickingen. Schottenloher, *Ritterschaftsbewegung*, 6.

MINOR CIVIL SERVANTS AND TECHNICIANS, MEN WITH SOME ADVANCED EDUCATION OR SPECIALIZED TECHNICAL SKILLS

Alber, Erasmus
   Schoolmaster. Clemen, *Flugschriften*, 3, 359.
Bossler, Ulrich [von Hassfurt]
   Apothecary. Self-identified.
Gaismair, Michael
   Administrator for the Bishop of Brixen; leader of Peasants' War. ADB, 8, 313–314.
Gengenbach, Pamphilus
   Printer in Basel. K. Lendi, *Die Dichter Pamphilus Gegenbach*.
Greff, Joachim
   School teacher and playwright. ADB, 9, 624.
Hergot, Hans
   Printer. ADB, 12, 210–212, Laube, *Flugschrift der Bauernkriegszeit*, 545.
Herman, Nicolaus
   Cantor, songwriter, teacher. Clemen, *Flugschriften*, 2, 248ff.
Marschalck, Haug (genannt Zoller)
   Officer for imperial troops in Augsburg, tax collector. Russell, *Lay Theology*, 10–16.
Meldeman, Nicolaus
   Engraver, printer. ADB, 21, 292.
Motschidler, Jörg
   Master gunner, Wittenberg. Clemen, ARG, 9 (1911–12): 277.
Scharffenstein, Heinz von
   Official in Mainz. Laube, 3, 1332.
Stanberger, Balthasar
   Secretary at ducal castle, Weimar. Self-identified. See also Laube, 1, 225.
Sturm, Caspar
   Imperial herald. ADB, 37, 41–42.
Vogtherr, Heinrich der älter
   Engraver, printer, doctor. ADB, 40, 192–194.
Weyda, Ursula
   Wife of tax collector in Eisenberg, ducal Saxony. Russell, *Lay Theology*, 201–203.
Zell, Katherina [Katherina Schutz]
   Daughter of Strasbourg carpenter, wife of the reformer Matthias Zell.
   Chrisman, ARG 63 (1972): 156–157.
Anonymous author of #47, *Teütscher Nation Notturft*.
   The name of Georg Rixner, called Jerusalem, herald of the empire, appears at the
   end of the articles in the pamphlet. Rixner was the herald of the Count Palatine
   and regent of the *Reichsregiment*. Laube 2, 788, summarized the evidence against
   Rixner as author. See also Klaus Arnold, "Reichsherold und Reichsreform," 107.
   T. Scott and B. Scribner attribute the pamphlet to Friedrich Weigant, official in
   Miltenberg for the Archbishop-Elector of Mainz (*German Peasant's War*), 259.

URBAN ELITE

Nützel, Kaspar [pseudonym Philadelphus Noricus]
  Patrician, active in Nuremberg *Rat*. Clemen, *Kleine Schriften*., 2, 295–298.
Rem, Bernhard
  Patrician Augsburg family. *ADB*, 28, 187.
Rem, Katherina
  Sister of Bernhard Rem. Self-identified.
Wurm von Geudertheim, Matthias
  Noble patrician, Strasbourg. J. Rott, "De quelques pamphletaires nobles," *Grandes Figures de l'humanisme Alsacien*, 1978, 139ff.
Anonymous author of #13, *Ayn bezwungene antwort . . . eyner Closternonnen*.
  Laywoman of honorable estate. Schottenloher, *Sachs/Hötzel*, #4, 249.
Anonymous author of #43, *Ain Sendbrieff von ainer erbern frawen*.
  Self-identified as an honorable patrician woman.

STADTSCHREIBER, UNIVERSITY EDUCATED PROFESSIONALS

Brandeck, Hieronymus [von Strassfurt]
  Upper civil servant. Identified by written style and emphasis on reason.
Burger zu Erfurt
  Burgher close to Erfurt *Rat*. Laube, 2, 1316–1322.
Copp, Johannes
  Astronomer, doctor of medicine, compiler of prognostications. Self-identified.
Gretzinger, Benedictus
  Stadtschreiber of Reutlingen. Clemen, *Beiträge*, 3, 24–34.
Karg, Ottmar
  University educated Swiss burgher. Self-identified.
Scharpf, Heinrich [von Klingau]
  Learned professional, university educated. Identified in preface to his pamphlet, #178, *Ain gryme, gross Ketten*.
Schorr, Jakob
  Landsschreiber for the Duke of Zweibrücken. *ADB*, 32, 384–386.
Spengler, Lazarus
  Stadtschreiber of Nuremberg. H. Grimm, *Lazarus Spengler*.
Steger, Lucius
  Learned professional. Identified in introduction to pamphlet #178.
Vögeli, Jörg
  Stadtschreiber of Constance. Jörg Vögeli, *Schriften zur Reformation in Konstanz*, ed., A. Vögeli, 1, Halbband, 39–53.

ARTISANS, MIDDLE-RANKING BURGHERS, AND POPULAR POETS

Bechler, Hans [von Scholbrunnen]
  Layman, urban middle rank. Private communication with H.-J. Köhler.
Breuning, Jörg
  Weaver. Self-identified.
Büllheym, Steffan von [pseudonym]
  Popular social level, artisan. M. Lienhard, "Mentalité populaire," 37ff.
Bürger zu Nürnberg
  Middle-rank burgher. Lack of organizational skills indicates little formal education.

Butzbach, Dietrich
  Middle-level burgher or artisan. Self-identified. Asks to have his writing read to the *Gesellen*, journeymen or companions. See also Laube, 2, 1987.
Distelmair, Conrad
  Artisan. *ADB*, 5, 256.
Felbaum, Sebastian [von Breten]
  Catholic, middle-burgher rank according to his style of writing.
Fincken, Michael
  Self-identified as burgher from outside Miltenberg at time of bishop's attack.
Füssli, Hans
  Bell-maker, artisan. *Hist.-Biog. Lexikon der Schweiz*, 3,356.
Gerhardt, Hans
  Wegmaster (weigh-master or road builder) and wagoner in Kitzingen. My thanks to Dr. Christoph Weisman, Stadtarchiv Reutlingen, who located Gerhardt in the Steuerbuch (St. B Ki 1530 S. 3).
Goltschmit, Bastian
  Burgher of Worms. Self-identified as ordinary burgher of Worms.
Graff, Jörg
  Landsknecht, popular poet. *ADB*, 9, 570–571.
Greiffenberger, Hans
  Artisan, painter. *ADB*, 9, 651.
Hass, Cuntz
  Clothmaker, weaver, *Meistersinger*. *ADB*, 10, 753–754.
Johim, Bernhart
  Self-identified as a burgher from Burgstat, visiting Miltenberg at the time of the bishop's attack.
Kattelsburger, Nikolaus
  Carpetweaver. Arnold, 319f.
Kolb, Hans
  Popular songwriter. Folger Library, *Catalogue*, #330.
Lotzer, Sebastian
  Furrier. Russell, *Lay Theology*, 90ff.
Manuel, Niklaus
  Painter in Bern, playwright. *ADB*, 20, 275–277.
Morlin, Hans
  Linen weaver. Arnold, 296.
Nagel, Hans
  Tanner. Folger Library, *Catalogue*, #575.
Reychart, Peter
  Furrier. Rothenburg, Arnold, 305.
Rychssner, Utz
  Weaver. Russell, *Lay Theology*, 120–121; Laube, 1, 439.
Sachs, Hans
  Shoemaker, *Meistersinger*, playwright in Nuremberg. K. Wedler, *Hans Sachs*, and numerous other biographies.
Schnewyl, Johann [von Strassburg]
  Burgher of Strassburg. Identified by Adolf Laube in personal communication.
Schöpfer, Hans
  Popular poet. Folger Library, *Catalogue*, #168.

Staygmayer, Hans
   Baker at Reutlingen. Self-identified. Confirmed by Herr Brühl, Staatsarchiv
   Reutlingen.
[Tauber, Caspar]
   Burgher of Vienna. *ADB*, 37, 423–429.
Ulem, Hans
   Unidentified. Writes to warn the *gemeyn armen Mann.*"
Ziegler, Clement
   Gardener, guildsman Peter, 256ff.
Ziegler, Jörg [pseudonym Hans von Schore]
   Tailor, brother of Clement Ziegler. J. Rott, *Investigationes Historicae*, 1, 521 ff.
Zierer, Wolfgang
   Landsknecht. Self-identified.
Anonymous author of #17, *Das ist ein Spruch von der Evangelische lere.*
   Popular poet. Identified by style and vocabulary.
Anonymous author of #18, *Dialogus zweischen einem Vatter und Sohn.*
   Clemen, *Flugschriften*, 1, 21, accepts the self-identification of the upper peasant
   father and his student son. Since I have no peasant classification I placed the
   author with the artisans and middle burghers because he comes from a popular
   milieu and speaks for the lower ranks.
Anonymous author of #39, *Ein neuer spruch von Sickingens Handlung.*
   Burgher milieu because of sharp criticism of the knights. Schottenloher,
   Ritterschaftsbewegung, 12.
Anonymous author of #36, *Ain n new Gedicht.*
   Popular writer. Identified by style and content.
Anonymous author of #45, *Ain Strafred.*
Unlearned but not a peasant. Probably from Weissenburg in Franconia. Schade, 2,
175ff.
Anonymous author of #50, *Welcher das Evangelium hat für gut.*
   Self-identified as a common layman and day worker.

Primary Sources

The primary source bibliography is divided into four sections. The first lists the sources used to find the pamphlets and gives the abbreviations for these in the entries which follow. The second section gives a small sample of pamphlets directed to lay readers written before the Reformation. These give some insight into the writers' and printers' concepts of the popular reading market. Much more work needs to be done on this, including careful examination of the large corpus of popular poems, songs and *Fastnachspiel*. The pamphlets used in this study begin with the third section which lists those by anonymous authors. That there were forty authors who were unwilling to sign their work is indicative of the fear which marked the decade. The fourth section lists pamphlets with identified authors. Each entry in sections two, three and four includes information on where the pamphlet can be located. In most cases this refers to the full text of the treatise. In some cases, however, such as Schottenloher's monograph on the *Ritterschaftsbewegung*, and Rudolphe Peter's work on Clement Ziegler, the texts are not included and references are bibliographical. These titles have been included to show the range of the pamphlets.

Titles in the bibliography were transcribed from the title pages of each pamphlet. Misspellings were carefully maintained. In terms of punctuation, a slash is used, as it was by the printer, as a comma. A double slash denotes the end of a line. Long titles, for reasons of space, had to be abbreviated; some slashes were deleted. The ampersand was transcribed as "etc." The complex "d" symbol was transcribed as "der," "m" or "n" were added where a bar appeared over the penultimate "e" or the superscript "e" to make the title more readable. Additional printings are listed below each entry. NCA means no copy available in the sources used.

This bibliography does not attempt to cover all lay pamphlet writers in the period 1500–1530. It represents only the pamphlets used in the database for this study. After 1993, I added no new pamphlets since my own analysis of individual pamphlets was then complete. Full bibliographic references appear in Hans-Joachim Köhler's *Bibliographie der Flugschriften des 16. Jahrhunderts*, 3 vols. (Tübingen: Bibliotheca Verlag, 1991—). Köhler includes lay pamphlets, particularly journalistic accounts of events, which I did not use. Köhler lists each pamphlet edition separately with data on printers and place of publication. References are also given for pamphlets listed in VD16, *Verzeichnis der im Deutschen Sprachbereich ershienenenen Drucke des XVI Jahrunderts.* These appear at the end of an entry. Multiple editions are included in the numbers given.

My list does not claim to be exhaustive but is a point of departure for further work on lay writers and their pamphlets.

SOURCES WITH ABBREVIATIONS

ADB   *Allgemeine Deutsche Biographie.*, vols. 1–56, Leipzig: Duncker und Humblot, 1904; Berlin: Duncker und Humblot, 1967.
ARG   *Archiv für Reformation Geschichte.*
Arnold   Martin Arnold, *Handwerker als theologische Schriftsteller: Studien zu Flugschriften der frühen Reformation (1523–1525).* Göttingen: Vandenhoek und Ruprecht, 1990.
Baechthold   Jacob Baechthold, ed., *Niklaus Manuel in Bibliothek altere Schriftwerke der deutschen Schweiz,*vol. 2. Frauenfeld: J. Haber, 1878.
Benrath   Gustav Adolf Benrath, "Zwei Flugschriften des Reichsritters Hans Landschad von Steinach von 1522 und 1524," *Ebernburg-Hefte* 6./7. Folge, 1972–1993, 66–96.
Benzing, Köbel   Josef Benzing, *Jakob Köbel zu Oppenheim, 1494–1553: Bibliographie seiner Drucke und Schriften.* Wiesbaden: G. Pressler, 1962.
Böcking   Eduard Böcking, ed., *Opera Ulrichi Huttens equitis Germani.* 5 vols. Leipzig, 1859–1862. Two supplemental volumes, Leipzig, 1869–1870.
CRR   Center for Reformation Research, St. Louis, Mo.
Clemen, Beiträge   Otto Clemen, *Beiträge zur Reformationsgeschichte aus Büchern und Handschriften der Zwickauer Ratsschulbibliothek.* 3 vols. Berlin: C.A. Schwetschke, 1901–1903.
Clemen, Faksimile   Otto Clemen, ed. *Flugschriften der Reformationszeit in Faksimiledrucken.* Leipzig: O. Harrasowitz, 1921–1922.
Clemen, Flugschriften   Otto Clemen, ed. *Flugschriften aus den ersten Jahren der Reformation.* 4 vols. 1907–1911. Reprint, Nieuwkoop: B. de Graaf, 1967.
Clemen, Kleine Schr.   Otto Clemen, *Kleine Schriften zur Reformationsgeschichte, 1897–1944,* ed. Ernst Koch, 1982–1984, 5 vols. Leipzig: Zentralantiquariat der DDR, 1982–1984.
Demant/Rublack   Dieter Demandt and Hans-Christoph Rublack, *Stadt und Kirche in Kitzingen, Darstellung und Quellen.* . . . Stuttgart: Klett-Cotta, 1978.
Fiche/#   Number of pamphlet in Hans-Joachim Köhler, ed. *Flugschriften des frühen 16. Jahrhunderts,* Microfiche Serie, 1978–1988. Zug: Interdokumentation AG, 1978–1988.
Folger   *Reformation,* Catalogue of the Emanuel Stickelberger Collection purchased by The Folger Shakespeare Library, Washington, D.C. Basel: Haus der Bücher, 1977.
Goetze   *Sebastian Lotzer's Schriften,* ed. A. Goetze. Leipzig, 1902.
Grimm   Harold J. Grimm. *Lazarus Spengler: A Lay Leader of the Reformation.* Columbus, Oh.: Ohio University Press, 1978.
Hieronymus   Frank Hieronymus. *Basler Buchillustration 1500 bis 1545.* Universitätsbibliothek Basel Austellung 31. März bis 30. Juni 1984, Katalog. Basel: Universitätsbibliothek, 1984.
Koch   Copy kindly supplied by Gustave Koch. See Gustave Koch, *Eckhart zum Drübel, témoin de la Réforme en Alsace: Biographi, textes et traductions.* Strasbourg: Assoc. des Publications de la Faculté de Theologie Protestante, 1989.
Köhler, Bibliog.   Hans-Joachim Köhler, *Bibliographie der Flugschriften des 16.*

Jahrhunderts, Teil I, Das Frühe 16. Jahrhundert (1501–1530), Band 1 & 2, *Druckbeschreibung*, *A-L*. Tübingen: Bibliotheca Academica Verlag, 1991, 1993–.

Kolde Th. Kolde, "Der Reichsherold Caspar Sturm und seine literarische Tätigkeit," *Archiv für Reformationsgeschichte* IV (1906–1907),117–148.

Laube Adolf Laube and Annerose Schneider, eds. *Flugschriften der frühen Reformationsbewegung 1518–1524*. 2 vols. Berlin: Akademie-Verlag, 1983.

Laube, Flug. der Bauernkrieg Adolf Laube and Hans-Werner Seiffert, eds. *Flugschriften der Bauernkriegszeit*. Berlin: Akademie Verlag, 1975.

Lenk Werner Lenk, ed. *Die Reformation in zeit-genössischen Dialog*. Berlin: Academie Verlag, 1968.

NCA No copy available.

Panzer Georg Wolfgang Panzer, *Annalen der ältern deutschen Literatur*. 6 vols., 1788–1885. Reprinted, 6 vols. in 3, Hildesheim: Georg Olms, 1961.

Peter Rodolphe Peter. "Le Maraîcher Clément Ziegler: L'homme et son oeuvre." *Revue d'histoire et de philosophie religieuses* 34 (1954). 256–282.

Röhrich Timotheus Wilhelm Röhrich. "Matthias Wurm von Geudertheim." *Mittheilungen aus der Geschichte der evangelischen Kirche des Elsasses*. Vol. 3 of 3. Strassburg: Treuttel und Würtz, 1855. 6–18.

Rott Jean Rott. *Investigationes Historicae: églises et société au XVIe siècle. Gesammelte Aufsätze*. Strasbourg: Librairie Oberlin, 1986.

Russell Copy kindly supplied by Paul Russell. The entry lists the library where the pamphlet was photocopied.

Russell Paul Russell. *Lay Theology and the Reformation*. Cambridge: Cambridge University Press, 1986.

Schade Oskar Schade, ed. *Satiren und Pasquille aus der Reformationszeit*. 3 vols. Hannover: Carl Rümpler, 1868.

Schottenloher, Ritterschaft Karl Schottenloher. *Flugschriften zur Ritterschaftsbewegung des Jahres 1523*. Reformationsgeschichtliche Studien und Texte, 53. Ed. Albert Ehrhard. Münster: Aschendorffschen Verlagsbuchhandlung, 1929.

Simmler, Mss, CRR. Simmler Manuscript Collection on Film at Center for Reformation Research, St. Louis, Mo.

Strasbourg, BM Strasbourg, Bibliothèque Municipale.

Strasbourg, BNU Strasbourg, Bibiothèque Nationale et Universitaire.

Strasbourg, St. Guillaume Strasbourg, Bibliothèque du Seminaire protestante.

Strauss Gerald Strauss, ed. and trans. *Manifestations of Discontent in Germany on the Eve of the Reformation*. Bloomington, Ind.: Indiana University Press, 1971.

Studer J. Studer. "Der Schulmeister Johannes Buchstab von Winterthur. ein Gegner U. Zwinglis." *Schweizerische Theologische Zeitschrift* 29 (1912): 198–219.

VD 16 *Verzeichnis der im Deutschen Sprachbereich erschienenen Drucke des XVI Jahrhunderts*. VD 16. Eds. Bayer. Staatsbibliothek in München in Verbindung mit d. Herzog August Biblikothek in Wolfenbüttel. 21 vols. Stuttgart: Anton Hiersemann, 1983—.

Weller Emil Weller, *Annalen der poetischen National Literatur . . . im XVI/XVII Jh.*. 2 vols. Reprinted 1964, vol. 1, Part III.

Yale, Beinecke Yale University, Beinecke Library.

Zurich, ZB Zurich, Zentralbibliothek.

PRE-REFORMATION PAMPHLETS FOR LAY READERS

1. *Das biechlin ist ge-//nant Der fußpfadt zu der ewigen se-//ligkait/*. . . . Augsburg: J. Nadler, 1521. [Fiche 1233/#3109]

2. *Dis biechlin saget von Bru//der Rauschen und was er//wunders getriben hat in einem Closter.* . . . Strassburg, M. Flach, 1508. [Fiche 1303/#3368]

3. *Das buchlin sagt von//des Endkrists leben und regierung durch verhengniß//gottes/ wie er die welt dut verkeren mit synerfalsche ler//und rat des tüfels/.* . . . Strassburg, M. Hupfuff, 1503. [Fiche 1299/#3349]

4. *Der Geystlich flüß//.* . . . N.p.: n.p., n.d. [Fiche 1296/#3338]

5. *Der text des Passions oder Lidens Christi aus den vier Evangelisten.* Strassburg: J. Knobloch, 1506. [Strasbourg, BNU]

6. *Von dem kremer//Christi was er gut-//tes zuvorkauffen hat.* Strasbourg: M. Hupfuff, 1510. [Zurich, ZB]

7. *Ein wahrhafftiger tractat wie man//das hochwirdig heiligthum verkundet und geweist/ /in der heiligenstadt Trier im thum.* N.p.: n.p., n.d. [Fiche 1301/#3357]

8. Gengenbach, Pamphilus. *Die X Alter dieser Welt.* N.p.: n.p., n.d. [Fiche 933/ #2324]

9. Hass, Cuntz. *Hierin vindet mon die ursach wo durch alle hendel yetz in der welt verkert und verderbt werden.* Nuremberg: A. Huber, 1500? [Fiche 1317/#3431]

10. Manuel, Nicolaus. *Die war History von den vier//Ketzer prediger ordens, zu Bern in der//Eydgenosschafft verbrant.//Ein schön lied von den vnbeflecten//entpfengknuß Marie.* N.p.: n.p., 1509. [Zurich, ZB]

ANONYMOUS PAMPHLETS

11. *Absag brieff des Fürsten diser wel//te etc. wider Martinum// Luther.* Nuremberg: H. 1524.(?). [Fiche 1261/#3231] VD 16, A 1468–1475.

12. *Anklag und//ernstliches ermanen Got-//tes Allmechtigen/zu einer gemeinen// Eydgnoschafft/das sy sich vonn//ire sunden/zu im//keere//.* N.p.: n.p., 1528. [Fiche 1459/ #3851] Attributed to Heinrich Bullinger d. A in VD 16, B 9544–9547.

13. *Ayn bezwungene ant-//wort uber eynen Sendtbrieff/eyner//Closter nunnen/an jr schwester im Eelichen//standt zugeschickt/.* . . . N.p.: n.p., 1524. [Zurich,ZB; Fiche 1382/ #3653] VD 16, B 2539.

14. *Das biechlin hat gemacht der nar der//gut lutherisch ist/.* . . . Augsburg: E. Öglin Erben, 1521. [Laube, 2, 742–746; Fiche 49/#138] VD 16, G 4146. Editions with title *Der gut frum Lutherisch Pfaffennarr haysz ich*: VD 16, G 4147–4149.
   Augsburg: E. Öglin Erben, n.d.
   Augsburg: J. Nadler, 1521.
   Strassburg, J. Prüß II, n.d.
   Erfurt, M. Maler, n.d.

15. *Das biechlin zaiget an wer der//lebendig martrer sey auff erdtrich/und//betrifft den Christenlichen//glauben.* Augsburg: E. Oeglin Erben, 1521. [Fiche 984/#2493]

16. *Das ist yetz der gemain und//new gebrauch. in welch//em das volck der welt//zu dissen gezeiten//ganntz leer be-//laden ist.* N.p.: n.p., n.d. [Fiche 1314/#3413] VD 16, D 1450. N.p.: n.p., n.d. [Fiche 1314/#3414]

17. *Dis ist ein Spruch von der Euan//gelischen lere . . . yetz gegen disem newen iar///was ich euch wünsch//das werd vch//war.* N.p.: n.p., n.d. [Fiche 1808/#4634] VD 16, D 1450.

18. *Eynn Dialogus ader ge//sprech zwischen einem//Vatter unnd Sun dye//Lere Martini Luthers . . . belangende.* Erfurt: M. Buchfürer, n.d. [Clemen, 1, 21–52; Lenk, 153–167; Fiche 266/#748] VD 16, D 1331.

19. *Dialogus der//Rede unnd gesprech//so Franciscus von Sick//ingen/vor deß himmelß/ /pfortten/mit sant//Peter/ und dem//Riter sant Jör//gen gehalten//Zuuor: und//ee dan er eingelassen ist//worden.* Augsburg: Melchior Rammiger, 1523. [Fiche 1346/#3540] VD 16, D 1319–1322.

N.p.: n.p., 1523.
Colmar: A. Farckall, 1523.
Speyer: J. Schmidt, 1523.
Altenburg: G. Kantz, 1526.

20.   *Dis seind etlich erschrockenliche wun.//derzaichen so got uns//zewarnen für augen gestelt hat/*. . . . N.p.: n.p., n.d. [Fiche 569/#1458]

21.   *Dise der Graven:herren//gemainer Ritterschafft/und anderer . . . so in dem. xxiii. jar zu Nürm-//berg versamelt gewest/uberant-//wort worden.* N.p.: n.p., 1523/24. [Fiche 1211/#3063] VD 16, R 713–715.

22.   [Herbst, Hans]. *Eyn gesprech von dem//gemeynen Schwabacher kasten.* . . . Erfurt: M. Maler, 1524. [Schade, 3, 196ff.; Fiche 1316/#3427; Fiche 985/#2499] VD 16, H 2226–2228. Nürnberg: H. Höltzel, 1524.

23.   *Der Gotzferchtige//Eerentreiche fraw//Hilgart von Frey//burg seiner cri//stenliche al//lerliebsten//schwester.* Augsburg: M. Ramminger, 1524. [Fiche 1252/#3191] VD 16, G 2682.

24.   *Ein grosse clag der armen//Leyen. Zu Gott dem herren//Von der pfaffen wegen.* . . . Basel: T. Wolf? 1523. [Fiche 1779/4580]

25.   *Hab Gott lieb//unnd diene//jm al-//lein.* Speyer: J. Eckhart, 1522. [Fiche 612/#1576] VD 16, H 5.

26.   *Hübsch Argument, Red, Frag und Antwurt dreier Personen, nämlich Curtisan, Edelman Burger, alles D.M. Luthers Lehre betreffend.* Augsburg: M. Ramminger, 1522. [Fiche 267/#753] VD 16, H 5676.
    Coburg: A. Fellenfürst bzw. Bamberg: G. Erlinger, 1522. [Fiche 267/#753]
    Wien: J. Singeriener der Ä., 1522. [Fiche 1588/#4098]

27.   *Ich kan nit vil neues erdenken//ich musz der katzen dschellen anhenken.* Augsburg: J. Schönsperger, 1523. [Schade, 1, 13–18; Fiche 937/#2340] VD 16, K 1204–1208.
    Strassburg: M. Schürer Erben, 1524. [Fiche 1315/#3418]
    Nürnberg: H. Guldenmund, c. 1535. [Fiche 980/#2475]

28.   *Ein klarlich anzeygung//und außweysung eines Christlichen//unnd unchristlichen lebens . . . auch . . . ob der//Endchrist kom//men/oder zu//kommen//künff//tigt sey.* Speyer: J. Schmidt, c. 1523? [Fiche 223/#624] VD 16, K 1236.

29.   *Lieder. Das Eesonet//Papistisch.//Das Eesonet//Lutherisch.* N.p.: n.p., n.d. [Fiche 1505/#3960]

30.   ———. *Ein new Christlich lied . . . verantwurtet den gots lesterer schmehung/so// der Baurer auffrür dem Evangelio fälschlich//zu legendt.* N.p.: n.p., n.d. [Simmler Mss. CRR, H 3000, V 13, #110]

31.   ———. *Ein news lied von bekerung des Gaistlichen stands.* N.p.: n.p., n.d. [Simmler Mss, CRR, H 3000, v. 17a #141]

32.   ———. *Ain new lied/gemacht zu eren den hochgelerten Doctor Martin Luther.* . . . N.p.: n.p., 1524. [Weller, 3, #47]

33.   ———. *Das ist ein spruch von der Evangelischen lere/von dem wurt Gottes/zu trust den frommen Christen.* . . . N.p.: n.p., 1524. [Weller, 3, #48]

34.   ———. *Nüw zeitung betreffend die absterbende papistische Messen zu Strassburg bysshar loblichen von in gehalten.* N.p.: n.p., 1525. [Weller, 3, #54]

35.   *Ain Lieplicher sch-//oner auszug in gesetzts weysz ge-//macht/von ersten anfangs/von ainen Engelschlich//en leerer/der gotlichen warhait . . . der .x. Gebot gottes/mit sampt et-//llichen schonen prophetischen . . . sprüchn//zu horen. etc.* N.p.: n.p., n.d. [Fiche 1311/#3400] N.p.: n.p., n.d. [Fiche 1311/#3401]

36.   *Ain n new gedicht//des da spricht/Nach des//Luthers ler/und got zu her.* . . . N.p.: n.p., n.d. [Fiche 1314/#3415]

37. *Eine neue wahrhaftige und wunderbarliche Geschichte von Jörgen Wagner, zu München als Ketzer verbrannt.* N.p.: n.p., 1527? [Fiche 282/#809]

38. *Ein//newer//Spruch von//Boxspergk und//von landt-//stall.//Im. xxxiii. Jahre.* Bamberg: G. Erlinger, 1523. [Schottenloher, Ritterschaft, p. 12] VD 16, N 1146–1147.

39. *Ein newer spruch von//Frantzen von Sickingens//handlung.* Würzburg: J. Lobmeyer, 1523. [Schottenloher, Ritterschaft, 23] VD 16, N 1148.

40. *Der Ritterschafft brüderliche//verainigung . . . jüngst zu Landaw/für-//nemlich got zu lob/und denn folgend//meerung gemaines nutzs . . . auff-//gericht.* Augsburg: S. Otmar, 1522. [Fiche 1375/#3623] VD 16, R 2543–2546.
   Augsburg: H. Steiner, 1522.
   Mainz: J. Schöffer, 1522.

41. *Ain schenes und//nutzliches büchlin von//dem Christlichen//glauben.* Augsburg: P. Nehart? (1522?) [Fiche 69/#180] VD 16, S 3681.

42. *Ain schöner newer Passion.* N.p.: n.p., c.1521/22. [Schade, 2, 108–113; Fiche 1258/#3220]

43. *Ain Sendbrieff von//Ainer erbern frawen im Eelichen stat/an ain//Klosterfrawen/gethon. . . .* N.p.: n.p., 1524. [Regensburg, Kreisbibliothek; Russell Copy] VD 16, S 5720–5721.

44. *Ain Sendbrieff//von aym Jungen Student//ten zu Wittemberg, an seine öltern//ym land zu Schwaben von//wegen der Lutheri//schen leer zu ge-//schriben.* Augsburg: M. Ramminger? 1523. [Clemen, 1, 5–20; Fiche 67/#176] VD 16, S 5719.

45. *Ain Strafred und ain underricht//Wie es des bapsts junger auf geiz hond zu gericht. . . .* N.p.: n.p., 1521. [Schade, 2, 175–189] VD 16, S 9370.

46. *Teütscher nation//beschwerd von//den Geistlichen.//Durch der Weltlichen Reichs//stand/Fürsten und Herren//Bapst Adriano schrifftlich//überschickt/nechst vergang//nen Reichstag zu//Nürenberg//im xxii. jar angefangen/. . . .* Strassburg: J. Schott II, 1523. [Fiche 983/#2488] VD 16, R 725.

47. *Teütscher Nation notturft://Die Ordnung und Re-//formation aller Stendt ym Römischen//Reych. Durch Kayser Fridrich//den driten/. . . .* Zwickau: J. Gastel, n.d. [Laube 2, pp. 760–792; Fiche 531/#1355] Bamberg, G. Erlinger, n.d.

48. *Ein tractat in dem//kürtzlich durch die heyligen ge-//schrifft anzeygt würt/wie der inwendig//und ußwendig mensch wider ein-//ander und bei einander sein. . . .* N.p.: n.p., 1524. [Russell Copy, München, Bibl. Paulina] VD 16, T 1828–1831.

49. *Die Verteütschten Text//aus den Bebstlichen//Rechten: und vil//andren glaubwirdigen ge-//schrifften:daraus sich meni//klich allerley mag erkun//den wie erbarlich bis//her mitt gemeiner//Christenheyt ist//gehandlet//worden.* N.p.: n.p., n.d. [Fiche 1040/#2514] VD 16, V 590.
   Von der Gült. See Sachs, *Hie kompt ein Beüerlein.*

50. *Welcher das Evangelium hat für gut. . . den haist man jetzt ain Filtzhut.* N.p.: n.p., n.d. [Fiche 221/#615]

51. *Wer hören will wer//die ganze Welt arm hat gemacht. . . .* Augsburg: E. Öglin Erben, 1521. [Laube, 2, 731–741; Fiche 221/#619–620]
   Strassburg: M. Schürer Erben, 1521.
   Strassburg: M. Flach II, 1521.

52. *Wie Hieronimus von Prag ain//anhanger Johannis Huss durch das concilium//zu Constentz für ain Ketzer verurtailt un//verprant worden ist.* N.p.: n.p., 1530. [Z,ZB]

53. *Wiltu etwas newes habenn//Laß diß büchlein nicht vor über draben . . . Von dreyen dingen wirt es genandt//Wie offenbar wirt wrrdi all zu handt.* N.p.: n.p., n.d. [Fiche 1257/#3213]

54. *Zwo Christenlich Trostschrifften an//die Oberkeyten, die in dess//Evangelions sachen . . .*

vom Wort Gottes zufallen//täglich getrieben und gereytzt//werden. Nuremberg: J. Gutknecht, 1530. [Fiche 363/#1021]
See also #179 [Jacob Köbel]

PAMPHLETS WITH IDENTIFIED AUTHORS

A

55.   Alber, Erasmus. *Absag/oder vhed schrifft/ Des Hellischen//Fürstenn Lucifers/Doctor//Martin Luther ietzt zu//gesandt.* Speyer: J. Fabri, 1524. [Clemens III, 355–67] VD 16, A 1468–1475. See also #11.
    N.p.: n.p., 1524 or 1525.
    Zwickau, J. Gastel, n.d.
    Nürnberg: H. Hölzel, 1524.

56.   ———. *Gesprech büchlein von einem Bawern, Belial,//Erasmo Rotterodam vnd doctor Johann Fabri . . . anzeygend,//was Eraßmum vnd Fabrum zu verleugnung des gots worts//bewegt hatt.* Speyer: J. Fabri, 1524. [Clemens I, 315–338; Lenk, 215–223] Speyer: J. Fabri, n.d. VD 16, A 1490–1491.

57.   ———. *Schöne Dialogus von Martino Luther und der geschickten Botschaft aus der Hölle.* Zwickau, n.p., 1525. [Summarized in Clemens, III, p. 356] VD 16, A 1523–1526.
    Erfurt: M. Buchführer, 1523.
    Three other editions.

B

58.   Bechler, Hans [von Scholbrunnen]. *Ein Gesprech eyneß Fuchs//und Wolffs . . . M.D.XXiiij.* Nürnberg, H. Hergot, n.d. [Schade 2, pp. 60–72; Fiche 1378/#3633] VD 16, B 1328–1334.
    Augsburg: M. Ramminger, 1524 (two editions).
    Nürnberg: F. Peypus, 1524.
    Erfurt: M. Maler, 1524 (two editions).
    Würzburg: J. Lobmeyer, 1524.

59.   Bossler, Ulrich [von Hassfurt]. *Dialogus oder gesprech des Apposto//licums Angelica und anderer Specerey der Appotecken An-//treffen Doctor M. Lutterers ler. . . .* Speyer: J. Eckhart, 1521. [Fiche 261/#734] VD 16, B 6782–6783.

60.   Brandeck, Hieronymus (von Strassfurt). *Ain Nutzli-//che Ermanung zü handt-//habung . . . allen Oberkaiten und//Regimenten in disen Schwerlichen zyten. . . .* N.p.: n.p., n.d. [Fiche 1459/#3853] VD 16, B 6897.

61.   Breuning, Jörg. *Dreü gar Nützliche//und fruchtbare lieder . . . in welchen die menschen//besonder gründtlich leer und//unterweysung/Gott zu//suchen und erkennen em-//pfahen. . . .* Augsburg: P. Ulhart d.Ä. 1526. [Fiche 1317, #3432]

62.   Buchstab, Johannes, *Das nit alle Crist//glöbige menschen gleich prie-//ster seyend. . . .* Strassburg: J. Grüninger, 1527. [Fiche 1289/#3312] VD 16, B 9048–9049. Strassburg: J. Grüninger, 1527. [Fiche 1496/#3934]

63.   ———. *Dass die Biblischen Geschrifften müssen eyn geystliche usslegung han. . . .* N.p.: n.p., 1529. [Studer, 10] VD 16, B 9047.

64.   ———. *. . . . Kundschaft. . . . dass M. Ulrich Zwinglein eyn falscher Prophet und verfürer des christlichen Volkes ist.* N.p.: n.p., 1528–29. [Studer, 211] VD 16, B 9051–9052. [Hagenan: W. Seltz, 1529] [Fiche 1205/#3050]

65.   ———. *Ein kurtze underrichtung, uss den alten und nüwen testament//dass die mess ein opffer ist. . . .* Strassburg: J. Grüninger, 1527. [Studer, 209; Fiche 1396/#3681] VD 16, B 9053.

66.   ———. *Vier Artikel/einem jeglichen christlichen Menschen not ze thun und ze halten.* [Strassburg: J. Prüss II] 1528. [Fiche 751/#1920] VD 16, B 9054.

67. ————. *Von becleidung der Priester, liechter* . . . *mess früme gesang und bildnissen/ so in d'Cristenlichen kilchen got zulob und ze eer gebrucht werden*. . . . Strassburg: J. Grüninger, 1527. [Fiche 1021/#2580] VD 16, B 9055–9056.

68. ————. *Von dem fegfeür//mit sampt einem bescluß über//zehen ußgangen büchlin Johann Buch//stab von Winthertur*. . . . Strassburg: J. Prüss II, 1528. [Fiche 1289/ #3314] VD 16, B 9057.

69. ————. *Von Fürbit der mutter gotess Maria*. . . . [Strassburg: J. Grüninger] 1528? [Fiche 1070/#2709] VD 16, B 9060.

70. ————. *Vom Hochwir//digen Sacrament des leibs vnd//bluts Christi unsers herren/ wie dz in zeit der apostlen//und seid har/glaubt ist worden*. . . . [Strassburg: J. Grüninger] 1527. [Fiche 1289/#3313] VD 16, 9058–9059. [Strassburg: J. Grüninger, 1527] [Fiche 1446/#3832]

71. Büllheym, Steffan von. *Ein brüderliche warnung an//meister Mathis Pfarrherren/ /zu sanct Lorentzen im Münster zu Straß-//burg/sich vor seinen widersacheren zu//verhüten und bewaren*. Strassburg: J. Knobloch, 1523. VD 16, B 9137. Strassburg: J. Schwann, 1523/24.

72. Bürger zu Erfurt. *Ain new Ge-//dicht wie die gaystlich//ait zu Erffordt* . . . *Gesturmbt ist worden//*. . . . [Augsburg: M. Ramminger] 1521. [Clemen, 1, 361–369; Laube 2, 1316–1320; Fiche 221/#616]

Bürger zu Nürnberg see #48.

73. Butzbach, Dietrich. *Neu tzeytung//vom Reichstag tzu//Wormbs*. Leipzig: M. Landsberg, 1521. [Laube 2, 1285–1287] VD 16, B 9994.

C

74. Carion, Johannes. *Bedeütnus vnd Offenbarung* . . . *M.D.xl.jar*. . . . N.p.: n.p., 1529. [Fiche 1245/#3165] VD 16, C 961, C 964–967, C 969–970.

N.p.: n.p., n.d. (4 editions.) [Fiche 1239/#3132; Fiche 1244/#3162; Fiche 1244/ #3163; Fiche 1245/#3164]

N.p.: n.p., 1530. [Fiche 965/#2415]

75. ————. *Prognosticatio und Erklerung der//grossen wesserung: Auch anderer// erschrockenlichenn würckungen/so sich begeben nach Christi* . . . *geburt/funfftzehenhundert und .xxiiii.iar*. . . . Leipzig: W. Stöckel, 1522. [Fiche 858/#2171] VD 16, C 1031– 1033. N.p.: n.p., n.d. (2 editions.) [Fiche 858/#2170; Fiche 920/#2285]

76. Cattelspurger, Nicolas. *Ain Missive* . . . *darinn* . . . *durch hailig geschrift angezaygt wirt//von den falschen leeren byssher gehalten* . . . *seiner schwe//ster* . . . *umb rechtes// glaubens verstand//geschriben.//1524*. N.p.: n.p., 1524. [Russell copy; Arnold; 318– 326; Fiche 725/#1845] VD 16, K 542.

77. Copp, Johannis. *Practica deutsch* . . . *auff das Tausentfunff//hundert und .xxii. Jare*. Leipzig: W. Stöckel, 1521. [Fiche 1237/#3124] VD 16, C 5022.

78. ————. *Twe nyge nutte und//lustige Dialogi*. [Halberstad: L. Stuchs, c. 1522.] [Fiche 833/#2090] VD 16, C 5032.

79. ————. *Twe nyge nutte vnd//lustige Dialogi/edder gesprecke*. . . . N.p.: n.p., n.d. [Fiche 883/#2080]

80. Cronberg, Harmuth von. *Ableynung des vermein//lichen unglimpffs so dem Andechtigen* . . . *Doctor//Martin Luther* . . . *von vielen zugelegt/jn dem das er* . . . *den Babst ein Vicari//des Teüfels vnd Antecrists//etc. genant hat*. Strassburg: J. Schwan, c. 1524. [Fiche 1889/#4824] VD 16, C 5903.

81. ————. . . . *Tzwen//Brieff/Eyner an Romische Kayser-//liche Maiestat/vnd der ander an//Franciscus von Sickin-/gen* . . . *der//gotlichen vnd Euan-//gelischen ler vnd//warheit* . . . *zu//furderung geschrieben.//Ein schrifft von hansen von Doltzck://vnnd Bernhardt von*

Hirßfeldt an Joachim//Marschalck zu Pappenheym etc. auß-//gegangen wie folget. Augsburg: M. Lotter, d.J., 1521. [First letter in Laube, 2, pp. 748–753; entire pamphlet, Fiche 337/#952.] VD 16, C 5911.

82. ———. *Ein ernstliche Schrifft an all//stend des Romischen reychs.* . . . Basel: A. Petri, 1524. [Zurich,ZB; Fiche 231/#645] VD 16, C 5927.

83. ———. *Eyn hüpsch Cristenliche . . . erinnerung vnd warnung///so Kayserlicher Maiestat von eynem//iren Kayserlichen Maiestat ar//men Reüterlyn . . . beschicht.* Strassburg: J. Prüss II, 1520/21. [Zurich,ZB; Fiche 3/#8] VD 16, C 5928.

84. ———. *Ein kurtz/treüwe/Christliche vermanung///an die Eydgnossen.* . . . Basel: A. Petri, 1522. [Zurich, ZB; Fiche 1951/#4981] VD 16, C 5929–5930.

85. ———. *Ein schrifft und Christlich ver-//manung an die . . . Ersamen vnnd weisen// Meister vnnd Rath zu//Straßburgk.* . . . Strassburg: J. Schott, 1523. [Strasbourg, BNU; Fiche 1387/#3669] VD 16, C 5932.

86. ———. *Schrifften . . . wider Doctor Peter Meyer/Pfarrher zu//Franckfurt/sein . . . unchristlich leer//betreffend.* . . . Strassburg: J. Schott, 1522. [Zurich, ZB] VD 16, C 5933.

87. ———. *Ein Sendbrieff an Bapst Adria-//num/daryn . . . angezaygt würt ein . . . weg zu außreuttung//aller Ketzereyen/vnd zu hayl//samer rettung gantzer//Christenhait von//des Turcken//tyranney.* . . . Nuremberg, J. Gutknecht,1523. [Zurich, ZB; Fiche 7/#33] VD 16, C 5934–5937.

[Augsburg: P. Ulhart der ä., 1523.] [Fiche 83/#225]
Erfurt [J. Loersfeld] 1523. [Fiche 231/#644]
Wittenberg: [L. Cranach and C. Döring], 1523. [Fiche 146/#404]

88. ———. *Ein trewe vermanung an alle stende vnd geschick//ten auff den Reichstage yetzund zu Nürn-//berg . . . von aller//Edlen wegen/die keinen standt im/Reich haben.* Augsburg: S. Grimm, 1522. [Fiche 231/ #642] VD 16, C 5938–5942.

[Augsburg: P. Ulhart der älter, 1523.] [Fiche 611/#1572]
[Erfurt: M. Buchfürer, 1523.] [Fiche 1105/#2813]
[Strassburg: J. Schott, 1523.] [Fiche 1103/#2807]
[Basel: A. Petri, 1522.] [Fiche 931/#2318]

89. ———. *Vier Christliche schrifft . . . Die erst an Bapst Leo des//names den zehenden.// Die ander an die inwoner zu Cronenberg.//Die drit an die Bettel//orden.//Die vierd an Jacob// Kobeln//Wittemberg.* [Augsburg: S. Grimm und M. Wirsung, 1522.] [Fiche 1061/#2677] VD 16, C 5922.

Title Variation:
Drey Christli//che schrifft . . . Die erst an Ba//pst Leo des names den zehenden.//Die ander an die ein//woner zu Cronenburg//Die dritte an die bettel orden//Die vierd an iacop Kobeln.// Wittenberg, Strassburg: M. Flach, 1522. [Fiche 1174/#2953] VD 16, C 5920–5921, C 5923–5924.

[Wittenberg: M. Lotter d.J., 1522.] [Fiche 611/#1570]
Cuntz von Oberndorf. See Kuntz von Oberndorf

D

90. Distelmair, Conrad. *Ain gesprechbuch//lein von aim Xodtschneyder vnd aim// Holtzhawer . . . Von wegen/warumb Petrus//dem Malcho das or hat//abgehawen.//1523.* Augsburg: H. Steiner, 1523. [Zurich, ZB; Fiche 1828/#4687] VD 16, D 2062–2064.

[Augsburg: H. or S. Froschauer] 1523. [Fiche 1180/#2962]
Zwickau: J. Gastel [1523]. [Fiche 1066/#2697]

91. ———. *Ain trewe erma//nung/das ain yeder Christ selbs zu seiner seel//hail sehe/ vnd das schwert (das ist die hai//lig geschrifft) auch selbs zu seinen // handen neme.* . . . 1523.//[Augsburg: H. Steiner] 1523. [Fiche 223/#625] VD 16, D 2065–2066.

92.   Dolzig, Hans von. *Ein Schrift an Joachim Marshalek zu Pappenheim.* N.p.: n.p., n.d. [Fiche 337#952] See Hartmuth von Cronberg, *Tzwen Brieff.* VD 16, D 2172.

93.   Dorfmeister und Gemeind zu Wendelstein. *Dorffmayster unnd//Gemaind zu wendelstains fürhal-//ten den Amptleüten zu Schwa-//bach vnd irem new angeen-//dem Pfarrherrn gethan.* N.p.: n.p., 1524. [Fiche 1116/#2853]

94.   Drübel, Eckhart zum. *Anzeige Bericht and Antwort aus dissen Inhalt/gegen aller menniglich da es Not erfordert.* Hündesheim: n.p., 1538. [Koch, 137–141]

———.   *Bericht und anzey//ge/zu lob vnd eeren/vnd preiß//Gottes.* . . . Strassburg: J. Fröhlich, 1539. [Koch 144–155]

95.   ———.   *Ein Christlich: bryederlich://treüwlich warnung vor auffrur vnnd//trostlich bestendig bey dem//Euangelio zu be-//harren an ein//gemeyn//leyschafft.* . . . Hagenau: A. Farckall, 1525. [Koch 51–57]

96.   ———   [Eckhart zum Treybel]. *Ein Christelich lob vnd verma//nung an die hochberümpte Christe-//liche statt Straßburg.* . . . Strassburg: M. Flach II, 1524. [Strasbourg, Bibl. Mun.; Laube 2, 952–963; Koch 29–45; Fiche 233/#649]

97.   ———.   [Eckhart zum Treubel]. *Da gloriam Deo. Von dem eynigen Gott. Von dem Sun Gottes.* . . . N.p.: n.p., 1534. [Koch, 121–131]

98.   ———.   *Ein demütige ermanung an//Ein gantze gemeine Christen//heit. Von Eckhart zum//Drübel etc.* Strassburg: M. Flach d.J., n.d. [Laube, 1, 218–221; Koch, 21–25; Fiche 1946/#4960]
Strassburg: M. Flach d.J., 1521–1523?
[Laube attributes undated edition to Augsburg: M. Ramminger, 1523; Laube 1, p. 220.]

99.   ———.   *Eckart der trew sagt dir//verwar//Wie es im M.D.XXXiiij. Jar/ //Sol erghan auff erd durch all Ständ* . . . *Mit auszlegung desz Cometen disz iar gesehen.* Strassburg: J. Cammerlander, 1538. [Koch, 105–117]

100.   ———.   *Ein sendt Brieff an treffende des//selbuchs Jarmarckt geschriben vonn Mathis//Sittich Pfarher zu hindeßheym Ann denn//Edlen vnnd vesten Eckharten//zum Tribell etc. Unnd uff das//sein antwort.* Hagenau: A. Farckall, 1526. [Koch 59–65]

101.   ———   [Eckhart zu Tribell]. *Ein vetterliche gedruge gute///zucht/lere/und bericht/ Christlich//zuleben vnnd sterben/an//meine kynder vnd//alle frumme//Christen.* Hagenau: W. Seltz, 1528. [Strasbourg, Bibl. Mun.; Koch 59–65; Fiche 1232/#3105]

E

102.   Eidgenossenschaft. *In disem büchlein findt//man etliche mandat wider die newe emporunng//des Glaubens/so außgangen/nämlich von Her//tzog Ferdinando inn dem Hertzogthumb von//Wirrtemberg/* . . . *Item von den. xii. orten gemeyner//Eydnoschafft zu Lucern.//versamlet.* Nürnberg: H. Hergot, 1524. [Fiche 567/#1447]
Four other editions.

103.   Eidgenossenschaft. Stetten und Landen der 12 orten. *Ein Christlicher abschaid/ durch//vil Artigkl begriffen/der loblichen//Aydgnoßschafft/ wider den Luther* . . . *Der selbigen Aydgnoßschafft Sendt-//brieff/ an den Bischoff zu Costentz.* . . . [Ingolstadt: A. Lutz, 1524.] [Fiche 1723/#4487]
[München: H. Schobser] 1524. [Fiche 1438/#3818]

104.   Eidgenossenschaft. *Entschuldigung//gemeyner Eydtgnossen: über//die artickel so jnen von etlichen geltsüchtigen//Pfarrherrn* . . . *zu Lucern* . . . *felschlich zu ge-//schriben vnd vßgebreyt//werden.//.* [Strassburg: W. Köpfel, 1524.] [Fiche 1898/#4861]
[Strassburg: J. Schwan, 1524?] [Fiche 172/#474]

105.   Endorf, Hieronymus von. *Axiomata oder sitig begerungen.* . . . Augsburg: S. Ruff, 1525. [Fiche 1298/#3346] VD 16, E 1175.

106. ———. *Ain Christliche vermanung//an Ro. K. M. vnd die stend//des hayligen Reychs.* . . . Augsburg: S. Ruff, 1525. [Fiche 1401/#3689] VD 16, E 1176.

107. ———. *Ain Missif/ansagend ain gemail/ne fryds botschafft/zu hinlegung//Gotlichs zorns/auch gemayne zwitracht.* . . . Augsburg: S. Grimm, 1523. [Fiche 1367/#3607] VD 16, E 1177.

108. ———. *Eins schonn vnd//des rechtenn zehents bringung//jnn Reichstag gen Nürmberg* . . . *des. 1524 .jars.* . . . Nürnberg: F. Peypus, 1524. [Fiche 1204/#3049] VD 16, E 1178.

109. ———. *Ain wunderbar schön: not-//dürfftig Prophetisch schaydung/gantz unpartheysch///zwischen allenthalben auffruriger Bawrschafft/vnd//irer Herren.* . . . Augsburg: P. Ulhart, 1525. [Fiche 1202/#3040] VD 16, E 1179–1180.

F

110. Fassnacht, N. [pseud.]. *Dem Edlen vnd Vesten//Ersamen vnd weysen//Wolff Christoffel von Wissenthaw genannt// Amptman/Bürgermaistern vnd Rathe//zu Schwabach bekannt.* . . . Nürnberg: H. Höltzel, 1524. [Fiche 1316/#1524] VD 16, F 630.

111. Felbaum, Sebastian [von Breten]. *Ein nutzliche//rede frag vnd antwort//von dreyen personen sich vben in lutrischen// sachen.* . . . Strassburg: J. Grüniger, 1524. [Fiche 1027/#2588] VD 16, F 694.

112. Fincken, Michael. *Bericht Michel Fincken wie die Christen von Miltenberg des Rechten glaubens halben gesturmbt seyn.* N.p.: n.p., 1523. [Follows account of Bernhart Johim, Fiche 1187/#2981.]

113. [Fränkischen Adel]. *Entschuldigung des Adels//zu Franken, der bei dem// Schweinfurter Vertrag gewest sindt.* Bamberg: G. Erlinger, 1523. [Schottenloher, Ritterschaft #11] VD 16, E 1379.

114. ———. *Vertrag und Einigung der gefürsten Gravven, Herren und gemeyner Ritterschaft der Ort im Land zu Francken* . . . *im 23. Jahr zu Schweinfurt aufgerichtet.* Nürnberg: F. Peypus, 1523. [Schottenloher, Ritterschaft #3]. VD 16, F 2294.

115. Füssli, Hans. *Antwurt eins Schwy//tzer Purens/über die vngegründten//geschrifft Meyster Jeronimi Geb-//wilers Schulmeisters zu Straßburg* . . . *Ein Epistel Huldrich Zuinglis.* Zurich: J. Hager, 1524. [Fiche 341–342/#960]

116. Füssli, Hans, und Martin Seger O.c. *Das hond zwen Schweytzer bauren gmacht/ Für war sy hond es wol betracht.* Zurich: C. Froschauer, before 1521. [Hieronymus #214, p. 185; Fiche 279/#794]
    [Augsburg: M. Ramminger, 1521.] [Fiche 1041/#2620]
    [Speyer: J. Eckhart, 1521.] [Fiche 784/#1968]

G

117. Die Gemein von Rotwyl. *Ein Christenlich Suplication//von den vertribnen Rotwylern/Gmeinen Eydgnossen//und andern Christenlichen burgern und Stotten zuge// stelt.* . . . N.p.: n.p., 1529. [Fiche 1423/#3769]

118. Die Gemeyn der Statt Franckfort. *Sechs und viertzig Artickel: so//die Gemeyn/ einem ersamen Rath der loblichen Statt Franckfort* . . . *fürgehalten.* . . . Mainz: J. Schöffer, 1525. [Fiche 1418/#3749] VD 16, F 2308.
    [Leipzig: M. Blum] 1525. [Fiche 843/#2114]
    Title variation [Augsburg: M. Ramminger, 1525]. [Fiche 968/#2435]

119. Gemigger, Lux von Heinfelt. *Ob einer wissen wolt wie der hieß//Der dissen spruch auß gen ließ//Das hat gethon ein freyer student//Auß ursach Das man luther seine bucher//hat verbrent.* [Strassburg: R. Beck, c. 1522.] [Zurich, ZB; Fiche 1036/#2606] VD 16, G 1074–1076.
    Title variation:

Zu lob den Luther//und eeren der gantzen//Christenhait//etc. Augsburg: Erhard Öglin Erben, 1521? [Laube,1, 548–557; Fiche 728/#1856]

Strassburg, J. Prüß d.J., n.d.

Strassburg, J. Prüß d.J., after 1520.

120.   Gengenbach, Pamphilus. *Disz new Bockspyl ist gemacht zu lob und eren dem aller . . . groszmächtigosten herren, Herr Carle, erwolter Römischer Küng.* Basel: P. Gengenbach, 1519 or 1520. [Hieronymus #197]

121.   ———. *Der alt Eidgenoss/Das ist ein neu Lied von den alten Eidgenossen und allen Fürsten und Herren.* Basel: P. Gengenbach, 1514. [Fiche 933/#2326] VD 16, G 1167–1169.

122.   ———. *[Ein] christlich biech//lin Sancti: Hieronymi, dz er zu einem Priester/ Nepotianus genannt/geschrieben hat//Der Pfaffen Spiegel.* Basel, P. Gengenbach, c. 1520. [Hieronymus #256; Fiche 243/#671]

123.   ———. *Diss ist ein ie-//merliche clag über die Todtenfresser.* [Strassburg: J. Prüss d.J., 1522.] [Fiche 24/#674] VD 16, G 1180–1181.

124.   ———. *Der Ewangelischburger.* Basel, P. Gengenbach, 1523. [Hieronymus #318; Fiche 243/#672] VD 16, G 1182–1185.

[Augsburg: J. Nädler, 1524?] [Fiche 624/#1619]

Zwickau: J. Gastel, 1524. [Fiche 4631/#125]

125.   ———. *Der gestryfft Schwitzer Baur//Disz büchlin hat gemacht einBaur auss dem Entlibuch////Wem es nit gefall der küsz im die bruch.* Basel: P. Gengenbach, 1522. [Hieronymus #343 attributes this to Gengenbach; Fiche 1259/#3225.] VD 16, G 1188–1190.

[Basel: P. Gengenbach, 1522.] [Fiche 623/#1612]

[Basel: P. Gengenbach, 1522.] [Fiche 988/#2506]

126.   ———. *Ein kläglichs Gespräch von einem Apt/Curtisanen//vnd dem Teüfel/wider den//frommen Pabst Hadrian. . . .* Basel, n.p., 1522. [Zurich ZB; Fiche 1820/#4669] VD 16, G 1192–1193.

Title variations:

Wie der Hailig Vater Bapst-Adrianus ein geritten ist zu Rom. Augsburg, M. Ramminger, 1522. [Fiche 264/#745]. VD 16, G 1219–1221; 1224.

Ein Dialogus/wie d' Heilig vatter Papst Adrianus/eingeritten zeu Rom. Erfurt: W. Stürmer, 1522. [Fiche 985/#2500] VD 16, G 1222–1223.

127.   ———. *Ein kurtzer begriff wie//der Schultheiß vnd die gemein deß dorffs Frid// husen . . . erwelt haben ein schoffel irs dorffs mit na-//men Hans Knüchel/ dz der selbig an stat ires// Pfarrers sol verkünden vnd predigen die Ewa-//gelische leer . . . biß zu der/ / zu kunfft irers Pfarrers.//* [Basel: P. Gengenbach, 1523.] [Fiche 1548/#4015] VD 16, G 1194.

128.   ———. *Ein newes lied gemachet durch Pamphilum Gengenbach zu lob dem aller hochgebornsten, grossmachtigen Carolo, erwelter römscher Küng, Küng in Hyspanien.* Basel: P. Gengenbach, 1519. [Hieronymous # 331a] VD 16, G 1204.

129.   ———. *Der Nollart/Dies sind die Propheteien Sancti Methodii und Nollard:* Basel: P. Gengenbach, 1517. [Fiche 936/#2336] VD 16, G 1205, G 1208–1210.

Title variation: [Augsburg: J. Schönsperger d.J.] 1522. [Fiche 1428/#3784]

130.   ———. *Von dreien Christen//Dem Römischen Christen//Dem Böhemischen Christen//den Thürkischen Christen.* Basel: P. Gegenbach, 1523. [Hieronymus #328; Laube 2, 227–243] VD 16, G 1216.

131.   ———. *Der Welsch Fluss.* [Basel: P. Gengenbach, 1513.] [Fiche 933/#2325] VD 16, G 1217–1218.

132.   Gerhardt, Hans. *Schone Frag vnd//Antwort/Was ain warhafftiger Christenn//der*

recht Glaub/vnnd seyn frucht sey. . . . Augsburg: H. Steiner, 1525. [Regensburg Kreisbibliothek Russell copy] VD 16, G 1484–1487.
    Wittenberg: H. Lufft, 1525.
    Zwickau: J. Gastel, 1525.

133. Goltschmit, Bastian [Sebastian Goldschmidt]. *Eyn vnderweisung etzlicher ar// tickel/so bruder Matteiß/prior des prediger//closters zu Worms/ungegründt in hei-//liger gschrifft/offentlich gepredigt//hat . . . zu nichts gemacht.* . . . [Worms: P. Schöffer d.J.] 1525. [Fiche 1476/#3879] VD 16, G 2571–2572.

134. Graff, Jörg. *In diesem tractetlin sind drey//hübsche lieder new gemacht . . . von Bapst Cardinal Bischoff prelaten/Pfaffen//vnd Münch.* . . . [Strassburg: J. Prüss d.J., c. 1523.] [Fiche 1130/2890] VD 16, G 2744.

135. ———. *Von dem aller heyligsten in//Got vater babst Leo etc. Unnd dem gross-//mechtigen Keyser Maximilian etc. Und//vonn den Türcken.* . . . [Nürnberg: J. Stuchs, 1518.] [Fiche 1296/#3339] VD 16, G 2756.

136. Greiffenberger, Hans. *Diss biechlin zaygt an//was vns lernen vnd gerlernet ha-// ben vnsere maister der ge-//schrifft.* . . . München: H. Schobser, 1523. [Zurich, ZB; Fiche 313/#897] VD 16, G 3159.

137. ———. *Dies Büchlin sagt von den falschen kamesierern die sich auss thund vil guts mit fasten peten messlesen.* N.p.: n.p., 1523. [Fiche 314/#899] VD 16, G 3156–3157.

138. ———. *Diss buechel zaygt an//wie wir allso weyt gefuert sind von//der lere vnnsers maysters Cristo//jm gepet/vn andern sachen.* . . . München: H. Schobser, 1523. [Fiche 2736/#1079] VD 16, G 3164.

139. ———. *Ein Christenliche Antwordt//denen/die da sprechen/das Euangelion//hab sein krafft von der kirchen.* . . . N.p.: n.p., 1524. [Fiche 254/#712; 1199/#3022] VD 16, G 3149.

140. ———. *Ein kurzer Begriff von Guten Werken.* [Augsburg: M. Ramminger] 1524. [Fiche 343/#967; Fiche 750/#1916] VD 16, G 3151–3152.
    [Nürnberg: J. Gutknecht] 1524. [Fiche 343/#967]

141. ———. *Eintrostliche ermanung//den angefochten im gewissen/von we//gen gethoner sünd.* . . . [Augsburg: M. Ramminger] 1524. [Fiche 1083/#2742] VD 16, G 3154–3155.
    [Nürnberg: J. Gutknecht] 1524. [Fiche 1198/#3020]

142. ———. *Ein warnung vor//dem Teüffel/der sich wider//vbt mit seinem dendel-marckt.* . . . [Nürnberg: J. Gutknecht] 1524. [Fiche 1198/#3019] VD 16, G 3158.

143. ———. *Die welt sagt Sy sehe//kain besserung von den//die sy Luterisch nen-// net/was besserung//sey/ain wenig//hierin be-//griffen.* Augsburg: S. Ottmar, 1523. [Fiche 1293/#3330] VD 16, G 3160–3163.
    [Nürnberg: J. Gutknecht] 1523. [Fiche 107/#277]

144. Gretzinger, Benedikt. *Hauptartikel und fürnemlich Punkten der göttlichen Geschrift.* Wittenberg, J. Rhau-Grunenberg, 1524. [Fiche 1137/#2910] VD 16, G 3253, G 3259, G 3263.
    [Wittenberg: J. Rhau-Grunenberg, 1525.] [Fiche 1055–1056/2665]

145. ———. *Houet artikel//vndede Vornehmely-//kesten stocke/unses Christen-// domes.* . . . Wittenberg: H. Baerth, 1525. [Fiche 1053/#2663] VD 16, G 3266–3268.
    [Wittenberg: H. Weiss, 1526.] [Fiche 904/#2263]
    [Wittenberg: H. Baerth, 1528.] [Fiche 1056/#2666]

146. ———. *Ain vnüberwint//lich Beschirm buchlin von//haubt Artickeln/vnd für-// nemlichen puncten der got-lichen geschrifft Auß dem//Alten vnnd newen Testa-//ment.* . . . Augsburg: H. Steiner, 1525. [Fiche 1384/#3568(1)]

Augsburg: Heinrich Steiner, 1525. [Fiche 679/#1773] These are the authentic editions. There were 6 abridged editions, see Köhler, Bibliog. VD 16, G 3248–3252, G 3254–3258, G 3260–3265.

147.   Grumbach, Argula von. *An den edlen//und gestrengen Herren Adam/von Thering/ ein Sendbrief.* [Augsburg: P. Ulhart d.Ä., 1523.] [Fiche 967/#2427] VD 16, G 3655.

148.   ―――. *An ain Ersamen//Weysen Radt//der stat Ingolstat//ain sandtbrief von Fraw von Grunbach geborne von Stauffen.* [Augsburg: P. Ulhart d.Ä., 1523.] [Fiche 5/#19] VD 16, G 3658.

149.   ―――. *[Ein] Antwort in//gedichtsweis/einem aus der// Hohenschul zu Ingol/stadt auf einen Spruch,//neulich von ihm ausgangen.* [Nürnberg: H. Höltzel] 1524. [Fiche 285/#820] VD 16, G 3660.

150.   ―――. *Ein christlich und ernstlich Ermahnung und Geschrift an die ganze Universität zu Ingolstadt.* [Basel: A. Cratander, 1523.] [Fiche 1345/#3539] VD 16, G 3677.

151.   ―――. *Christliche ermanungenn//an Hertzog Friderichen Churfürsten//zu Sachsen/ /. . . .* Strassburg: W. Köpfel, 1524. [Fiche 1841/#4706] VD 16, G 3659.

152.   ―――. *Ain Christenlich schrifft//ainer Erbarn frawen//vom Adel// darin sy alle Christenliche Stendt//vnd obrigkeyten//ermant Bei//der warhait/vnd dem wort//Gottes//zu bleyben. . . .* [Augsburg: P. Ulhart d.Ä.] 1523. [Fiche 16/#66] VD 16, G 3661–3665.
    [Bamberg: G. Erlinger] 1523. [Fiche 69/#183]
    [München: H. Schobser] 1523. [Fiche 751/#1922]

153.   ―――. *Dem Durchleichtigisten hoch gebornen Fursten//-vnd Heern//Friderichen Hertzogen zu Sachsen . . . meinem Gnedigsten herren.* N.p.: n.p., 1523. [Zurich, ZB; Fiche 1808/ #4631] VD 16, G 3670–3671.

154.   ―――. *Dem Durchleuchtigsten Hochgeboren//-Fursten vnd herren Herrn Johansen/ /Pfaltzgrauen bey Reyn Herzoge zu Beyern. . . .* [Erfurt: W. Stürmer, 1524.] [Fiche 1808/#4630] VD 16, G 3666–3668.
    [Augsburg: P. Ulhart der Ä., 1523.]
    [Bamberg: G. Erlinger, 1523.] [Fiche 566/#1444]

155.   ―――. *Wie Ain//Christliche Frau des Adels//in Bayern durch iren in//Götlicher schrift wolgegrundte//Sendbrieffe die hohenschul zu Ingoldstat . . . haben straffet.* [Augsburg: P. Ulhart d.Ä., 1523.] [Fiche 49/#135] VD 16, G 3676, G 3678–3684, G 3686.
    [Nürnberg: F. Peypus, 1523.] [Fiche 285/#819]
    [Nürnberg: F. Peypus, 1523.] [Fiche 1199/#3023]
    See also #150, title variant.
    Editions with the articles presented by Schoffer:
    [Erfurt: M. Maler, 1523.] [Fiche 1002/#2543]
    [Leipzig: W. Stockel, 1523.] [Fiche 283/#814]

H

156.   Hass, Cuntz. *Von dem Eelichen standt. . . .* Augsburg: P. Ulhart, 1525. [Fiche 1252/#3194] VD 16, H 751.

Herbst, Hans. See #22.

157.   [Hergot, Hans]. *Von der new//en wandlung///eynes Christlichen//lebens. . . .* Leipzig: M. Blum, 1526/27. [Laube, Flug. der Bauernkriegs, 547–557] VD 16, V 2614.

158.   Herman, Nicolaus. *Ain Mandat Jhesu Chirsti/an alle seyne//getrewen Christen. . . .* N.p.: n.p., 1524. [Clemen, 2, pp. 260–273; Fiche 1062/#2680] VD 16, H 2390–2402.
    Nine other editions in 1524 alone; including:
    Wittenberg: L. Cranach und C. Döring, 1524. [Fiche 854/#2142]

Wittenberg: J. Rhau-Grunenberg, 1524. [Fiche 891/#2244]
Zwickau: J. Gastel, 1524. [Fiche 829/#2069]
N.p.: n.p., n.d. [Fiche 1105/#2811]
Magdeburg: U. Walther, 1530. [Fiche 972/#2448]
Hirssfeldt, Bernhard von [Bernhard von Hieschfeld]. *Ein Schrift an Joachim Marschalk zu pappenheim*, see #81.
159. Hornung, Katharina. *Ein antwort//Kacherinen//Hornung/auff D. Marti. Luthers// notbriefe/An Wolff//Hornung.* Wittenberg: N. Schirlentz, 1530. [Fiche 14/#62] VD 16, H 4996.
160. Hutten, Ulrich von. *Abschied//auf gehaltenem Reichs-Tag zu Augspurg Anno 1518. . . .* N.p.: n.p., 1518. [Böcking, 5, 202–204]
161. ———. *Botschaft an den Kurfürsten.* N.p.: n.p., 1522. [Fiche 116/#310]
162. ———. *Ein Clagschrift des Hochberum//ten . . . herrn Ulrichs von Hutten . . . an alle stend//Deütscher nation/Wie . . . Er mit eignem tyrannischen//gewalt/von dem Ro-//manisten/an leib//eer/vnd gut . . . beno//tiget/wer//de.* Strassburg: M. Flach, 1520. [Fiche 115/#308] VD 16, H 6265.
163. ———. *Clag und vor-//manung gegen dem über//mässigen vnchristlichen gewalt des//Bapstes zu Rom/vnd der vngeist-//lichen geistlichen. . . .* Strassburg: J. Knobloch, end of 1520. [Böcking, 3, 473–526; Fiche 115/#307] VD 16, H 6371–6374.
Strassburg: J. Schott, Oct./Nov. 1520.
Strassburg: J. Knobloch, Nov. 1520.
Strassburg: J. Schott, Nov./Dec. 1520.
164. ———. *Concilia, wie man halten sol . . . Ermanung das ein yeder bey den rechtlich alten Christlichen glauben bleiben und sich zu keiner newerung bewegen lassen soll . . . in 76 artikel.* Strassburg: J. Schott, 1521. [Fiche 534/#1367]
165. ———. *Das ist der hoch türen Babel, id est confusio Pape darinn Doctor Luther gefangen ist.* Strassburg: M. Schurer, 1521. VD 16, H 6308.
166. ———. *Ein clag und vormanung an//ein gemeine stat Wormß von//Ulrich von Hutten.//zugeschriben.* Strassburg: J. Knobloch, 1522. [Böcking, 3, 473–526; Fiche 244/#677] VD 16, H 6317–6319.
167. ———. *Entschuldigung Ulrichs von Hutten wyder etliche unwarhafftiges auszgeben von ym als soll er wider alle geystlichheit und priesterhafft sein.* Strassburg: M. Flach, 1521. [Fiche 1924/#4920] VD 16, H 6323–6324.
Worms: H. von Erfurt, 1521. [Fiche 593/#1539]
168. ———. *Gespräch buchlin//her Ulrichs von Hutten//das erst Feber genant.* Liepzig: M. Landsberg, 1519. [Böcking, 4, 29–41; Fiche 973/#2451] Title variations. VD 16, H 6338–6341.
Mainz: J. Schöffer, 1519. [Fiche 1883/#4807]
169. ———. *Gespräch buchlin//her Ulrichs von Hutten/das ander Feber//genant.* N.p.: n.p., 1519. [Böcking, 4, 101–143] VD 16, H 6342.
170. ———. *. . . Vadiscum//oder//die Römische Dreyfaltigkeit.* Strassburg: J. Schott II, 1521. [Böcking, 4, 145–268] VD 16, H 6345.
Under titles *Die Römische Dreyfaltigkeit* or *Trias Romana*: Also in VD 16, H 6342, H 6344, H 6346–6347.
N.p.: n.p., n.d.
N.p.: n.p., 1521.
171. ———. *Hienachuolgt ain anzaigung//wie alwegen sich die Römisch//en Bischoff oder Bapst//gegen den Teütsche kai-//sern gehalten haben. . . .* Erfurt: M. Maler, 1521. [Böcking, 5, 364–384; Fiche 594/#1541] (Title variations) VD 16, H 6269–6277.
Anzeig wie allweg sich die Römischen Bischoff . . . [title variation]. Strassburg:

J. Schott, 1520. [Fiche 826/2060]
 Strassburg: J. Schott, before April 1521.
 Augsburg: S. Grimm und M. Wirsung, 1521. [Folger #282]
172. ———. . . . *Uber vnd gegen vorgewaltigung des Bapsts/vund des//Romanissten/ Klagschrifft an Keyserliche maiestat.//Ein andere klagschrifft auch in//die selbigen sach/an gemeyne Teütsch nation.//Ermanung an Hertzog Fride//rich Churfürst zu Sachßen/zu vorfechtung gemeyn-//er freyheit wider die Romanisten.* . . . Strassburg: J. Schott, 1522. [Fiche 116/310] VD 16, H 6239.
173. ———. *Ein Klag über den Luteri-//schen Brandt zu Mentz//Durch herr Ulrich// von Hutten.* Zurich: C. Froschamer der Ä., 1521. [Böcking, 3, 455–459; Fiche 116/ #311] VD 16, H 6365–6370.
 Wittenberg: J. Rhau-Grunenberg, 1521. [Fiche 196/#560]
 Schlettstadt: M. Küffer, 1521. [Fiche 1894/#4840]
 Augsburg: J. Nadler, 1521. [Fiche 246/#682]
174. ———. *Das teüsch Requiem der ver-//branten Bullen und Bepst-//lichen Rechten.* Strassburg: R. Beck, 1520? [Böcking, 3, 470–472; Fiche 116/#312]
175. ———. *Die verteutscht clag Ul-//richs von hutten an Hertzogen//Fridrichen von Sachsen.* Strassburg: J. Schott, 1520. [Fiche 116/#310] VD 16, H 6251–6254.
 Basel: V. Curio, 1520/21. [Fiche 593/#1540]
 Augsburg: E. Oeglin Erben, 1521. [Fiche 444/#1191]
 Coburg: A. Fellenfurst bzw. Bamberg: G. Erlinger, 1522. [Fiche 973/#2452]
176. ———. *Vormanung an die//freien und reich Stette//teuts//cher nation.* Strassburg: J. Knobloch, 1522. [Fiche 841/#2108] VD 16, H 6418.

J

177. Johim, Bernhart. *Warhafftig bericht Bernhart Jo-//hims wie die Christen zu Miltenberg//von Herrn Albrechts Cardinals vnd Erzbischoffs//zu Mentz Thumberrn oder Stathaltern das Recht glaubens halben gestürmbt seyn.//Anclage der Stat Miltenberg// widder die Pfaffen daselbst.//Ein ander unterricht von Michel//Fincken Recitirt/wie die Christen von Milten//berg gesturmet seyn.* N.p.: n.p., n.d. [Fiche 1187/#2981] VD 16, J 861–862. See also Fiche 109/#288 for the Reformed preacher Johannes Karlstadt's account.

K

178. Karg, Ottmar, and Lucius Steger. *Ain grÿme/grosse//Ketten/darzu die hert gefancknuss/über die Kinder//Gottes auffgericht/seynd.* . . . Augsburg: H. Steiner, 1524. [Fiche 280/#798] VD 16, K 120.
Kattelspurger, Nicolas, see Cattelspurger, Nicolas.
179. [Köbel, Jacob] *Zu Kayserlicher Maie-//stat . . . Carolo/dem fünfften etc.* . . . *Doctor Martin//Luthers lere . . . ware antzeig.* . . . Oppenheim: n.p.,1520. [Weller, 1, #60; Fiche 963/#2409] See 53-x.
180. ———. *Eine zierliche Rede und Ermahnung zu den Grossmachtigen Carolo . . . mit anzeigung, was Tugend und Geschicklichkeit ein oberster Regierer an ihm haben soll.* . . . Oppenheim: n.p., 1519. Preface by J. Köbel to U. von Hutten. [Jöcher,3; NCA]
181. Kolb, Hans. *Ein Reformation notturfftig in//der Christenheit mit den Pfaffen/vnd jren//Magten.* . . . Strassburg: M. Schürer Erben, 1523. [Fiche 328/#924] VD 16, K 1921.
182. Kunz von Oberndorf. *Dialogus ader ein//gespreche, wieder//Doctor Ecken Buchlein das er zu entschuldigung des Con-//cily zu Costnitz etc. außge-//hen hat lassenn.* . . . [Leipzig: W. Stöckel, 1520.] [Fiche 375/#1043] VD 16, K 2572–2575.

L

183. Landschad von Steinach, Hans. *Ain Missive . . . an den . . . Herren Ludwygen/ /von Gottes genaden Pfaltzgrauff bey Reyn.//Hertzog in Bairen. Des Hailigen Römisch// en Reichs . . . Churfürst//en. Von wegen der gotliche leer zu be/schirmen. . . .* Augsburg: M. Ramminger, 1522. [Benrath, 66–86] [Fiche 53/#151] VD 16, L 225.

184. ———. *Ursach warum etlich hartt-//nickichen dem auffgehend//Evangelio so zuwider/ /sindt. . . .* Strassburg: J. Prüß II, 1524. [Benrath, 86–96] VD 16, L 226.

185. Lenhart zu der Eych. *Kegel spill gepractiziert auß dem yetzi-//gen zwytracht des glaubens. . . .* Speyer: J. Schmid, 1522. [Clemen, 3, 219–261; Fiche 1003/#2548]
   Augsburg: M. Ramminger, 1522. [Fiche 1045/#2640]

186. Lotzer, Sebastian. *Ayn außlegung uber//dz Euangelium. So man//lyßt und singt/ nach brauch der kyr//chen am zwayntzigisten Sontag//nach der hayligen Trivaltigkait// . . . [Matthew xxii].* Augsburg: M. Ramminger, 1524. [Fiche 389/#1063] VD 16, L 2877.

187. ———. *Ain christlicher sendbrief//darinn angetzaigt wirt/dz die lay//en macht vnd recht haben von//dem hailigen wort gots re-//den/lern/vn schreiben. . . .* Augsburg: M. Ramminger, 1523. [Fiche 224/#629] VD 16, L 2878.

188. ———. *Entschuldigung einer frommen christlichen Gemein zu Memmingen.* Augsburg: M. Ramminger, 1525. [Fiche 464/#1257] VD 16, L 2879.

189. ———. *Ain hailsame Ermanun//ge an die ynwoner zu horw das sy be//stendig beleyben an dem hailigen//wort Gottes. . . .* Augsburg: J. Nadler, 1523. [Laube 1, 252– 264] [Fiche 1493/#3921] VD 16, L 2881.

190. ———. *Ain vast haylssam trostlich christlich unüberwynndlich beschyrmbüchlin, Auff ainvnddreyssig Artyckel. . . .* Augsburg: M. Ramminger, 1524. [Goetze, 47–75; Fiche 1306–1307/#3382] VD 16, L 2880.

M

191. Manuel, Niklaus. *Ein Faßnacht schimpff, so zu Bern//uff der alten Faßnacht gebrucht ist im xxij. jar. . . .* N.p.: n.p., 1525. [Baechtold, 103–111] VD 16, M 709.
   Von Papst und Christe Gegensatz. . . . N.p.: n.p., 1522.

192. ———. *Ein Faßnacht spyl/so zu Bern uff//der Herren Fassnacht in den M.D.XXII./ /jar/von burgers sünen offentlich gemacht ist//Darinn die warheyt in schimpffs wyss//von Babst und siner priester-//schafft gemeldet wurt.* Meyen: n.p., 1522. [Baechtold, 29– 101; Fiche 938/#2345] VD 16, M 704–708, M 710–711.
   N.p.: n.p., 1524.
   N.p.: n.p., 1524.
   N.p.: n.p., 1525.
   N.p.: n.p., 1529.
   Zurich: C. Froschauer, 1525.
   Bern: M. Apiarus, 1540.

193. ———. *Ein gesprech/vonn einer muter//mit ir tochter/sy ein kloster zubringen . . . Vnd wz die toch-//ter uß dem Evangelio zu antwurt gibt.* Zurich: C. Froschauer, 1526. [Zurich, ZB] VD 16, M 695, M 697.
   N.p.: n.p., 1538.
   N.p.: n.p., 1543.
   Editions under title of *Barbali*: VD 16, M 699–703.
   Strassburg: C. Müllers Erben, n.d.
   Zurich: A. Fries, n.d.
   Zurich: A. Fries, n.d.

194. ———. *Ein hüpsch lied . . . das Fa-//bers vnd Eggen Baden-//fart betreffende.*

Zurich: C. Froschauer, 1526. [Baechthold, 203–215] VD 16, M 727.

195. ———. *Ein hüpsch nüw//lied vnd verwantwortung desz//Sturms halb beschähen zu Pig-//goga*. . . . N.p.: n.p., 1522. [Baechthold, 21–28]
N.p.: n.p., n.d.
Zurich: R. Wyssenbach, c. 1600.

196. ———. *Ein Klegliche Bot//schafft an Babst/die Selmes//betreffendt/welche kranck/ /ligt vnd wil sterben*. . . . N.p.: n.p., 1528. [Schade, 2, 253–263; Baechthold, 216-231; Fiche 1263/#3242] VD 16, M 738.
Ain klegliche Botschafft . . . [accompanied by another pamphlet]. N.p.: n.p., 1528. [Fiche 1877;#4791] VD 16, M 752.

197. ———. *Klagred der armen Gotzen//wie es jnen gadt . . . die Christgloubigen vast bittende///das sy von jrem bosen fürnemmen abstandind*. . . . N.p.: n.p., 1526?. [Zurich, ZB; Baechthold, 237–254; Fiche 1875/#4787] VD 16, M 744.
Klag und bekanntnis der Armen Götzen. . . . Strassburg: J. Cammerlander, 1538.

198. ———. *Sendbrieff///Von der Messz//kranckheit/vnd jrem let-//sten willen/dem Bapst/ /zukommen*. N.p.: n.p., 1528. [Fiche 1929/#4928] VD 16, M 739.

199. Marschalk, Haug. *Durch betrachtung vnd//Bekarung der boßen gebreych in//schweren sünden/Ist Gemacht Dy-//ser Spyegel Der Blinden*. Augsburg: M. Ramminger, 1522. [Zurich, ZB] VD 16, M 1099.
Editions under title *Der Spiegel der Blinden*: VD 16, M 1100–1103.
Augsburg: M. Ramminger, 1523. [Weller, 2689]
Basel: A. Peter, 1523. [Weller, 2691]
Strassburg: W. Köpfel, 1523. [Weller, 2690]

200. ———. *Eyn Edles/Schönes///lieplichs Tractatlein/von den//raynen/hymlischen/ewigen wort//(Verbum Domini) zu lob Got*. . . . N.p.: n.p., 1521. [Fiche 109/#2783] VD 16, M 1083–1089.

201. ———. *Eyn Ermanung . . . an unsern aller gnedigsten hern Caro-//lum/Römischen Keyser/Ferdinandum sey-//ner Maiest. bruder . . . All geystlich vnd weltlich Chur-//ben/alle Geystich vnd weltlich Oberkeyt///Damit yhn Got der almechtig yn dissem//ytz angehenden vnd furgenomen//Keyserlichen Reychsdag vnd Concilio tzu//Augsburg/den heyligen geyst/ das wort//Gottes tzu erhalten*. . . . N.p.: n.p., 1530. [Fiche 1080/#2738] VD 16, M 1081.

202. ———. *Das heilig ewig wort//gottis/was das in ym krafft/stercke//tugent/fryd/freud/ erleuchtung vnd leben/in//eym rechten Christen zu erwecken vermag, etc*. . . . Zwickau: n.p., 1524. [Fiche 1111/#2836] VD 16, M 1090–1092
N.p.: n.p., n.d.
N.p.: n.p., n.d.
Augsburg: M. Ramminger, 1523. [Fiche 272/#777]
Constance: Schäffer, 1524.

203. ———. *Pfaffenklag//Der Pfaffen Klag heyss ich//Wer mich find der kauff mich*. . . . Altenburg: G. Kantz, 1525. [Laube, 1, 569–574] VD 16, M 1092–1093, M 1095.

204. ———. *Die Scharf Metz wider die//(die sich evangelisch nennen) und//doch dem Evangelio ent//gegen sind*. N.p.: n.p., 1525? [Clemen, I, 95–130] VD 16, M 1095–1098.
N.p.: n.p., 1525?
Strassburg: J. Schott, 1525?

205. ———. *Von dem weyt//erschollen Namen//Luther/wz er bedeut//vnnd wie er wirt/ /mißbraucht*. . . . Erfurt: J. Loersfeld, 1523. [Laube, 2, 563–569; Fiche 10/#41] VD 16, M 1107.

206. Meldeman, Niclaus. *Ein kurtzer bericht uber//die recht warhafftig Contrafactur/ Tur-//ckischer belegerung der Stat Wien.* . . . N.p.: n.p., n.d. [Fiche 1333/#3496] VD 16, M 4443.

Meyer, Peter. See Hartmuth von Cromberg #86.

207. Mörlin, Hans. *Sendt brieff eines leyen//Hansen Mörlins Leynewebers zu Schweyn-// furt/An herrn Valentin Kreydner Cap-//lan daselbst/und Prediger des//Geytzs in den Kasten //der Geystlichen.* Nürnberg: H. Hergot, 1524. [Summarized in Arnold, 295–303]

208. Motschidler, Jörg. *Eyn newer Dialo-//gus oder gesprech/zwischen//einem verprenten/ vertrib-//nem Edelman vnd ey-//nem Munch.* . . . N.p.: n.p., 1525. [Schade, 3, 101ff; Fiche 1196/#3009] VD 16, M 6455–6456.

   Nürnberg: H. Höltzel, 1525.
   Erfurt: L. Trütebul, 1525.
   Also see #26, Hübsch Argument.

209. ————. *Ein vnderred des Bapsts vnd//seiner cardinelen wie im zu thun//sey/vnd das wort Gottes vnder zu trucken.* . . . N.p.: n.p., 1524. [Schade, 3, 74–100; Fiche 568/#1453]

N

210. Nagel, Hans, and Hans, Krüsi. *Von dem Glawbenn//Gotes Der allein selig// machett/vnd nur//von hymel geben//würdt.* . . . N.p.: n.p., 1525. [Fiche 1357/#3580] VD 16, K 2466.

211. Niklaus under dem Rotten hütt [pseud.]. *Ich bin der Strigel//Im teütschen landt.* . . . N.p.: n.p., 1521. [Fiche 279/#795]

Noricus, Philadelphus [pseud.]. Identified by Clemen (*Kleine Schriften* 2, 295–298) as Kaspar Nützel of Nuremberg. See Nützel, Kaspar.

212. Nützel, Kaspar. *Wie alle Closter/vnd sonderlich Junck-//frawen Closter in ain Christ//lichs wesen mochten//durch gottes gna//den bracht//werden.* N.p.: n.p., 1524. [Fiche 291/#844]

P

Preuning, Jorgen. See Jörg Breuning.

R

213. Rem, Bernhard. *Ain Sendtbrieff an ettlich//Closterfrawen zu sant//Katherina vnd zu//sant Niclas in//Augspurg.* N.p.: n.p., n.d. [Fiche 225/#632] VD 16, R 1084.

214. Rem, Katherina and Veronica. *Antwurt zwayer Closter frau-//wen im Katheriner Closter zu Aug-//spurg an Bernhart Remen///Vnd hernach syn ge-//gen Antwurt.* N.p.: n.p., n.d. [Fiche 751/#1921] VD 16, R 1063.

215. Reychart, Peter. *Ain Cristenlich ge//sprech Buchlin vonn zwayen//Weybern/Mit namen Mar-//gretha Bohemn vnnd Anna//Kollerin/wie sy von dem wort//gots geredt hand.* . . . Augsburg: H. Steiner, 1523. [Arnold, 304, pr. 3; Fiche 734;#1876] VD 16, R 1552.

216. Ritter, Hans. *Welcher gern wissen well//Von armutz nott vnd ungefell//Auch von almusens bracht wesen.* . . . N.p.: n.p., 1525. [Fiche 1428/#3783] VD 16, R 2530.

217. Rychssner, Utz. *Ayn ausszug/auss der//Cronicka der Bapst un//iren gesatzen, wie gleych//formig sy den gsatze gots und leer der apostel seyen.* . . . N.p.: n.p., 1524. [Russell copy] VD 16, R 2210.

218. ————. *Ain gesprech buchlin von ainem Weber//vnd ainem Kramer über das Büchlin Doctoris//Mathie Kretz von der haimlichen Beycht.* . . . N.p.: n.p., 1524. [Fiche 835/#2094] VD 16, R 2211–2212.

219. ———. *Ein schöne unterweysung//wie und wir in Christo alle Gebrüder//und Schwester seyen.* . . . N.p.: n.p., 1524. [Fiche 737/#188] VD 16, R 2215.

S

220. Sachs, Hans. *Ein Dialogus/des inhalt/ein argument//der Römischen/wider das Christlich heüflein/den//Geytz* . . . *betreffend.* Nürnberg: H. Höltzel, 1524. [Fiche 1537/#4000] VD 16, S 209–212.

    Augsburg: P. Ulhart d.Ä, 1524. [Fiche 666/#1758]

    Nürnberg: J. Gutknecht, 1524. [Fiche 208/#592]

221. ———. *Disputacion zwyschen ainem Chorherre//vnd Schuchmacher Darinn das wort//gottes ain recht Christlich wesenn//verfochten wirt.* N.p.: n.p., 1524. [Fiche 1321/#3452] VD 16, S 213–224.

    Eilenberg: N. Widemar, n.d. [Fiche 1078/#2730]

    Augsburg: M. Ramminger, 1524. [Fiche 1050/#2654]

    Augsburg: M. Ramminger, 1524. [Fiche 835/#2093]

    Bamberg: G. Erlinger, 1524. [Fiche 1094/#2779]

222. ———. *Ain Gesprech aines Euangeli-//schen Christen/mit ainem Lutherischen.* . . . Augsburg: P. Ulhart d. A., 1524. [Fiche 13/#53] VD 16, S 296–303, S 305.

    N.p.: n.p., 1524. [Fiche 1051/#2656]

    Nürnberg: H. Höltzel, 1524. [Fiche 1044/#2634]

223. ———. *Eyn gesprech von den Scheinwercken//der Gaystlichen/vnd jren ge-lübdten.* . . . N.p.: n.p., 1524. [Fiche 1322/#3454] VD 16, S 315–323.

    N.p.: n.p., n.d. [Fiche 1322/#3455]

    N.p.: n.p., n.d. [Fiche 1322/#3456]

    Bamberg: G. Erlinger, 1524. [Fiche 210/#595]

    Nürnberg: H. Höltzel, 1524. [Fiche 1196/#3010]

224. ———. *Hie kompt ein Beüerlein zu//einen reichen Burger von der güldt/den wucher//betreffen.* . . . N.p.: n.p., 1522. VD 16, H 3466–3468. [Schade 2, 73–79; English trans. Strauss, *Manifestations,* 109–115; Fiche 165/#448]

    Wedler, *Hans Sachs* (1976), attributes this to Sachs.

    Other editions (sometimes with title *Von der Gült*):

    Strassburg: J. Prüß, 1522.

    Nürnberg: n.p., 1522.

    Colmar: A. Farckall, 1522.

225. ———. *Ein lobspruch der statt//Nurnberg.//Der Stadt Nurmberg ordnung vnd wesen//Findtsu in disem gdicht zulesen.* . . . Nürnberg: W. Resch, 1530. [Fiche 1094/#2780] VD 16, S 441–450.

226. ———. *Underweysung der ungeschickten vermeinten Lutherischen so in eüsserlichen sachen zu ergernuss ires nechstin, freüntlich handlen.* [Printed with Hans Greiffenberg, *Ob das Evangelium sein krafft von der Kirchen hab.* . . .] N.p.: n.p., 1524. [Fiche 1189/#3022] VD 16, S 304.

227. ———. *Die Wittember//gisch nachtigall//Die man yetz//höret uberall:* Zwickau: J. Gastel, 1523. [Fiche 1310/#3395] VD 16, S 645–651.

    Augsburg: P. Ulhart d.Ä, 1523. [Fiche 10/#2672]

    Bamberg: G. Erlinger, 1523? [Fiche 1096/#2784]

    Eilenberg: N. Widemar, 1523. [Fiche 964/#2412/]

228. ———. *Ein wunderliche weissa-//gung/von dem Bapstum/wie es//yhm bis an das ende der welt gehen sol ym figu-//ren odder gemelde begriffen gefunden zu//Nürnberg ym Cartheuser Kloster* . . . *Ein vorred Andreas Osianders.//Mit gutter verstendlicher auslegung durch gelerte//lewt verklert Wilche Hans Sachs yn Deud-//sche reymen gefasset vnd darzu gesetzt hat.* . . . N.p.: n.p., 1527. [Fiche 1257/#3214]

Satrapitanus, Heinrich, pictor [pseud.]. See Vogtherr, Heinrich.
229.   Scharffenstein, Heintzen von. *Warhaftiger be-//richt* . . . *wie vnd aus was ursachen dye//Milternberger durch die Mentztischen//Rathe in hafft auff gepurlich straff//genommen sey.* N.p.: n.p., 1522. [Fiche 1547/#4013] VD 16, S 2288.
Scharpf, Heinrich [von Klingnau]. See Karg, Ottmar, *Ain grÿme grosse Ketten.*
230.   Schaumburg, Adam. *Dyses buchlein wirdt genent der//Leyen Spiegell.* . . . N.p.: n.p., 1522. [Fiche 1117/#2855] VD 16, S 2373.
231.   ———. *Mein . . . Antwort. vff das unchristlich//vnd vnwarhafft zuschreiben Philipi/ /Gutenums . . . wider//mich vßgangen.* N.p.: n.p., 1526. [Fiche 1089/#2760]
232.   Schenck von Stauffenberg, Jacob. *Sendtbrieff//an seyne Geschwyhen.* Strassburg: M. Schürer Erben, 1524. [Zurich,ZB] VD 16, S 2617.
233.   Schnewyl, Johann [von Strassburg]. *Wer gern wolt wissin wie ich hieß//zu leesen mich hett nit verdrieß.* . . . N.p.: n.p., n.d. [Fiche 42/#110] VD 16, M 1108.
234.   ———. *Wider die vnmilte verdammung.//Nach art vnd aygenschaff* . . . *erdicht auß aygnem kopff* . . . *Jacob Straussen/allen denen die auß warer erkantnuß Christlichs glaubens/nit//glauben den warhafften leyb Christi//unsichtbarlich sein blut vnd flaisch//// gegenwirtig vnder dem brot//vn wein des herrn genent//sacrament zu trost den//gefangnen irri-//gen selen ant-wort.* N.p.: n.p., 1526. [Fiche 1549/#4018] VD 16, M 1109.
235.   Schönichen, Georg. *Allen brudern zcu dresden//dy den Ewangelio Holt.* . . . Grimma: N. Widemar, 1523. [Arnold, 193, pr. 317; NCA] VD 16, S 3740.
236.   ———. *Auff die vnderricht des-//hoch-gelerten Docto//ris* . . . *Hieronimy tungirß- //heym/von Ochsenfart Col//ligat vnd prediger zu//leyptzick//Anthworth.* . . . Grimma: N. Widemar, 1523. [Arnold, 194; Fiche 1066/#2695] VD 16, S 3741.
237.   ———. *Den achtbarn vnd//hochgelerten zu Leypßck///Petro Mosellano Re//ctgori/ Ochsenfart//prediger zu S.//Nicolao/An//dree Ca//miciano/mey-//nen günstigen herrn//vnnd lieben brudern in//Christo Jhesu etc.* Grimma: Nicolaus, Widemar, 1523. [Arnold, 194; Fiche 116; #313, Fiche 737/#1883] VD 16, S 3738.
    Augsburg: H. Steiner, 1523. VD 16, S 3737.
    Erfurt: J. Loersfeld, 1523. VD 16, D 3739.
Schore, Hans von. See Ziegler, Jörg.
238.   Schorr, Jakob M. *Ratschlag vber den//Lutherischen handel/dem Durch//leuchtigen Hochgebornen Fürsten vnd Her//ren/herrn Ludwigen Pfaltzgraven bey//Rheyn* . . . *zu weylent//fürgenomenem Speyrischen//Reychßtage.* . . . N.p.: n.p., 1525. [Fiche 1880/#4801] VD 16, S 3957–3965.
Schütz, Katharina. See Zell, Katharina.
239.   Sickingen, Franciscus von. *Ain Sendbrieff* . . . *dem Edlen vnd Ern-//uesten Junnckherr Diethern//von Henschüchßheim/zu vnderrichtung//etlicher arti-//ckel Christ// liches//Gelaubens.* . . . N.p.: n.p., 1522. [Fiche 79/#212] VD 16, S. 6309–6316.
    N.p.: n.p., n.d. [Fiche 450/#1217]
    N.p.: n.p., n.d. [Fiche 1178/#2959]
    Wittenberg: n.p., 1522. [Fiche 215/#606]
240.   ———. *Auß schreiben vnd verannt=//würtung* . . . *vff//Rugklich verclagen* . . . *vnnd vnbillich verunglimpfung//seiner widerwertigen vnnd mißgünder.* N.p.: n.p., 1522. [Fiche 1219/#3085] VD 16, S 6306.
241.   ———. *Eruorderung vnd verkundung* . . . *an vnd wider Provincial//prioren vnd Conuenten Prediger ordens//teütscher nation vnd sunderlichen bru//der Jacoben von der Hochstraten* . . . *von wegen//vnd namen des hochgelerten* . . . *Johan Reüchlins bey//der Rechten doctor//seiner erlangten//Executorial//halben.* N.p.: n.p., 1519. [Fiche 926/#2303] VD 16, S 6307–6308.
    N.p.: n.p., n.d. [Fiche 968/#2430]

242. ———. *Warhafftiger bericht//Francisci von Sickingen//vff das vngegründt//vßschryben deren von//Worms/wyder//jnen bescheen//Anno.1515.* N.p.: n.p., 1515. [Fiche 1304/ #3372] VD 16, S 6317.

243. Spengler, Lazarus. *Eyn Kurtzer//außzug/auß dem//Babstlichen Rechten der De-// cret vnd Decretalen/Inn den//artickeln die vngeuerlich Got-//tes wort vnd dem Euangelio ge//meß seind.* . . . Wittenberg: J. Clugk, 1530. [Fiche 990/#2510] VD 16, S 8234– 8238.

244. ———. *Ein kurtzer begriff//wie sich ein warhaffter//Christ/in allem seinem//wesen vnd wandel///gegen Got vnd sei-//nem nechsten//halten sol.* . . . N.p: G. Kantz, n.d. [Fiche 1156/#2929] VD 16, S 8241–8246.

Erfurt: M. Sachs, 1526. [Fiche 950/#2361]

245. ———. *Die haubt//artickel durch//welche gemeyne Chri//stenheyt byßhere//verfuret wor-//den ist.//Daneben auch grund vnnd antzeygen eyns gantzen//rechten Christenlichen/ /weßens.* Wittemberg: N. Schirlentz, 1522. [Yale, Beinecke; Laube, 1, 156–185] VD 16, S 8230–8232.

246. ———. *Schutzrede vnd Christenli-//che antwort* . . . *mit antzeygung/Warumb/ Doctor Mar//tini Luthers lere/nit szam vnchristlich//verworffen/Sunder meher/als Chris- ten//lich gehalten werden solle.//Apologia.* Augsburg: S. Ottmar, 1519. [Yale, Beinecke; Laube, 1, 501–516]. VD 16, S 8250–8251, S 8253–8254, S 8256–8257.

Nürnberg: J. Gutknecht, 1520.

Nürnberg: S. Ottmar, 1520.

247. ———. *Ain trostliche Chri-//stenliche anweisung//vnd ertzney in allen//widerwertig// kaiten.* Nürnberg: F. Peypus, 1521. [Yale, Beinecke] VD 16, S 8258–8259.

248. ———. *Verantwortung* . . . *etlicher//vermainter Argument* . . . *So//zu widerstandt vnnd verdruckung des//wort Gottes vnd hailigen Euan//gelions/Von denen die nit Cri-// sten sein gebraucht werdenn.//1524.* Bamberg: G. Erlinger, 1524. [Clemen, 2, 44; Fiche 746/#1908] VD 16, S 8262–8265.

249. ———. *Wie sich eyn Christen mensch inn trübsal und widerwertikayt trösten/ und wo er die rechten hilff und Ertznay derhalben suchen soll.* Nürnberg: J. Gutknecht, 1529. [Fiche 1184/#2969] VD 16, S 8266.

250. Stadt Bern. *Gemein Reformation: vnd ver//besserung der bißhergebrachten verwan- //ten Gotsdiensten/vnd Ceremonien* . . . *der Statt Bern* . . . *uss gereutet sind/vnd also dyse Refor-//mation in jren stetten/landen vnd gebiet-//en/hinfür zehalten/angesehen vnnd vßgesandt.* N.p.: n.p., 1528. [Fiche 1281/#3298] VD 16, B 1882–1889.

N.p.: n.p., 1528. [Fiche 1281/#3297]

N.p.: n.p., 1528. [Fiche 1454/#3841]

251. Stadt Constanz. *Burgermeiysters unnd Radts der statt Costentz verantwurtung/ etlicher//maren/die über sy vnd über die Prediger deß//wort Gottes bey jnen/neüwlich//on grund der warheit//außgangen//seind.* N.p.: n.p., 1526. [Fiche 1298/#3344]

N.p.: n.p., 1526. [Fiche 1298/#3345]

252. Stadt Kitzingen.*Ein Cristen-//liche Ordenung der//Betler halben/vber den auffge- //richten gemainen Kasten/in//der Stat Kitzingen zu//Francken.* . . . Nürnberg: J. Gutknecht, 1523. [Laube, 2, 1078–1085] VD 16, K 1114.

253. Stadt Leisnig. *Ordenung eyns gemey-//nen kastens.//Radschlag wie die gey-//stlichen gutter zu han-//deln sind.//Martinus Luther.* . . . Wittenberg: L. Cranach d. Ä. und C. Döring, 1523. [Laube 2, 1051–1071]

254. Stadt Nürnberg. *Eyn lobliche vnd//Christliche Ordnung der hochbe-//rumpten stat Nurmberg/von//dem hußarmer vnd ander Bet//tellüt Almusen.* . . . N.p.: n.p., 1522. [Fiche 1418/#3748] VD 16, N 2017.

255. Stadt Strassburg. *Ordnug des herren//Nachtmal: so man die Messz//nennet/sampt*

der Tauff vnd Insegung//der Ee/Wie yetzt die diener des wort//gottes zu Strasszburg/ Erneü-// wert/vnnd nach gottlicher//geschrifft gebessert haben. . . . Strassburg: J. Schwan, 1525. [Strasbourg BNU]

256. Stadt Wittenberg. *Ain lobliche ordnung//der Fürstlichen stat Wittemberg//Im tausent fünfhundert vnd zway vnd//zwaintzigsten jar auffgericht.* Augsburg: M. Ramminger, 1522. [Laube 2, 1033–1037]
See also entries under "Die Gemein," "Zünfte," "Dorfmeister" und "Gemein," "Eydgenossenschaft," and "Stetten. . . ."

257. Stanberger, Balthasar. *Dialogus zwischen Petro und eynem//Bawrn, darinne angezeigt wurdt wie man auß Petro einen Juden gemacht hat, vnd nie sie ken Roem kommen.* . . . Erfurt: M. Buchfürer, 1523. [Clemen, 3, 198–217] VD 16, S 8540.

258. ———. *Ein Dialogus oder gesprech zwischen//einem Prior, Leyenbruder und Bettler dz wort Gottes belanget.* . . . Erfurt: M. Buchfürer, 1522. [Fiche 1003/#2546] VD 16, S 8539.

259. ———. *Ein Epistel oder Sendtbrieff Balta-//sar Stanberger von der lieb Gottes/ und des nechsten/seinem//geliebten brüder in Christo Michel Buchfürer von Weimar aus den Furstlichen Schloss . . . zu geschriben.* Erfurt: M. Buchfürer, 1523. [Clemen, 3, 192; Laube 1, 222–225; Fiche 983/#2487] VD 16, S 8541–8542.

260. Staygmayer, Hans. *Ain kurtze un-//derrichtung von der//waren Christliche bru-// derschaft.* . . . N.p.: n.p., 1524. [Fiche 142/#391] VD 16, S 8714.

261. ———. *Ain Schoner Dialogus oder//Gesprech/von aynem Münch vnd//Becken/ wolcher die Oster//ayer Samlen//wollt.* . . . N.p.: n.p., 1524. [Fiche 4/#17] VD 16, S 8715.

Stauffen. See Grumbach, Argula von.

Steger, Lucius. See Karg, Ottmar, *Ain grÿme, grosse Ketten.*

Steger, Martin. See Füssli, Hans.

262. Stetten und Landen der Zwölff Orten. *Ein Christlicher ab-//schaid/durch vil Artigkl be//griffen/der loblichen ayd//gnosschafft/wider den//Luter/vnnd seiner//anhenger geyeb-//te jrrtungen.//Derselbigen Aydgnosschafft//Sandtbrieff/an den Bischof//zu Costentz gleyche Cristliche//erberkait anzaygendt.* N.p.: n.p., 1524. [Fiche 1436/#3818]

263. Sturm, Kaspar. *Ain kurtze anzaygung vnd beschreybung//Romischer Kayserlicher Maiestat einreyten//Erstlich von Innßpruck . . . vnd zu letst gen Augspurg auff//den Reychstag.* . . . Augsburg: J. Schönsperger d.J., 1530. [Fiche 6/#26]
N.p.: n.p., n.d. [Fiche 666/#1756] VD 16, S 10013.

264. ———. *Römischer Kai.Mai. verhö//rung Rede und Wider-//Rede Doctor Martini Lu-//thers Augustiner Ordens zu Witten//bergk, in gegenwürdt der Chur-//fürsten, Fürsten und Stenden//des heylige Reichs, auff//dem Reychstag zu Wurms//besche//hen.MD 21 Jahr.* N.p.: n.p., 1521. [NCA. Kolde, 125]

265. ———. *Warlicher bericht//wie von den dreyen Churfürsten//vnd Fürsten/nämlich Tryer/Pfaltz und Hessen//weylandt Frantz von Sickingen überzogen//Auch was sich im selbigen mit eröberung//seiner vnd anderer Schlosser . . . begeben.* . . . N.p.: n.p., n.d. [Fiche 583/#1516; expanded and illustrated edition of Fiche 966/#2419] VD 16, S 10018–10019.
N.p.: n.p., 1523. [Kolde, p. 129]

266. ———. *Wie die drey Kriegsfürsten, Nemlich//Trier, Pfaltz und Hessen, Frantzen/ /von Sickingen uberzogen, /Inen//und seine anhenger eyns tayls ge//strafft, auch etlich Schlösser//gewunnen und Erobert//haben.* . . . Worms: H. von Erfurt? 1523. [Fiche 966/ #2419] VD 16, S 10020.
N.p.: n.p., n.d. [Fiche 1900/#4865]

T

267.   [Tauber, Casper.] *Ain Christenlich Lied, das bewainlichen Tod Casper Taubers genant. Burger zu Wien.* . . . N.p.: n.p., 1525. [Weller, 2, #42]

268.   ———. *Ein hüpsch new lied von//eine Christenlichen man mit namen//Caspar Tauber genant.* N.p.: n.p., 1524. [Zurich, ZB]

269.   ———. *Eyn warhafftig geschicht//wie Casper Tawber/Burg//er zu Wien in Osterreich/ /fur ain Ketzer/vnd zu//dem todt verurtaylt/vnd außgefurt//worden ist.//1524.* N.p.: n.p., 1524. [Fiche 1405/#3705]

Treubel, Eckhart zum. See Drübel, Eckhart zum.

U

270.   Ulem, Hans. *Merckt jr leyen habt euch jn hutt//Seeht der geistlichen vber mutt.* . . . Speyer: J. Eckhart, 1522. [Fiche 843/#2117]

V

271.   Vögeli, Jörg. *Dry missiuen ains lay//eschen Burgers zu//Costantz betreffen//de den pfarrer zu//Almanßdorff.//der nit nun//Martin//lutrer//Besunnder auch alle//seiner schrifften le-//sere ketzer halt.* N.p.: n.p., 1524. [Fiche 1740/#4525]

272.   ———. *Schirmred ains lay-//eschen burgers zu Costantz/wie//den pfarrer von uberlingen//der one grund der schrifft//etlich Costantzisch pre//diger/vnd in dem/ire//zühorere/ offenlich//gscholtten hat.* . . . N.p.: n.p., n.d. [Fiche 1556/#4035]

273.   ———. *Ain schrift der kaiserlichen Regierung, in Hailigen Reich zugeschickt darinn sich Burgermeister und Radt der Stadt Constanz ettlicher Hendel, deren sy verunglimpfft sind, entschuldigent.* . . . Konstanz: J. Spitzenberg, 1528. [Russell]

274.   Vogtherr, Heinrich d.Ä. *Ain Cristliche//anred unnd ermanung///sich vor den grossen Lutherischenn//Schreyern und Cantzel schendern zu ver-///hütten.* . . . Augsburg: H. Steiner, 1524. [Laube, I, 480–490; Fiche 125/#335] VD 16, V 2175.

275.   ———. *. . . eines Christlichen//Loßbuchs/nach ordnung eines Alphabets oder.A.B.C. Jn//reimen gestelt. Darinnen mann/der wunderbaren Krefften//Gottes/sampt gantzen Christlichen leben nach berichtet wurt.* . . . Strassburg: H. Vogtherr, 1539. [Strasbourg, BNU] VD 16, V 2187.

276.   ———. *Ein Christlich büchlin//wie man sich in guten wercken hal//ten/vnnd wem man sie zu-//schreyben sol.* . . . N.p.: n.p., 1523? [Fiche 833/#2089] VD 16, V 2176, V 2177.
   N.p.: n.p., 1523. [Fiche 587/#1524]

277.   ———. *Ain Fruchtbar bü//chlin, wie ain Christen mensch//in Got widerumb neüw ge//poren/vnd in die jnnerlich//erkantnus gots ge-//fürt.* . . . Augsburg: M. Ramminger, 1523. [Fiche 587/#1525] VD 16, V 2185.

W

Wendelstein. See Dorfmeister und Gemein zu Wendelstein.

278.   Weyda, Ursula. *Apologia Fur die//Schöfferin zu Eysenbergk//Auf das gotlose Büchlin . . . Simon . . . schreybt . . . Apt zu Pegaw.* . . . N.p.: n.p., 1524. [Russell, *lay Theology*] VD 16, W 1445.

279.   Wurm von Geudertheim, Matthias. *Balaams Esel . . . Von dem Bann///und das aller geystliche stand schuldig ist, der weltlicher oberkait zu gehorsamen.* Strassburg: W. Köpfel, 1523. [Fiche 1497/#3940]

280.   ———. *Christenlich//kurtz vermanung Mat-//this Wurmen von Geydertheim . . . an den würdi-//gen vnd gelerten herr Jacob//kornkauff pfarrherrn zu//Geidertheim.* . . . Strassburg: J. Schwan, 1524. [Zurich, ZB]
   N.p.: n.p., 1524. [Fiche 797/#2005]

281. ———. *Christlich Schreiben, so ain Evangelischer bruder seiner schwestern, ainer Closter junckfrawen zugeschickt.* Strassburg: n.p., 1523. [Fiche 1550/#4019]
282. ———. *Jesus. Auszlegung der geschrifft. dem anderen Capitel S. Jacob's Epistel anfahend.* . . . Strassburg: J. Schwann, 1524. [Strasbourg, St. Guillaume]
Strassburg: M. Schürer Erben, 1525.
283. ———. *Trost Closterge-//fangner.* . . . Strassburg: n.p., 1523. [Zurich, ZB]

Z

284. Zell, Katherina. *Entschuldig//ung Katharina Schütz inn/für M. Matthes Zellen/ jren Eege-//mahel/der ein Pfarrher vnd dyener ist im//wort Gottes zu Straßburg.* . . . Strassburg: W. Köpfel, 1524. [Zurich, ZB]
285. ———. *Den Leydenden Christglaubigen Weybern der Gemain zu Kentzigen Meinen Mitschwestern in Christo Jhesu zu handen.* Strassburg, n.p., 1524.
N.p.: n.p., 1524. [Fiche 737/#1882]
286. Zell, Katharina (ed.), and Michael Weisse. *Von Christo Jesu unserem säligmacher . . . etlich Christliche Kostliche lobgesäng ausz einem vast herrlichen Gsangbuch gezogen.* Strassburg: J. Fröhlich, 1534. [Strasbourg, BNU]
Strassburg: J. Fröhlich, 1534, 1535, 1536 (2 editions).
287. Ziegler, Clement. *Ein fast schon büch-//lin in welchen yederman findet ein hel-//len vnd claren verstandt von dem leib und blut Chri-//sti.* . . . Strassburg: J. Schwann, 1525. [Strasbourg, BNU; Fiche 1915/#4902]
288. ———. *Ein fast schöne uszlegung und betrach-//tung des Christlichen gebetts.* . . . N.p.: n.p., 1525. [NCA; cited in Peter, 256]
289. ———. *Ain Kurtz Register/vnd außzug der Bibel in wolchem//man findet was Abgoterey//sey/vnnd wa man yedes//suchen soll.* . . . Strassburg: W. Köpfel, 1524. [Strasbourg, BM]
Strassburg: J. Schwann, 1524. [Strasbourg, BM]
290. ———. *Von der vermehe-//lung Marie und Josephs//Darzu von der unverruckte/ /Junckfrawschafft Marie://vor, yn und nach der Geburt.* Strassburg: J. Schwann or J. Prüss, 1524. [NCA; cited in Peter, 256]
291. ———. *Von der waren nyessung//beyd leibs vnd bluts//Christi.* . . . Strassburg: J. Schott, 1524. [Strasbourg, B.M; Fiche 1107/#2824]
292. Ziegler, Jörg. *Was stebn jr da mich zgaffen an?//Ich wolt ein jeder gieng sein ban.* . . . N.p.: n.p., n.d. [Rott, 1, 521–527]
293. Zierer, Wolfgang. *Ein Christenlich Ge-//sprech/von ainem Waldbrüder/vnd ainem waysen der//von seinen vorgengern verlassen ist/die in solten le//ren vnd speisen/mit dem gotlichen wort des dann//ist ain Speiß der seel.* . . . N.p.: n.p., 1522. [Fiche 7/#31]
294. Zünfte [Basel]. *Supplication ettlicher Zunfften an ein Ersamen Rath zu Basel abzustellen das zwispeltig predigen unnd die Mess.* Strassburg: B. Beck, 1529. [Chrisman P3.3.25]

Works Cited

Abray, Lorna Jane. *The People's Reformation: Magistrates, Clergy and Commons in Strasbourg, 1500–1598.* Ithaca, N.Y.: Cornell University Press, 1985.

Agricola, Johann. *Die Sprichwörter Sammlugen.* Sander L. Gilman, ed., Berlin: De Gruyter, 1971.

Allgemeine deutsche Biographie. 56 vols. Leipzig, 1875–1912. Berlin: Duncker und Humblot, 1967–1971.

Alves, Abel. "The Christian Social Organism and Social Welfare: The Case of Vives, Calvin and Loyola." *Sixteenth Century Journal* XX, I (1988): 5–21.

Anker, Karl. *Bann und Interdikt im 14. und 15. Jahrhundert als Voraussetzungen der Reformation.* Inaugural-Dissertation Universität Tübingen. Tübingen: Druck von H. Laupp Jr., 1919.

Arnold, Klaus. "Reichsherold und Reichsreform. Georg Rixner und die sogenannte Reform Kaiser Friedrichs III." *Bericht des Historische Vereins Bamberg* 120 (1984): 91–109.

Arnold, Martin. *Handwerker als theologische Schriftsteller: Studien zu Flugschriften der frühen Reformation (1523–1525).* Göttingen: Vandenhoek und Ruprecht, 1990.

Augsburger Stadtlexikon. Wolfram Baer et al., eds. Augsburg: Perlach Verlag, 1985.

Bainton, Roland. *Here I Stand: A Life of Martin Luther.* New York, Nashville: Abingdon Press, (1950).

———. *Women of the Reformation in Germany and Italy.* Minneapolis, Minn.: Augsburg Publishing House, 1971.

Balzer, Bernd. *Bürgerliche Reformationspropoganda: Die Flugschriften des Hans Sachs in den Jahren 1523–1525.* Stuttgart: J. B. Metzler, 1973.

Barnes, Robin B. *Prophecy and Gnosis: Apocalypticism in the Wake of the Lutheran Reformation.* Stanford: Stanford University Press, 1988.

Batori, Ingrid. "Herren, Meister, Habennichtse. Die Bürgerschaft der Reichstadt Nördlingen um 1500." *Rieser Kulturtage* VI/I. Nördlingen: Steinmeier, 1986. 252–269.

Bauer, Augustus. *Deutschland in den Jahren 1517–1525 im Lichte . . . anonymer und pseudoanonymer Volks- und Flugschriften.* Ulm, 1872.

Bebb, Phillip N. "The Lawyers, Dr. Christoph Scheurl and the Reformation." In Lawrence P. Buck and Jonathan Zophy, eds., *The Social History of the Reformation.* Columbus: Ohio State University Press, 1972. 52–72.

Bellot, Josef. "Humanismus-Bildungswesen Buchdruck-und Verlagsgeschichte." In Gunther Gottlieb et al., ed., *Geschichte der Stadt Augsburg.* Stuttgart: Konrad Theiss Verlag, 1985: 340–345.

Benzing, Josef. *Bibliographie Strasbourgeoise.* Baden-Baden: Valentin Koerner, 1981.

———. *Die Buchdrucker des 16. und 17. Jahrhunderts im Deutschen Sprachgebiet.* Wiesbaden: Otto Hassarrowitz, 1963.

———. *Lutherbibliographie: Verzeichnis der gedruckten Schriften Martin Luthers bis zu dessen Tod.* Baden-Baden: Heitz, 1965–1966.

———. *Ulrich von Hutten und seine Drucker; eine Bibliographie des Schriften Huttens im 16. Jahrhundert.* Wiesbaden: O. Harrosowitz, 1956.

Berger, Arnold E., ed. *Die Schaubühne im Dienste der Reformation.* 2 vols. Deutsche

Literatur: Sammlung literarischer Kunst- und Kulturdenkmäler in Entwicklungsreihen. Reihe 9: Reformation. Bände 5–6. Leipzig: Philipp Reclam jun., 1932.

———. *Die Sturmtruppen der Reformation: Ausgewählte Flugschriften der Jahre 1520–25*. Deutsche Literatur: Sammlung literarischer Kunst- und Kulturdenkmäler in Entwicklungsreihen. Reihe 9: Reformation. Band 7. Leipzig: Philipp Reclam jun., 1931.

Bernstein, Eckhard. *Hans Sachs*. Reinbek: Rowohlt, 1993.

———. *Ulrich von Hutten*. Reinbek: Rowohlt Verlag, 1988.

Blaschke, Karlheinz, ed. *An den christlichen Adel deutscher Nation*. In Hans-Ulrich Delius, ed., *Martin Luther, Studienausgabe*. 3 vols. Berlin: Evangelische Verlagsanstalt, 1979–1983. Vol. 2, 89–95.

Blickle, Peter. Biblicism versus Feudalism." In Bob Scribner and Gerhard Benecke, eds., *The German Peasant War 1525: New Viewpoints*. London: George Allen and Unwin, 1979: 137–143.

———. *Communal Reformation: The Quest for Salvation in Sixteenth-Century Germany*. Trans. Thomas Dunlap. Atlantic Highlands, N.J.: Humanities Press, 1992.

———. *Gemeindereformation: Die Menschen des 16. Jahrhundert auf dem Weg zum Heil*. Münich: R. Oldenbourg Verlag, 1985.

———. *Revolte und Revolution in Europa*. Historische Zeitschrift Beiheft 4, 1975.

———. *The Revolution of 1525: The German Peasant's War from a New Perspective*. transl. Thomas A. Brady, Jr., and H. C. Eric Midelfort. Baltimore. Md.: The Johns Hopkins University Press, 1981.

Blickle, Peter, ed. *Bauer, Reich und Reformation*. Festschrift für Günther Franz. Stuttgart: Ulmer, 1982.

Böcking, Eduard, ed. *Opera Ulrichi Hutteni equitis Germani*. 5 vols. Leipzig, 1859–1862. Two supplemental volumes, Leipzig, 1869–1870.

Bode, Helmut. *Hartmut XII. von Cronberg, Reichsritter der Reformationszeit*. Frankfurt am Main: Verlag Waldemar Kramer, 1987.

Bogler, Wilhelm. *Hartmuth von Kronberg: ein Charakterstudie aus der Reformationszeit*. Schriften des Vereins für Reformationsgeschichte, 57. 14jg. (4), 1897.

Boucher, Pierre. "Mes Dernier Volontez." in Louis Lalande. *Une vieille seigneurie; Boucherville, chroniques, portraits et souvenirs*. Montréal: Cadieux et Derome, 1890: 57–70.

Bouwsma, William J. *John Calvin: A Sixteenth Century Portrait*. New York: Oxford University Press, 1988.

Brady, Thomas A. Jr. "Patricians, Nobles, Merchants: Internal Tensions and Solidarities in South German Ruling Classes at the Close of the Middle Ages." In Miriam U. Chrisman and Otto Gründler, eds., *Social Groups and Religious Ideas in the Sixteenth Century*. Studies in Medieval Culture XIII. Kalamazoo, Mich.: Medieval Institute, 1978. 38–46, 159–164.

———. *Ruling Class, Regime and Reformation at Strasbourg, 1520–1555*. Leiden: E. J. Brill, 1978.

———. *Turning Swiss, Cities and Empire, 1450–1550*. Cambridge/London: Cambridge University Press, 1985.

———. "'You hate us priests': Anticlericalism, Communalism and the Control of Women at Strasbourg in the Age of the Reformation." In Peter A. Dykema and Heiko Oberman, eds., *Anticlericalism in Late Medieval and Early Modern Europe*. Leiden: E. J. Brill, 1993. 167–208.

Brant, Sebastian. *The Ship of Fools*. English translation by Ediwn Zeydel. New York: Columbia University Press, 1944.

Brecht, Martin. "Luthertum als politische und soziale Kraft in den Städten." In

Franz Petri, ed., *Kirche und Gesellschaftliche Wandel in deutschen und niederländischen Stätden der werdenden Neuzeit*. Cologne/Vienna: Böhlau Verlag, 1980. 1–21.

Broadhead, Philip. "Popular Pressure for Reform in Augsburg, 1524–1534." In Wolfgang J. Mommsen et al., eds., *Stadtbürgertum und Adel in der Reformation: The Urban Class, the Nobility and the Reformation*. Publications of the German Historical Institute, London, Vol. 5. Gerlingen for Klett-Cotta,1979. 80–87.

Brunner, H., and E. Strassner. "Volkskultur vor der Reformation." In Gerhard Pfeiffer, ed., *Nürnberg-Geschichte einer europäischen Stadt*. Münich: C. H. Beck, 1982.

Bucer, Martin. *Deutsche Schriften*, ed. Robert Stupperich. 7 vols. Gütersloh: Gerd Mohn, 1960–.

Cellarius, H. *Die Reichsstadt Frankfurt und die Gravamina der Deutschen Nation*. Schriften des Vereins für Reformationsgeschichte, Vol. 55. Heft 1, 163, 1938.

Chrisman, Miriam Usher. *Bibliography of Strasbourg Imprints*. New Haven: Yale University Press, 1982.

———. *Lay Culture, Learned Culture: Books and Social Change in Strasbourg, 1480–1599*. New Haven: Yale University Press, 1982.

———. "Lay Response to the Protestant Reformation in Germany, 1520–1528." In Peter N. Brooks, ed., *Reformation Principle and Practise*. Essays in honour of Arthur Geoffrey Dickens. London: Scolars Press, 1980.

———. *Strasbourg and the Reform*. New Haven: Yale University Press, 1967.

———. "Women and the Reformation in Strasbourg 1490-1530." *Archive for Reformation History* 63 (1972): 143–168.

Clemen, Otto. *Beiträge zur Reformationsgeschichte aus Büchern und Handschriften der Zwickauer Ratsschulbibliothek*. 3 vols. Berlin: C. A. Schwetschke, 1901–1903.

———. *Flugschriften aus den ersten Jahren der Reformation*. 4 vols. Leipzig, 1907–1911; NieuwKoop Reprint, B.de Graaf, 4 vols., 1967.

———. *Flugschriften aus der Reformationszeit in Faksimiledrucken*. Neue folge der "Flugschriften aus den ersten Jahren der Reformationszeit." Leipzig: O. Harrasowitz, 1921–1922.

———. *Kleine Schriften zur Reformationsgeschichte*. 1897–1944. New edition ed. Ernst Koch. Leipzig: Zentralantiquariat der DDR, 1982–1984; Cologne: Böhlau Verlag, 1982–1984.

———. *Unbekannte Drucke, Briefe und Akten aus der Reformationszeit*. Leipzig: O. Harrasowitz, 1942.

Crossan, John Dominic. *The Historical Jesus: The Life of a Mediterranean Jewish Peasant*. San Francisco: Harper, 1992.

Darlow, T. H., and H. F. Moule. *Historical Catalogue of the Printed Editions of Holy Scripture in the Library of the British and Foreign Bible Society*. 2 vols. London: The Bible House, 1911.

Decker, Klaus Peter. "Die Besitzungen der Familie von Hutten . . . um 1500." In Peter Laub, ed., *Ulrich von Hutten, Katalog zur Ausstellung des 500. Geburtstag*. Kassel: Hessischer Museums verband e.V., 1989. 113–118.

Demandt, Dieter, and Hans-Christoph Rublack. *Stadt und Kirche in Kitzingen*, Josef Engel und Ernst-Walter Zeeden, eds. Darstellung und Quellen zu Spätmittelalter und Frühe Neuzeit 8. Tübinger Beiträge zur Geschichtsforschung 10. Stuttgart: Klett-Cotta, 1978.

Deutscher Biographischer Index, ed. Willi Gorzny. 4 vols. with microfiche. Munich: K. G. Sauer, 1986.

Dickens, A. G. *The German Nation and Martin Luther*. New York: Harper and Row, 1974.

Die Chroniken der Fränkischen Städte. Nürnberg. Unveränderte Auflage. 5 vols. Göttingen: Vandenhoeck & Ruprecht, 1961.

Dykema, Peter A., and Heiko Oberman, eds. *Anticlericalism in Late Medieval and Early Modern Europe.* Leiden: E. J. Brill, 1993.

Edwards, Mark U. Jr. *Luther's Last Battles: Politics and Polemics, 1531–1546.* Ithaca, N.Y.: Cornell University Press, 1983.

Endres, Rudolf. "Sozialstruktur Nürnbergs." In Gerhard Pfeiffer, ed., *Nürnberg-Geschichte einer europäischen Stadt.* Munich: C. H. Beck, 1982. 194–199.

———. "Zur Lage der Nürnberger Hanswerkerschaft zur Zeit von Hans Sachs." *Jahrbuch für fränkischer Landesforschung* 37 (1977): 107–123.

Evans, Austin Patterson. *An Episode in the Struggle for Religious Freedom: The Secretaries of Nuremberg, 1524–1528.* New York: Columbia University Press, 1924.

Flood, J. L. "Le monde Gérmanique." In Jean-Francois Gilmont, ed., *La Réforme et le livre.* Paris: Editions Cerf, 1990, 29–104.

Folger Shakespeare Library. *Catalogue of the Emanuel Stickelberger Collection purchased by the Folger Library, Washington, D.C.* Basel: Haus der Bücher A.G., 1977.

Franz, Guenther. *Der Deutsche Bauernkrieg: Aktenband.* Munich and Berlin: R. Oldenbourg, 1935.

Fuchs, Francois-Joseph. "Les critères du choix des secrétaires de la ville (*Stadtschreiber*) au XVIᵉ siècle." In Marijn de Kroon and Marc Lienhard, eds., *Horizons Européens de la Reforme en Alsace.* Strasbourg: Librarie Istra, 1980. 9–17.

Füssel, Stephan, ed. *Ulrich von Hutten 1488–1988.* Akten der Internationalen Ulrich-von-Hutten Symposions, 15–17 Juli, 1988. *Pirckheimer-Jahrbuch.* Band 4. Munich: Wilhelm Fink Verlag, 1989. 37–57.

Garland, Sarah. *The Complete Book of Herbs and Spices.* New York: Viking, 1979.

Gäbler, Ulrich. *Huldrych Zwingli: His Life and Work,* trans. Ruth C. L. Gritsch. Philadelphia: Fortress Press, 1986.

Gawthorp, Richard, and Gerald Strauss. "Protestantism and Literacy in Early Modern Germany." *Past and Present* 104 (August 1984): 29–55.

Geck, Elisabeth, ed. *Festschrift für Josef Benzing zum sechzigsten Geburtstag.* Wiesbaden: G. Prissler, 1964.

Geertz, Clifford. *Local Knowledge: Further Essays in Interpretative Anthropology.* New York: Basic Books, 1983.

Genée, Rudolph. *Hans Sachs und seine Zeit: Ein Lebens- und Kulturbild aus der Zeit der Reformation.* Leipzig: J. J. Weber, 1894.

Gensicke, Helmuth. "Der Adel in Mittelrheingebiet." In Helmuth Rössler, ed., *Deutscher Adel 1430–1555.* Darmstadt: Wissenschaftliche Buchgesellschaft, 1965. 127–152.

Ginzburg, Carlo. *The Cheese and the Worms: The Cosmos of a Sixteenth-Century Miller,* transl. John and Anne Tedeschi. New York: Penguin Books, 1982.

Goertz, Hans-Jurgen. *Pfaffenhass und gross Geschrei: Die Reformatorische Bewegungen in Deutschland, 1517–1529.* Munich: C. H. Beck, 1987.

Gottlieb, Gunther et al., eds. *Geschichte der Stadt Ausburg von der Römerzeit bis zur Gegenwart.* Stuttgart: Konrad Theiss Verlag, 1985.

Gravier, Maurice. *Luther et l'opinion publique. Essai sur la littérature satirique et polémique en langue allemand pendant les années decisives de la Réforme (1520–1530).* Paris: Aubier, 1942.

Grenzman, Ludgar, and Karl Stackman, eds. *Literatur und Laienbildung im Spätmittelalter und in der Reformationszeit.* Symposium Wolfenbüttel 1981. Stuttgart: J. B. Metzler, c. 1984.

Grimm, Harold J. *Lazarus Spengler: A Lay Leader of the Reformation*. Columbus OH: Ohio State University Press, 1978.

Grimm, Heinrich. *Ulrich von Hutten. Wille und Schicksal. (Persönlichkeit und Geschichte, Band 60/61)*. Göttingen: Musterschmidt 1971.

Grüneisen, C. *Niclaus Manuel: Leben und Werke*. Stuttgart & Tübingen: J. G. Cotta, 1837.

Guggisberg, Hans, and Gottfried Krodel, eds. *The Reformation in Germany and Europe: Interpretations and Issues*. Special volume. *Archive for Reformation History*. Gütersloh: Gütersloher Verlaghaus, 1993.

Haeusler, Martin. *Das Ende der Geschichte in der Mittelalterlichen Weltchronistik*. Cologne: Böhlau Verlag, 1980.

Hamm, Berndt. "Humanistische Ethik und Reichsstädtische Ehrbarkeit in Nürnberg." *Mitteilungen des Vereins für Geschichte der Stadt Nürnberg* 76 (1989): 65–148.

———. "Lazarus Spengler und Martin Luther's Theologie." In Volker Press and Dieter Stievermann, ed., *Martin Luther: Probleme seiner Zeit*. Spätmittelalter und Frühe Neuzeit. Bd. 16. Stuttgart: Klett-Cotta, 1986. 129–136.

———. "Reformation 'von unten' und Reformation 'von oben': zur Problematik reformationshistorischer Klassifizierungen." In Hans Guggisberg und Gottfried Krodel, eds., *The Reformation in Germany and Europe*. 1993. 256–293.

———. "Stadt und Kirche unter dem Wort Gottes." In Ludwig Grenzmann und Karl Stackmann, eds., *Literatur und Laienbildung im Spätmittelalter und in der Reformationszeit*. Symposium Wolfenbüttel. 1981. Stuttgart: J. B. Metzler, 1982. 710–729.

Hampe, Theodor. "Der blinde Landknecht-Dichter Jörg Graff und sein Aufenthalt in Nürnberg (1517–1542)." *Euphorion* 4 (1887): 457–469.

Hannenman, Manfred. *The Diffusion of the Reformation in South-Western Germany, 1518–1534*. University of Chicago, Department of Geography Research Paper No. 167. Chicago: University of Chicago Press, 1975.

Harms, Wolfgang. "Der kundige Laie und das naturkundliche illustrierte Flugblatt des frühen Neuzeit." *Berichte zur Wissenschaftsgeschichte* 9 (1986): 227–246.

Hasak, Vicenz. *Der christliche Glaube des deutschen Volkes beim Schlusse des Mittelalters, dargestellt in deutschen Sprachdenkmalen*. Regensburg: Georg J. Manz, 1868.

Hashagen, Justus. "Zur Characteristik der geistlichen Gerichtbarkeit vornemlich im späteren Mittelalter." *Zeitschrift der Savigny-Stiftung für Rechtsgeschichte, Kanonistische Abteilung* 6 (1916): 205–292.

Heckel, A. W. *Die Martyrer der evangelischen Kirche in den ersten Zeiten nach der Reformation*. Nuremberg: Haubinstricker und von Ebner, 1828.

Heimpel, Hermann. *Studien zur Kirchen-und Reichsreform des 15 Jh.s, II. Zu zwei Kirchenreform-Traktaten des beginnenden 15 JH.s*. Sitzungsberichte der Heidelberger Akademie der Wissenschaften. Phil.-hist. Kl. Jg., 1974. 1. Abhandlung. Heidelberg, Winter, 1974.

Hieronymus, Frank. *Oberrheinische Buchillustration 2. Basler Buchillustration 1500 bis 1545*. Catalogue of exhibition, Universitäts-Bibliothek Basel, March 31–June 30, 1983. Basel: Universitätsbibliothek, 1983.

Hillerbrand, Hans. *Anabaptist Bibliography 1520–1630*. St. Louis: Center for Reformation Research, 1991.

———. "The Antichrist in the Early German Reformation: Reflections on Theology and Propaganda." In Andrew Fix and Susan C. Karant-Nunn, eds., *Germania Illustrata: Essays in Early Modern Germany Presented to Gerald Strauss*. Sixteenth Century Essays and Studies, vol. XVIII, Kirksville, Mo.: Sixteenth Century Journal Publishers, Inc., 1992. 3–17.

Hirschmann, Gerhard. "Archivalische Quellen zu Hans Sachs." *Hans Sachs und Nürnberg: Bedingungen und Problem. Reichstädtischer Literatur. Hans Sachs zum 400.* Nuremberg: M. Edelmann, 1976. 14–54.

Historisch-biographisches Lexikon der Schweiz. Heinrich Türler et el eds. Neuenburg: Administration des Historisch-Biographischen Lexikons der Schweiz, 1921–1934. 7 vols.

Hitchcock, William R. *The Background of the Knight's Revolt.* University of California Publications in History, Vol. 61. Berkeley & Los Angeles: University of California Press, 1958.

Hofman, Hans H. "Der Adel in Franken." In Hellmuth Rössler, ed., *Deutscher Adel 1440–1555.* Darmstadt: Wissenschaftliche Buchgesellschaft, 1965. 95–126.

Holborn, Hajo. *Ulrich von Hutten and the German Reformation,* trans. Roland H. Bainton. New York: Harper Torchbooks, 1967.

Holeczek, Heinz. "Erasmus von Rotterdam und die volkssprachliche Rezeption seiner Schriften in der deutschen Reformation 1519–1536." *Zeitschrift für Historische Forschung* Band II; Heft 2 (1984): 129–165.

Holstein, H. "Hieronymus von Endorf." *Zeitschrift für Kirchengeschichte* 10/3 (1839): 453–462.

Holzberg, Niklas. *Hans-Sachs Bibliographie.* Beiträge zur Geschichte und Kultur der Stadt Nürnberg 20. Nuremberg: Stadtbibliothek Nürnberg, 1976.

Honemann, Volker. "Der deutsche Lukian. Die volkssprachigen Dialogi Ulrichs von Hutten." In Stephen Füssel, ed., *Ulrich von Hutten 1488–1988.* Munich: Wilhem Fink, 1989. 50–60.

Höss, Irmgard. "Religiös Leben vor der Reformation." In Pfeïffer, ed., *Nürnberg-Geschichte,* 137–146.

Hsia, R. Po-chia. *The Myth of Ritual Murder: Jews and Magic in Reformation Germany.* New Haven: Yale University Press, 1988.

Junghans, Helmar. "Der Laie als Richter im Glaubenstreit der Reformationszeit." *Lutherjahrbuch* 39 (1972): 31–54.

Jütte, Robert. *Poverty and Deviance in Early Modern Europe.* Cambridge: Cambridge University Press, 1994.

Kalkoff, Paul. *Ulrich von Hutten und die Reformation: eine kritische Geschichte seiner wichtigsten lebenszeit und der entscheidungsjahre der Reformation (1517–1523).* Leipzig: R. Haupt, c.1925. Johnson Reprint, 1971.

Kamen, Henry. *European Society, 1500–1700.* London: Hutchinson & Co., 1984.

Kawerau, Waldemar. *Hans Sachs und die Reformation.* Verein für Reformationsgeshichte Schriften 26; 7;1. Halle, 1889.

Kellenbanz, Herman. "Gewerbe und Handel am Ausgang des Mittelalters," in Pfeiffer, ed., *Nürnberg-Geschichte.* 178–186.

———. "Wirtschaftsleben im Zeitalter der Reformation." in Pfeiffer, ed., *Nürnberg-Geschichte.* 186–193.

Kiessling, Rolf. *Bürgerliche Gesellschaft und Kirche in Augsburg im Spätmittelalter: ein Beitrag zur Strukturanalyse der oberdeutschen Reichstadt.* Abhandlung zur Geschichte der Stadt Augsburg 19. Augsburg: H. Mühlberger, 1971.

Klaniczay, Tibor. "Die Reformation und die volkssprachlichen Grundlagen der Nationalliteraturen." In Robert Weimann, Werner Lenk, and Joachim-Jürgen Slomka, eds., *Renaissanceliteratur und frühbürgerliche Revolution.* Berlin: Aufbau-Verlag, 1976.

Knox, Ellis Lee. "The Guilds of Augsburg." Ph.D. Dissertation. University of Massachusetts, 1984.

Koch, Gustave. *Eckhart zum Drübel, témoin de la Réforme en Alsace.* Strasbourg: Publications de la faculté de Théologie Protestante, 1989.

Köhler, Hans-Joachim, et al., eds. *Flugschriften des frühen 16. Jahrhunderts.* Microfiche Serie, Zug, 1978–1987.

Köhler, Hans-Joachim, ed. *Flugschriften als Massenmedium der Reformationszeit.* Beiträge zum Tübinger Symposion 1980. Spätmittelalter und Frühe Neuzeit. Tübinger Beiträge zur Geschichtsforschung, Vol. 13. Stuttgart: Klett-Cotta, 1985.

———. "'Der Bauer wird witzig': Der Bauer in den Flugschriften der Reformationszeit." In Peter Blickle, ed., *Zugänge zur Bäuerlichen Reformation.* Zurich: Chronos, 1987, 187–218.

———. *Bibliographie der Flugschriften des 16. Jahrhunderts.* 3 Parts. Part I. Das Frühe 16. Jahrhundert (1501–1530) in 3 vols. Vols. 1 and 2, *Druckbeschreibung A–L.* Tübingen: Bibliotheca Academica Verlag, 1991–1993.

———. "Die Flugschriften der frühen Neuzeit." In W. Arnold et al., ed., *Die Erforschung der Buch- und Bibliotheksgeschichte in Deutschland.* Wiesbaden: W. Arnold u.a., 1987. 307–344.

Kolde, Theodor. "Der Reichsherold Caspar Sturm und seine literarische Tätigkeit." *Archiv für Reformationsgeschichte* 4 (1907): 117–161.

Könneker, Barbara. *Hans Sachs.* Stuttgart: Metzler, 1971.

———. "Ulrich von Hutten Gesprächbuchlin und Novi Dialogi." In *Die Deutsche Literatur der Reformationszeit, Kommentare zu einer Epoche.* Munich: Winkler Verlag, 1975. 90–100.

———. "Vom 'Poeta Laureatas' zum Propagandisten, die Entwicklung Huttens als Schriftsteller in seinen Dialogen von 1518 bis 1521." In *L'humanisme allemand (1480–1540).* XVIII Colloque International de Tours. Munich: Fink Verlag; and Paris: Librairie Vrin, 1979. 303–319.

Kopp, Arthur. "Jörg Grünwald, ein dichtender Handwerksgenosse des Hans Sachs." *Archiv für das Studium der Neuen Sprachen und Literaturen.* Jahrgang LV, Band CVII, Neuen Serie VII (1901): 1–32.

Kramm, Heinrich. *Studien über die Oberschichten der Mitteldeutschen Städte im 16. Jahrhundert: Saxony; Thuringia; Anhalt.* 2 vols. Cologne/Vienna: Böhlau, 1981.

Kück, Eduard. Zu Sickingens Sendbrief an Handschuchsheim." *Anzeiger fur deutsches Altertum und deutsche Literatur.* 30 (1906), 148.

Laub, Peter, ed., *Ulrich von Hutten: Ritter, Humanist, Publizist 1488–1523. Katalog zur Ausstellung des Landes Hessen anlässlich des 500. Geburtstag.* Kassel: Hessischer Museumsverband e.V., 1989.

Laube, Adolf. "Die Volksbewegung im Deutschland von 1470–1517." *Historische Zeitschrift Beiheft* 4, Nr. 84 (1975).

———. "Zur Rolle sozialökonomischer Fragen in frühreformatorischen Flugschriften." In *Flugschriften als Massenmediums der Reformationszeit,* ed. Hans-Joachim Köhler. Stuttgart: Klett-Cotta, 1981. 205–224.

Laube, Adolf, and Hans-Werner Seiffert, eds. *Flugschriften der Bauernkriegszeit.* Berlin: Akademie-Verlag, 1975.

Laube, Adolf, Annerose Schneider, and Sigrid Loos, eds. *Flugschriften der frühen Reformationsbewegung.* 2 vols. Berlin: Akademie-Verlag, 1983.

Lendi, Karl. *Die Dichter Pamphilus Gegenbach: Beiträge zu seinem Leben und seinen Werken.* Sprache und Dichtung: Forschungen zur Sprach- und Literaturwissenschaft, eds H. Mayne and S. Singer, Heft 39. Bern: Paul Haupt, 1926.

Lenk, Werner. "Frühbürgerliche Revolution und Literaturprozeß in Deutschland." In Robert Weimann, Werner Link, and Joachim-Jürger Slomka, eds.,

Renaissanceliteratur und frühbürgerliche Revolution: Studien zu den sozial- und ideolo-giegeschichtlichen Grundlagen europäische Nationalliteraturen. Berlin: Aufbau-Verlag, 1976. 145–169.

———. [ed.]. *Die Reformation in zeitgenössischen Dialog*. 12 Texte aus dem Jahren 1520 bis 1525. Berlin: Akademie Verlag, 1968.

Lenski, Gerhard E. *Power and Privilege: A Theory of Social Stratification*. New York: McGraw Hill, 1966.

Levine, Lawrence W. "The Folklore of Industrial Society: Popular Culture and its Audience." *American Historical Review* 97,5 (1992):1369–1399.

Lewis, Keith D. "Ulrich von Hutten, Johann Faber, und *Das Gyren Rupffen: A Knight's Last Campaign*." *Archiv für Reformationsgeschichte* 77 (1987): 124–146.

Liebhart, Wilhelm. "Stifte, Klöster und Konvente in Augsburg." In Gunther Gottlieb et al., eds., *Geschichte der Stadt Augsburg*. Stuttgart: Konrad Theiss Verlag, 1985. 198–206.

Lienhard, Marc. *Un temps, une ville, une Réforme. La Reformation à Strasbourg*. Variorum, Collected Studies 39. Great Yarmouth: Galliard Printers, 1990.

———. "Mentalité populaire, gens d'Eglise et mouvement évangélique à Strasbourg en 1522–1523; le pamphlet 'Ein bruderlich warnung an meister Mathis . . . de Steffan von Bullheym'". In *Un temps, une ville, une Réforme. La Reformation à Strasbourg*. 37–62.

Little, Lester K. *Religious Poverty and the Profit Economy in Medieval Europe*. London: Paul Elek, 1978.

Locher, Gottfried. *Zwingli's Thought: New Perspectives*. Studies in the History of Christian Thought, ed. Heiko Oberman, Vol XXV. Leiden: E. J. Brill, 1981.

Lucke, Peter. *Gewalt und Gegengewalt in den Flugschriften der Reformation*. Göppingen: A. Kümmerle, 1974.

Luther, Martin, "Eine treue vermahnung zu allen Christen, sich zu vorhuten for auffruhr unnd emporung." In *D. Martin Luthers Werke. Kritische Gesamtausgabe. (Weimar Ausgabe)*. Weimar: Hermann Böhlaus Nachfolger: 1883–1993. 65 Bänder. Band 8: 616–687.

———. "Judgement on Monastic Vows", James Atkinson, ed. and trans. In Jaroslav Pelikan et al., eds., *Luther's Works*. 56 vols. St. Louis: Concurdia Publishing House, 1955–1976. Vol 44. 243–400.

———. "An Open Letter to the Christian Nobility," trans. Charles M. Jacobs. *Three Treatises*. Philadelphia, Pa.: Fortress Press, 1943. 3–112.

———. "Ordinance of a Common Chest, Preface, 1523," transl. Albert T. W. Steinhauser. In Jaroslav Pelikan et al., *Luther's Works*, Vol. 45. 159–175.

———. "The Sacrament of Penance, 1519," E. Theodore Bachman, ed. and trans. In Jaroslav Pelikan et al., *Luther's Works*, Vol. 35: 9–22.

———. "Vom ehelichen leben." In *D. Martin Luthers Werke. Kritische Gesamtausgabe. (Weimarer Ausgabe)*. Weimar: Hermann Bohlaus Nachfolger, 1883–1993. 65 Bänder. Band 10: 275–310.

Lutz, Robert. *Wer war der gemeine Mann? Der dritte Stand in der Krise des Spätmittelalters*. Munich & Vienna: R. Oldenbourg Verlag, 1979.

Maschke, Erich. "Mittelschichten in deutschen Städten des Mittelalters." In Erich Maschke and Jürgen Sydow, eds., *Städtische Mittelschichten*. Stuttgart: W. Kohlhammer Verlag, 1972. 1–31.

———. "Die Unterschichten der mittelalterichen Städte Deutschlands." In Erich Maschke and Jürgen Sydow, eds. *Städte und Menschen: Beiträge zur Geschichte der Stadt, der Wirtschaft und Geseilschaft 1959–1977*. In Vierteljahrschrift für Sozial-

und Wirtshaftsgeschichte 68 Band. Wiesbaden: Franz Steiner Verlag, 1980; 306–379.

Maschke, Erich and Jürgen, Sydow eds. *Gesellschaftliche Unterschichten in den südwestdeutschen Städten.* In Veröffentlichungen der Kommission für geschichtliche Landeskunde in Baden-Württemberg, Reihe B, 41. Band. Stuttgart: W. Kohlhammer Verlag, 1967.

McCutcheon, R. R. "*The Responsio ad Lutherum*: Thomas More's Inchoate Dialogue with Heresy." *Sixteenth Century Journal* XXII, 1 (1991) 77–78.

McLaughlin, R. Emmet. *Caspar Schwenckfeld Relunctant Rebel: His Life to 1540.* New Haven: Yale University Press, 1986.

Midelfort, H. C. Erik. *The Mad Princes of Renaissance Germany.* Charlottesville: University Press of Virginia, 1994.

———. "The Reformation and the German Nobilty." In Hans R. Guggisberg and Gottfried Krodel, eds., *The Reformation in Germany and Europe.* 344–360.

Mitgau, Hermann. "Geschlossene Heiratskreise, sozialer Inzucht." In Hellmuth Rössler, ed., *Deutsches Patriziat 1430–1740.* Limburg: C. A. Startke, 1968.

Mitteis, Heinrich, and Heinz Lieberich. *Deutsche Rechtsgeschichte.* 15th edition. Munich: C. H. Beck Verlag, 1978.

Moeller, Bernd. "Das Berühmtwerden Luthers." *Zeitschrift für Historische Forschung* 15/1 (1988): 65–92.

———. *Imperial Cities and the Reformation.* H. C. Eric Midelfort and Mark Edwards, Jr., transl. and eds. Philadelphia: Fortress Press, 1972.

———. *Johannes Zwick und die Reformation in Konstanz.* Heidelberg: Gütersloher Verlagshaus Gerd Mohn, 1961.

Mohl, Ruth. *The Three Estates in Medieval and Renaissance Literature,* Columbia University Studies in English and Comparative Literature. New York: Columbia University Press, 1933.

Mollat, Michel. *The Poor in the Middle Ages: An Essay in Social History,* trans. Arthur Goldhammer. New Haven: Yale University Press, 1986.

Mommsen, Wolfgang, Peter Alter, and R. W. Scribner, eds. *Stadtbürgertum und Adel in der Reformation.* Stuttgart: Klett-Cotta Verlag, 1979. With English title, *The Urban Classes, The Nobility and the Reformation.*

Mullett, Michael. *Popular Culture and Popular Protest in Late Medieval and Early Modern Europe.* London & New York: Croom Helm, 1987.

Murphy, James J. *Renaissance Eloquence: Studies in the Theory and Practise of Renaissance Rhetoric.* Berkeley: University of California Press, 1983.

Nebelsieck, H. "Ein fürstlicher Laientheologie des 16. Jahrhunderts. Graf Wolfrad II von Waldeck." *Archiv für Reformationsgeschichte* 41 (1948): 58–93.

Nouveau dictionnaire de biographie alsacienne, ed. Jean-Pierre Kintz. 14-vols. Strasbourg: Société d'édition de la Basse-Alsace, 1982–.

Oberman, Heiko A., ed. *Forerunners of the Reformation: The Shape of Late Medieval Thought, Illustrated by Key Documents,* trans. Paul L. Nyhus. New York: Holt, Rinehart and Winston, 1966.

———. *The Dawn of the Reformation: Essays in Late Medieval and Early Modern Thought.* Edinburgh: T. & T. Clark, 1986.

———. *Masters of the Reformation: The Emergence of a New Intellectual Climate in Europe,* trans. Denis Martin. Cambridge. Cambridge University Press, 1981.

———. *Luther, Man between God and the Devil,* trans., Eileen Walliser-Schwarbart. New Haven: Yale University Press, 1989.

Oehmig, Stefan. "Der Wittenberger Gemeine Kasten in der ersten zweienhalb Jahrzehnten seines Bestehens (1522/23 bis 1547)." Part 1. "Seine Einnahmen und seine finanzielle Leistungs-fähigkeit. . . ." Part 2. "Seine Ausgaben und seine sozialen Nutzniessen." *Jahrbuch für die Geschichte des Feudalismus*, 1988, 260–295; 1989, 155–185.

Oelschläger, Ulrich. "Der Sendbrief Franz von Sickingens an seinem Verwandten Dieter von Handschuchsheim." *Ebernburg-Hefte* 4 Folge (1970): 71–85.

O'Malley, John W. *The First Jesuits.* Cambridge: Harvard University Press, 1993.

Ozment, Steven. "Pamphlet Literature of the German Reformation." In Steven Ozment, ed., *Reformation Europe: A Guide to Research.* St. Louis: Center for Reformation Research, 1982. 85–106.

———. *The Reformation in the Cities.* New Haven: Yale University Press, 1975.

———. *When Fathers Ruled: Family Life in Reformation Europe.* Cambridge: Harvard University Press, 1983.

Peter, Rodolphe. "Le Jardinier Clément Ziegler l'homme et son oeuvre." Unpublished baccalaureat thesis in theology presented to the Faculty of Protestant Theology of the University of Strasbourg, 1954.

———. "Le maraîcher Clément Ziegler: l'homme et son oeuvre." *Revue d'histoire et de philosophie Religieuses* 34 (1954): 255–282.

Pfeiffer, Gerhard. "Entscheidung zur Reformation," in Pfeiffer, ed., *Nürnberg-Geschichte.* Munich: C. H. Beck, 1982. 146–154.

———. *Quellen zur Nürnberger Reformationsgeshichte von der Duldung liturgischer Änderung bis zur Ausübung des Kirchenregiments durch den Rat (Juni 1524– Juni 1525).* Nuremberg: Verlag für bayerische Geschichte, 1968.

——— [ed.]. *Nürnberg—Geschichte einer europäischen Stadt.* Munich: C. H. Beck, 1982.

Philoom, Thurman E. "Hans Greiffenberger and the Reformation in Nuremberg." *The Mennonite Quarterly Review* XXXVI (January 1962): 62–75.

Piper, Ernst. *Der Stadt als Grundriss der Gesellschaft: Topographie und Sozialstruktur in Augsburg und Florenz um 1500.* Frankfurt am Main: Campus Verlag, 1982.

Pocock, J. A. "The Reconstitution of Discourse: Towards the Historiography of Political Thought." *Modern Language Notes* 96 (1981): 959–980.

Pohl, Hans, ed. *Gewerbe- und Industrielandschaften vom Spätmittelalter bis ins 20. Jahrhundert.* Beiheft 78. *Vierteljahrschrift für Sozial- und Wirtschaftsgeschichte.* Stuttgart: Franz Steiner Verlag, 1986.

Polke, Johannes "'Wiewohl es ein rühmlich und wohlgebaut Haus gewesen,' Das Ende der Ebernburg im Spiegel Hessische Dokumente." *Ebernburg-Hefte* 15 (1981): 133–195.

Potter, G. R. *Zwingli.* Cambridge: Cambridge University Press, 1976.

Press, Volker. "Franz von Sickingen, Wortführer des Adels, Vorkämpfer der Reformation und Freund Huttens." In Peter Laub, ed., *Ulrich von Hutten, Katalog zur Ausstellung des 500. Geburtstag.* Kassel: Hessischer Museumsuerband e.V., 1989. 293–305.

———. *Kaiser Karl V, König Ferdinand und die Entstehung der Reichsritterschaft.* Wiesbaden: Franz Steiner, 1980.

———. "Die Reichsritterschaft im Reich der frühen Neuzeit." *Nassauische Annalen* 87 (1976): 101–122.

———. "Ulrich von Hutten, Reichsritter und Humanist, 1488–1523." *Nasauissche Annalen* 85 (1974): 71–86.

Preu, Georg. "Die Chronik von Georg Preu." In Friedrich Roth, ed., *Die Chroniken der Schwäbischen Städte Augsburg.* 7 vols. Leipzig: S. Hirzel: 1865–1917. Vol. 6, 18–30.

Raillard, Rudolf. *Pamphilus Gegenbach und die Reformaton.* Abhandlung der Doctorwürde der Philosophischen Fakultät I der Universität Zürich. Heidelberg: Evangelische Verlag, 1936.

Rapp, Francis. "Über Bürger, Stadt und städtische Literatur im Spätmittelalter." In Josef Fleckenstein and Karl Stackmann, eds., *Bericht über Kolloqien der Kommission zur Erforschung der Kultur des Spätmittelalters, 1975–1977. Abhandlungen der Akademie der Wissenschaften in Göttingen.* Philologisch-historische Klasse. 3. folge. Nr. 121. Göttingen: Vandenhoeck & Ruprecht, 1980.

Reichel, Jörn. "Hans Rosenplüt genannt Schnepperer, Ein Handwerksdichter im Spätmittelalterlichen Nürnberg." *Mitteilungen des Vereins für Geschichte der Stadt Nürnberg* 67 (1980): 17–36.

Rendenbach, Karl Hans. *Die Fehde Franz von Sickingen gegen Trier.* Berlin: Emil Ebering, 1932.

Rieber, Albrecht. "Das Patriziat von Ulm, Augsburg, Ravensburg, Memmingen, Biberach." In Helmuth Rössler, ed., *Deutsches Patriziat 1430–1740.* Limburg: C. A. Startke, 1968. 302–330.

Ritter, François. *Histoire de l'imprimerie alsacienne, au XV et XVI siècles.* Strasbourg-Paris: F-X. Le Roux, 1955.

Ritter, Gerhard. *Nürnberg-Geschichte einer europäischen Stadt.* Munich: C. H. Beck, 1982.

Ritter, Suzanne. *Die kirchenkritische Tendenz in den deutschsprachigen Flugschriften der frühen Reformationszeit.* Tübingen: Diss. 1970.

Röhrich, Timotheus Wilhelm. *Mitteilungen aus der Geschichte der evangelischen Kirche des Elsasses.* 3 vols. Band III: Evangelische Lebensbilder. Strabourg: Treuttel und Würtz, 1855.

Roper, Lyndal. *The Holy Household: Women and Morals in Reformation Augsburg.* Oxford: The University Press, 1989.

Rössler, Hellmuth. "Adelsethik und Humanismus," In Hellmuth Rössler, ed., *Deutscher Adel 1440–1555.* 234–250.

——— [ed.]. *Deutscher Adel, 1430–1555.* Schriften zur Problematik der Deutschen Führungsschichten in der Neuzeit. 1. Darmstadt: Wissenschaftliche Buchgesellschaft, 1965.

——— [ed.]. *Deutsches Patriziat, 1430–1740.* Schriften zur Problematik der Deutschen Führungsschichten in der Neuzeit. 3. Limburg-Lahn: C. A. Starke Verlag, 1968.

Roth, Friedrich. *Augsburgs Reformationsgeschichte, 1517–1528.* Munich, 1881.

———. "Wer war Haug Marschalck, genannt Zoller von Augsburg?" *Beiträge zur Bayerischen Kirchengeschichte* 6 (1900): 229–234.

———. "Zur Lebensgeschichte des Augsburger Formschneider David Denecker." *Archiv für Reformationsgeschichte* 9 (1911): 189–230.

Rott, Jean. *Investigationes Historicae: églises et société au XVI siècle.* Gesammelte Aufsätze. 2 vols. Strasbourg: Librairie Oberlin, 1986.

———. "Après sept années de prédiction évangélique où en étaient les Strasbourgeois en 1528? Le pamphlet de Hans von Schore." In *Invesitgationes Historicae.* Vol. 1, 521–534.

———. "De quelques pamphlétaires nobles-Hutten, Cronberg et Mathias Wurm von Geudertheym." In *Grands Figures de l'humanisme Alsacien.* Strasbourg: Librarie Istra, 1978. 135–145. Reprinted in *Investigationes Historicae.* Vol. 2, 575–586.

Rublack, Hans-Christoph. "Anticlericalism in German Reformation Pamphlets." In Peter A. Dykema and Heiko Oberman, eds., *Anticlericalism in Late Medieval and Early Modern Europe*. Leiden: E. J. Brill, 1993. 461–489.

——. *Die Einführung der Reformation in Kontsanz von den Anfangen bis zum Anschluss 1531*. Gütersloh: Gerd Mohn, 1971.

——. "Political and Social Norms in Urban Communities in the Holy Roman Empire." In Kaspar von Greyerz, ed., *Religion, Politics and Social Protest*. London: George Allen and Unwin, 1984. 24–60.

Russell, Paul A. *Lay Theology in the Reformation: Popular Pamphleteers in Southwest Germany, 1521–1525*. Cambridge: Cambridge University Press, 1986.

Sachs, Hans and Jost Amman. *Das Ständebuch*. Facsimile Aufgabe. Leipzig: Insel Verlag, n.d..

Schade, Oskar. *Satiren und Pasquille aus der Reformationszeit*. 3 vols. Hannover, 1863.

Schanze, Helmut. "Problems and Trends in the History of German Rhetoric to 1500." In James J. Murphy, ed., *Renaissance Eloquence: Studies in the theory and Practise of Renaissance Rhetoric*. Berkeley: University of California Press, 1983. 105–125.

Schiff, Otto. "Forschungen zur Vorgeschichte des Bauernkrieges. III. Die unechte Reformation Friedrichs III." *Historische Vierteljahrschrift* 9 (1919/20): 189–219.

Schiller, Karl M., ed. *Hans Sachs Werke in zwei Bänder*. 2 vols. Berlin: Bibliothek deutscher Klassiker, 1972.

Schilling, Heinz. *Aufbruch und Krise: Deutschland 1517–1648*. Berlin: Siedler, 1988.

Schmoller, Gustav. *Die Strasburger Tucher-und Weberzunft: Urkunden und Darstellung*. Strassburg, 1876.

Schoebel, Martin. "Franz von Sickingen als Kurpfalzische Amtmann in Kreuznach und Böckelheim." *Ebernburg-Hefte* 15 (1981): 139–147.

Schön, Theodor. "Beiträge zur Reformationsgeschichte Württembergs." *Blätter für Württembergische Kirchengeschichte* Dritte Folge; Nr. 6; 9. Jahrgang (June 30, 1894): 44–46.

Schottenloher, Karl. *Bibliographie zur deutschen Geschichte im Zeitalter der Glaubensspaltung, 1517–1585*. 7 vols. Leipzig: Karl W. Hiersemann, 1933–1966.

——. "Flugschriften zur Ritterschaftsbewegung des Jahres 1523." In *Reformationsgeschichtliche Studien und Texte*, ed. Albert Ehrhard. Heft 53. Münster: Aschendorffschen Verlag, 1929. 1–29.

——. *Phillip Ulhart, ein Augsburger Winkeldrucker und Helfershelfer der "Schwärmer" und "Wiedertäufer" (1523–1529)*. 1921. Nieukoop: B. de Grauf, 1967.

Schwiebert, Ernest G. *Luther and His Times*. St. Louis, Mo.: Concordia Publishing House, 1950.

Scott, Tom. *Freiburg and the Breisgau: Town-Country Relations in the Age of Reformation and Peasant's War*. Oxford: Clarendon Press, 1986.

Scott, Tom, and Bob Scribner, eds. and transl. *The German Peasants' War*. Atlantic Highlands, N.J.: Humanities Press International, 1991.

Scribner, Robert W. "Civic Unity and the Reformation in Erfurt." *Past and Present* 66 (1975): 29–60.

——. *For the Sake of Simple Folk: Popular Propaganda for the German Reformation*.

Cambridge Studies in Oral and Literate Culture, Peter Burke and Ruth Finnegan, eds. Cambridge: Cambridge University Press, 1981.

———. *Popular Culture and Popular Movements in Reformation Germany.* London: The Hambledon Press, 1987.

———. "Understanding Early Modern Europe." *History Journal* 30 (1987): 743–758.

Seaver, Paul S. *Wallington's World: A Puritan Artisan in Seventeenth Century London.* Stanford: Stanford University Press, 1985.

Seyboth, Reinhard. "Ulrich von Hutten und sein Verhältnis zur Ritterschaftlichen Bewegung." In Stephan Füssel, ed., *Ulrich von Hutten 1488–1988.* 129–144.

Silver, Lawrence A. "'The Sin of Moses': Comments on the Early Reformation in a Late Painting by Lucas van Layden." *Art Bulletin.* 55 (Sept. 1973):

Sittler, Lucien. *L'artisanat en Alsace.* Strasbourg: Editions Mars et Mercure, n.d.

Skinner, Quentin. *The Foundations of Modern Political Thought.* 2 vols. London: Cambridge University Press, 1978.

Slater, Miriam. *Family Life in the Seventeenth Century: The Verneys of Claydon House.* London: Routledge and Kegan Paul, 1984.

Smith, Toulmin, ed. *English Guilds.* London: N.Trübner, 1870.

Sonnino, Lee A. *A Handbook to Sixteenth Century Rhetoric.* London: Routledge and Kegan Paul, 1968.

Stayer, James M. *The German Peasants' War and Anabaptist Community of Goods.* McGill-Queens Studies in the History of Religion, 6. Buffalo, N.Y.: McGill-Queen's University Press, 1991.

Steer, Georg. "Zum Begriff 'Laie' in deutscher Dichtung und prosa des Mittelalters." In Ludger Grenzmann und Karl Stackmann, eds., *Literatur und Laienbildung im Spätmittelalter und in der Reformationszeit.* Symposium Wolfenbüttel, 1981. Stuttgart: J. B. Metzler, c. 1984.

Steinmetz, Max. *Deutschland von 1476 bis 1648.* Berlin: Deutscher Verlag der Wissenschaften, 1965.

———. "Johann Virdung von Hassfurt, sein Leben und sein astrologischen Flugschriften." In Hans-Joachim Köhler, ed., *Flugschriften als Massenmedium der Reformationszeit. Spätmittelalter und Frühe Neuzeit.* Tübinger Beiträge zur Reformationszeit, Vol. 13. Stuttgart: Klett-Cotta, 1981. 353–372.

Stone, Lawrence, *The Family, Sex and Marriage in England, 1500–1800.* New York, Harper and Row, 1977.

Störmann, Anton. *Die städtischen Gravamina gegen den Klerus am Ausgange des Mittelalters und in der Reformationszeit.* Münster: W. Aschendorf, 1916.

Strauss, Gerald, ed. and trans. *Manifestations of Discontent in Germany on the Eve of the Reformation.* Bloomington: Indiana University Press, 1971.

———. *Law, Resistance and the State: The Opposition to Roman Law in Reformation Germany.* Princeton: Princeton University Press, 1986.

———. *Nuremberg in the Sixteenth Century.* New York: John Wiley, 1966.

Stromer, Wolfgang von. "Gewerbereviere und Protoindustrien in Spätmittelalter Industrieland und Frühneuzeit." In Hans Pohl, ed., *Gewerbe-und Industrielandschaften.* 39–111.

Studer, J. "Der Schulmeister Johannes Buchstab von Winterthur, ein Gegner Ulrich Zwinglis." *Schweizerische Theologische Zeitschrift* 29 (1912): 198–219.

Sullivan, Margaret A. *Bruegel's Peasants: Art and Audience in the Northern Renaissance.* Cambridge: Cambridge University Press, 1994.

Szamatólski, Siegfried, ed. *Ulrich von Hutten Deutsche Schriften.* Quellen und Forschungen zur Sprach- und Culturgeschichte der Germanischer Völker, Vol 67. Strassburg: K. J. Trübner, 1891.

Theiss, Winfried. "Der Bürger und die Politik zu den zeitkritischen Dichtung von Hans Sachs." In Horst Brunner et al., eds., *Nürnberger Forschungen.* Band 19. Nuremberg: Selbstverlag der Vereins für Geschichte der Stadt Nürnberg, 1976. 76–104.

Thiessen, Victor. "Stormy Days, Peaceful Knights: Noble Writers and the Reformation," Paper presented at the Sixteenth Century Studies Conference, Toronto. 29 October 1994.

Verzeichnis der in Deutschen Sprachverbereich erschienen Drucke des XVI. Jahrhunderts. Ed. Bayerischen Staatsbibliothek in München in Verbindung mit der Herzog August Bibliothek in Wolfenbüttel. I. Abteilung, Band 1– Band 8. Stuttgart: Anton Hierseman, 1984.

Vögeli, Jörg. *Schriften zur Reformation in Konstanz, 1519–1538.* Ed. Alfred Vögeli. 3 vols. Tübingen: Osiandersche Buchhandlung, 1972.

Vorberg, Axel. "Die Einfuhrung der Reformation in Rostock." *Schriften des Vereins fur Reformationsgeschichte* Jg. 15:58 (1897): 25–50.

Wandel, Lee Palmer. *Always Among Us; Images of the Poor in Zwingli's Zurich.* Cambridge: Cambridge University Press, 1990.

———. "The Reform of the Images: New Visualizations of the Christian Community at Zurich." *Archive for Reformation Research* 80 (1989): 105–124.

———. "Social Welfare." *Oxford Encyclopedia of the Reformation.* forthcoming.

Weber, Eugen. *My France: Culture, Politics, Myths.* Cambridge: Belknap Press, 1991.

Wedler, Klaus. *Hans Sachs.* Leipzig: Phillip Reclam, 1976.

Weickmann, Rudolf. *Hans Sachs: Leben und Werk des grossen Schusterpoeten leicht fassbar nacherzählt.* Schwabach: P. Gersbeck, c. 1875.

Weller, Emil Ottokar. *Annalen der poetischen National literatur der Deutschen im XVI. und XVII. Jahrhundert.* 2 vols. 1862–1864. Reprinted Hildesheim: Olms, 1964. Vol. 1, part 3.

———. *Index Psudonymorum: Wörterbuch der Pseudonymen oder Verzeichnis aller Autoren, die sich falscher Namen bedienten.* Leipzig: Falcke und Rössler, 1856.

Werner, Heinrich. "Die sogenannte' Reformation des Kaisers Friedrich III.', ein Reichsreformplan der westdeutschen Ritterschaft." *Westdeutsche Zeitschrift fur Geschichte und Kunst* 28 (1909): 29–70.

Wiesflecker, Hermann. *Kaiser Maximilian I. Das Reich, Osterreich und Europa an der Wende zur Neuzeit.* 5 vols. München: Oldenbourg Verlag, 1986.

Wiesner, Merry E. "Beyond Women and the Family: Towards a Gender Analysis of the Reformation." *Sixteenth Century Journal* XVIII, 3 (1987): 311–322.

———. "Ideology Meets the Empire: Reformed Convents and the Reformation." In Andrew C. Fix and Susan Karant-Nunn, eds., *Germania Illustrata: Essays on Early Modern Germany Presented to Gerald Strauss.* Sixteenth Century Essays and Studies, Vol. XVIII. Kirksville, Mo.: (Sixteenth Century Journal Publications, 1992. 181–195.

Williams, George H. *The Radical Reformation.* London: Weidenfeld and Nicolson, 1962. 2nd ed., Kirksville, Mo.: Sixteenth Century Journal Publications, 1992.

Winkler, Hannelore. "Zum soziologischen Aspekt von Flugschriften aus der Zeit der Reformation und des Bauernkrieges." *Beiträge zur Geschichte der deutschen Sprache und Literatur* 94 (1972): 37–54.

Wittmer, Charles and Meyer, J, Charles, eds. *Le livre de bourgeoisie de la ville de Strasbourg, 1440–1530.* 3 vols. Strasbourg: P. H. Heitz, 1948–1966.

Zedler, Johann Heinrich. *Grosses Universal Lexicon aller Wissenschaften und Künste, welche bisshero durch menschlichen Verstand und Witz erfunden worden.* 64 plus 4 supplemental vols. Halle & Leipzig: Verlag Johann Heinrich Zedler, 1732.

Zimmerman, Walter. *Die Reformation als rechtlich-politisches Problem in den Jahren 1524–1530/31.* Göppinger Akademische Beiträge #106. Göppingen: Kämmerle.

Zophy, Jonathan W. *Patriarchal Politics and Christoph Kress 1484–1535 of Nuremberg.* Studies in German Thought and Culture, Vol. 14. Lewiston, N.Y.: The Edwin Mellen Press, 1992.

Zorn, Wolfgang. *Ausburg Geschichte einer deutschen Stadt.* Ausburg: H. Mühlberger Verlag, 1972.

Index

absolution, declared unnecessary: God forgives sins (sawyer), 167–68

Adrian VI, pope: Cronberg's letter to, 80

aims of city secretaries: order and peace through law, 216

aims of common people for reform: discipline of the Roman clergy, 199; increase pay of day laborers, 199; no lay persons to be cited by an ecclesiastical court, 195–96; pastor to distribute the Sacrament according to Testament of Christ, 195; pastor to preach the Gospel without human additions, 195, 196; right to elect own pastor, 194–95, 196

Ain schenes und nutzlichen büchlin von dem Christen glauben, 73–75

Ain Sendbrieff von Ainer erbern frawen in Eelichen stat an ein Klosterfrawen, 147–48

Alber, Erasmus (schoolteacher), 115; *Absag oder Fehdschrifft*, 116; *Schone Dialogus von Martini Lutheri und der geschickten Botschaft aus der Holle*, 116

Aleander, Hieronymus: assigned to publish bull *Exsurge Domine*, 54; burns Luther's books at Louvain, 54

Alsace: and Peasant's War, 123

Anabaptist writers: omission of, 4

analysis of pamphlets: by context, 5; by genre, 5; by sequence of ideas, 5; religious ideas expressed in, 5–6; word choice and grammar, 5

anonymous honorable woman: *Der Gotzferchtige eerentreiche fraw Hilgart von Freyburg seiner cristliche . . . schwester*, 96–99, 99–100

anonymous pamphlets: placed by form, language and content, 6

Anthony (vicar of provincial Dominicans, Constance): ordered by city council to preach only from Scripture, 217; preaches against order of the city council, 217

anticlericalism: artisans condemned venality of village priests, 184; artisan deplores concubines of local clergy (Büllheym), 183; clergy bought up the food in the market (Ulem, Ritter), 187; clergy destroyed justice and order (knights), 76; clergy should work with their hands, 120, 121; criticism of artisans directed at local clergy, 183; denial of papal supremacy (minor civil servants), 121; knights accuse priests of failure to teach, 74; knights condemn greed of clergy, 77; knights denounce church landholdings, 65, 76; moral corruption of papacy condemned by minor civil servants, 117; of minor civil servants and technicians exceeded that of other classes, 117; treachery and violence of papacy depicted by minor civil servants, 118

anti-Lutheranism: preachers calling themselves Lutheran criticized for arrogance and avarice (Vogtherr), 122

Aquila, Kaspar (reformer): appointed tutor to Sickingen's son, 69

Archbishop of Mainz: Cronberg family served at his court, 67; Hutten (counsellor at his court), 66

Archbishop of Trier: defeats Sickingen, 82; territory beseiged by Sickingen, 82. *See also* Greiffenklau, Richard von

Arnold, Martin, 2

articles for communal reform: Articles of Bamberg, 196; Articles of Chur, 195–96; Frankfurt Articles, 199;

277